TRADITION IN TRANSITION

D1598524

ROGER LONSDALE
Photograph by Rob Judges

Tradition in Transition
Women Writers, Marginal Texts, and the Eighteenth-Century Canon

EDITED BY

ALVARO RIBEIRO, SJ

AND

JAMES G. BASKER

CLARENDON PRESS · OXFORD
1996

*This book has been printed digitally and produced in a standard design
in order to ensure its continuing availability*

OXFORD
UNIVERSITY PRESS

Great Clarendon Street, Oxford OX2 6DP

Oxford University Press is a department of the University of Oxford.
It furthers the University's objective of excellence in research, scholarship,
and education by publishing worldwide in

Oxford New York

Athens Auckland Bangkok Bogotá Buenos Aires Cape Town
Chennai Dar es Salaam Delhi Florence Hong Kong Istanbul Karachi
Kolkata Kuala Lumpur Madrid Melbourne Mexico City Mumbai Nairobi
Paris São Paulo Shanghai Singapore Taipei Tokyo Toronto Warsaw
with associated companies in Berlin Ibadan

Oxford is a registered trade mark of Oxford University Press
in the UK and in certain other countries

Published in the United States
by Oxford University Press Inc., New York

Jacket illustration: Detail from Colley Cidder and
his daughter Charlotte *by Edward Fisher. By
courtesy of the National Portrait Gallery, London.*

To ROGER LONSDALE

Scholar, Mentor, and Friend

Preface

ON the occasion of Professor Roger Harrison Lonsdale's sixtieth birthday, this volume collects eighteen commissioned essays written by his pupils on eighteenth-century English literature, a subject that Lonsdale has made so eminently his own. Having enjoyed the privilege to have been taught by Lonsdale, the contributors to this volume, now pursuing academic careers of their own in various parts of the world, here join together in offering their work as a grateful tribute in honour of their mentor.

From his tutorial room in Balliol College, Oxford, and his accustomed perch in the Upper Reading Room of the Bodleian Library, Lonsdale, without fanfare, has prepared and published ground-breaking scholarly work in several areas of eighteenth-century studies. His first major book, *Dr Charles Burney: A Literary Biography* (Oxford, 1965), re-established a neglected but important literary figure who had been relegated exclusively to the world of music history; his recent anthologies—*The New Oxford Book of Eighteenth-Century Verse* (Oxford, 1984) and *Eighteenth-Century Women Poets: An Oxford Anthology* (Oxford, 1989)—have redefined the canon of eighteenth-century English poetry. In between these publications have come important critical editions of works by Thomas Gray, William Collins, Oliver Goldsmith, John Bampfylde, and William Beckford, as well as a stream of critical studies on Alexander Pope, Oliver Goldsmith, Samuel Johnson, John Cleland, and Thomas Gray, and on topics that include the history of criticism, journalism, and poetry.

While Lonsdale continues to be a very productive scholar, his work over the last three decades has already fundamentally altered the shape of eighteenth-century literary studies. This Festschrift volume therefore takes as its organizing principle the three areas of scholarship in which Lonsdale's work has had the greatest impact: women writers, marginalized texts, and the canon of eighteenth-century literature.

Lonsdale's revolutionary anthology of *Eighteenth-Century Women Poets* restored to view scores of women poets and radically redirected the whole discussion of women writers in the eighteenth century. Five chapters in this volume take up Lonsdale's lead by concentrating on the work, in different genres, of marginalized women writers. Each chapter focuses both on the achievement of the individual woman writer and on the nature of her relationship to the mainstream of eighteenth-century literary history. Carolyn Williams considers Elizabeth Carter's response to the competing demands of a literary career and the conventional role of women. Alvaro Ribeiro studies the correspondence of Mrs Hester Thrale and Dr Charles Burney from the dual perspectives of literary history and criticism. James Basker explores the surprising affinities, both intellectual and psychological, between Mary Wollstonecraft and Samuel Johnson, while April London examines the novels of Jane West against the volatile politics of the 1790s. Marilyn Butler completes this panel of our triptych with her investigation of Maria Edgeworth's ambivalence towards the personal and literary influence of Thomas Day.

In the second frame of this volume's tripartite arrangement, Lonsdale's commitment to the recovery of marginal authors and neglected texts, a scholarly pursuit which has brought to light a wealth of lost eighteenth-century writing, provides the inspiration for a set of essays on a wide variety of 'marginal texts'. Katherine Armstrong makes the case for regarding *Colonel Jack* as a literary and historical text comparable in stature to *Robinson Crusoe* and *Moll Flanders*. Shirshendu Chakrabarti draws to our attention the central importance of Swift's little-known *Directions to Servants* as a key to understanding Swift's ironic view of social mobility and master–servant relations. Ian McGowan, on the other hand, takes a Boswellian text that has been eclipsed by the *Life of Johnson*, and finds in its author's preparations for publication significant new light on Boswell's authorial priorities and anxieties. Katherine Turner's chapter explores the boundaries between fiction and non-fiction in a Sternian narrative of the 1760s, while Nicholas Hudson traces the emergence in the period of oral tradition as an acknowledged literary mode. The question of generic categories is raised in both Richard Wendorf's treatment of Sir Joshua Reynolds's hitherto forgotten 'Apologia' and in Katherine Reimann's analysis of Lieutenant Bligh's narratives of self-construction. Both chapters challenge, as Lonsdale has done in his own scholarship, our hitherto settled notions of what constitutes a 'literary' text.

Future literary historians will undoubtedly point to Lonsdale's redefinition of the eighteenth-century poetic canon as his greatest contribution to the field. His anthologies not only reshaped the canon of English poetry, but opened to question the whole process of canon-formation. Essays in the final section of this volume therefore pursue topics arising from the history of the evolving canon. Christine Gerrard examines the manipulating influence of Pope's editorial practices in determining Thomas Parnell's place in the canon, while Anthony Barker maps the countervailing populist pressure on the poetic canon exerted through the poetry pages of the *Gentleman's Magazine*. The classical influence of

Neoplatonism on a canonical poet such as William Collins, featured in Paul Williamson's contribution, plays against Nick Groom's piece on the yearning for a home-grown British poetics evident in the Celtic and Gothic poetry of Macpherson, Percy, and their circles. Michael Suarez's study of the impact of Robert Dodsley's *Collection of Poems by Several Hands* on the mid-century definition of the poetic canon leads, finally, to David Fairer's examination of the way in which the early Romantic poets sought to reimagine the canon they had inherited.

As the chapters in this volume cohere around these three critical issues, they collectively address a larger question that challenges every student of literature today: 'After Postmodernism and the New Historicism, what?' While it would be pretentious and serve no useful purpose to claim that a 'Lonsdale School' of criticism exists, the contributors to this volume represent a new generation of scholarship influenced by Lonsdale and united by certain methodological assumptions: a desire to renew and extend historical scholarship; a commitment to the close reading of texts; and a receptiveness to the best insights of recent schools of critical thought. In the light of current concerns in literary criticism we hope this volume articulates a persuasive vision of traditional eighteenth-century studies in transition and, by implication, points the way forward neither hidebound by the old complacencies and certainties nor mesmerized by the stampede to the latest fashionable orthodoxies.

A.F.V.R.
J.G.B.

Acknowledgements

In the preparation of this volume the editors have incurred many debts of gratitude which they wish to acknowledge: The Master and Community of Campion Hall, Oxford; The Master and Fellows of Sidney Sussex College, Cambridge; President Ellen Futter and Dean Robert McCaughey of Barnard College; Co-Masters Steven Mitchell and Kristine Forsgard and the members of Eliot House, Harvard University; Randall Bass, Lynne Hirschfeld and the Department of English, Georgetown University; Remington Patterson, Connie Budelis, and the English Department of Barnard College; and the staffs of the Beinecke Library, Bodleian Library, Cambridge University Library, and Sidney Sussex College Library and Muniments Room.

We should also like to thank the following individuals for much needed assistance: Robert Araujo, SJ; Judith Basker; Elise Buchman; Philip Endean, SJ; Steven Epley; Jm Gregorio; Julia Hore; Charles Lonsdale; Gregory Maertz; Alan Mitchell, SJ; Lee Morrissey; Claire Preston; Marie Ribeiro; Pat Rogers; Jennifer Thorn; Lars Troide; Angela Vallot; Kevin Van Anglen; Kim Warner; Sir Edgar Williams and Lady Williams.

Contents

Notes on Contributors

KATHERINE A. ARMSTRONG (Lecturer in English, Chester College of Higher Education). A member of New College, Oxford, Armstrong wrote her D.Phil. thesis on self-consciousness in eighteenth-century fiction. She has taught for New College and Worcester College in Oxford, for Stanford University, and at Manchester University. She has published articles in *Factotum* and the *Library Review*, has worked on the Eighteenth-Century Short Title Catalogue, and is now completing a book-length study of the political and ideological implications of Defoe's historiography entitled *Daniel Defoe: Writer as Agent*.

ANTHONY D. BARKER (Associate Professor, Universidade de Aveiro). Barker completed his D.Phil. at Christ Church, Oxford, on Edward Cave, Samuel Johnson, and the *Gentleman's Magazine*. He subsequently went to Cambridge, where he was the Munby Fellow in Bibliography, and later to Portugal, where he is now Head of English Studies at Aveiro. Currently the President of the Portuguese Association of Anglo-American Studies (APEAA), he has written and lectured on a wide range of topics, from Edward Cave, Samuel Johnson, and eighteenth-century publishing history, to Thomas Hardy, Tom Stoppard, and the films of Alfred Hitchcock.

JAMES G. BASKER (Professor of English, Barnard College, Columbia University). After the D.Phil. at Christ Church, Oxford, supported by a Rhodes Scholarship, Basker worked at Harvard University as Assistant Professor in English and Senior Tutor in Eliot House before moving to Barnard College, Columbia University. He co-authored the Johnson exhibition catalogue *He has Long Outlived his Century* (1984), and his book, *Tobias Smollett, Critic and Journalist* (1988) won a *Choice* award. He has contributed essays to many learned journals and volumes, and is currently editing *Roderick Random* for the Georgia Works of Smollett and writing a book on *Samuel Johnson and the Common Reader*.

MARILYN BUTLER (Rector of Exeter College, Oxford). One of Roger Lonsdale's first graduate students, Butler has pursued a distinguished career in literary scholarship; until recently she was King Edward VII Professor of English Literature at Cambridge University. Her many books include *Maria Edgeworth: A Literary Biography* (1972), *Jane Austen and the War of Ideas* (1975), *Peacock Displayed: A Satirist in his Context* (1979), and *Romantics, Rebels and Reactionaries: English Literature and its Background, 1760–1830* (1981), as well as scholarly editions of *Burke, Paine, Godwin and the Revolution Controversy* (1984), and, with Janet Todd, *The Works of Mary Wollstonecraft* (1989).

SHIRSHENDU CHAKRABARTI (Reader in English, University of Delhi South Campus). Educated at Presidency College, Calcutta, and St Stephen's College, Delhi, Chakrabarti earned his D.Phil. at Trinity College, Oxford, as an INLAKS Scholar in 1980. On returning to India, he was elected Reader in English at Jadavpur University, Calcutta, and, since 1991, has been Reader in English at the University of Delhi South Campus. He has written on Shakespeare, Montaigne, Swift, and Johnson, among others; has an essay on George Herbert and an edition of *Gulliver's Travels* under way; and is currently finishing a book on Swift and the Renaissance Humanist tradition for Oxford University Press (Delhi).

DAVID FAIRER (Senior Lecturer in English, University of Leeds). Fairer's publications include *Pope's Imagination* (1984), *The Poetry of Alexander Pope* (1989), and, as editor, *Pope: New Contexts* (1990), as well as numerous articles in a wide variety of scholarly journals. His Oxford D.Phil., an edition of *The Correspondence of Thomas Warton*, is forthcoming at the University of Georgia Press. He is currently writing a biography of Thomas Warton, has been commissioned to write the volume on *Eighteenth-Century Poetry* for the Longman 'Literature in English' Series, and, with Christine Gerrard, is preparing a teaching anthology of eighteenth-century English poetry.

CHRISTINE GERRARD (Fellow and Tutor in English, Lady Margaret Hall, Oxford). Gerrard followed her undergraduate work at Oxford with an MA in American Literature at the University of Pennsylvania. She received her D.Phil. from Oxford in 1987, and has published a number of articles on the eighteenth century. Editor of the *English Review*, she has recently published *The Patriot Opposition to Walpole: Politics, Poetry, and National Myth, 1725–1742* (1994), and is currently writing a literary biography of Aaron Hill.

NICK GROOM (Lecturer in English Literature, University of Exeter). Groom was a Baring Senior Scholar at Hertford College, Oxford, where, under the supervision of Roger Lonsdale, he researched his D.Phil. on the subject of Thomas Percy's *Reliques of Ancient English Poetry*. He was successfully *viva*'d for his doctorate in 1994. Since then Groom has published various articles on eighteenth-century literature, critical theory, and Postmodernism, and is a contributing editor of the pan-European journal *Angelaki*. He is currently completing a history of the Rowley Controversy, editing a collection of new essays on Thomas Chatterton, revising his doctoral thesis for a monograph on Percy, and working on an edition of the *Reliques*.

NICHOLAS HUDSON (Associate Professor, University of British Columbia). Since obtaining in 1984 his D.Phil. at Pembroke College, Oxford, on Samuel Johnson, Hudson has published essays about Defoe, Swift, Fielding, Richardson, and Johnson, among others, in leading scholarly journals. His first book, *Samuel Johnson and Eighteenth-Century Thought*, appeared at the Clarendon Press in

1988; and he has co-edited with Rosena Davidson, *Man and Nature: Proceedings of the Canadian Society for Eighteenth-Century Studies* (1989). His current book-length project, *Writing and Enlightenment: Changing Perceptions of Written Language, 1600–1830*, is under contract with Cambridge University Press.

APRIL LONDON (Associate Professor, University of Ottawa). After writing her Oxford D.Phil. on landscape in the eighteenth-century novel, London joined the English Department of the University of Ottawa. She has since contributed essays to scholarly books and journals and is currently working on a major book on *Women and Property in the Eighteenth-Century British Novel*.

IAN McGOWAN (Senior Lecturer in English Studies, University of Stirling). After winning the Robert Browning Senior Studentship at Pembroke College, Oxford, and later completing a Ph.D. on Boswell at Stirling, McGowan was appointed in 1988 Director of the Centre for Publishing Studies at Stirling University. His publications include *Charles Dickens: 'Little Dorrit'* (1984) and *The Restoration and Eighteenth Century: An Annotated Anthology of English Literature* (1989), as well as articles on Sterne, Austen, and Dickens, among others. He is a Member of the Scottish Arts Council and Chair of its Literature Committee and Grants to Publishers Panel. His scholarship includes commissioned reports on 'Public Policy and Literary Culture in Scotland' for *Publishing Research Quarterly* and 'Publishing in the Later Twentieth Century' for the *New Companion to Scottish Culture*.

K. A. REIMANN (Sometime Junior Dean, St Hugh's College, Oxford). Reimann has completed her Oxford D.Phil. thesis entitled 'On their own Account: Pirate Narratives and Pirate Writers of the Long Eighteenth Century'. She received her BA at Yale University and the M.Phil. in Eighteenth-Century Studies at Oxford. She has worked as an Assistant Cataloguer on the Eighteenth-Century Short Title Catalogue Project. Her first novel will be published in 1995, by Tom Doherty Associates.

ALVARO RIBEIRO, SJ (Assistant Professor, Georgetown University). A priest of the Society of Jesus, Ribeiro's academic career has taken him from his native Hong Kong to a D.Phil. at Balliol College, Oxford. After working as Research Assistant to the late James M. Osborn at Yale University, he joined the Burney Papers Project at McGill University and is now its Associate Director. Theological degrees were followed by appointment as Warden of Ricci Hall, University of Hong Kong, before his recent move to Georgetown University. In addition to other publications, he co-edited with René Wellek, *Evidence in Literary Scholarship: Essays in Memory of James Marshall Osborn* (1979). The first volume of his edition of *The Letters of Dr Charles Burney* appeared in 1991, and he is currently editing the subsequent three volumes for the Clarendon Press.

MICHAEL F. SUAREZ, SJ (Campion Hall, Oxford). A Marshall Scholar and winner of the Matthew Arnold Prize at Oxford, Suarez in 1987 became the first person in the history of Oxford University to win both the Newdigate Poetry Prize and the Chancellor's Essay Prize in the same year. He has published scholarly articles and reviews in *The Age of Johnson, Review of English Studies, Papers of the Bibliographical Society of America, Johnsonian News Letter,* and *Eighteenth-Century Studies.* Ordained a priest of the Society of Jesus in 1994, Suarez has now been elected a Junior Research Fellow in English at St John's College, Oxford.

KATHERINE S. H. TURNER (Lecturer, St Hugh's College, Oxford). One of Roger Lonsdale's current graduate students, Turner is writing on 'Travel Literature and the Politics of Subjectivity, 1750–1800', a thesis topic that grew out of her successful work for the M.Phil. in Eighteenth-Century Studies. Winner of the Goldsmith Exhibition and the Elton Shakespeare Prize at Balliol, she has worked on the Wing and Eighteenth-Century Short Title Catalogue projects, and taught for Balliol, Brasenose, Mansfield, and St Hilda's at Oxford, and at Royal Holloway, University of London.

RICHARD WENDORF (Librarian, The Houghton Library, Harvard University). After taking a B.Phil. in Eighteenth-Century Studies at Worcester College, Oxford, in 1972, and a Ph.D. at Princeton in 1976, Wendorf rose to Professor of English and Art History at Northwestern University before being appointed director of the Houghton Library. He has written and edited several books, including *The Works of William Collins* (with Charles Ryskamp, 1979), *William Collins and Eighteenth-Century English Poetry* (1981), *Articulate Images: The Sister Arts from Hogarth to Tennyson* (1983), *The Elements of Life: Biography and Portrait-Painting in Stuart and Georgian England* (1990), *Rare Book and Manuscript Libraries in the Twenty-First Century* (1993), and *Sir Joshua Reynolds: The Painter in Society* (1995). Wendorf is now working on two book-length projects: a collection of essays on visual and verbal encounters, and a study of printing history and cultural change.

CAROLYN D. WILLIAMS (Lecturer in English, University of Reading). Supervised by Roger Lonsdale, Williams completed her Oxford B.Litt. thesis in 1972 on Dr John Arbuthnot and the Scriblerians. Since then she has written widely on Swift, Gay, Pope, and Richardson for such journals as *Critical Quarterly, Essays in Criticism, Studies in English,* and the *Yearbook of English Studies,* and contributed essays to *John Gay and the Scriblerians* (1988) and *Pope: New Contexts* (1990). She has published *Pope, Homer, and Manliness: Some Aspects of Eighteenth-Century Classical Learning* (1993) and is currently working on eighteenth-century benevolence, early modern childbirth, Thomas Chatterton, and an edition of Elizabeth Carter's *Epictetus.*

PAUL WILLIAMSON (Lecturer in English, University of Vienna). After receiving his first degree and the Woodall Prize for the highest result in his year at Manchester University, Williamson completed his D.Phil. thesis in 1990 at Balliol College, Oxford, on 'The Metaphysical Basis of Mid-Eighteenth Century English Poetry'. His most recent publication is an essay entitled 'Gray's *Elegy* and the Logic of Expression', in *Thomas Gray: Contemporary Essays* (1993). He has taught for the British Council in Jordan, is currently Lecturer in English at the University of Vienna, and is working on a book-length study of mid-eighteenth-century literature.

PART ONE

Women Writers

1   Poetry, Pudding, and Epictetus: The Consistency of Elizabeth Carter

CAROLYN D. WILLIAMS

No woman in eighteenth-century Britain matched the attainments of Elizabeth Carter (1717–1806): she was 'poet, scholar, translator, essayist, and letter writer',[1] a doyenne of the bluestockings. She had other skills, besides. Hearing a lady praised for her learning, Dr Samuel Johnson observed: 'A man is in general better pleased when he has a good dinner upon the table than when his wife talks Greek. My old friend, Mrs Carter, could make a pudding as well as translate Epictetus.'[2] Roger Lonsdale believes she 'is perhaps doomed to be best remembered' for this 'intended compliment'.[3] Elizabeth Carter, however, might have regarded this doom as a triumph, celebrating her struggle to balance the disparate, often contradictory, claims of matter and spirit, combining them in a harmonious unity. At first glance, her task appears impossible. The precepts of Epictetus (c.55–c.153), as recorded by Flavius Arrianus (fl. second century AD), advocate the doctrine of stoicism, one of the most austere pagan philosophies. They do not seem conducive to good housekeeping. Yet in Carter's correspondence with Catherine Talbot (1721–70), her 'Dialogue' (1741) between Body and Mind, and her translation of All the Works of Epictetus (1758), the reader can trace a developing pattern of conflict and reconciliation that finally reveals closer and more intricate connections between pudding and philosophy than Dr Johnson's antithesis implies.

'The science of puddings'

To a great extent, Carter shared her society's tendency to elevate the abstract and general, deeming many forms of engagement with the material universe trivial and degrading. A philosophical basis for this attitude can be traced back to Plato, who considers ideal form infinitely

---

[1] Editorial preface to the section on Elizabeth Carter in Robert W. Uphaus and Gretchen M. Foster (eds.), The 'Other' Eighteenth Century: English Women of Letters 1660–1800 (East Lansing, 1991), 213.
[2] James Boswell, The Life of Samuel Johnson, ed. George Birkbeck Hill (6 vols.; Oxford, 1887), i. 122–3 n. 4.
[3] Eighteenth-Century Women Poets: An Oxford Anthology, ed. Roger Lonsdale (Oxford, 1989), 167.

superior to physical object,[4] and whose *Timaeus* depicts creation as a 'Compromise of Teleology with Necessity'.[5] Class distinction fostered this belief: in societies where practical tasks were delegated to inferiors, indifference and ignorance about such affairs indicated gentility. Many areas of eighteenth-century life were affected. A 'liberal' education, based on classical texts and concentrating on words rather than things, conferred higher social and professional status than technical training. The public revered theoretical investigators like Isaac Newton, who discovered natural laws; inventors who tried to put them to use might be scorned as misguided or fraudulent 'projectors'. Poets attempting the high style conformed to neo-classical concepts of decorum derived from 'an ancient epistemological principle concerning the inverse relation between the importance of objects and their capacity to be known or apprehended by the senses'.[6]

Of course, all these instances were subject to change. The Classics were losing their monopoly of polite education;[7] celebrities like John Theophilus Desaguliers, lecturer in experimental philosophy, made new technology profitable, as well as socially and intellectually respectable;[8] William Blake, with his insistence that 'Singular & Particular Detail is the Foundation of the Sublime',[9] heralded a new approach to literature. But Elizabeth Carter took little interest in such developments: it is evident from her literary theory and practice that she took for granted the low status and pettiness of material concerns. Most of the writing which she intended for publication (with the significant exception of *Epictetus*, which will be discussed later) was formal in tone, with a strong tendency to abstraction: her 'Ode to Wisdom' (1747) contains twelve personifications in ninety-six brief lines. She found the detailed descriptions of animal husbandry and household management in Homer's *Odyssey* thoroughly wearisome, and ludicrously inappropriate to her concept of epic dignity:

really it does not seem of any great importance to the reader whether Telemachus (like a notable housewifely young man as he was) hung his cloaths upon a peg, or was sloven enough to throw them on the floor; or whether Mr. Trulliber (I have forgot his Greek name) took exact care of the hogs. (5 September 1746)[10]

[4] *Republic* 5.22.
[5] Gregory Vlastos, *Plato's Universe* (Oxford, 1975), 28.
[6] Stephen Shankman, *Pope's 'Iliad': Homer in the Age of Passion* (Princeton, NJ, 1983), 57.
[7] See Penelope Wilson, 'Classical Poetry and the Eighteenth-Century Reader', in Isabel Rivers (ed.), *Books and their Readers in Eighteenth-Century England* (Leicester, 1982), 72–3.
[8] See Larry Stewart, *The Rise of Public Science: Rhetoric, Technology and Natural Philosophy in Newtonian Britain, 1660–1760* (Cambridge, 1992).
[9] William Blake, 'Annotations to *The Works of Sir Joshua Reynolds*, ed. Edmond Malone: London, 1798', in *The Poetry and Prose of William Blake*, ed. David V. Erdman (Garden City, NY, 1965), 637.
[10] *A Series of Letters between Mrs. Elizabeth Carter and Miss Catherine Talbot*, ed. Montagu Pennington (4 vols.; London, 1809), i. 166.

This perception of materiality would be particularly galling to an intelligent woman, since spiritual and intellectual concerns were normally monopolized by upper-class men, leaving females of all classes to concentrate on handicrafts—a custom justified by the belief that women were inferior to men in spirit and reason. Again, this theory had an ancient pedigree: Aristotle set out the physiological causes of female inferiority in his *Generation of Animals* 765^b. With stronger passions than men, and less self-restraint, women needed constant male supervision and control. Avarice was perceived as a related female failing. According to the apocryphal *Problems of Aristotle*, 'The nature of women (as we have often said) is imperfect, therefore they think it impossible fully to satisfy themselves; and therefore they gather together and keep that by which means they may help their need; and by industry and art they covet to get that which nature does not give them.'[11] Material and materialistic, women were doubly contaminated.

Carter was born into a world where feminine capacities for higher interests were acknowledged and encouraged by the increasingly frequent publication of edifying books for, and even by, women. One celebrated example was her own *Sir Isaac Newton's Philosophy Explain'd, for the Use of the Ladies* (1739), translated from the Italian of Francesco Algarotti. Nevertheless, serious doubts still shadowed the femininity, if not the virtue, of women who studied the 'learned' languages (Latin, Greek, and Hebrew), indulged in creative writing, or sought publication. Carter's friend Samuel Richardson frequently addresses the issue of female education in his novels, but even his *Sentiments* (1755), where he speaks *ex cathedra* rather than in character, are ambiguous. *Pamela* (1740–1) gives rise to a radical view of domesticity as a distraction from learning, rather than vice versa: 'when a poor girl, in spite of her narrow education, breaks into notice, her genius is immediately tamed by trifling employments, and she is kept back, as if it were apprehended she would become the envy of her own sex, and raise the jealousy of the other.'[12] *Sir Charles Grandison* (1753–4) provides a more conservative compromise. Although reading and writing are acceptable female occupations, they must not interfere with household affairs, involve strenuous exertion, or be taken seriously:

Young women who are writers, should not suffer their pen to run away with their needle. . . .

[11] 'Aristotle', *The Problems of Aristotle*, in *The Whole of Aristotle's Works, Complete* (London, 1782), 105.
[12] Samuel Richardson, *A Collection of the Moral and Instructive Sentiments or Maxims, Cautions, and Reflexions, Contained in the Histories of Pamela, Clarissa, and Sir Charles Grandison* (London, 1755; repr. New York, 1980), 28.

Nor is their love of reading to interfere with that housewifery which is indispensible in the character of a good woman ...

When no duty is neglected for the acquirement; when modesty, elegance, and a teachable spirit are preserved, it is not a disgrace to a woman to be supposed to know something ...

[T]he easy productions of a fine fancy, not made the business of life or its boast, confer no denomination that is disgraceful; but very much the contrary.[13]

By these standards, Carter was a failure. From the outset, the demands of learning and domestic duty set up tensions which she resolved only partially, and with enormous effort. Having devoted her daylight hours to family affairs, she pored over the learned languages far into the night, taking snuff to keep awake.[14] She had no leisure for the acquisition of the elegant manners required by Richardson: she confessed to Catherine Talbot, 'an excess of good huswifry has prevented me from ever using a fan' (9 May 1752).[15] Her father, however, was content. He trusted her in matters great and small, allowing her to decide for herself whether to marry, and writing a shopping list whose conclusion gave her complete discretion in stocking the family larder: 'Peper. Morells. Best Almonds. Raisins, Coffee. And anything else, of whatever kind you think is wanting.'[16] In 'To the Rev. Dr. Carter' (1762), she addresses him gratefully as a kind parent who treats her as a reasonable being:

> Ne'er did thy Voice assume a Master's pow'r;
> Nor force Assent to what thy Precepts taught;
> But bid my independent Spirit soar,
> In all the Freedom of unfetter'd Thought.[17]
>
> (ll. 17–20)

Despite the absence of paternal pressure, Carter knew learned ladies had a dubious image, and anxiously rebutted every hint of domestic incompetence. In reply to a remark on puddings, she told Catherine Talbot:

I wish I could send you one piping hot to Cuddesden, as a specimen of my abilities in the science of puddings. One would think you had a mind to insult me upon a misfortune that happened to me some fifteen years ago, when I produced a pudding of a new invention, so overcharged with pepper and brandy

---

[13] Ibid. 309.

[14] Montagu Pennington, *Memoirs of the Life of Mrs. Elizabeth Carter, with a New Edition of her Poems* (2 vols.; 2nd edn., London, 1808), i. 9.

[15] Carter, *Letters*, ii. 78.

[16] Barbara Collins, 'Letters to a Famous Daughter', in *Deal and its Place in European Architectural Heritage* (Deal Society, n.d.), 8, quoted in Sylvia Harcstark Myers, *The Bluestocking Circle: Women, Friendship, and the Life of the Mind in Eighteenth-Century England* (Oxford, 1990), 47.

[17] Elizabeth Carter, *Poems on Several Occasions* (London, 1762), 63. All poems except the 'Dialogue' are quoted from this edition, but the names in the titles have been added after reference to the versions in Pennington's *Memoirs*.

that it put the whole family in a flame. The children all set up their little throats against Greek and Latin, and I found this unlucky event was like to prove my everlasting disgrace, for they made a perfect æra of it, and every remarkable thing that was quoted for a month after, was always sure to happen on the same day '*my sister made the brandy pudding.*' So to stop their clamour, I happily applied myself to the forming a special good sweet cake, with such success, that the former mishap was forgot, and I was employed to make every christening cake that happened in the family ever after. And though I say it, that should not say it, several grave notable gentlewomen of unquestionable good housewifery have applied to me for the receipt. I hope you will not infer from my story that I am fond of brandy, for I put it in out of pure good management to save milk. (15 September 1747)[18]

The most likely cause of the great pudding disaster was youthful inexperience: Elizabeth was then about 15, an age when even the demanding Richardson believed a girl was not yet fully qualified 'discreetly to conduct the affairs of a family'.[19] Her siblings, however, were very much of their period in their assumption that knowledge of ancient languages automatically entailed culinary incompetence. For Elizabeth herself, the incident encapsulated all the familial and social pressures that could be brought to bear on a girl who aspired to classical learning. She internalized those pressures at an early age, and they drove her ever after; the vivid detail of her letter to Catherine reveals the painful clarity with which the incident was etched on her memory. Her subsequent culinary exploits probably had a double aim: to vindicate both her reputation for good housekeeping and her right to study. Delicious puddings and cakes were solid arguments in defence of female education.

Pudding cannot always be enlisted, however covertly, in the service of enlightenment. It may symbolize female bondage to triviality and, more generally, human subjection to the demands and dangers of corporeality:

I have had vile head-aches which have confined me most days for some hours to such a lifeless state of *faineantise* as might have appeared sufficiently mortifying to me, if I had not felt a more sensible pain from the sad apprehensions of losing one of my best friends by the small-pox; this with a constant succession of illness in our own family, has left me but little leisure for that variety of employments which amuse me agreeably enough at another time. Indeed I cannot tell when I shall be able to get into my former track again, for this long confinement has rendered me so extremely plodding and stupid, that I begin to fear all my gay whimsical ideas, now I am tolerably at ease, will dwindle into a sober relish for comfortable life. I don't know that for this week I have formed any one scheme but what has been entirely practicable, or said or done any one thing that people

---

[18] Carter, *Letters*, i. 218–19.
[19] Samuel Richardson, *Familiar Letters on Important Occasions*, ed. Brian W. Downs (London, 1928), 89.

could either be offended or pleased with. It is not to be described how perfectly muzzy I look, nor what a strange fondness I have lately acquired for dumplings. (9 October 1744)[20]

Carter has been subjected to the most demoralizing concomitants of physical materiality: pain, sickness, and fear of death. She claims to have been reduced to such thorough submission that she is actually capable of enjoying her lot; the tone lightens as her intellectual pursuits are ironically dismissed as 'whimsical' follies, while mundane existence promises (or threatens?) the joys of 'comfortable life'. The final item in this bill of complaint initially appears more hopeful: a 'strange' fondness suggests interesting exoticism. Then, with brilliant comic timing, the objects of this mysterious desire are revealed as dumplings—the nadir of domesticated bathos. For all its gallant wit, this is a thinking woman's *de profundis*.

Pudding is served with even more bitter sauce when Carter describes the humiliation awaiting any woman who ventures into the traditionally masculine domain of classical learning. A young man, who had recently left university, was asked to subscribe to her *Epictetus*. He refused, making it quite clear that the translator's sex accounted for his decision:

he would have done it, if the book had been some treatise of œconomy for the use of the ladies. Is not this a most notable youth? And might not one be sure, by applying to him, of getting the best receipt extant for making modern dumpling; for I believe he has much too good a taste to have been perverted at Oxford by the soups and sauces of the ancients. (n.d.)[21]

Superficially, this attack expresses a wilful misunderstanding: the young man maintains excessively strict gender boundaries by refusing to encourage women to publish on any subject but housekeeping; Carter affects to believe he is violating these boundaries by acquiring cookery books for his own use. In fact, she makes a much graver charge: in emerging from Oxford unperverted by the cookery of the ancients (and, by implication, ignorant of all other ancient lore), he has squandered his masculine heritage of classical, or 'manly', learning. He may be the better woman in jest, but she is the better man in earnest.

Carter's adventurous vigour as a woman writer and classicist was matched by her taste for physical exercise. Long country walks were essential to her health, but people about her did not acknowledge her needs. She complains about their well-meaning interference:

To reject the advice of those who profess to love one and to have a regard for one's happiness, has such an appearance of perverseness and ingratitude, that it requires some degree of fortitude to persevere in a resolution taken up on ever

[20] Carter, *Letters*, i. 71–2.   [21] Pennington, *Memoirs*, i. 211.

such reasonable grounds, when they oppose it so strongly. . . . I have had the complaisance out of attention to the opinions of others to be less constant in my walking this summer than usual, and the consequence is, I have never been free from a head ach and a slow fever. (5 July 1746)[22]

For most women, marriage presented the greatest threat to personal freedom. Carter chose a single life: Sylvia Harcstark Myers attributes her decision to a 'perception that marriage involved a power relationship in which men dominated women. . . . She dared not risk the loss of independence.'[23] In fact, her independence was already limited: she was vulnerable to social and moral pressure, which sometimes forced her to modify her behaviour in ways that did not suit her; until the publication of *Epictetus* she was unable to support herself. But she still had too much to lose. Her father never attempted to control her by physical force, legal sanctions, or financial penalties; a husband might not be so indulgent. Eighteenth-century wives might lawfully be confined, isolated, or beaten. Even if matters did not come to such a brutal head, husbands might abuse their authority in other ways:

If I have suffered from the troubles of others, who have more sense, more understanding, and more virtues than I might reasonably have expected to find, what might I not have suffered from a husband! Perhaps be needlessly thwarted and contradicted in every innocent enjoyment of life: involved in all his schemes right or wrong, and perhaps not allowed the liberty of even silently seeming to disapprove them! (21 May 1751)[24]

Furthermore, marriage involved women in practical domesticity more intimately and irreversibly than single life. The custom of associating man with spirit, woman with matter, became ironically reversed when marriage was regarded from the wife's viewpoint: in her efforts to provide his creature comforts, she was confronted with her husband's materiality at every turn. However lofty and important the concerns which elevated him above the need to make pudding, they never disqualified him from eating it.

'The dull Fatigue of Life'

The idea of marriage as a system enabling a coarse, stupid husband to tyrannize over an intelligent, long-suffering wife provides the controlling image for Carter's 'Dialogue' between Body and Mind. When she wrote the poem, she was an attractive girl in her early twenties, admired by men and women in London society; marriage was a thoroughly practical

[22] Carter, *Letters*, i. 156.   [23] Myers, *Bluestocking Circle*, 111.   [24] Carter, *Letters*, ii. 29.

proposition, but she was clearly having doubts about the benefits of this institution for women. Body complains,

> We're so nearly related yet never agree,
> But lead a most wrangling strange sort of a life,
> As great plagues to each other as husband and wife.[25]

(ll. 2–4)

Body is never explicitly defined as male, but it is hard not to hear such utterances in a male voice; their language is appropriate to a bullying husband in Restoration comedy. Mind, addressed as 'your ladyship' (l. 5), rebuked for rambling 'abroad' (l. 30), and threatened with 'force' (l. 18) to make her more attentive to household affairs, is cast in the role of wife. Body scores a few debating points, as in this account of the disturbing effect of the imagination:

> you hourly call in a disorderly crew
> Of vagabond rogues, who have nothing to do
> But to run in and out, hurry-scurry, and keep
> Such a horrible uproar, I can't get to sleep.

(ll. 9–12)

The other party in the dispute is described as 'Poor Mind, who heard all with extreme moderation' (l. 19)—an introduction calculated to engage the reader's sympathy. But this engagement is not uncomplicated; it must be admitted that her language makes her seem rather flighty:

> I did but step out, on some weighty affairs,
> To visit, last night, my good friends in the stars,
> When, before I was got half as high as the moon,
> You despatched Pain and Languor to hurry me down.

(ll. 23–6)

Carter wittily plays off human vehicle against abstract tenor. Stepping out to the stars, taken literally, sounds ridiculous; the gravitational associations of 'weighty affairs' make matters worse, suggesting the pretext is either frivolous or fraudulent: truly 'weighty' matters could never get off the ground. But a personification of Mind is fully entitled to say such things. Besides, the translator of Algarotti considers the stars a legitimate subject of enquiry for all human beings, including women.

In fact, Body's case is extremely weak. Even claims to be acting in self-defence backfire: 'unless I had closely confined you in hold, | You had left me to perish with hunger and cold' (l. 31). This admission of

---

[25] All references to this poem are taken from *Eighteenth-Century Women Poets*, ed. Lonsdale, 168.

vulnerability exposes Body as the inferior partner. Since Mind is immortal, separation holds no terror for her:

> 'I've a friend', answers Mind, 'who, though slow, is yet sure,
> And will rid me at last of your insolent power:
> Will knock down your walls, the whole fabric demolish,
> And at once your strong holds and my slavery abolish:
> And while in the dust your dull ruins decay,
> I'll snap off my chains and fly freely away.'
>
> (ll. 33–8)

On this dramatic note, with death envisaged as the dissolution of an oppressive marriage, the poem ends. Read allegorically, Mind's fierce retort represents the spirit's noble contempt for earthly life; in human terms, it displays a grim practicality well suited to an age of infrequent divorce and high mortality. Body's failure to reply fits in with the disputants' gender roles: it was proverbial that 'Women will have the last word.'[26] Carter does not challenge sexual stereotypes when they suit her artistic or polemic purpose.

Comparison with other poets' treatment of related subjects reveals unusual features in Carter's use of sexual roles, connected with a strikingly intense hostility to the body. She was consciously taking her place within an old-established, and traditionally male-dominated, literary tradition—a tradition which she then reappraised from a woman's viewpoint. The duality of human nature was a perennially attractive theme, which had recently received memorable treatment in Pope's *An Essay on Man* (1733–4):

> With too much knowledge for the Sceptic side,
> With too much weakness for the Stoic's pride,
> He hangs between; in doubt to act, or rest,
> In doubt to deem himself a God, or Beast;
> In doubt his Mind or Body to prefer,
> Born but to die, and reas'ning but to err.[27]
>
> (ll. 5–10)

A less distinguished, though closely related, composition was 'ΓΝΩΘΙ ΣΕ'ΑΥΤΟΝ. Know Yourself' (1734) by Dr John Arbuthnot. Here, too, physical limitations put a stop to star-gazing:

---

[26] See e.g. *The Oxford Dictionary of English Proverbs* (3rd edn., Oxford, 1970), 911.
[27] *The Poems of Alexander Pope*, ed. John Butt (London, 1968), 516.

> I trace the blazing comet's fiery trail,
> And weigh the whirling planets in a scale;
>
> .   .   .   .   .   .
>
> Some beastly want, craving, importunate,
> Vile as the grinning mastiffs at my gate,
> Calls off from heavenly truth this reasoning me,
> And tells me I'm a brute as much as he.[28]

(ll. 37–8, 43–6)

Arbuthnot, however, uses a very different form of sexual representation:

> Thy parents right, I own a mother, earth;
> But claim superior lineage by my Sire,
> Who warmed the unthinking clod with heavenly fire.[29]

(ll. 24–6)

This unflattering reference to motherhood might well have provoked a response from Carter, but it does nothing to suggest why she should have cast her poem in dialogue form. Precedents were, however, available elsewhere.

The Body–Soul dialogue was a popular form of medieval *débat* which enjoyed a resurgence of popularity in the seventeenth century.[30] There are two versions: either 'a virtuous soul overcomes and chastises a guilty and spiritually obtuse body', or there is a less decisive encounter in which 'the Soul shares guilt with the Body and often deserves more blame'.[31] Carter's poem shows resemblances to both forms; this will be demonstrated in comparison with works by Andrew Marvell and Francis Quarles. Both were reprinted in the eighteenth century; if Marvell had higher critical acclaim (albeit for his political works),[32] Quarles's *Emblems* (1635) and other devotional poems had a wider circulation. Readers familiar with the strictures of Joseph Addison[33] and Pope should remember that they do not reflect the opinion of the book-buying public: Pope's remark that 'Quarles is saved by Beauties not his own'[34] is not a gibe at obscure mediocrity, but a protest at undeserved success. In Marvell's 'Dialogue between the Resolved Soul and Created Pleasure', the Soul triumphantly rejects every form of earthly bliss, from gross

---

[28] George A. Aitken, *The Life and Works of John Arbuthnot* (Oxford, 1892), 437.
[29] Ibid. 436.
[30] See Rosalie Osmond, 'Body and Soul Dialogues in the Seventeenth Century', *English Literary Renaissance*, 4 (1974), 364–403.
[31] Barbara Kiefer Lewalski, 'Marvell as Religious Poet', in C. A. Patrides (ed.), *Approaches to Marvell: The York Tercentenary Lectures* (London, 1978), 258.
[32] See Elizabeth Story Donno (ed.), *Andrew Marvell: The Critical Heritage* (London, 1978).
[33] See *Spectator* 58.
[34] *Dunciad* (1743), bk. i, l. 140, in Pope, *Poems*, 516.

sensuality to the gratification of intellectual pride and curiosity. Although Carter's 'Dialogue' aligns intellectual pursuits with spiritual rather than corporeal concerns, her Mind adopts a similarly uncompromising stance. Marvell's 'Dialogue between the Soul and Body' is more enigmatic. Body displays a flair for injured innocence, posing such unanswerable questions as

> What but a soul would have the wit
> To build me up for sin so fit?[35]
>
> (ll. 41–2)

The poem is inconclusive, perhaps to mimic the futility of their endless bickering, perhaps because it simply lacks a conclusion.[36] We can be sure only that there are faults on both sides. Carter also recounts a quarrel between implacable foes, but without leaving moral issues in doubt. In her conviction that it is a poet's duty to teach clear ethical lessons, rather than to indulge in beautiful ambiguities, she is more akin to Quarles, who was driven by a perennial mission to explain. In his *Emblems*, iii. 14, Flesh amuses herself by looking at the world through a prism whose colours represent evanescent earthly pleasure, while her sister Spirit gazes through a telescope at Death and Judgement. The poem ends with Spirit's plea to 'Break that fond glass, and let's be wise together' (l. 52).[37] Even closer to Carter's 'Dialogue' in content, if not form, is *Emblems*, v. 8: the picture shows the soul as a little girl enclosed in a skeleton, and surmounts the verse, '*O wretched man that I am! who shall deliver me from the body of this death?*' (Rom. 7: 24).[38] The accompanying texts emphasize the distress and bewilderment engendered by the soul's predicament, demonstrating that the sooner it can be freed from the body's degrading influence, the better. The next two emblems show a little girl chained to a massive globe, then cooped up in a tiny cage, adding further images of imprisoned femininity. All these works provide useful contexts, if not specific sources, for Carter's 'Dialogue'.

Carter differs most significantly from her predecessors on the issue of physical pleasure. Her Mind perceives the connection with Body solely in terms of pain, coercion, and confinement. All the others, however, air the possibility that the material world has something desirable to offer. Pope's Man might 'prefer' either mind or body. Arbuthnot's persona participates fully, if sporadically, in brutish desires. Marvell's Resolved

---

[35] Andrew Marvell, *The Complete English Poems*, ed. Elizabeth Story Donno (Harmondsworth, 1976), 104.

[36] Ibid. 259.

[37] Francis Quarles, *Emblems, Divine and Moral; The School of the Heart; and Hieroglyphics of the Life of Man* (London, 1866), 138.

[38] Ibid. 208.

Soul, like Quarles's Spirit, acknowledges the attractions of the earthly temptations, arguing only that they are inferior in quality or durability to heavenly joys. As for Marvell's Body and Soul, 'their mutual recriminations point to a past history of temptation and fall'.[39] In this tradition, temptation is sometimes specifically associated with sexuality, especially in women. Quarles's Spirit is depicted as modestly clad, while Flesh is voluptuously naked. Marvell's Resolved Soul is an armed warrior, resisting 'The batteries of alluring sense' (l. 49);[40] Created Pleasure combines them in a woman:

> All this fair, and soft, and sweet,
> Which scatteringly doth shine,
> Shall within one beauty meet,
> And she be only thine.[41]
>
> (ll. 51–4)

The poem in Quarles's *Emblems*, v. 8, describes both temptation and redemption in sexual terms. Firstly, the Soul is a besotted man, Body a predatory mistress:

> Behold thy darling, who, when clad by thee,
> Derides thy nakedness; and when most free,
> Proclaims her lover slave; and being fed
> Most full, then strikes the indulgent feeder dead.[42]
>
> (ll. 15–18)

Then the Soul becomes female, Body her adored but unworthy lover:

> And wilt thou prostrate to the odious charms
> Of this base scullion? shall his hollow arms
> Hug thy soft sides? shall these coarse hands untie
> The sacred zone of thy virginity?[43]
>
> (ll. 37–40)

If already married, Soul is urged to 'Annul, at least avoid, thy lawless act' (l. 49).[44] Body will be supplanted by a formidable rival, as soon as Soul recognizes his merit:

> The Son and Heir to Heav'n's Triune JEHOVE
> Would fain become a suitor for thy love.[45]
>
> (ll. 31–2)

---

[39] Christine Rees, *The Judgment of Marvell* (London, 1989), 64.
[40] Marvell, *Poems*, 26.   [41] Ibid. 27.   [42] Quarles, *Emblems*, 209.
[43] Ibid. 209.   [44] Ibid. 210.   [45] Ibid. 209.

These poems provide only a tiny fraction of the contexts in which representations of female sexuality are associated with the meretricious attractions of the material universe: the Garden of Eden, the Judgement of Paris, the Choice of Hercules, and the enchanted bowers of Circe, Alcina, Armida, and Acrasia would spring to the liberally educated eighteenth-century mind. But Carter defends female dignity and virtue by refusing to show a female personification as either tempting or tempted. Furthermore, despite frequent allusions in the Christian tradition to redeemed souls as brides of Christ, she does not associate Mind's liberation with marriage. Her feminized image of the human spirit is neither rapacious, sensual, nor foolish; at death it will achieve full autonomy. Together, these deviations from tradition form a passionate yet decorously oblique protest against the degradation and subjection of women.

Although 'A Dialogue' is allegorical, its texture is translucent, not transparent. Readers who stay their eye on the surface may detect a plea for real women to be allowed more liberty. The monotonous efforts required to look after the bodies entrusted to them intensify their need for occasional release from domestic labours. Carter testifies elsewhere to the depressing effect of mundane cares. In 'To Miss Hall. 1748. Written at an Oratorio', she acknowledges,

> I droop beneath the dull Fatigue of Life,
> And wish the quiet Refuge of the Grave.[46]
>
> (ll. 19–20)

Many poets have enumerated the agonies that made existence unendurable; few have mentioned anything as numbingly prosaic or hideously convincing as 'dull Fatigue', where 'Fatigue' is not merely a negative state of low energy, but the distressing presence of turmoil and anxiety. She shows in 'To Miss Wilbraham. 1747' that poetry offers an escape from material concerns:

> There Forms, that never struck the Sense
> Of vulgar Sight, appear:
> And Music breathes, that never charm'd
> The dull untutor'd Ear.
>
> No puzz'ling Schemes of low-born Cares
> Distract the peaceful Mind,
> Whose Thoughts are by the gentle Pow'rs
> Of Harmony refin'd.[47]
>
> (ll. 33–40)

---

[46] Carter, *Poems*, 65.   [47] Ibid. 44.

Like 'A Dialogue', but in more solemn mood, these lines suggest the indignity, and perhaps the futility, of attempting to chain an immortal being to the kitchen sink. Yet they fall rather short of their author's normally scrupulous moral standards. Carter voices her yearnings for intellectual exploration and spiritual fulfilment as abhorrence of everything 'dull', 'low-born', 'vulgar', or 'untutor'd'. However metaphorically deployed, her words imply contempt for social and intellectual inferiors. Worse still, from the viewpoint of an eighteenth-century Christian lady, is the use of this language to express discontent with the lowly tasks which she usually perceives as her divinely ordained duty. In aspiring to rise above base materiality, is she falling into the sin of pride? Fortunately, these expressions of frustration and resentment, while perfectly understandable, do not tell the whole story. Other writings, especially her *Epictetus*, show her attempts to establish a very different perspective on the claims of body and mind.

'That warm and practical spirit'

Carter tried to convince herself and Catherine Talbot that, since the ultimate criterion of all behaviour was its tendency to promote salvation, no field of human endeavour was inherently better than any other. Human needs must have their due: it would be arrogant and irresponsible to neglect one's own physical and psychological welfare, or that of others. She refused to agree when Talbot accused herself of wasting time:

A long ride sweeps away all the morning, and then I prowl about the garden. After this I determine, like Pyrrhus, to sit down and enjoy myself, write, read, and be quiet. But then Anne Such-a-one has brought a pound of spinning, there is a new brood of chickens just hatched, Phillis is ill, powders must be weighed out, or Shaw consulted; Flora wants to talk to me; Polly or Dicky are good children, and I must gather a posie to reward them. Thus is unsteady idleness blown out of its path by every breath. (28 September 1750)[48]

Carter pronounces these activities morally superior to any amount of study:

First then, that same ride and walk in the garden, of which you express yourself in such discontented fashion, as sweeping away the whole of the morning, I deem no other than a necessary means for a cheerful enjoyment of the rest of the day. . . . Then in attendance upon Polly, and Flora, and Phillis. . . . Now is there any one person in the world, except the injured one I am defending, whom you would have stigmatized with the title of *unsteady idleness*, for an attention to the virtue, the health, and the happiness of the more helpless part of mankind? In any other case you would have allowed such an employment to have been a very

---

[48] Carter, *Letters*, i. 353.

profitable, and very noble use of time, and would have agreed that the deepest theories, and most sublime contemplations, have not half the merit of that active social virtue that generously exerts itself for the good of others. (26 October 1750)[49]

The importance of establishing a correct ratio between contemplation, comfort, and active duties appears at every stage of Carter's dealings with Epictetus. The project was never envisaged as an exercise of intellect for its own sake; her chief priority was utility. The translation began some time between November 1748 and April 1749, when Carter was in London with Talbot, trying to console her for the death of her mother. Sylvia Myers finds the dating significant:

Although Elizabeth Carter believed deeply that only Christianity offered true solace from life's unhappy events, she also believed that stoicism, though a pagan philosophy, helped people learn how to discipline themselves. Her willingness to translate Epictetus must have arisen from her feeling that she would be undertaking a task that would help her friend gain mental fortitude.[50]

An important contributor to the enterprise was the learned and pious Thomas Secker, who rose from Bishop of Oxford to Archbishop of Canterbury, and brought up Catherine Talbot in his household, looking upon her as a daughter. Secker and Carter frequently communicated with each other, either directly, when he provided detailed comments on her translation, or through her correspondence with Talbot, who often added opinions of her own. With such an impeccably respectable background, *Epictetus* was bound to be an improving work.

Carter's task was made more difficult by incompatibilities between stoicism and Christianity. The disciples of stoicism were taught that the real self was the spirit, a portion of divine fire. Nothing in the material universe, including their own bodies, should have the power to affect their judgement. They must cultivate 'apathy', freedom from joy or sorrow at external phenomena. This philosophy was greatly respected in eighteenth-century Europe, since it promoted self-denial, integrity, and indifference to worldly ills. Many critics, however, maintained that its uncompromising severity expected too much of mere mortals. Jonathan Swift observed, 'The stoical scheme of supplying our wants, by lopping off our desires, is like cutting off our feet, when we want shoes.'[51] Carter conceded that 'nothing can excuse their Idolatry of human Nature'.[52]

---

[49] Ibid., i. 359–60.   [50] Myers, *Bluestocking Circle*, 160.

[51] 'Thoughts on Various Subjects' (1706), in *The Works of Jonathan Swift*, ed. W. Scott (19 vols.; Edinburgh, 1814), ix. 436.

[52] *All the Works of Epictetus, Which are now Extant; Consisting of His Discourses, preserved by Arrian, in Four Books, The Enchiridion, and Fragments. Translated from the Original Greek, by Elizabeth Carter* (2 vols.; 3rd edn., London, 1768), i, p. xxiv.

Nor did she consider apathy a worthwhile goal: she had 'no sort of ambition for the great wisdom of becoming insensible' (13 July 1743).[53] She did, however, realize that apathy might have served an important purpose for pagans:

I know not however whether some of the Stoic extravagancies which carry the appearance of self sufficiency and pride, might not have been the effects of piety, and a zeal to vindicate the ways of Providence. To persons unacquainted with the doctrines of a future state, there seemed to be no other effectual way of reconciling the apparently unequal distribution of things, with the justice and goodness of God, than by renouncing the affections, contradicting the feelings of the human heart, and denying that pain which was often the lot of virtue, to be an evil. (20 December 1752)[54]

As Carter well knew, Epictetus was born into slavery, crippled by a cruel master, and lived through the tyrannical reigns of Nero and Domitian; he must have seen and suffered evil in many forms. In order to ensure that all her readers would learn the correct lessons from Epictetus, she added notes and an introduction to her translation. At first she considered this unnecessary, since she modestly believed that 'none but very good Christians' would trouble to read her work (July 1755),[55] but she yielded to the arguments of Secker and Catherine Talbot, who feared lest ignorant or sceptical readers might lose respect for Christian doctrine. Some of her critical apparatus deals with scholarly matters; the rest, like this attack on the élitism of stoic philosophers, asserts the superiority of Christianity:

A very slight Examination of their Writings is sufficient to convince any impartial Reader how little the Doctrines of this Sect were fitted to influence the Generality of Mankind. But indeed, about the Generality of Mankind, the Stoics do not appear to have given themselves any kind of Trouble. . . . How unlike was this to the diffusive Benevolence of the Divine Author of the Christian Religion, who adapted his Discourses to the Comprehension, and extended the Means of Happiness, to the Attainment of all Mankind![56]

Only readers aware of its limitations could make proper use of stoicism.

The biography and correspondence of Carter show how even questions of literary taste were resolved by appeals to moral utility. Finding her first attempts more polished than was warranted by the ruggedness of the original, Secker demanded, 'why would you change a plain, home, awakening preacher into a fine, smooth, polite writer, of what nobody will mind?'[57] She argued that an ornamental style would enhance

[53] Carter, *Letters*, i. 34.
[54] Ibid. ii. 106–7.
[55] Pennington, *Memoirs*, i. 188.
[56] Carter, *Epictetus*, i., pp. xviii–xix.
[57] Pennington, *Memoirs*, i. 165.

Epictetus' impact: 'books of morality, which have no sacred authority to recommend them, will find it difficult to recommend themselves without some little external helps.'[58] Secker persisted: 'plain and home exhortations and reproofs . . . such as they might be supposed to come extempore from the fulness of the old man's good heart, will be more attended to and felt, and consequently give more pleasure, as well as do more good, than any thing sprucer that can be substituted in their room.' Only these would truly express 'that warm and practical spirit' which he considered 'the characteristick of this book'.[59] To her eternal credit, Carter abandoned her ladylike scruples and gave the world a translation that conveyed, as faithfully as contemporary notions of decency would permit, Epictetus' abrupt manner, his predilection for concrete references and imagery, his penchant for blistering personal insult, and his reckless disrespect of persons. No other style could do justice to the contempt of worldly goods and values that permeated his philosophy.

Epictetus emerges from Arrian's records as a crusty old man whom people accosted at their peril, and Carter does little to soften this image. She renders with merciless accuracy his response to an aspiring student:

For what can I see in you, to encourage me, as spirited Horses do their Riders? Your Person? That you disfigure. Your Dress? That is effeminate. Your Behaviour? Your Look? Absolutely nothing. When you would hear a Philosopher, do not say to him, 'You tell me nothing;' but only show yourself worthy, or fit, to *hear*; and you will find how you will move him to *speak*.[60]

When the Governor came to see him, Epictetus refused to acknowledge the value of his credentials:

Cæsar hath given me a Commission.
    Let him give you a Commission to judge of Music; and what Good will it do you? But how were you made a Judge? Whose Hand have you kissed?[61]

Epictetus' notion of the correct mode of address to a tyrant is little short of suicidal: 'I had forgot, that one is to pay Regard to you as to a Fever, or the Cholic; and that there should be an Altar erected to you, as there is to the Goddess *Fever* at *Rome*.'[62]

Carter renders with unflinching brutality Epictetus' rebuke to an adulterer who defended himself by claiming all women were meant to be held in common:

---

[58] Ibid. i. 166.
[59] Ibid. i. 168.
[60] *Discourses* 2. 24. 2, in Carter, *Epictetus*, i. 263–4.
[61] *Discourses* 3. 7. 3, in ibid. ii. 32.
[62] *Discourses* 1. 19. 1, in ibid. i. 81.

I admit it: and so is a Pig at Table common to those who are invited. But, after it is distributed, go, if you think proper, and snatch away the Share of him who sits next you; or slily steal it, or stretch out your Hand, and taste; and, if you cannot tear away any of the Meat, dip your Fingers and lick them. A fine Companion![63]

She even gives a literal version of Epictetus' suggestions that a man who epilated his body might as well castrate himself or allow himself to be sodomized by other men:

But the whole Affair displeases you. Go to work upon the Whole then. Remove what is the Cause of these Hairs; and make yourself a Woman entirely, that we may be no longer deceived, nor you be half Man, half Woman. To whom would you be agreeable? To the Women? Be agreeable to them as a Man.
   Ay: but they are pleased with smooth pretty Fellows.
   Go hang yourself. Suppose they were pleased with Pathics, would you become one?[64]

Carter does baulk, however, at Epictetus' allusion to defecation. The philosopher, who is discussing the obligation to be true to one's character, considers how different men might react to their master's command that they should hold his chamber-pot for him. She translates the action vaguely as 'submit to a dirty disgraceful Office'. Her revulsion slightly distorts Epictetus' argument, since he is showing that, since men differ from each other, there are some for whom such an action would not be a disgrace, but sensible and appropriate behaviour. She attempts to balance the claims of decorum and scholarship by adding a footnote: 'The Translation here gives only the general Sense, as a more particular Description would be scarcely supportable in our Language.'[65] Her original readership would have applauded her refusal to offend their refined sensibilities. This restraint is probably more a matter of class than of gender: through most of this translation, Carter does not allow femininity to cramp her style.

   At first, it is hard to see why Carter and Catherine Talbot hoped Epictetus' tenets would enable them to accept a situation which obliged them to spend so much time and energy on domestic pursuits. He regards all material concerns as distractions from the pursuit of virtue. He claims that, if his disciples really saw the point of his lessons, they would have to be restrained from instant suicide; they would come to him, saying,

'*Epictetus*, we can no longer bear being tied down to this paultry Body: feeding and resting, and cleaning it, and hurried about with so many low Cares on its Account. Are not these Things indifferent, and nothing to us: and Death no Evil? Are not we Relations of God: and did we not come from him? Suffer us to go

---

[63] *Discourses* 2. 4. 2, in ibid. i. 147.   [64] *Discourses* 3. 1. 6, in ibid. ii. 8–9.
[65] *Discourses* 1. 2. 2, in ibid. i. 9.

back thither from whence we came: suffer us, at length, to be delivered from these Fetters, that chain and weigh us down. . . .'

And in this Case it would be my Part to answer: 'My Friends, wait for God, till he shall give the Signal, and dismiss you from this Service: then return to him.'[66]

With aggressive asceticism, he defines life's little luxuries, and even comforts, as trivia that a true philosopher would find expendable: '*Socrates* lived in his own House, patiently bearing a furious Wife, a senseless Son. For what were the Effects of her Fury? The throwing as much Water as she pleased on his Head, the trampling a Cake under her Feet.' Carter annotates, '*Alcibiades* sent a fine great Cake, as a Present to *Socrates*: which so provoked the Jealousy of the meek *Xantippe*, that she threw it down, and stampt upon it. *Socrates* only laughed, and said, "Now you will have no Share in it yourself." '[67] It is hard to believe Carter would have preserved her equanimity if one of her own cakes had received such mortifying treatment; here, however, in her capacity as classical translator, she enters fully into the spirit of Epictetus' contempt for materiality. She even adds to the joke by her ironical reference to Xanthippe (an archetypal shrew) as 'meek'.

It was the concept of duty that marked the intersection between Epictetus' philosophy and Carter's life-style. While indifferent to pleasure, Epictetus would not excuse irresponsibility. The body might be a nuisance, but its problems must be solved without fuss:

Oh, but my Nose runs.
    And what have you Hands for, Beast, but to wipe it?
    But was there then any good Reason, that there should be such a dirty Thing in the World?
    And how much better is it that you should wipe your Nose, than complain?[68]

Epictetus' insistence on the obligation of caring for others appears in his exposure of self-indulgent emotionalism. An affectionate father deserted his sick daughter, claiming his conduct was natural and right because 'All, or most of us Fathers, are affected in the same Way'.[69] The subsequent inquisition is devastating:

Did you, then, from an Affection to your Child, do right in running away, and leaving her? Hath her Mother no Affection for the Child?
    Yes, surely, she hath.
    Would it have been right, then, that her Mother too should leave her; or would it not?

---

[66] *Discourses* 1. 9. 3–4, in ibid. i. 42–3.   [67] *Discourses* 4. 5. 5, in ibid. ii. 202–3.
[68] *Discourses* 1. 6. 6, in ibid. i. 29–30.   [69] *Discourses* 1. 11. 1, in ibid. i. 49.

It would not.
And doth not her Nurse love her?
She doth.
Then ought not she likewise to leave her?
By no means.
And doth not her Preceptor love her?
He doth.
Then ought not he also to have run away, and left her: and so the Child to have been left alone, and unassisted, from the great Affection of her Parents, and her Friends; or to die in the Hands of People, who neither loved her, nor took care of her?
Heaven forbid!⁷⁰

It is noteworthy that Epictetus looks to the disenfranchised for examples of people who can be trusted to do their duty: the mother is a woman, the preceptor a slave, while the nurse labours under both disadvantages. His precepts fully vindicate Carter's opinion that time spent assisting 'the more helpless part of mankind'⁷¹ is never wasted. Epictetus judges philosophy, and philosophers, by practical results.

In translating Epictetus, close acquaintance with mundane affairs might actually prove helpful. Carter's house wifery joins forces with her scholarship in her treatment of a crux in *Discourses* 3. 6. 4. In the Loeb *Epictetus* (1925–8), W. A. Oldfather translates, 'It is not an easy thing to prevail upon soft young men; no, and you can't catch soft cheese on a fishhook either.'⁷² In the original, the word for cheese, τυρὸν, is used, without an accompanying adjective. In order to make sense of this passage, it is necessary to infer the intended texture of the cheese; scholars sometimes add the word ἁπαλός, 'soft'. Carter conveys the proverbial pungency of the phrase in her own way: 'It is not easy to gain the Attention of effeminate young Men; for you cannot take Custard by a Hook.'⁷³ For all his boasted indifference to material things, Epictetus revealed keen sensitivity to their potential as illustrations for his arguments; it is ironically fitting that he should find such a sympathetic translator in a famed maker of puddings.

As far as Catherine Talbot was concerned, Carter's *Epictetus* fully achieved its original purpose of increasing her emotional resilience. Catherine's enthusiastic response to Carter's translation of *Discourses* 1. 12. 2 shows that Epictetus could even reconcile her to the inanities of the London season:

⁷⁰ *Discourses* 1. 11. 2, in ibid. i. 52.
⁷¹ See above, n. 49.
⁷² Epictetus, *The Discourses as Reported by Arrian, the Manual, and Fragments*, ed. and trans. W. A. Oldfather (2 vols.; London, 1925–8), ii. 49.
⁷³ Carter, *Epictetus*, ii. 26.

What dignity and authority of reason, and common sense! And what an excellent reproof and lesson has the honest, plain old man given to me, (thank you a thousand times for transmitting it.) Whenever I am seized with an impertinent, untimely fit of reformation, or with a splenetic dissatisfaction either with the company or tedious lowliness, methinks I hear his voice sounding in my ears— 'But you are wretched and discontented; be pleased, and make the best of every thing. Call society an entertainment and a festival.'—You are right, most revered Epictetus. In society our hearts should be open to every cheerful, good-humoured kind affection. 'Tis a time of festivity when our business is to delight and do good to one another. What an idea, and how does it brighten up London to me! (5 December 1749)[74]

The translation proceeded very slowly: nearly a decade elapsed between its commencement and its publication. Carter never gave Epictetus precedence over more urgent tasks, such as sewing shirts[75] or preparing her brother Henry for entrance to Cambridge University.[76] Her sense of priorities revealed her as both a true Christian and a worthy disciple of Epictetus. Christians, like stoics, learnt that earthly ambitions were trivial and foolish. Boys, incited to emulate their peers, to cram every precious moment with the acquisition of useful knowledge, and to compete for professional goals, found this lesson easy to forget. Carter, like other women among the early bluestockings, took the lesson to heart; it enabled them to avoid the bitterness which might otherwise have accompanied the thought of so much wasted female talent. The life to come was the proper sphere for their abilities. We can see how literally Carter understood this in her 'Ode to Melancholy':

> In Death's soft Slumber lull'd to Rest,
> She [the soul] sleeps, by smiling Visions blest,
> That gently whisper Peace:
> Till the last Morn's fair op'ning Ray
> Unfolds the bright eternal Day
> Of active Life and Bliss.[77]
>
> (ll. 73–8)

Meanwhile, she felt under no pressure to maximize her potential by speedy publication. Morally speaking, the tasks which interrupted her translation might be equally valuable, if only as a form of spiritual discipline:

If it be considered that with these petty employments, these idle amusements, which in some views we are apt to look upon as so trifling and insignificant, and below the dignity of our nature, are necessarily interwoven innumerable occa-

---

[74] Pennington, *Memoirs*, i. 172.   [75] Carter, *Letters*, ii. 54.
[76] Pennington, *Memoirs*, i. 158.   [77] Carter, *Poems*, 83.

sions for the improvement of it; that in the most ordinary occurrences of conversation there is always some irregularity of temper to be corrected, some impropriety of behaviour to be avoided, some good disposition to be called forth, we shall find no reason to treat the daily exercises of life as low and contemptible, even where there are no opportunities from great and distinguished talents, and advantages, of rising to any remarkable degrees of excellence. (21 October 1751)[78]

Although Carter was destined to live another fifty years after the publication of *Epictetus*, she never again embarked upon a major publication. This work remained her 'crowning achievement'.[79] It is hard to imagine a man of similar talent being content to rest on his laurels at this stage of his career.

From the perspective of eternity, was Elizabeth Carter's *Epictetus* equivalent to another pudding? Only in the afterlife could she hope to achieve final resolution of the tensions generated by the conflicting claims of intellectual and domestic endeavour. Meanwhile, she would probably have accepted Dr Johnson's compliment in the spirit in which it was intended.

[78] Carter, *Letters*, ii. 54–5.
[79] Claudia Thomas, ' "Th'Instructive Moral, and Important Thought": Elizabeth Carter reads Pope, Johnson, and Epictetus', *The Age of Johnson*, 4 (1991), 166.

2 The 'Chit-Chat way': The Letters of Mrs Thrale and Dr Burney

ALVARO RIBEIRO, SJ

'You are a delightful Man, and write delightful Letters.' So begins, by happy accident of preservation, the first of a run of sixty-nine sparkling letters which constitutes the surviving correspondence between Mrs Hester Lynch Thrale, the centre of the literary circle at Streatham, and Dr Charles Burney, the historian of music. The preserved correspondence is unevenly divided: fifty-one letters of Mrs Thrale to Dr Burney have come down to us, as against eighteen of his to her, and while the Burney side of the correspondence has recently been published, the letters of Mrs Thrale still await a full edition.[1]

Mrs Thrale, after her opening declaration of delight in Burney the man as well as Burney the letter-writer, proceeds to contrast his busy public life in the great world to her own rural and private pursuits at Streatham Park. Writing on 18 September 1777 from Streatham she continues:

but then you run about and bustle, and see Churches, and chat with Dr Warton, and dine twenty at Table, and take a dip in the Sea: while London and its Environs are nearly deserted, & none of our Rovers returned from Furlow . . . We therefore are mostly alone & should be reading, to make ourselves (as the Ladies say) companions for *Men of Sense!* instead of that I sent for a Fiddler last Night from the Village & set the Men & Maidens to dancing because it was Hester's Birthday. Sophy was much entertained, and asked—if any Balls were grander?

Delightful as all this might be, Mrs Thrale finally gets to the main point of her letter: an invitation. She writes: 'Well! on the 30th Day of this

I am grateful to the following public and private manuscript collections for permission to quote from unpublished materials in their possession: Family collection of John R. G. Comyn; the Donald and Mary Hyde Collection, Four Oaks Farm, Somerville, New Jersey; Collection of W. G. S. Macmillan; the James Marshall and Marie-Louise Osborn Collection, Yale University Library; Collection of H. L. Platnauer; the John Rylands University Library of Manchester.
[1] Of the eighteen surviving letters of Dr Burney to Mrs Thrale, twelve are preserved in the John Rylands University Library of Manchester and are described in W. Wright Roberts, 'Charles and Fanny Burney in the Light of the New Thrale Correspondence in the John Rylands Library', *Bulletin of the John Rylands Library*, 16 (1932), 115–36. Sixteen of Burney's letters to Mrs Thrale have appeared in *The Letters of Dr Charles Burney*, i. *1751–1784*, ed. Alvaro Ribeiro, SJ (Oxford, 1991) (hereafter *LCB* i). Of the fifty-one surviving letters of Mrs Thrale to Dr Burney, thirty-seven are preserved in the Osborn Collection at Yale. Only three of these letters date from the time of Mrs Thrale's second marriage and find their place in the chronological run of *The Piozzi Letters*, ed. Edward A. and Lillian D. Bloom, i (Newark, Del., 1989). A critical edition of Mrs Thrale's letters remains a great desideratum.

Month we do actually and absolutely set out for Brighthelmston . . . but do come a little before hand for Kindness's sake, and for Shame's sake, and for ev'ry sake, and so adieu till then, unless you send a *Promissory Note* or so.'[2]

Mrs Thrale's letter, in addition to its wit, its easy conversational tone, its concern with private versus public life, and its interest in family matters, might also be regarded as a suitable introduction to her correspondence with Dr Burney as a whole. I should like to note especially how it touches on the two features of the correspondence that I wish to consider in this contribution to honour Roger Lonsdale, whose *Dr Charles Burney: A Literary Biography* (1965) first brought to light the full extent of the literary quality of Burney's campaign for friendship with women.

In the first place, Mrs Thrale raises the issue of 'delight'. The pleasure that she and Dr Burney took in writing to one another, 'to *throw notes* at each other', as Burney put it,[3] is everywhere apparent in the short seven-year span of their close friendship and correspondence. They delighted in each other's company and when apart revelled in the continuation of their conversation by letter. They called this epistolary conversation, significantly enough, 'chat' or 'prattle'. In these letters, written in 'a true Chit-Chat way',[4] Mrs Thrale and Dr Burney can be seen to reach out to one another over distances and to fashion with delight a private, rhetorically constructed world of shared concerns equipped with its secret language-code, allusions, and echoes of remembered conversation. This little private world is, however, constantly threatened by the irruption into it of the great world of public affairs.

Secondly, Mrs Thrale's letter of 18 September 1777 reveals on her part an understanding of the familiar missive letter as mediated presence. 'Do come', she writes, 'a little before hand . . . and so adieu till then, unless you send a *Promissory Note* or so'. That expected '*Promissory Note*', Mrs Thrale implies, might stand temporary proxy for Burney himself should he be unable soon to 'come' in person to Streatham. The notion of the letter as mediating the presence of the letter-writer to the recipient, and vice versa, is central to this correspondence.

In touching on the two aspects of delight and epistolary mediation of personal presence, Mrs Thrale raises for us the central issue that faces every critic who comments on the eighteenth-century familiar letter.

[2] Mrs Thrale to Dr Burney, Streatham, 18 Sept. 1777 (Collection of W. G. S. Macmillan).
[3] Dr Burney to Mrs Thrale, [Chessington], 29 [Aug. 1779] (*LCB* i. 277).
[4] The phrase itself occurs in Dr Burney to the Revd Thomas Twining, Queen Square, 28 Apr. 1773 (*LCB* i. 127).

Mrs Thrale's 'delight' in Burney as a writer of letters might be taken as a token of the rhetorical and literary aspects of their correspondence; her notion of Burney's *'Promissory Note'* as mediating his personal presence might be construed as representative of the historical or documentary dimension of the missive letter. The Thrale–Burney correspondence thus exemplifies a problem in current critical thinking on the letter, for the paucity of comment on this art form in English might be traced to the problem of its generic placement and the consequent lack of appropriate criteria for judgement. The critic of correspondences has to take into account both the literary and the historical features of the genre. To be fruitfully studied the letter must be considered *both* as a rhetorically written and read literary artefact *and* as a historical document which records a moment in the life of its writer and of its recipient. Two recent publications have begun to redress the critical neglect of the letter and to suggest further avenues of investigation: Bruce Redford's *The Converse of the Pen* (1986) and Alan T. McKenzie's collection of critical essays entitled *Sent as a Gift* (1993).[5] From these works the present study gleans some of its critical method in its attempt to illuminate the Thrale–Burney correspondence, noticing especially how letters delicately negotiate various kinds of 'distance' between correspondents; how they forge and rupture relationships; and how a letter held in the hand of its recipient might function as a powerful metonymical symbol of its writer's presence.

'Delightful Letters'

The friendship between Mrs Thrale and Dr Burney had begun a year earlier than the date of the first preserved letter. In January 1776, at a dinner party given by Sir Joshua Reynolds, Burney had met Henry Thrale, the wealthy brewer and MP for Southwark. At the end of the month the first volume of Burney's celebrated four-volume *A General History of Music, from the Earliest Ages to the Present Period* (1776–89) was published to universal acclaim, and later in the year the 50-year-old musician was introduced, by the young littérateur William Seward, to the Thrale home at Streatham, where he met the 35-year-old Hester Lynch Thrale, accomplished, vivacious, literary, and descended of ancient aristocratic Welsh stock. On 12 December 1776 Burney journeyed to Streatham to give his first music lesson to the Thrales' eldest daughter, Hester

---

[5] For especially helpful comments on epistolary critical theory, see Bruce Redford, 'Introduction' in *The Converse of the Pen* (Chicago, 1986), 1–15; Alan T. McKenzie, 'Introduction', and Janet Gurkin Altman, 'Postscript' in *Sent as a Gift: Eight Correspondences from the Eighteenth Century*, ed. Alan T. McKenzie (Athens, Ga., 1993), 1–20 and 201–28 respectively.

Maria, called by Samuel Johnson 'Queeney'.[6] Professional contact soon led to close family friendship between the Thrales and the Burneys. Mrs Thrale's particular favourite early in the relationship was the music teacher's youngest son, the 9-year-old Richard Thomas ('Dick') Burney, a strikingly handsome child, who became a playmate for Mrs Thrale's daughters. In 1778, after the sensational appearance of *Evelina*, Burney's second daughter, Frances ('Fanny'), was virtually adopted by Mrs Thrale as a female companion.

It must not, however, be forgotten that Mrs Thrale's and Dr Burney's increasing intimacy in their epistolary exchanges was conducted against the background of the relationship between employer and employee.[7] The distance that had to be bridged in the correspondence was therefore not only geographical (occurring when Mrs Thrale and Dr Burney happened to be apart), but more significantly social and emotional. The letters of Mrs Thrale and Dr Burney show how they forged their friendship by 'prattle': by finding common ground in the delightful artless chatter of the nursery and the inconsequential talk of their children. Seen in this light the description that Mrs Thrale and Dr Burney themselves give of their exchanges of letters makes sense. They are constantly pleased to call their correspondence by such names as 'chat', 'nonsense', 'prating', 'schtofe', and 'jargon'.

We do not know whether Burney turned up early at Streatham or had to send a '*Promissory Note*' by way of proxy in late September 1777, but we do know that he travelled on the 30th of that month with the Thrales to Brighton. After spending a fortnight's holiday there, Burney returned on his own to London on 12 October but took almost three weeks to get around to thanking his hostess for the jaunt. He writes in the guise of a sulking child from his home in St Martin's Street:

If my long Silence has *traust* into your head any suggestions of my Friendship being like that of many others, only local & temporary, believe them not; for something tells me Daily that however business, disagreeable Situations, or a relaxed & flaccid Mind may prevent me from writing, you will never be forgotten. When I was at Bright^n, I was too happy to write . . . One Peg lower w^d perhaps have made me wish for Pen Ink & Paper; but two or three lower have made me shudder at the thoughts of them. . . . When things go wrong, I find relief from nothing so much as Silence and Sulkiness. . . . I very much want some

---

[6] For a full account of the Thrale–Burney friendship, see Roger Lonsdale, *Dr Charles Burney: A Literary Biography* (Oxford, 1965), ch. 6; James L. Clifford, *Hester Lynch Piozzi (Mrs. Thrale)* (2nd corr. edn., Oxford, 1968), 149–93. See also Mary Hyde, *The Thrales of Streatham Park* (Cambridge, Mass., 1977), 172; *LCB* i. 235 n. 1.

[7] For an invaluable account of Burney as Queeney's keyboard teacher at Streatham, see Valerie Rumbold, 'Music Aspires to Letters: Charles Burney, Queeney Thrale and the Streatham Circle', *Music and Letters*, 74 (1993), 24–38.

Bright^n news, however; for one can read, you know, & still be silent & sulky—& yet a Letter from you w^d let me be neither. . . . I wish you were at Streatham: I w^d then fly thither, & if the foul Fiend followed me, you w^d instantly send him a packing.—You w^d ferment Pleasanter Ideas, & set me a prating as usual—& we'd have our Pastoral, & our Rondeau again; *that's* what we w^d. And let those be wise that will.[8]

To which Mrs Thrale, still on holiday in Brighton, replies:

What News shall I tell you of a Place that will as General Burgoyne says— *Physically* speaking, be soon as much *evacuated* as Philadelphia? we have had Dukes & Dutchesses, but nobody has made us amends for Doctor Burney. . . . The Balls are over, and the Rooms expire tonight; but Mr Thrale does not mean to stir till next Monday or Tuesday sevennight—we have a *Lame* Lord left, a *deaf* Gentleman, and Mr Palmer who *squints*; my Master therefore *compels* them to come in & we play at Cards in the best Parlour. . . . You will see Mr Johnson before I do . . . I wish you would bring him to Streatham yourself on Wednesday or Thursday sennight . . . & would give me a View of the People I most wish to see—after my own Family. . . . Let me—(tho' in *this* Commerce you would rather receive than give I believe) Let me have one Letter more before I listen once again to the Pastoral & Rondo, and before I make you listen to the Nonsense of Your most Faithful | humble Servant | Hester: L: Thrale[9]

We follow Mrs Thrale as she disposes of the distant thunder of the war in America in the first lines of her letter; defuses its threat through her ludicrous news account of the emptiness of Brighton, populated now, it would seem, only by the lame, the deaf, and the cross-eyed; and ends with reassuring Burney her correspondent that all will soon be well at Streatham when they and Johnson reassemble there again to listen to her 'Nonsense'. These are the soothing sounds of the nursery.

The absent-mindedness of children, a certain innocent insouciance, is another characteristic note of this correspondence. In a letter remarkable for its rhetorical control and structure, Burney, exercising the considerable art of seeming artless, writes to Mrs Thrale: 'I forget that I am writing, & my Pen prattles away your Time about *Tweedledum* & *Tweedledee*.'[10] Mrs Thrale in her turn, after writing some two pages of what she calls 'Chat', concludes a letter with, 'I meant only to say I

---

[8] Dr Burney to Mrs Thrale, St Martin's Street, 1 Nov. 1777 (*LCB* i. 235–7).

[9] Mrs Thrale to Dr Burney, Brighton, 6 Nov. [1777] (Osborn Collection).

[10] Dr Burney to Mrs Thrale, St Martin's Street, 11 Jan. 1778 (*LCB* i. 243). For an analysis of the structure of this letter, see my 'Real Business, Elegant Civility, and Rhetorical Structure in Two Letters by Charles Burney', in *Sent as a Gift*, ed. McKenzie, 90–108.

should not like you to call tomorrow when I begun, but see what it is to have to do with such a Prattler as your faithful & Obedᵗ H:L:T.—'¹¹

All these letters, it should be noticed, antedate Johnson's oft-quoted letter to Mrs Thrale of 15 October 1778: 'I never said with Dr. Dodd that *I love to prattle upon paper*, but I have prattled now till the paper will not hold much more, than my good wishes which I sincerely send you.'¹² Johnson might have picked up from the Thrale–Burney correspondence the happy notion of epistolary prattling upon paper. He was probably made privy to some of this exchange, for on three separate occasions Mrs Thrale goes out of her way to enjoin Dr Burney to keep her letters secret from Johnson. In November 1778 she says, 'I write to our Dear Doctor by this Post—don't shew him my Letters though nor say anything of them to him.'¹³ Almost a year later she writes again, 'Are you come from Oxford, & have you been very busy there? have you seen our Dear Dʳ in Bolt Court & is he laid fairly by the Heels? . . . do not read him this nonsense tho', for he will not like we should make Quibbles, while he is making faces with the Gout.'¹⁴ And finally in 1780, writing from Bath, where the Thrales had taken Fanny Burney:

I suppose you think you have all the Music to yourselves, no such Thing: here is Jerningham the poet, & he sings Songs to a Harp—& now he will have the Carpet removed, & then He will have the Fire put out, & then he must wet his Lips with some Cat-Lap, and then he must have two Candles placed by him to shew off his Figure—& when all's done, he sings Arne's Ballads in a Voice so low, so tender & so delicate, that though the Room we sat in was not 20 Feet long—Miss Burney was forced to move her Seat that she might hear the Dear Creature at all. . . . don't tell Seward this Stuff any more than Johnson——We must be *private* you see, as when you shut the Blinds to, & sate with me in your Wrapper. . . . Company coming in relieves you, but distresses me: you will read no more Nonsense and I must break off & go to talk fine.¹⁵

This is surely like two children giggling over a private joke behind the furniture out of sight of the adults. The barely suppressed laughter at the Jerningham performance, the admonition to tell neither Seward nor Johnson of it, and the reminder to be '*private* . . . as when you shut the Blinds to, & sate with me in your Wrapper', constitute what Mrs Thrale

---

¹¹ Mrs Thrale to Dr Burney, [Southwark?], 18 [Feb. 1778] (Osborn Collection).
¹² *The Letters of Samuel Johnson, with Mrs. Thrale's Genuine Letters to Him*, ed. R. W. Chapman (3 vols.; Oxford, 1952), ii. 258; *The Letters of Samuel Johnson*, iii. *1777–1781*, ed. Bruce Redford (Princeton, NJ, 1992), 128.
¹³ Mrs Thrale to Dr Burney, Brighton, 21 Nov. [1778] (Comyn Collection).
¹⁴ Mrs Thrale to Dr Burney, Brighton, 13 [Oct. 1779] (Osborn Collection).
¹⁵ Mrs Thrale to Dr Burney, Bath, [20 Apr. 1780] (Platnauer Collection).

calls her epistolary 'Nonsense' conversation with Dr Burney, from which delightful occupation 'Company coming in' interrupts her and obliges her to 'break off & go to talk fine'.

The use of the metaphor of undress, such as the instance of it just quoted, also features in this correspondence as a token of the delightful intimacy achieved in these talking letters: undress in the writing and undress in the receiving. Here is Burney, early in the correspondence: 'What a too good Creature you are to enquire after your seemingly Naughty Friend! Well, but 'tis now near one & I am still in my Robe de Chambre—But you know *that* gives one an opportunity of saying foolish things—'[16] And Mrs Thrale's undress on the receiving end in Brighton: 'By the way of waking me agreably this Morning my Master brought me your Letter . . . and so you sit up at Night to say & send kind Words away to Brighthelmstone, when you have been harrassed and driven about all Day long.'[17]

The nursery 'prattling', the secrecy enjoined, as well as the undress deemed necessary for this correspondence all serve a deeper purpose. By their means Mrs Thrale and Dr Burney seek to 'advance' and 'prolong' their friendship. Ever mindful of the contrast between Burney's frantically busy life as a music teacher and her own of affluent leisure, Mrs Thrale solicitously seeks ways to relieve Burney of the burden of letter-writing itself, thereby helping to narrow the distance between their two life-styles: 'A Thousand Thanks my Dear Sir—but don't steal from your Sleep to write to me, and think you are doing a good Thing: how will that advance or prolong our Friendship? just the Reverse.'[18] In fact the issue had quickly become part of Mrs Thrale's and Dr Burney's little world of in-jokes. She writes, for example, from Brighton in October 1778: 'how is my sweet Evelina? . . . when you have been kept up late either by Business or Prattle make her write to me, & do not wear your Eyes out to delight mine.'[19] To this suggestion, Burney, in Oxford on a research trip, replies: 'Having commissioned Secretary Fanny to answer your last Charming Letter, or at least to thank you for it in her best Eveline Manner, I came hither on Tuesday Even^g to run my Nose into Cobwebs, & consult the Learned.'[20]

On his return to St Martin's Street later in November 1778, Burney, despite his protestations of lack of time, sends a long letter to Mrs Thrale in Brighton:

[16] Dr Burney to Mrs Thrale, [St Martin's Street, 4 Mar. 1778] (*LCB* i. 244).
[17] Mrs Thrale to Dr Burney, Brighton, 21 Nov. [1778] (Comyn Collection).
[18] Mrs Thrale to Dr Burney, Bath, [20 Apr. 1780] (Platnauer Collection).
[19] Mrs Thrale to Dr Burney, Brighton, 28 Oct. [1778] (Osborn Collection).
[20] Dr Burney to Mrs Thrale, Oxford, 6 Nov. 1778 (*LCB* i. 259).

Ah, my dear Madam! it is lucky for you that I am not an idle man, for you w^d then be *so* pestered with Letters in order to provoke you to quick & ample returns as w^d make you rue the Day you ever learned to write or read. . . . Whether Johnson can tell you that the Hist^y of Music is in a *thriving* state or no, I very much doubt.—But we'll discuss these Points & a 1000 more anon—& so without a flourish I end *tout plat*, with only a hearty wish that now your frolick is nearly at an end, you may be eager to enjoy your own domestic comforts, & even long for a homely Chat with your constant & every-Day Friends, including the Cats, Dogs, chickens, & your affectionate & faithful Servt | C.B.[21]

   This scintillating letter to Mrs Thrale, of which only the opening and closing are here quoted, is undated, as are the majority of Mrs Thrale's letters to Burney. The casual fashion with which these correspondents inscribe their letters 'Brighton 6: Nov.', or 'Wed^y Noon', or even 'Wednesday 13 or 14' represents not only a delightful and informal absent-mindedness, but is part and parcel of their converse of the pen. A private world of 'schtoof' and 'nonsense', a 'chat' or 'prattle' in the fashion of children, an intimate *tête-à-tête* conducted *en robe de chambre* having first 'shut the Blinds to' has no need to be pinned down by place and date.[22] In this manner Mrs Thrale and Dr Burney escape the time-and-place-bound self in their correspondence in order to create, through their letters, their own private world, free from temporal and spatial limitation. Inasmuch as that private sphere is fashioned by 'delightful Letters', it is a world rhetorically constructed by literary art. The pleasure we receive from reading these letters derives then from the slightly illicit delight we take in eavesdropping on private conversation. We position ourselves behind the arras and overhear their epistolary voices in which they render absence or distance, through the medium of the letter, presence and closeness.

Mediated Personal Presence

'Well & now what signifies all this Rattle?' asks Mrs Thrale of Dr Burney in a letter characteristically dated 'Monday Noon 30: August'.[23] The letters themselves suggest an answer to her question: they create a private 'world' in order to bridge distances between the correspondents and to mediate their personal presence to one another. It becomes abundantly

---

[21] Dr Burney to Mrs Thrale, [St Martin's Street, 19 Nov. 1778] (*LCB* i. 261–4).

[22] Mrs Thrale was notorious for not dating her letters. Samuel Johnson, as can be seen from his letters to her, was annoyed enough by her to mount a campaign in 1779–80 to get Mrs Thrale to give a full place and date to her letters. See Johnson, *Letters*, ed. Chapman, ii. 325, 341, 346, 349, 352, 363, 366; ed. Redford, iii. 214, 237, 244, 250, 261, 265.

[23] Mrs Thrale to Dr Burney, [Streatham], 30 Aug. [1779] (Osborn Collection).

clear as we read through this correspondence that part of the logistics involved in their campaign for intimacy engaged Mrs Thrale and Dr Burney in frequent comment on the acts of letter-writing and letter-reading. Mrs Thrale and Dr Burney seem to be keenly conscious while writing to each other that the very act of putting pen to paper brings the intended recipient close to the writer of the letter. As James L. Clifford once remarked of Mrs Thrale, 'she wanted her correspondent to imagine that he was for a few minutes actually in the same room with her and enjoying that most desirable of all pleasures—unrestrained talk'.[24] This vivid presence of the recipient in the consciousness of the letter-writer might take various forms. In one instance, for example, it assumes the shape of an invitation by Dr Burney to Mrs Thrale to witness with him a blunder in the very act of writing his letter to her. He starts the letter on the recto of a standard double sheet, and dates it, typically, 'Thursday Night'. He proceeds to fill his first page, and then opens the double sheet: 'Hey day!' he exclaims, 'here's a trick indeed! I began my Letter on the 1st paper I c^d find, & the other $\frac{1}{2}$ sheet happen'd to have a Page of Hist^y on it—& I am in too great a hurry to be able to take a fresh sheet—' With Mrs Thrale, as it were, looking over his shoulder, Dr Burney goes on to fill the rest of the verso, then cuts away the half-sheet bearing the offending page of draft *History of Music*, and completes his letter to Mrs Thrale on another leaf of paper. It is not surprising that the John Rylands Library has catalogued the resulting bibliographical monstrosity as fragments of two separate letters![25]

A much more complex situation arises in an exchange of letters in late August 1779. On 10 August Mrs Thrale suffered the agonizing miscarriage of an infant son at Streatham.[26] As she convalesced from the ordeal she occupied herself by composing a six-line verse translation of the celebrated epigram 'Animula vagula blandula', attributed to the dying Emperor Hadrian, and wrote out her translation in a letter dated 'Streatham/Wednesday 18: Aug.' to Dr Burney. Mrs Thrale begins by situating herself neatly between Paul Scarron (1610–60), the French burlesque writer long bedridden with paralysis, and the dying Roman Emperor:

When Scarron was dying his Friends lamenting round his Bed; Dear Creatures! says he, tender as you are, I shall never make you cry as much as I have made you laugh.—Adrian was in another Key you know, & wrote the sweet Sonnet so often paraphrased, & never translated.

---

[24] 'Mrs. Piozzi's Letters', in James Sutherland and F. P. Wilson (eds.), *Essays on the Eighteenth Century Presented to David Nichol Smith in Honour of his Seventieth Birthday* (Oxford, 1945), 157.
[25] Dr Burney to Mrs Thrale, [St Martin's Street, 28 Oct. 1779] (*LCB* i. 289).
[26] See *Thraliana: The Diary of Mrs. Hester Lynch Thrale (Later Mrs. Piozzi) 1776–1809*, ed. Katharine C. Balderston (2 vols.; 2nd edn., Oxford, 1951), i. 400–1.

As for myself who am neither Poet nor Emperor, when I thought as I did last Week, that I should no more live two hours than two Centuries—I felt the Inclination though not the power of doing the Latin Sonnet with Less Amplification at least if with less Skill than my Predecessors.—here is my *sickly* Performance; we will as you say not be Voluminous: like the Suzette's Singing, no need to put Cotton in our Ears at least.

> Gentle Soul a moment stay,
> Whither wouldst thou wing thy way?
> Chear once more thy House of Clay,
> Once more prattle and be gay;—
> See! thy fluttring Pinions play
> Oh my Soul! a Moment stay!—

To translate a Sonnet or an Epigram is as you know the highest flight of my Genius—I can say nothing of my own Accord but that I am with all affection & Esteem | Dear Sir | Your ever Faithful | Friend Servant &c &c | H:L:T.[27]

Mrs Thrale seems to offer Dr Burney in this letter much more than simply a six-line verse translation of a classical poem: she seems to present her very self to him. And if, perchance, Burney might not immediately take the point of Mrs Thrale's gift of self in the letter, she adds a remarkable postscript to Burney, who, she knows, is working busily on the second volume of his *History of Music* in his summer retreat at Chessington:

If you love *any* body here at Streatham you may look through the Telescope & see Master J: Acky's fine house upon the Hill—fifty Yards behind which white House live your Friends & your Daughter.
  Look out at the parlour Window this Minute its very fair, & clear, & the Sun shines just right.

The interest of the postscript lies neither in whether or not Streatham is physically visible by telescope from Chessington, nor, indeed, how long it might take for Mrs Thrale's letter to reach Burney at Chessington via his town address in St Martin's Street. By the device of a stage-direction like her postscript, Mrs Thrale telescopes the spatial distance that separates them. By disregarding the time that it takes for her letter to reach Burney at Chessington, and directing him to 'Look out at the parlour Window this Minute', Mrs Thrale nullifies the passage of time. Mrs Thrale and Dr Burney are made spatially and temporally present to one another, and Burney, holding in his hand Mrs Thrale's translation of

[27] Mrs Thrale to Dr Burney, Streatham, 18 Aug. [1779] (Osborn Collection). An almost verbatim transcription of this letter appears in Mrs Thrale's private diary (*Thraliana*, i. 402).

Hadrian's epigram, holds in his hand, in a powerfully symbolic way, Mrs Thrale's proffered 'Gentle Soul'.

The significance of Mrs Thrale's gesture conveyed through her letter of 18 August was certainly not lost on Dr Burney, as is evident in his reply from Chessington:

> Sunday 29th as I
> really believe—
>
> I thought, as how, we were to *throw notes* at each other. I have so long been a dealer in Notes, & am now so beset wth them, that if you liked their fashion, I w^d send you some to *un*bother, as I have had partly enough of them. But, unluckily, a million of my notes w^d not be worth one of yours—*such* a one as I carried off with me, unread, on Tuesday, dated 18 Aug^t—& I found your sweet, dear, innocent, sportive little *Soul*, wrapt up in it!—Well, 'tis a good little Soul, as *eefer vaas*—& I likes it.—Who, but a Swan, c^d sing so sweetly, when dying?—indeed who but the truely innocent & tranquil can sing at all, in such a situation?—Pray content yourself, as you will delight me, with singing *worse*, & being *better*.[28]

Again, whether or not Burney actually picked up Mrs Thrale's letter of 18 August on a visit to town and carried it off, unopened, with him on Tuesday 24 August when he returned to Chessington is not ultimately material to this exchange of correspondence.[29] Burney needs to respond to Mrs Thrale by letting her know that he 'carried off' her 'sportive little *Soul*, wrapt up in' her letter, which, in view of its postscript, must be answered from Chessington.

Such precise manipulation of space and time in the epistolary exchange might serve, conversely, to bridge social and emotional distances from the safe haven that actual geographical distance affords. A striking instance occurs in the Thrale–Burney correspondence in January 1778, when a Burney music lesson with Queeney has been disrupted by some of Mrs Thrale's other guests at Streatham. How is Burney, the employee, to tell his employer and hostess the unpalatable news that her other guests are a confounded nuisance? And how is Mrs Thrale's embarrassment, as recipient of Burney's protest, to be ameliorated? Burney retreats on this occasion to the geographical distance of his town residence and sends a letter.[30] He begins by referring to Mrs Thrale's and Dr Johnson's kind efforts to get young Dick Burney accepted at Winchester, and then places the real business of his letter at the centre:

---

[28] Dr Burney to Mrs Thrale, [Chessington], 29 [Aug. 1779] (*LCB* i. 277).

[29] For the satisfaction of inveterate fact-seekers such as unreconstructed literary historians and traditional editors of correspondence, the sequence of events outlined here appears indeed to have happened. See *LCB* i. 277 n. 2.

[30] Dr Burney to Mrs Thrale, St Martin's Street, 11 Jan. 1778 (*LCB* i. 241-3). See also my 'Real Business' in *Sent as a Gift*, 99-103.

But now, to transfer my Thoughts in a more particular Manner to Streatham: Do you know, my good Mad^m, that I returned from that dear Habitation more dissatisfied with myself than usual, at the thoughts of the little Service I had been able to do Miss T[hrale] during my last Visit? It is neither pleasant to a Pupil to hear, nor a Preceptor to tell Faults, in *Public*—Pray, if you can, let us fight our A, B, C-Battles in private, next Time. Miss B[row]ns are very goodnatured Girls, & as little in the way as Possible; but yet it is not easy for Miss T[hrale] or myself to forget that they are in the Room. When *real Business* is over, I shall rejoice to talk, laugh, sing, or play with them, till the Instant I am obliged to depart—But let our downright *Drumming* be first finished.

By couching his highly crafted letter in terms of mutual concern for the education of their children, Burney bridges the social distance between employer and employee and defuses the emotional distance that might arise from the awkwardness of the situation. This act of social and emotional intimacy is accomplished from the safe haven furnished by the geographical distance between Streatham and St Martin's Street and by Burney's writing to Mrs Thrale in a seemingly artless 'Chit-Chat way'. Yet the message is nevertheless delivered perfectly clearly: when Burney is to teach, 'private' space must be made available to him.

The rebuke must have been received by Mrs Thrale in good part. As far as we can judge from the chronology of the friendship, Burney felt bold enough only a few weeks later, in February 1778, again 'with something between pleasantry and severity', to stifle Mrs Thrale's exuberance when she mimicked the Italian singer Gabriel Piozzi behind his back at the celebrated and embarrassing evening party in St Martin's Street.[31]

Study of the Thrale–Burney correspondence shows that both Mrs Thrale and Dr Burney took seriously, and went beyond, Samuel Johnson's opinion that 'the purpose for which letters are written when no intelligence is communicated, or business transacted, is to preserve in the minds of the absent either love or esteem'.[32] Their letters, it seems to me, serve the function in a literary medium not merely of passively 'preserving' the love or esteem of the absent friend, but of actively telescoping distances of various kinds and thereby fostering presence. The purposes of bringing absent friends close in active memorializing are served in another artistic medium by the famous series of thirteen Reynolds portraits which adorned the walls of the library at Streatham. Burney himself, at the behest of the Thrales, had his portrait painted by

---

[31] See the accounts in *The Early Diary of Frances Burney 1768–1778*, ed. Annie Raine Ellis (2 vols.; rev. edn., London, 1907), ii. 284–7; Madame d'Arblay, *Memoirs of Doctor Burney* (3 vols.; London, 1832), ii. 101–14; and, for the modern reconstruction of the incident, Virginia Woolf, 'Dr. Burney's Evening Party', in *The Second Common Reader* (London, 1932), 108–25.

[32] *Rambler* 152, in *The Yale Edition of the Works of Samuel Johnson*, v, ed. W. J. Bate and Albrecht B. Strauss (New Haven, Conn., 1969), 47.

Sir Joshua at Streatham in January 1781. He is shown in this painting dressed in the spectacular cream and pink robe of his Oxford D. Mus., and he writes the following month to his son Charles:

I have lately sate for my Picture to Sr Jos. Reynolds, for my Friend Mr Thrale . . . who has a Library furnished wth 12 or 14 portraits of Persons with whom it is a great honour to be placed . . . y^r Coz. Ned is now making *two Copies* of my picture, (wch every body says is very like . . .)[33]

The outstanding exception to the chorus of praise of 'every body' for Reynolds's likeness of Burney was Dr Johnson, who 'grumbled at it much— "we want to see *Burney* & he never comes to us in that dress" '.[34] Johnson, as usual, hits the nail on the head. If Burney in real life 'never comes to us in that dress', neither did he, in his letters, ever 'come' to Mrs Thrale 'in that dress', but, as we have seen, rather in his undress *robe de chambre*.

Two months later, on 4 April 1781, Henry Thrale died and the charmed circle at Streatham began slowly to disperse. The little private epistolary world, set apart from but not immune to the depredations of time and space, came to an end when, in July 1784, Mrs Thrale married Gabriel Piozzi, he whom she had mimicked behind his back at Dr Burney's evening party in St Martin's Street. The letter Burney writes on this momentous occasion to Mrs Piozzi is full of pathos and repays close scrutiny. It bears a full-dress date, and is signed in full.

Friday Night
July 30. 1784

Dear Madam.
If my wishes for your felicity sh^d seem to arrive late, I hope you will not imagine that I was slow in forming them; but ascribe my silence to the true cause: my not being certain that the Event had taken place. For, till this evening that I saw it announced, seemingly with authority, in my own Paper, the Morning Chronicle, I had nothing but slight & uncertain rumour to depend on. Fanny is still at Mr Lock's, & I have been shut up in the *Spidery* scribling in the utmost hurry an Acc^t of the late Commemoration of Handel, for immediate publication, so that I gain but little information from mixing wth the world, & still less from news-papers, into wch I have hardly time to look once in a Week. This it seems necessary to say in apology to you, dear Mad^m, & my friend, Mr Piozzi, to whom I most heartily wish every species of happiness wch this world can allow.[35]

Burney locates himself in his study, his '*Spidery*', which used to be the comfortable, secluded place where, in one another's presence, he and

---

[33] Dr Burney to Charles Burney, [St Martin's Street], 25 Feb. 1781 (*LCB* i. 321). The original by Reynolds now hangs in the National Portrait Gallery, London (no. 3884).
[34] Dr Burney to Charles Burney, [Chelsea College, 12 Oct. 1801] (Osborn Collection). See *LCB* i. 321 n. 27.
[35] Dr Burney to Mrs Piozzi, [St Martin's Street], 30 July 1784 (*LCB* i. 421–3).

Mrs Thrale had spun, out of nonsensical epistolary 'Chit-Chat', the interconnected web of their private world. This private world is now shattered by the irruption of the great world in the shape of the *Morning Chronicle*; public 'rumour'; and publication of the account of the glamorous musical event-of-the-century that was the 1784 Commemoration of Handel chronicled by Dr Burney at the command of King George III. This is the public world that Burney now wishes might 'allow' the newly married couple 'every species of happiness'.

Burney proceeds to a second paragraph in which he begs Mrs Piozzi to make his peace with Piozzi for neglect as a correspondent. It comes as no surprise that the central paragraph of this letter is about letter-writing: 'I fear M^r P[iozzi] is displeased with me for not writing to him at Milan in answer to the Letter wth wch he favoured me from that City early last Winter.'

Nothing but a familiarity with the entire Thrale–Burney correspondence which precedes it can, however, expose the full pathetic weight of Burney's astonishing final paragraph. In it he weaves together those two strands of artistry and history that constitute the eighteenth-century familiar letter at its best. Before he concludes his letter with his signature, Burney seems to cast one last longing look back at that private Streatham world of face-to-face encounter, continued, supplemented, and elaborated by the gift of self in the correspondence. He takes one last peep through the telescope at happier days. Burney comes finally to Mrs Piozzi in 'that dress' deplored by Johnson, in the form of his portrait now engraved by Bartolozzi—and awaits Mrs Piozzi's orders for the 'future disposal' of himself in the Reynolds original:

I had not time to thank you for your last Letter, or the agreeable Visit it procured me from Mr Lysons, who is a charming young man. I had the honour of sending to you, by him, a *proof Print* from Bartolozzi's engraving of me from your picture by Sr Joshua. It will not be published or presented to any one else till my last Vol. [of the *History of Music*] comes out; an event not yet within my ken. Bartolozzi has the Picture still; but is to return it to Sir Jos[hua] & your orders for its future disposal will be instantly & implicitly obeyed.

I beg you will present my best Comp^{ts} of congratulation to Mr Piozzi, & ever regard me as your most obliged & affectionate Servant. | Chas Burney.

The personal presence to one another, hitherto mediated exclusively by the correspondence between Mrs Thrale and Dr Burney, is here given over to the charge of third parties such as the new friend Lysons, who carries Burney as an engraved proof-print to Mrs Piozzi. She, on her part, replies from Bath in a letter that pointedly mentions neither the engraving nor the Reynolds original:

The Compliments of Congratulation which we have received from many friends—from most indeed; have been less dear to both of us than the kind Letter which came this Moment to my hands from dear Dr Burney . . . the Inhabitants of this Place . . . stifle us with tenderness & Civility. Business however will call us from hence in a few days when I shall at least have to make me amends—the Pleasure of saying with how much Sincerity I am ever Dear Dr Burney's | most affec^{te} & faithful Servt | H: L: Piozzi.[36]

Mrs Piozzi seems, sadly, to look forward to maintaining the epistolary intimacy that she and Burney had known. She holds in her hands his letter of 30 July, and hopes it might lead them back to regular friendly encounter by letter. It was not to be.

Postscript

After the 1784 lapse in their relationship, the surviving documentation shows that Mrs Piozzi and Dr Burney met only twice more, and then by chance encounter. They attended the same concert in April 1794, and met for the last time in Bath early in 1807.[37] On 21 January 1807 Mrs Piozzi was a week away from her sixty-sixth birthday, and the ailing Burney was 80 years old. On that date they exchanged correspondence once again, and, as it was to transpire, for the last time.[38] Burney begins with apologies:

I was so animated by the honour of your visit, after losing sight of each other for so many years, that I fear you thought me less an invalide than I really am, and must have imagined me rude & ungrateful for not returning your visit . . . As soon as I am able to go out like other Christians, with safety, be assured, dear Madam that nothing will afford me more pleasure than the renewal of old friendships, and the talking over old times; and I shall wait on my ingenious and worthy friend Mr Piozzi with the utmost pleasure. . . . I am grieved that with his other blessings he does not enjoy better health . . . You will excuse, it is to be hoped, the garrulity of an *Octogenaire* . . .

To which Mrs Piozzi answers immediately:

Dear Doctor Burney | has no Reason to complain while he can write such Letters . . . all Thanks for kind Enquiries & Adieu——If Sir Walter James had not given me to understand that you went out in an Evening, You should have had another Call from your old Friend & ever | faithful Servt | H:L:P.

---

[36] Mr and Mrs Piozzi to Dr Burney, Bath, 2 Aug. [1784] (Osborn Collection); see also *The Piozzi Letters*, ed. Bloom, i. 106.

[37] Lonsdale, *Dr Charles Burney*, 368–9, 461.

[38] Dr Burney to Mrs Piozzi, Bath, 21 Jan. 1807 (Rylands Eng. MS 545/13; draft, Osborn Collection); Mrs Piozzi to Dr Burney, Bath, 21 Jan. 1807 (Osborn Collection); Dr Burney to Mrs Piozzi, [Bath], 21 Jan. 1807 (Hyde Collection; draft, Osborn Collection).

And Burney writes back the same day:

We are not come to a right understanding yet. . . . I know not how my good friend, Sir Walther James, c^d construe, or rather *mis*construe anything I said about evening visits. I have made no one evening, or even morning Visit, but to the Pump, since I came hither . . . This being 'the truth, and nothing but the truth &c' let not dear Madam, cold Etiquette, after we have fortunately met, keep us asunder. If you will kindly honour me with a call any time after one O'clock, and receive this as a *promissory note* of payment; whenever, *if* ever I am able, you will very much oblige & gratify, you[r] old, your *very* old and obliged servant | Chas Burney

Again, the full literary and human significance of this exchange of letters emerges only after we take into account the brief seven-year flourishing of the Thrale–Burney letters. Mrs Piozzi's compliment on the quality of Burney's letter and his reply, duly invested with the private signal of that '*promissory note*', take them almost thirty years back in space and time, all the way to the beginning of their correspondence in 1777.

In his *Rambler* essay on the familiar letter, Johnson had observed of the genre, 'the pebble must be polished with care, which hopes to be valued as a diamond'.[39] To us, as readers of the conclusion to the letters of Mrs Thrale–Piozzi and Dr Burney, the literary and the historical aspects of the eighteenth-century familiar letter here tug against one another and at our heartstrings. Even in their old age, and after their private 'Chit-Chat' epistolary world had long ceased to exist, we find these correspondents still polishing the pebble of their letter-writing art, and leaving behind them a few diamonds.

[39] *Rambler* 152, in *Yale Works*, v. 47.

3 Radical Affinities: Mary Wollstonecraft and Samuel Johnson

JAMES G. BASKER

The continuing recovery of the works of eighteenth-century women writers, exemplified in such projects as Roger Lonsdale's *Eighteenth-Century Women Poets* (1989) and Janet Todd's and Marilyn Butler's seven-volume edition of *The Works of Mary Wollstonecraft* (1989), poses new problems even as it rectifies old imbalances. With the uncovering of lost or forgotten texts, new complexities emerge that destabilize our understanding of writers we thought we knew with categorical certainty. This chapter seeks to explore a dramatic example of such complexity: the unexpected but profoundly important presence of Samuel Johnson in the mind and writings of Mary Wollstonecraft.

At first glance such a connection seems almost incredible. 'More unlikely allies could hardly be imagined,' a Wollstonecraft scholar concluded, while noting one point on which their opinions had coincided.[1] What connection could one expect between Johnson, the stern moralist and critical dictator, a devout Anglican, arch-conservative Tory, and pro-monarchist who once compared a woman preacher to a dog walking on its hind legs, and Mary Wollstonecraft, the literary and political radical, religious Dissenter and apologist for the French Revolution, ardent feminist, social nonconformist, and 'scandalous' woman? One might well imagine that Samuel Johnson, who died before Wollstonecraft had published a word, is being mistaken for Joseph Johnson, the liberal publisher and close friend of Wollstonecraft who gave her professional, intellectual, and emotional support throughout her career.

But it is *Samuel* Johnson who, for all their differences, turns up everywhere in her thought and writing, and who seems to have held such a powerful appeal—intellectually and psychologically—for Wollstonecraft. This chapter pursues two aims: first, to map the intertextual connections between them and thus show the extent to which Johnson informs Wollstonecraft's mind and work; and, second, to examine three

---

[1] Moira Ferguson, 'Introduction', *Maria, or the Wrongs of Woman* (New York, 1975), 12. Since then the scholarly neglect or denial of links between Wollstonecraft and Johnson has continued, with two slight exceptions: the notes to Janet Todd's and Marilyn Butler's edition of *The Works of Mary Wollstonecraft* (New York, 1989) (hereafter *Works*); and a very perceptive note by Stuart Sherman entitled 'Wollstonecraft and Johnson', *Johnsonian News Letter*, 52/1 (Mar. 1992), 11–15.

areas in which their affinity seems most remarkable—Wollstonecraft's deliberate affiliation with Johnson as critical authority; as commentator on the condition of women; and, in her own life, as kindred spirit and consoling presence during moments of personal crisis and depression.

The story of connection between Johnson and Wollstonecraft begins not in the writings but, rather surprisingly, in their lives. In 1784, when he was at the height of his fame and she had yet to begin her writing career, Johnson and Wollstonecraft actually met and spent an afternoon talking together. William Godwin describes this meeting, which took place years before he had ever met Mary, in an early chapter of his *Memoirs of the Author of A Vindication of the Rights of Woman* (1798), obviously recounting it as Mary had told it to him. Mary had been living in the community of Dissenters and intellectuals gathered around Richard Price in Newington Green, where she and her sisters and Fanny Blood conducted a school and socialized in Price's circles. 'It was during her residence at Newington Green', Godwin tells us,

that she was introduced to the acquaintance of Dr Johnson, who was at that time considered as in some sort the father of English literature. The doctor treated her with particular kindness and attention, had a long conversation with her, and desired her to repeat her visit often. This she firmly purposed to do; but the news of his last illness, and then of his death, intervened to prevent her making a second visit.[2]

One can only imagine what the 75-year-old Johnson, who very much enjoyed the company of intelligent women, and the 25-year-old Wollstonecraft, who was drawn to intellectual mentors, talked about in their 'long conversation' that afternoon, or what might have developed in this remarkable friendship—potentially one of the most extraordinary in literary history—had it not been cut short by Johnson's death soon after in December 1784. Perhaps Godwin's description of Johnson as 'in some sort the father of English literature' also resonates on the level of Wollstonecraft's personal response to Johnson—she who had been so brutalized and rejected by her own father. But certainly this account of their first meeting suggests her disposition towards Johnson, whom she still remembered more than a dozen years later in the most positive terms, as having treated her 'with particular kindness and attention' and having asked her 'to repeat her visit [to him] often'. Her attraction to Johnson after just one afternoon's conversation is implicit in the language (which Godwin had no reason to exaggerate) of her resolution: 'This [i.e. to visit Johnson often] she firmly purposed to do.' Wollstonecraft scholars tend

[2] Godwin, *Memoirs of the Author of A Vindication of the Rights of Woman*, ed. Richard Holmes (Harmondsworth, 1987), 216.

to agree, as one has written, that 'she cherished the memory of meeting him, but turned decidedly against his view of life'.[3] But, in fact, Wollstonecraft's response to Johnson in person foreshadows the pattern of response she was to exhibit to his writings, visiting and revisiting them again and again, over the rest of her life.

When we turn to her writings, we can trace Johnson's presence throughout Wollstonecraft's career, from the very first of her imaginative writings in 1786, to the novel she began and left unfinished in the last year of her life. A chronological survey is in itself quite revealing. For example, when Wollstonecraft first decided to become a writer and started on a novel in 1786, she laid out an allegorical fiction—'The Cave of Fancy'—modelled closely on Johnson's *Rasselas*. In the fragment that survives we can see that, like Johnson, she sets the scene 'in a sequestered valley, surrounded by rocky mountains' and her protagonist is an elderly sage who, like Rasselas's mentor Imlac, finds it wisest to live withdrawn from the world. But it is in the first lines of the novel, an address to her readers, that Wollstonecraft echoes Johnson exactly. *Rasselas* begins with these lines:

Ye who listen with credulity to the whispers of fancy, and pursue with eagerness the phantoms of hope; who expect that age will perform the promises of youth, and that the deficiencies of the present day will be supplied by the morrow; attend to the history of Rasselas prince of Abissinia.[4]

Wollstonecraft's 'Cave of Fancy' opens this way:

Ye who expect constancy where every thing is changing, and peace in the midst of tumult, attend to the voice of experience, and mark in time the footsteps of disappointment; or life will be lost in desultory wishes, and death arrive before the dawn of wisdom.[5]

From here 'The Cave of Fancy' becomes a story in which the hermit sage finds washed up on the beach, amidst a slew of corpses, a little girl who is the sole survivor of a shipwreck that has killed her family and all the other passengers. The sage rescues the little girl, and begins to raise and educate her. There, however, the story is left in suspense because, for whatever reason, Wollstonecraft never got beyond the third chapter of this psychologically suggestive little tale. (One might wonder whether this story is an early expression of a fantasy—the orphaned little girl rescued by an elderly sage—that was to manifest itself more than once in Wollstonecraft's life and whether that fantasy had anything to do with

---

[3] Claire Tomalin, *The Life and Death of Mary Wollstonecraft* (London, 1974), 34.
[4] *The History of Rasselas*, in *The Yale Edition of the Works of Samuel Johnson*, xvi, ed. Gwin J. Kolb (New Haven, Conn., 1990), 7.
[5] 'The Cave of Fancy', in *Works*, i. 191.

her affinity for the life and writings of Johnson himself, the elderly sage she had met in 1784.)

Thereafter, though she turned to other and less overtly Johnsonian forms of writing, Wollstonecraft never completely dropped Johnson from her frame of reference or, apparently, from her unconscious mind. Quotations, echoes, and comments about Johnson crop up everywhere. These include Johnsonian echoes and allusions in her first published novel *Mary* (1788), her children's book *Original Stories* (1788), her anthology *The Female Reader* (1789), seventeen different book reviews she wrote for the *Analytical Review* between 1788 and 1796, five separate allusions in *A Vindication of the Rights of Woman* (1792), at least one in her travel book *Letters Written during A Short Residence in Sweden, Norway, and Denmark* (1796), and a key section of her critical essay 'On Poetry' (1797), as well as passages in her private correspondence and in her unfinished novel *The Wrongs of Woman: or, Maria*, published posthumously in 1798.

Some of these allusions are admittedly slight. One of her *Original Stories* for children is about a beautiful girl who becomes so vain she neglects her education, only to be ruined when she loses her looks to smallpox; the plot is taken from one of Johnson's *Rambler* essays, the same essay that Wollstonecraft selected for the anthology she was then preparing, *The Female Reader* (1789).[6] There are routine citations from Johnson's *Dictionary* and various casual allusions, including one in her *Letters Written in Sweden, Norway, and Denmark* in which she mistakenly attributes to Johnson a remark that is actually by Swift.[7]

But even the slightest of these allusions to Johnson can be quite telling. In discussing the Portuguese people in chapter 14 of her novel *Mary*, Wollstonecraft contrives not only to draw in Johnson (who had never commented on the Portuguese) but to align herself with his way of thinking. She writes: 'The Portuguese are certainly the most uncivilized nation in Europe. Dr Johnson would have said, "They have the least mind." '[8] Her appropriation of Johnson in this way seems all the more significant in the last chapter of *Mary*, where, apparently unconsciously, Wollstonecraft closes the novel with a melancholy distillation of the last chapters in *Rasselas* and the final lines of *The Vanity of Human Wishes*. Where Johnson had enjoined us to pray for (among other blessings)

[6] *Original Stories*, in *Works*, iv. 391; 'On the Loss of Beauty' i.e. *Ramblers* 130, 133, *Female Reader*, in *Works*, iv. 102–8.

[7] Wollstonecraft quotes from Johnson's *Dictionary* a definition of the word *pretty* in a 1788 book review in the *Analytical Review*; see *Works*, vii. 42–3. *Letters Written in Sweden, Norway, and Denmark*, in *Works*, vi. 264.

[8] *Mary*, in *Works*, i. 36. Wollstonecraft is adapting a remark Johnson makes in Boswell's *Journal of a Tour to the Hebrides, with Samuel Johnson* (1785).

'faith', 'a will resigned', and 'Love, which scarce collective man can fill', Mary is left with 'a heart in which there was a void, that even benevolence and religion could not fill. The latter taught her to struggle for resignation; and the former rendered life supportable.' Where Nekayah at the end of her travels in *Rasselas* had resolved to shift her focus from 'the choice of life' to 'the choice of eternity' and, on the practical level, to found a women's college in which she could 'converse with the old' and 'educate the young', Mary, after her travels, undertakes a life in which 'she visited the sick, supported the old, and educated the young' and meanwhile shifts her thoughts from the trials of this world to life in the next, a 'world where there is neither marrying, nor giving in marriage'.[9]

Wollstonecraft's Johnsonian allusions are denser and more overt in her critical writings. Book reviews for the *Analytical Review* were her main vehicle for critical expression from 1788 to 1792, a period during which she wrote at least 200 articles and perhaps as many as 400 or more.[10] Almost certainly at her own request, Wollstonecraft took charge of reviewing most of the books that seemed to have anything to do with Johnson during these years. Among them were:

A Sermon, written by the late Samuel Johnson for the Funeral of his Wife . . . ed. by the Rev. Samuel Hayes (Aug. 1788).

Johnson's Sermons on Different Subjects . . . ed. by Hayes (Sept. 1788).

The Beauties of the Rambler, Adventurer, Connoisseur, World, and Idler (Oct. 1788).

Johnson's Sermons on Different Subjects . . . ed. by Hayes, vol. 2 (Sept. 1789).

[Cornelia Knight], *Dinarbas; A Tale: Being a Continuation of Rasselas* (June 1790).

Arthur Murphy, *An Essay on the Life and Genius of Samuel Johnson* (July 1792).

[Anon.], *The Character of Dr Johnson, with Illustrations from Mrs Piozzi, Sir John Hawkins, and Mr Boswell* (July 1792).[11]

Through these anonymous reviews her view of Johnson emerges most directly: her sympathy and admiration for the man (repeated expressions of 'esteem and respect'); her particular regard for his views on marriage (singling out his 'excellent sermon on Matrimony, which he compares to

[9] *Vanity of Human Wishes*, ll. 359–64; *Rasselas*, 175; *Mary*, in *Works*, i. 73.
[10] Todd, 'Prefatory Note', in *Works*, vii. 14–18.
[11] *Works*, vii. 32–3, 36–42, 48, 257–9, 443–6, 446–7. Wollstonecraft's review of the second volume of *Johnson's Sermons on Different Subjects*, which appeared in the *Analytical Review*, 5 (Sept. 1789), 64–7, was unaccountably omitted from the *Works*, perhaps by an oversight. Wollstonecraft's authorship has been well established and the article meets the same criteria laid down by the editors for inclusion of her other reviews. See Todd, 'Prefatory Note', in *Works*, vii. 14–18.

friendship'); her appreciation of his many published works ('from which we had often received instruction'); her sense that the *Rambler* 'claims the first place' among his writings and that *Rasselas* ('so well known . . . [that] comments on it might appear to be almost impertinent') was so accomplished a novel that no satisfactory sequel to it could 'have been done [except] by Dr Johnson himself'. But she does not only praise him. Wollstonecraft faults Johnson for aspects of his religion (too 'gloomy, narrow . . . [and] superstitious'), his personality ('overbearing ferocity', 'growling petulance', and a 'propensity to contradict'), his prose style (e.g. in the *Life of Savage*, 'dogmatical interruptions . . . sententiously thundered out'), his critical views (e.g. in the *Lives of the Poets* 'a grossness in Johnson's taste . . . led him into many errors'), and his lack of true poetic sensibility ('he had not a poetic eye'). On balance, Wollstonecraft seems to feel that we must neither exaggerate nor overlook Johnson's faults, for, as she says in reviewing Murphy's biography, 'Posterity will doubtless allow, that Dr Johnson was both a wise and good man, a respectable moralist and tolerable critic; but may not hyperbolically add, that his defects were only spots in the sun.'[12]

What reveals another dimension in Wollstonecraft's attraction to Johnson are the dozen or more book reviews in which, although the book under review has nothing to do with Johnson, Wollstonecraft none the less manages to cite, quote, or somehow invoke him. In reviewing *The Life of Baron Frederick Trenck*, for example, she cites Johnson from memory on autobiography: 'Dr Johnson has somewhere remarked, that the life of the most insignificant fellow creature, sketched by himself, would certainly convey many instructive lessons to the reader.'[13] (She is recalling *Idler* 84 and perhaps *Rambler* 60.) At times her affinity with Johnson becomes something nearer identification with him. Discussing a book about Defoe, she invokes Johnson's populist critical standards, probably derived from her memory of Johnson's remarks in the *Preface to Shakespeare*: 'A book, Dr Johnson would say, that is generally read, must have merit: and who has not heard of *Robinson Crusoe?*'[14] Elsewhere she borrows a critical model from Johnson to apply to a poem under review: 'Dr Johnson's criticism on Cato may be applied to this story. The reader is more anxious to hear what the characters, who people the scenes, say, than to know what they do.'[15] In part, no doubt, Wollstonecraft cites Johnson as a rhetorical device to add authority, or at least flair, to her anonymous critical opinions. But it is telling that the added authority is anti-élitist: in each of these instances the Johnsonian opinion that Wollstonecraft incorporates is populist, reader-centred,

[12] *Works*, vii. 32, 37, 360, 257–8, 36, 110, 445, 110, 303, 445–6.
[13] Ibid. 75.   [14] Ibid. 307.   [15] Ibid. 248.

even democratic. Here, on the level of intuitive sympathy, Johnson's humanist universalism meets Wollstonecraft's democratic egalitarianism. In finding her own voice as a critic, she has appropriated elements of Johnson's voice and thus extended his influence to her readers while also, in subtle ways, transforming the nature of that influence. Wollstonecraft's Johnson-as-critic sounds more the friend of the common reader than the literary dictator.

Wollstonecraft's reading in Johnson was unusually deep and extensive. At one point or another in her published writings she shows specific familiarity—often from memory—with virtually every one of Johnson's works: *The Life of Savage*, the translation of Lobo's *Voyage to Abyssinia*, *The Vanity of Human Wishes*, the *Rambler*, *Idler*, and *Adventurer*, the *Dictionary*, *Rasselas*, the *Preface to Shakespeare*, the *Lives of the Poets*, his posthumously published *Sermons* and *Prayers and Meditations*, even his failed tragedy *Irene* and minor lyric poems, as well as Hester Thrale Piozzi's *Anecdotes of the Late Samuel Johnson* (1786), Arthur Murphy's *Essay on the Life and Genius of Samuel Johnson* (1792), and of course Boswell's *Life of Johnson* and his *Journal of a Tour to the Hebrides*.[16] There is no other writer—even allowing for those such as Rousseau, whom she treats so extensively in the *Vindication* and elsewhere—with whom she exhibits such a thoroughgoing familiarity. Whatever the stage of life at which she accomplished this detailed reading of his works, Wollstonecraft truly was schooled in Johnson.

Wollstonecraft's embrace of Johnson poses many challenges, but none greater than how to interpret the use, in her feminist writings, of a writer often supposed to be a misogynist. One of Wollstonecraft's first major projects was *The Female Reader* (1789), designed as the female counterpart to a widely used school anthology, Enfield's *The Speaker*, and composed of a large number of pieces in prose and verse 'selected [the title-page announces] from the best writers, for the improvement of young women'. This collection has been called the first feminist anthology, a designation earned not only for the orientation of its contents but, as Moira Ferguson has pointed out, for the unusually high proportion of texts selected from women authors—about a third.[17]

What is more surprising to some, however, is that Wollstonecraft included five pieces by Johnson: a poem called 'The Natural Beauty', a speech from his tragedy *Irene*, and three *Rambler* essays (nos. 102, 130, and 133). Each is designed to instil enlightened values in young women, none more so than *Rambler*s 130 and 133, which tell the story of

[16] Ibid. i. 36, 191; iv. 102, 142, 155; vii. 9–10, 32–3, 36, 41, 42–3, 48, 109, 187–8, 307, 360, 443, 444, 445.
[17] Moira Ferguson, 'Introduction', *The Female Reader* (1789) (Delmar, NY, 1980), pp. xix–xx.

Victoria, a beauty who neglects her education and thus is ruined when smallpox disfigures her.[18] Johnson's five pieces are far more than those included from Richardson (one), Sterne (one), or Goldsmith (two), writers we more readily associate with women readers than we do Samuel Johnson, and almost as many as the eight that Wollstonecraft included from her own writings. Apparently Wollstonecraft regarded writings by Johnson as essential to the formation of young women's minds, something we find less surprising if we go back and read the more than forty essays in the *Rambler* and *Idler* that Johnson devoted to women's issues, most of them written in women's voices and all of them sympathetic to the condition of women in eighteenth-century society.[19] Johnson's 'Victoria', with its indictment of sexist social values, is a powerful example, as Wollstonecraft saw. Its message to young women about proper values, self-respect, and uncompromising virtue is reiterated in his poem 'The Natural Beauty' and the exemplary Aspasia's speech from *Irene* (III. viii. 26–35), while *Rambler* 102 (often anthologized in schoolbooks for boys) allegorizes about life as a dangerous sea voyage threatened by the Gulph of Intemperance and the Rocks of Pleasure.

Wollstonecraft's reading of Johnson as sympathetic to the condition of women forces us to re-examine the myth of Johnson the misogynist, a myth that had almost hardened into received truth when the editors of the highly influential *Norton Anthology of Literature by Women*, in their introduction to 'The Seventeenth and Eighteenth Centuries', could invoke Johnson's 'women preachers–dancing dogs' remark to conclude that Johnson 'was assuming that creativity and femininity were contradictory terms'.[20] And if, as we follow Wollstonecraft's lead in rereading Johnson's *Rambler*s and other works on women, we notice carefully where we have to go to find them—that is, to the complete works of Johnson because no selected editions include them—we begin to see a contributing factor to the distortion of his reputation concerning women. As recent scholarship has shown, few of Johnson's editors over the past two centuries have shared Wollstonecraft's sense of Johnson's interest in women and thus have systematically, if unintentionally, suppressed his essays on women's issues.[21] Wollstonecraft's inclusion of Johnson in her feminist anthology is not only a corrective to our misreading of him, it is a reminder—in an era of canonical self-consciousness—of our responsibilities as editors and anthologists.

[18] *The Female Reader*, in *Works*, iv. 102–8, 142, 155, 164–7.
[19] Basker, 'Dancing Dogs, Women Preachers, and the Myth of Johnson's Misogyny', *The Age of Johnson*, 3 (1990), 63–90. See especially App. A, 80–4.
[20] Sandra M. Gilbert and Susan Gubar (eds.), *The Norton Anthology of Literature by Women* (New York, 1985), 53.
[21] Basker, 'Dancing Dogs', 78–80, 84–7.

Modern readers are perhaps even less prepared to find Wollstonecraft quoting Johnson in her most famous book, *A Vindication of the Rights of Woman* (1792). Though the writings of Jean-Jacques Rousseau, Catherine Macaulay, and others are more frequently cited in the *Vindication*, it is again Johnson's intertextual presence that startles, because it is so unexpected in this classic text of feminism. Wollstonecraft's uses of Johnson are various. She turns to Johnson's *Dictionary*, as was perhaps inevitable for writers even many decades after its first publication, for a definition of the word *sensibility*, only to criticize it as inadequate (ch. 4, 'Observations on the State of Degradation to Which Woman Is Reduced by Various Causes').[22] In chapter 11, 'Duty to Parents', she enlists Johnson the moralist in support of her observation that 'I never knew a parent who had paid more than common attention to his children, disregarded.' 'Dr Johnson makes the same observation,' says Wollstonecraft in a footnote, alluding to *Rambler* 148, in which he discusses the pitfalls of parent–child relations.[23]

But again what strikes the modern reader is the way in which Wollstonecraft resorts to Johnson even when discussing a feminist topic. Thus in chapter 9, 'Of the Pernicious Effects Which Arise from the Unnatural Distinctions Established in Society', Wollstonecraft exposes the false values and vacuities in the lives of conventional upper- and middle-class women this way:

What can be a more melancholy sight to a thinking mind, than to look into the numerous carriages that drive helter-skelter about this metropolis in a morning full of pale-faced creatures who are flying from themselves. I have often wished, with Dr Johnson, to place some of them in a little shop with half a dozen children looking up to their languid countenances for support.[24]

Here she alludes to *Rambler* 85, 'On the Mischiefs of Total Idleness', revealing once again how thoroughly steeped she is in Johnson's *Rambler* essays and how often she agrees with his views on human psychology and social values.

The *Vindication* contains one further Johnsonian allusion that suggests that Wollstonecraft's attachment to Johnson ran deeper than mere points of intellectual engagement, however numerous. In chapter 8, 'Morality Undermined by Sexual Notions of the Importance of a Good Reputation', Wollstonecraft devotes a long passage to the problem of how difficult it can be, in reading a biography, to discern the subject's true character, given the treachery of gossip, the vagaries of reputation, and the mixed motives of biographers. She concludes that 'the hills and dales, clouds and sunshine, conspicuous in the virtues of great men, set off each other; and though they afford envious weakness a fairer mark to shoot

---

[22] *Works*, v. 132.　　[23] Ibid. 224.　　[24] Ibid. 217.

at, the real character will still work its way to light, though bespattered by weak affection, or ingenious malice'.[25] Here Wollstonecraft's footnote reads: 'I allude to various biographical writings, but particularly to Boswell's Life of Johnson.' Beyond what the note reveals about her reading of Boswell's *Life of Johnson*, a biography generally seen then and now as positive and at times worshipful, is what it implies about her underlying allegiance to Johnson. That Wollstonecraft detected in Boswell 'an ingenious malice' and felt compelled to defend Johnson's character from its 'bespattering' effects surpasses the protectiveness of all but the most ardent Johnson admirers.

Repeatedly over the course of 1792, with Boswell's *Life of Johnson* (1791) still very much under discussion, Wollstonecraft was publicly to defend Johnson from Boswell and other biographers. In one article for the *Analytical* she derides Boswell's *Life* as 'desultory volumes', filled with 'the redundant prolixity of vanity'. In another she detects 'private pique' behind an anonymous compilation of extracts from Piozzi, Hawkins, and Boswell, and damns it as 'invidious [for] bringing a man's faults and follies into broad daylight, keeping back all the softening virtues, and extenuating circumstances'.[26] Most extraordinary is her defence (in a review of Arthur Murphy's biography) of Johnson's political and religious 'illiberality'. While overall she thought Murphy inclined to panegyric, she none the less finds unsatisfactory his efforts to explain Johnson's prejudice against Milton. Wollstonecraft intervenes and, with remarkable empathy and insight, analyses Johnson's 'partiality' against Milton's politics and religion in psychological terms:

For Johnson's illiberality there can be but one excuse admitted, and it must be obvious to those who know any thing of the human heart: his morbid melancholy, the spice of madness in his mind, falling into the channel of religious dread, he could not patiently bear to have the doubts stirred up that preyed upon him when alone:—hell and damnation were at *their* heels like blood hounds to run him down; but had he ever ventured to bring his religious opinions to the test of reason he might at least have kept them at bay.[27]

There is in all this defensiveness on Johnson's behalf something more than critical judgement and beyond sympathy, something verging on possessiveness, with just a hint of vicarious paranoia. (Godwin's well-intentioned but unusually candid biographical technique in his 1798 *Memoirs [of Wollstonecraft]* has obvious debts to Boswell, and thus the negative impact the book was to have on her posthumous reputation makes Wollstonecraft's uneasiness about the effects of biography on reputation seem eerily prescient.)

---

[25] Ibid. 205.   [26] Ibid. vii. 443–4, 447; see also vii. 420.   [27] Ibid. 445.

Wollstonecraft's sensitivity about representations of Johnson's life touches on the final area in which she identified with him, this one personal and psychological rather than intellectual. Johnson's deeply rooted place in Wollstonecraft's psyche surfaced in two dramatic episodes in her life, separated by several years. The first arose from a book review. In 1752 Johnson had written a sermon for the funeral of his wife Tetty, a sermon that he had been emotionally unable to deliver at her funeral and left unpublished at his death. In 1788, when Johnson's friend Samuel Hayes published it as *A Sermon, Written by the Late Samuel Johnson, L.L.D. for the Funeral of his Wife*, Wollstonecraft undertook to review it for the *Analytical*. Very likely she requested the assignment, given her heavy involvement with the journal, her influence with its publisher Joseph Johnson, and her frequent coverage of books to do with Samuel Johnson.

However she came to it, the intensity of her response shows that she was powerfully attracted to the text. In the review, her tone and manner depart completely both from the staid norms of eighteenth-century book-reviewing, dominated by voluminous quotation and summary, and from the disciplined, severe tone Wollstonecraft had cultivated as a reviewer (most famously, of a bad female novelist, 'Pray Miss, write no more!'), no doubt anxious in part to seem as 'manly' as her fellow anonymous reviewers, who were all male.[28] In this review her manner is remarkably personal and impassioned: 'It is natural [she writes] to sympathize with a fellow creature enduring what we are all liable to endure, some string of our own hearts is touched and vibrates,—and we may each mournfully repeat—"and I also am a man!" ' From here she proceeds to describe a sensitive, almost painful reading of Johnson's sermon during which she explicitly suspends critical judgement to empathize with his suffering. In her words:

We read this sermon deliberately, and paused at some passages to reflect, with a kind of gloomy satisfaction, that the heart which dictated those pathetic effusions of real anguish now ceased to throb, and that the mind we had often received instruction from, was no longer disquieted by vain fears.—After the emotions these reflections raised we *cannot* criticise; trifling remarks appear impertinent, when we tread as it were, on a grave recently closed, before the clods have formed one common mass.—A few quotations will be a silent, but forcible testimony of our esteem and respect.[29]

---

[28] *Analytical Review* (Nov. 1789), in *Works*, vii. 185. Similarly in October 1789 she advised a young female novelist 'to throw aside her pen and pursue a more useful employment' (*Works*, vii. 174). See other examples, *Works*, vii *passim*.
[29] *Analytical Review* (Aug. 1788), in *Works*, vii. 32–3.

The 'grave recently closed' Wollstonecraft so vividly evokes here is, of course, Johnson's own. In these lines her book review takes on qualities of both a graveyard meditation and a personal leave-taking. The philosophical reflections and personal grief expressed in Johnson's sermon on the death of his wife provide both the occasion and the material for Mary Wollstonecraft to perform a similar ceremony over the 'grave' of her dead friend Samuel Johnson. This momentary fusion of his grief and hers lends special poignancy to the passages from Johnson's sermon she goes on to single out for quotation, such as his comment that, when a mourner tries to console himself with the thought 'that he suffers only what the rest of mankind must suffer', it is, in Johnson's words, 'a poor consideration, which rather awes us to silence, than sooths us to quiet, and which does not abate the sense of our calamity, though it may sometimes make us ashamed to complain'. Further along she also quotes Johnson's haunting description of how, when we lose a loved one,

The whole mind becomes a gloomy vacuity, without any image or form of pleasure, a chaos of confused wishes, directed to no particular end, or to that which, while we wish, we cannot hope to obtain; for the dead will not revive, those whom God has called away from the present state of existence, can be seen no more in it, we must go to them; but they cannot return to us.

With that insight into the psychology of grieving, her review ends.

Behind this unusually personal book review, however, there was a deeper psychological drama that Wollstonecraft played out, in a sense with Johnson's help, during the night she actually wrote the article. In a personal letter addressed the following morning to her publisher Joseph Johnson, Wollstonecraft begins with some chat about book-review business—'I send you *all* the books I had to review [she writes] except Dr. J[ohnson]'s Sermons, which I have begun. If you wish me to look over any more trash this month—you must send it directly'—and then suddenly she drops into a very serious tone: 'I have been so low-spirited since I saw you—I was quite glad, last night, to feel myself affected by some passages in Dr. J[ohnson]'s sermon on the death of his wife—I seemed (suddenly) to *find* my *soul* again—It has been for some time I cannot tell where.' She then asks for some books and supplies to be sent to her because she is trying to fend off depression by occupying herself with work, a very Johnsonian method of coping: 'I am trying [she explains] to brace my nerves that I may be industrious.—I am afraid reason is not a good bracer—for I have been reasoning a long time with my untoward spirits—and yet my hand trembles.' The letter then closes, but, in a long postscript written a bit later, she shows her awareness that the review she has written is unusual in form; but she steadfastly stands by it on the grounds that it is the product of a unique spiritual kinship with Samuel Johnson. She writes:

If you do not like the manner in which I reviewed Dr. J[ohnson]'s s[ermon] on his wife, be it known unto you—I *will* not do it any other way—I felt some pleasure in paying a just tribute of respect to the memory of a man—who, spite of his faults, I have an affection for—I say *have*, for I believe he is somewhere— *where* my soul has been gadding perhaps;—but *you* do not live on conjectures.[30]

It is impossible to know to what degree her dark mood that night, stirred by Johnson's sermon and then by thoughts of his death, was compounded by her continuing grief over the death of her dear friend Fanny Blood two years earlier or by the onset of those deeper depressions that would drive her to attempt suicide twice in the 1790s. But in this letter her imaginative attachment to Johnson and the consolation she derives from him resonate with emotional intensity. Intellectual or philosophical affinities give way to deeper connections. Wollstonecraft goes beyond the Christian stoicism expressed in Johnson's writings to the way it bears up in such painful experience as the death of his wife; in other words, and in a manner much like his own, she reaches beyond the teachings of the moralist to the moral heroism of the lived experience, the life itself. And she expresses her feelings without embarrassment: much as Johnson was reported to have wept openly in company at the memory of friends who had died, Wollstonecraft emotionally declares that she has 'found her soul again' through Johnson and that it was his spirit which somehow got her through the night.

Wollstonecraft seemed to circle back to Johnson almost instinctively in times of crisis. Seven years later, at a time when she was recovering from a suicide attempt, and still depressed over her failed relationship with Imlay, her poverty, and the burden of raising her illegitimate daughter by herself, Johnson loomed again in her inner life. In an impassioned, nearly hysterical, letter to Joseph Johnson in 1795, Wollstonecraft describes her troubles and implores his help, while also resenting some offence he appears (like so many others) to have committed against her. Suddenly, seemingly out of nowhere, she begins to compare herself to Samuel Johnson:

I am not the only character deserving of respect, that has had to struggle with various sorrows—while inferior minds have enjoyed local fame and present comfort.—Dr. Johnson's cares almost drove him mad—but, I suppose, you

---

[30] To Joseph Johnson, [c. July 1788], *Collected Letters of Mary Wollstonecraft*, ed. Ralph M. Wardle (Ithaca, NY, 1979), 178–9. As early as 1787 Wollstonecraft had discussed Johnson's idea 'that the most trivial occupations such as collecting shells, &c . . . are of use, and even, promote the cause of virtue' (referring to *Rambler* 83); 'I agree with him,' she wrote. See To the Reverend Henry Dyson Gabell, 16 Apr. [1787], *Letters*, ed. Wardle, 149.

would quietly have told him, he was a fool for not being calm, and that wise men striving against the stream, can yet be in good humour.

Here the Johnson with whom Wollstonecraft identifies has become a kind of Romantic hero, a sensitive soul who bravely endured a life racked with grief, depression, and public neglect. It is his suffering, rather than his achievement, that validates his heroism. Her letter goes on in this vein, growing steadily more excited and incoherent until she closes in a desperate ramble: 'God of heaven, save thy child from this living death!—I scarcely know what I write. My hand trembles—I am very sick—sick at heart.'[31] In dramatizing her claim to heroic status comparable to Johnson's, Wollstonecraft takes the measure of her own pain and, at the same time, divulges something of her deepest internalized reverence for him—though whether as alter ego or heroic ideal, surrogate parent or saintly protector, is never finally made clear.

Happily, as we now know, Wollstonecraft lived through this desperate crisis, met Godwin, and moved on to a period of relative peace and happiness before her tragic death from puerperal fever in September 1797. But to the very end, even in those writings on which she was working in the last months of her life, Wollstonecraft showed how persistent a presence Johnson was in her mind and imagination. Five months before she died, in what may have signalled her arrival at a new level of confidence and critical authority, Wollstonecraft published the first and only free-standing [i.e. non-book-review] essay on aesthetics of her career: 'On Poetry, and Our Relish for the Beauties of Nature'.[32] At the centre of that essay, grappling with the concept of artistic genius, Wollstonecraft first turns to Johnson for an argument against the idea of innate genius (*Rambler* 25), with which she takes issue, and then, as if to resolve the question and somehow exculpate Johnson at the same time, she quotes from the *Lives of the Poets* to the effect that poets are indeed born with a unique power of vision.[33] His stature in her thinking is indicated by the fact that in the course of the essay Wollstonecraft quotes only two other sources—Shakespeare and the Bible—and then only fleetingly. Johnson was the literary giant she had to slay, or win over, to prove herself as a literary critic.

Johnson continued to live in her creative imagination as well. In the dark vision of her last novel, *The Wrongs of Woman*, still in draft when she died, Wollstonecraft intermittently falls back into Johnsonian terms

[31] To Joseph Johnson, [c. late 1795], *Letters*, ed. Wardle, 325–6.
[32] *Monthly Magazine* (Apr. 1797), 279–82; published also in *Posthumous Works of the Author of A Vindication of the Rights of Woman* (1798), ed. Godwin, and in *Works*, vii. 1–11.
[33] *Rambler* 25, in *Works of Johnson*, iii. 138–40; and 'Thomson', in *Lives of the English Poets*, ed. George Birkbeck Hill (Oxford, 1905), iii. 298. See also Boswell, *Life of Johnson*, 28 July 1763.

and concepts. In chapter 7 the heroine Maria moralizes to herself, she tells us, 'on the vanity of human expectations', an obvious echo of Johnson's *Vanity of Human Wishes*, and in chapter 16 she invokes *Rasselas* when she observes that humans inevitably get bored with ideal conditions and 'long to scale the rocks which fence the happy valley of contentment'.[34] As Wollstonecraft had begun her imaginative life confronting the issues raised in Johnson's philosophical novel, so she ended there too—with her own 'conclusion in which nothing was concluded'.

The affinities between Wollstonecraft and Johnson amount, finally, to more than a collection of textual allusions, and more than a mental habit of Wollstonecraft's. Despite the obvious differences between them, differences of which much could be made, it is their underlying bonds that prove more compelling. Beginning with points of intellectual agreement—on literature, on women's issues, on the vacuities of materialism and social conformity—one traces their origins to shared philosophical attitudes. Both were essentialists who moved beyond superficial details to address fundamental questions about human nature and the purpose of life. Wollstonecraft recognized this. She saw Johnson as a radical, as someone always taking us back to first principles, and she praised his writings for just this essentialism: they focus, she wrote, on 'the deceitfulness of the human heart, the danger of thoughtless procrastination, and a false estimate of the real end of life'.[35] Like Johnson, she acknowledged such human weakness in herself and fought heroically against it. At the deepest level, she rightly saw in Johnson's life a parallel and a consolation to her struggles—so like his—to overcome despair and depression, and the descent into madness. As Wollstonecraft's and Johnson's 'radical affinities' cast each of them in a new light and undermine old categorical boundaries, they force us to look with new eyes on the complexities of cultural history these two writers represent and on the fundamental questions of human existence they both sought to answer.

---

[34] *Works*, i. 131, 177. In describing *The Wrongs of Woman* and its projected readership in a letter to a friend, Wollstonecraft's use of the Johnsonian term *common reader*—which Virginia Woolf later found so attractive—may also have been borrowed from Johnson. If so, her usage certainly differs in emphasis from his. See 'Author's Preface', *The Wrongs of Woman*, in *Works*, i. 84.

[35] *Analytical Review*, 5 (Sept. 1789), 65.

4 Jane West and the Politics of Reading

April London

In the concluding pages of *A Tale of the Times* (1799) Jane West disparages the literary form she herself has adapted to her defence of domestic virtue:

the novel, calculated, by its insinuating narrative and interesting description to fascinate the imagination without rousing the stronger energies of the mind, is [by the radicals] converted into an offensive weapon, directed against our religion, our morals, or our government, as the humour of the writer may determine his particular warfare.[1]

The dedication of fiction to political purposes in fact defines the literary production of both radicals and conservatives in the 1790s as they contested for the allegiance of an audience envisioned as peculiarly susceptible to calls for institutional change. West's determination to contrive fictions capable of 'rousing the stronger energies of the mind' in order to defeat Jacobin principles, however, stands in potential conflict with the idealization of private life and female inwardness her works enforce, an ideal centred on the notion that 'virtues shunned observation, and only courted the silent plaudit of conscience'.[2] In each of the novels written in the 1790s—*The Advantages of Education: or, the History of Maria Williams* (1793), *A Gossip's Story* (1796), and *A Tale of the Times* (1799)—the conflict is resolved by invoking the 'muse of history' in aid of 'the muse of fiction'.[3] Constructing the discourse of private life in accordance with the model afforded by linear history allows her obliquely to confirm its consonance with the forces of tradition and continuity. But investing the quotidian with exemplary status also, and more problematically, grants to culturally marginalized women political significance. The desire to harmonize these competing impulses shapes West's commitment to the education of her female readers. This chapter will consider how attention to genre and history finally enables West to address the intersections of private and public in terms consistent with her advocacy of 'things as they are'.

---

[1] Jane West, *A Tale of the Times*, repr. of the 1799 edn., intro. Gina Luria (3 vols.; New York, 1974) (hereafter *Tale*), iii. 388.
[2] Ibid. 333.   [3] Ibid. ii. 5.

I

For those unfamiliar with West's novels of the 1790s, brief plot summaries may be helpful. In *Advantages of Education*, the recently widowed and impecunious Amelia Williams settles with her daughter Maria in the neighbourhood of the latter's wealthy and indulged friend, Charlotte Raby. Maria, pursued by the libertine Sir Henry Neville, recognizes, with the gentle guidance of her mother, his many faults and rejects him in favour of the worthy Edmund Herbert. Charlotte Raby, in contrast, is allowed to act on her passion for Major Pierpoint and makes a disastrous marriage. In *A Gossip's Story*, Louisa, raised by her father, Richard Dudley, possesses the solid virtues which her more flighty sister Marianne lacks as a result of sustained indulgence by her grandmother. Marianne rejects as dull the eminently virtuous Pelham in favour of the more 'romantic' Lord Clermont, only to discover that sentimental excess cannot be sustained in marriage. After the death of her father, Louisa's quiet steadiness is rewarded with marriage to Pelham. In *A Tale of the Times*, the ubiquitous paired heroines are Geraldine Powerscourt, who marries the unworthy Earl of Monteith, is seduced by the Jacobin villain Fitzosborne, and dies, and Lucy Evans, whose successful marriage to Henry Powerscourt is founded on mutual esteem and abilities.

In each of these three novels, the voice of the narrator, Prudentia Homespun, gives coherence to the various levels on which the texts operate, its idiosyncrasies allowing her at once to court and to deflect the charge of 'egotism' she levels against her radical opponents.[4] She represents herself both in personality and literary interests as existing at the edges of official culture: living in a small village in the north of England sufficiently insular to have generated its own 'vocabulary', she possesses an annuity of a hundred pounds a year, is unmarried, and delights in that quintessential form of female converse, gossip, for which she claims to be suited by virtue of 'a retentive memory, a quick imagination, strong curiosity, and keen perception'.[5] The insistent ordinariness of her life in turn infiltrates her writing, which she declares has 'no splendour of language, no local description, nothing of the marvellous, or the enigmatical'.[6] In avoiding the 'high heroick' mode of 'memoirs and adventures',[7] however, she claims to achieve not inconsequentiality but a moral purposiveness keyed to the needs of her female readers. More specifically, her 'narrative way'—the linear organization of events, their causes,

---

[4] *Tale*, iii. 388.
[5] Jane West, *A Gossip's Story, and a Legendary Tale*, repr. of the 1797 edn., intro. Gina Luria (2 vols.; New York, 1974) (hereafter *Gossip*), i. 13, 2.
[6] Ibid., pp. xi–xii.   [7] Ibid. 39.

and consequences—counters the pernicious influence (both literary and ideological) of 'those refined principles and delicate distinctions invented by several French writers'.[8]

Prudentia's attempted reformation of the public through redefinition of the private sphere attaches to the notion of scrutiny a powerful corrective influence. The 'actual observation of life'[9] to which she dedicates her fiction draws on terms familiar from Adam Smith's *Theory of Moral Sentiments*, where personality is stabilized by reference to two spectatorial presences, one located in the social world that surrounds the self, the other in the man 'within the breast'.[10] In West's formulation, women should act in accordance with the terms by which men currently 'educate their youth' and 'look to the general esteem of worthy people, and the approbation of their own hearts, for the recompense of their merit'. But in the process, they must guard against imbibing 'those notions which novel reading in general produces', especially that most invidious expectation that 'matrimony [is] the great desideratum of our sex'.[11] Despite her declaration to the contrary, the novels do reward good characters with happy marriages and assign to the misguided miserable ones. This seems to confirm Janet Todd's identification of West with the 'reactionary moral novel' whose characterized narrator allows her to avoid the 'self-centredness of sensibility'.[12] But Prudentia Homespun as she is developed over the course of West's novels is not simply a narrative expedient. She exists in a relationship to both reader and text whose multiple ironies allow her creator to mark out a stance more complex and purposive than the oppositional role of 'reactionary' suggests.

One of the earliest of these ironies turns on Prudentia's lineage. While she claims in *Advantages of Education* relationship to the Vicar of Wakefield,[13] contemporary readers might well recognize her affiliation with the unfortunate Harriet Homespun of Samuel Jackson Pratt's *Pupil of Pleasure* (1776). Harriet's fall originates in affective and uncritical reading; she rejects 'such *low* stuff' as *Joseph Andrews* and 'such old

[8] Ibid. 25.   [9] Ibid. 39.

[10] Adam Smith, *The Theory of Moral Sentiments*, ed. D. D. Raphael and A. L. Macfie (Oxford, 1976), 247.

[11] *The Advantages of Education: or, the History of Maria Williams*, repr. of the 1793 edn., intro. Gina Luria (2 vols.; New York, 1974) (hereafter *Advantages*), i. 3–4.

[12] Janet Todd, *The Sign of Angellica: Women, Writing and Fiction, 1660–1800* (New York, 1989), 233. Claudia L. Johnson also locates West 'among conservative novelists of Austen's generation'. While she characterizes her as 'the most distinguished to dramatize Burkean fictions', her emphasis is on West's 'idealiz[ation] of authority per se', rather than on the ironic qualifications for which I argue. See *Jane Austen: Women, Politics and the Novel* (Chicago, 1988), 6, 8.

[13] Isobel Grundy (*The Feminist Companion to Literature in English: Women Writers from the Middle Ages to the Present* (New Haven, Conn., 1990), 1151) suggests that West took the name from Charlotte McCarthy's *Letter* to the Bishop of London (?1767); Homespun is also the patronymic of the gentry exemplar in Mackenzie's *Lounger* essays.

things' as the *Spectator* in favour of the highly wrought sentimental novels that her clergyman husband disparages as the 'trash that circulates at a watering place amongst the women',[14] trash that the villain Sir Philip Sedley will use in conjunction with Chesterfield's *Letters* to effect her seduction. As the reference to circulation suggests, Harriet's credulous acceptance of sentimental fiction as authoritative has its roots in a commodity culture that Pratt represents as inciting women to emulation and egotism.[15] The implicit homology here between social and readerly relations by means of which textual infatuation figures class confusion also attracts Prudentia Homespun's attention. But she, unlike her name-sake in Pratt's novel, is the controller rather than the victim of the text. She advocates at every level the maintenance of evaluative distance by aligning herself with those 'sensible people' who deplore 'this inunda-tion of affected fashion, which sweeps away before it distinction and oeconomy'.[16]

Her attack on categorical confusion and advocacy of social difference extend beyond declarative statement to inform virtually all aspects of the novels' structure and meaning. Verbal irony affords one of the more obvious instances of this commitment to detachment, and Prudentia attends carefully to the compact between reader and narrator on which the success of such irony depends.[17] Addresses to the reader, whom she assumes to be drawn from 'the younger part of the female world',[18] occasionally take the form of unmediated admonitions, as in her com-mendation of '[t]hat philosophy which I wish my readers to possess, [which] is constantly occupied in assimilating our desires with our situations'.[19] More frequently, however, the disciplining of the implied reader proceeds indirectly through critical representations within the text of the characters' sentimental indulgence in romance.

Anti-Jacobin narratives such as Elizabeth Hamilton's *Memoirs of Modern Philosophers* (1800) and George Walker's *The Vagabond* (1799) often render the radical agenda in terms of pastoral romance. This

---

[14] [Samuel Jackson Pratt], *The Pupil of Pleasure; or, The New System Illustrated* (London, 1776), i. 30, 32, 26.

[15] The vilification of 'fashion' as destructive of social distinction reflects the historical significance of rapid changes in fashion to the growing commercialization of English society as documented by Neil McKendrick, John Brewer, and J. H. Plumb, *The Birth of a Consumer Society: The Commercialization of Eighteenth-Century England* (Bloomington, Ind., 1982). See also Colin Campbell, *The Romantic Ethic and the Spirit of Modern Consumerism* (Oxford, 1977), and James Raven, *Judging New Wealth: Popular Publishing and Responses to Commerce in England, 1750–1800* (Oxford, 1992).

[16] *Advantages*, i. 35.

[17] See e.g. the narrator's definition of a 'generous spirit', which, in the manner of Fielding's *Covent-Garden Journal* entries, is glossed as 'a man, who squanders, with undiscriminating prodi-gality, the superflux of wealth, which he knows not properly how to bestow'. Such an epithet, Prudentia adds with typical acerbity, is contingent on the person in question possessing 'rank and birth' (*Advantages*, ii. 4–5).

[18] *Gossip*, i. 4.   [19] *Advantages*, i. 109.

generic designation allows the conservative author to conflate the aristocratic origins of pastoral and the idealist constructs on which Jacobinism itself depended, suggesting in the process the mutual dependence of the supposed political extremes on the factitious and improbable. But while Hamilton's and Walker's satires marginalize romance by associating it exclusively with misguided radicals, West attends to its potentially invidious consequences for readers attracted by the seductive promise of heightened sentiment. Romances, Prudentia implies, despite their vaunted emotional intensity, actually inhibit genuine compassion by encouraging stock responses. The dulling effects of formulaic writing on characters within the text serve as covert warning to actual readers that fiction acquires value only to the degree that it intersects with the concerns of 'common life'.[20] For the more sympathetic characters, such as Marianne in *A Gossip's Story*, the consequences of responding to events only through the medium of the novels she has read are disastrous: 'the *spring* of [her] mind was entirely broken',[21] we are told, by the failure of actual experience to be contained within the frame afforded by pastoral romance. In less attractive characters, romance provides a vocabulary which excuses brutality by renaming it fine feeling. To Geraldine's assertion in *A Tale of the Times* that familiarity with the industrious poor makes apparent the empty satisfactions of luxury, Arabella responds that her 'sensibility' could not bear such proximity: 'You certainly must have very strong nerves, sister. I protest, when I have seen several little dirty, starved, naked children, peeping out of those smoky hovels which stand by the road side, I have often thought that it would be a great mercy to shoot them, as one does worn-out horses.'[22]

---

[20] *Gossip*, i. 33. The reference to 'common life' is typical of the anti-Jacobins' strategy of indirectly criticizing their opponents by appropriating the radical vocabulary and applying it to their own conservative arguments. The attentiveness of both radical and conservative to the 'powers of persuasion' heightened the tendency of each to draw on the nuances of the other's language in the defining of political difference. See John Brewer, ' "This Monstrous Tragi-Comic Scene": British Reactions to the French Revolution', in David Bindman (ed.), *The Shadow of the Guillotine: Britain and the French Revolution* (London, 1989), 11–25, at 14.

[21] *Gossip*, ii. 210.

[22] *Tale*, ii. 126. In Mary Robinson's *The Widow, or a Picture of Modern Times. A Novel in a Series of Letters, in Two Volumes* (London, 1794) Lord Woodly, a banal Lovelace, is similarly identified as pernicious by the parallel associations of him with pastoral and with contempt for the poor: 'It is no very difficult undertaking to break the fetters of a *romantic* passion, which is only inspired by the pure air of the mountains! Cherished by the odours of enamelled meadows! and sanctioned by the pastoral simplicity of the children of *nature*! Unhappy beings! how I pity them! they are the very cart horses of creation; formed to labour for *our* use; to drag their heavy souls through a life of toil, and, when worn out in our service, to sink unnoticed to their native clod! While *we*, of higher blood, race full speed over the course of delight; the wonder of the multitude, the pride of pedigree, and the ornaments of the pleasurable scene!' (ii. 89–90). Again, as in West's novels, the contempt stigmatized as characteristically aristocratic extends to overt misogyny: 'since I cannot tyrannize over my vassals, I will over the *women*; they shall at least, feel my dominion, and be subservient to my pleasures' (ii. 91).

The construction of reading as the quintessential female activity thus allows the narrator not only to consider such attendant issues as interpretation, authority, and judgement, but also to absorb actual readers within the discourse that governs the characters' existences. The sophistication with which Prudentia marshals good and bad readers (both actual and fictional) in order to reinforce the need for critical engagement with the text is most evident in the interpolated 'Rudolpho, Earl of Norfolk; A Legendary Tale' in *A Gossip's Story*. Her introductory comments expose the tenuousness of the compact between the writer and those readers 'who choose to skip over adventitious matter', while they cement the alliance with 'the few, who still love to see nobility clad in the respectable robe of virtue; and eminent rank described in unison with dignified sentiments and generous actions'.[23] These 'few', of course, must read ironically, understanding that the inflated style of 'Rudolpho' marks the tale, in one sense, as escapist romance. The circle of characters who listen to the story and serve as the actual readers' surrogates represents the potential range of responses: Captain Target tries to keep himself awake, while Marianne's 'eyes swam with tears'; only her sister, the heroine Louisa, deduces the moral import of the tale. The characters' responses, in turn, play out at the level of the audience the ethical core of 'Rudolpho', which has argued that man 'must from labour's strenuous grasp | The palm of triumph gain'.[24] In stark contrast to the effortless gratifications of pastoral, 'Rudolpho' argues that without industry there can be neither knowledge nor pleasure. For West, then, the conditions of reading particularize a more inclusive faith in the civilizing value of labour.

The multiple viewpoints of good and bad readers both inside and outside the text are further complicated in *Advantages of Education* and *A Gossip's Story* by Prudentia's location of her narratorial function within a version of the conversational circle used by Richardson in *Sir Charles Grandison*. Interpolated exchanges between Prudentia and her more severe friend Mentoria in West's first novel provide the narrator with an internal audience for her ruminations on the morality of fiction. With *A Gossip's Story* that audience has expanded to a group of 'single ladies' who gather in a 'very agreeable society, which meets three times a week, to communicate the observations which the levity of youth, the vanity of ostentation, or the meanness of avarice have suggested'.[25] Their field of enquiry is much expanded by the arrival of Richard Dudley, his elder daughter Louisa, and his younger one Marianne, the latter of whom, raised by her grandmother after her mother's death, has recently inherited £50,000 on condition that she be 'uncontrolled mistress' of the sum.[26] The narrator comments on the flurry of speculation that greets each new piece of information about the Dudleys: 'The incertitude of public opinion has been exemplified by histories of degraded heroes and persecuted patriots. I choose to illustrate it by an instance from common life'.[27] In giving to the intimate details of 'common life' dignity and substance, Prudentia at once marks out the explanatory limits of 'public opinion' (of degraded heroes, persecuted patriots, or new neighbours) and privileges her own private insights. In the process, she obliquely confirms the novel's centrality to the representation of inwardness and her own role as mediator between this subjectivity and the public world on which its consequences are visited.

Forsaking history for private life, Prudentia nevertheless assumes an intrinsic connection between the two, a connection formalized through her narratorial role. The seeming contraries of public and private, objective and subjective, real and fictional are consistently broken down by her double alliance with each of the opposed terms. She is thus at once a member of the gossips' circle and an ironic observer of the shifting grounds from which its judgements issue. She is, as well, both the authoritative medium through which the implied reader encounters the characters within the text and, as she ruefully admits in the novel's conclusion, the dependent creature of that same reader: 'I am afraid readers care little about an author's private history, and after all the civil things we *can* say, only appreciate our merit by our ability to entertain and instruct *them*.'[28] Patricia Meyer Spacks's comment that gossip 'epitomizes a way of knowing as well as of telling'[29] is apposite here, for Prudentia's recognition of her instrumental function closes the gap between narrator and character. Throughout *A Gossip's Story* the female characters have been urged to accept self-denial as normative and to avoid the specious illusion of power that romance grants its heroines. Prudentia's authority, having been exercised through acts of narration, now yields to the recognitions that identity is contingent on performance and that the efficacy of her performance is finally unknowable. Those readers who 'care little about an author's private history', in other words, also remain private to the author who has attempted to reform their reading habits.

The anxieties of authorship implicit in the ending of a *A Gossip's Story* acquire additional urgency in *A Tale of the Times*, where social collapse is depicted as frighteningly imminent. The undermining of authority to which the text obsessively refers touches even Prudentia, who shares her authorial gifts of acuteness and ability to intuit weakness and repressed

---

[26] Ibid. 19.   [27] Ibid. 33.   [28] Ibid. ii. 216.
[29] Patricia Meyer Spacks, *Gossip* (Chicago, 1986), 46.

emotion with the novel's Jacobin villain, Fitzosborne. This confusion of powers for good and evil disturbs the wry superiority of tone characteristic of the earlier work and makes more pressing the need, at the level of overt commentary, to align narrative with a clearly articulated vision of social order. Like Thomas MacDonald, who argues in *Thoughts on the Public Duties of Private Life with Reference to Present Circumstances and Opinions* (1795) that 'the utter destruction of political balance in Europe compels us at last to turn our eyes inward',[30] Prudentia works on the assumption that coherence in the public realm can be reaffirmed only through an intimate knowledge of private life. In reorienting her fiction towards representations of 'the times'—the realm of memorialist or historian—she thus abandons ironic distance to pursue the private not in its mediated form of gossip, but directly through the 'power of Gyges' magic ring, invariably possessed by all novel writers, [which] has enabled me to peep behind the curtain'.[31]

In keeping with this transformation from gossip to novelistic spy upon human hearts, Prudentia alters the tone of her address to the reader. She poses less often as the chiding observer of venial sins and more as the righteously angry prophet brooding over a world in which the 'torrent of enthusiastic sentiment' threatens all that she values.[32] The warm complicity provided by the gossip's circle also gives way to a world imaged as bristling with the offensive textual products of the 'new code' of Jacobinism against which she situates her own writing.[33] Her narratorial stance, then, draws together the perspectives of novelist and historian in order to revile the 'New Philosophy', which, in an elaborate paralipsis at the beginning of the novel, she stigmatizes for its rejection of 'filial and conjugal ties', of religion, of inherent female virtue, and of appropriately constraining clothes, the latter superseded by the 'loose drapery of Grecian Bacchanals'.[34]

In its confirmation of the reciprocal verities of private and public, novelist and historian, the narratorial voice acquires powerful ideological resonances that allow it to serve as a model of response to the complexities of 'the times' themselves. At the heart of the novel, Prudentia's scrupulously contextual judgement thus offers a focused instance of the link between individual action and social integrity which the plot more expansively represents. These formal and structural paradigms of mediation open into engagement with questions of historical representation. History itself is now understood as a process in which momentous political change originates in the seemingly inconsequential details of private life.

---

[30] Thomas MacDonald, *Thoughts on the Public Duties of Private Life with Reference to Present Circumstances and Opinions* (London, 1795), 1–2.
[31] *Tale*, ii. 24. [32] Ibid. 7. [33] Ibid. iii. 70. [34] Ibid. i. 4–5.

This conviction that altered relations in the sphere of private life are causally prior to changes in the public realm, or, as Edmund Burke suggests in *Letters on a Regicide Peace*, that a 'silent revolution preceded the political, and prepared it',[35] in turn gives both urgency and moral sanction to West's efforts to forestall an English revolution by rendering in fiction a single instance of its anticipated dire effects:

When posterity shall know that these principles characterize the close of the eighteenth century, it will cease to wonder at the calamities which history will then have recorded. Such engines are sufficiently powerful to overturn governments, and to shake the deep-founded base of the firmest empires. Should it therefore be told to future ages, that the capricious dissolubility (if not the absolute nullity) of the nuptial tie and the annihilation of parental authority are among the blasphemies uttered by the *moral* instructors of these times: should they hear, that law was branded as a vain and even unjust attempt to bring individual actions under the restrictions of general rule; that chastity was defined to mean only individuality of affection; that religion was degraded into a sentimental effusion; and that these doctrines do not proceed from the pen of *avowed* profligates, but from persons *apparently* actuated by the desire of improving the happiness of the world: should, I say, generations yet unborn hear this, they will not ascribe the annihilation of thrones and altars to the successful arms of France, but to those principles which, by dissolving domestic confidence and undermining private worth, paved the way for universal confusion.[36]

Prudentia's appeal here not only to the monumental achievements of the past, but also, and more unusually, to the future assumes that history and fiction draw on parallel notions of plot. The sequential logic underlying this shared narrative allows her novelistic version of 'the times' to serve both as cautionary tale and prescriptive antidote to the threat of 'universal confusion'.

The counter-attack she mounts against the 'illustrious sophists'[37] adapts the terms of Burke's 'commercial humanism' with its stigmatizing of speculation and advocacy, as J. G. A. Pocock writes, of an 'aristocratic and commercial order which could be represented as at once natural and

[35] Edmund Burke, *Letters on a Regicide Peace*, in *The Works of the Right Honourable Edmund Burke: A New Edition* (16 vols.; London: C. and J. Rivington, 1826), viii. 259–60.

[36] *Tale*, ii. 274–5. Marilyn Butler's reading of this passage suggests that West's allusion to the 'domestic confidence' and 'private worth' is accidental rather than integral to her meaning: 'her reference to the successful "arms of France" has given the larger part of her case away. The immediate events which provoked the reaction headed in 1798 by the *Anti-Jacobin* were surely political and military rather than private or theoretical' (*Jane Austen and the War of Ideas* (Oxford, 1987), 105). I would argue that West's narratorial stance formally replicates and so confirms the connection of private and political, theoretical and actual. For an analysis of the Scottish moralists' engagement with the notion that private life 'was the proper school for virtue', see John Dwyer, *Virtuous Discourse: Sensibility and Community in Late Eighteenth-Century Scotland* (Edinburgh, 1987), 100.

[37] *Tale*, i. 163.

progressive and defended by reference to a system of civilized manners'.[38]
But despite the clear rhetorical need for characters capable of resisting
speculation in the economic sphere and licentious Jacobinism in the
sexual–political one, the exemplary commercial humanists of West's
novels appear rearguard apologists, retired from public life and defending their integrity by reference to past accomplishments. Richard Dudley
in *A Gossip's Story*, who 'united the character of a true Gentleman to the
no less respectable name of the generous conscientious merchant'[39]
'glor[ies] in having stimulated the industry of thousands; increased the
natural strength of [his] country; and enlarged her revenue and reputation, as far as a private individual could'.[40] But Dudley has been undone
by others' speculative activity and finally proves an inept defender of his
'remaining treasure', his daughter Louisa.[41]

If men possess an identity conferred by commercial enterprise, women
by the same logic are denied coherence and forced, by their legal status
as property, to resign their disposition to men. When Louisa Dudley begs
her father not to marry her off to the odious Sir William Morton, he
responds: 'Am I too sanguine in supposing that a man, who can make the
liberal offers he has done, will be influenced by the sweet and candid
partner he has purchased with his liberty and his fortune?'[42] In the event,
Morton is unmasked by the fortuitous revelation of a cast-off mistress,
and his 'purchase' is refused. While the contingencies of plot thus allow
the terms of fiscal exchange to remain unchallenged, the confirmation of
Louisa's initial response offers a covert rebuke to the emotionally unin-
flected masculine world of commercial enterprise. Yet another of the
signs of its potential to pervert and diminish can be found in the
increasingly active female participation in the commerce of the sexes that
A Tale of the Times sees as evidence of contemporary decadence: 'a
wife's affections, in this age', we are told, 'are but a transferable commodity of little permanent value'.[43]

II

What then is the appropriate form of the female enterprise which, at least
potentially, serves as corrective to its male equivalent? How can it be
represented in narrative in terms that respect West's desire at once to
sanction female inwardness and to argue for its centrality in the resistance to revolutionary change and in the construction of history as the

[38] J. G. A. Pocock, 'The Political Economy of Burke's Analysis of the French Revolution', in *Virtue, Commerce, and History: Essays on Political Thought and History, Chiefly in the Eighteenth Century* (Cambridge, 1985, repr. 1986), 194, 209.
[39] *Gossip*, i. 14. [40] Ibid. 182. [41] Ibid. 181. [42] Ibid. 65. [43] *Tale*, ii. 200–1.

product of individual effort? Genre provides the solution. By discrediting the responses variously elicited by Gothic, Jacobin, and pastoral and by espousing in their stead the redemptive power of labour central to georgic, West is able to formulate a coherent politics of reading. Such a politics at once confirms the central role women play in the constitution of private life and excuses their incursion into the domain of public speech by reference to the threat posed by French revolutionaries. As her *An Elegy on the Death of the Right Honourable Edmund Burke* (1797) suggests, Burke himself apparently recognized and encouraged the key role of women in the censuring of the French:

> Daughters of Britain! let the grateful Tear
>   Of kindred Worth your Champion's Ashes dew;
> His Breast, like your's, impassion'd and sincere,
>   Glow'd with the Virtues he rever'd in you.

> Like you, he sorrow'd for a noble Train,
>   Once the bright Gems that grac'd the Gallic Throne,
> Now scorn'd and slander'd by the Base and Vain,
>   Chas'd from all Countries, and proscrib'd their own.[44]

Gothic, Jacobin, and pastoral attract West's censure because each engages with the reader in terms that are represented as insufficiently rigorous given the acuteness of the danger now menacing Britain. William Beckford's *Azemia* (1797) mocks even as it exploits this studied inconsequentiality; Gothic, he maintains, allows him 'to fill up my little book without a word of politics, revolutions, or counter-revolutions, and prattle through my volumes as prettily, and beat up my literary *pap* with as innoxious ingredients as the most strait-laced matrons or religious elders, can recommend for their babes and sucklings'.[45] West's objections are less playfully expressed, but grow out of a parallel recognition of the genre's preciosity: Gothic, with its 'ghosts and dungeons, incident without character, or character without effect'[46] is culpably escapist in its focus on the 'terrific and romantic [rather than] the moral and the probable'.[47] Jacobin writings offer an even greater threat to the susceptible reader:

---

[44] Jane West, *An Elegy on the Death of the Right Honourable Edmund Burke* (London, 1797), 15. See Linda Colley, *Britons: Forging the Nation 1709–1837* (New Haven, Conn., 1992), for the political construction of patriotism as a form of social control.

[45] [William Beckford], *Azemia, A Novel: Containing Imitations of the Manner, Both in Prose and Verse, of Many of the Authors of the Present Day; With Political Strictures. By J. A. M. Jenks in Two Volumes* (2nd edn., London, 1798), i. 64–5.

[46] *Tale*, i. 163.   [47] Ibid. 11.

Combining Pagan superstitions with the exploded reveries of irrational theorists, they place at the head of their world of chance a supine material God, whom they recognize by the name of Nature, and pretend that its worship supersedes all other laws human and divine. By the side of this circumscribed Deity they erect the idol shrine of its viceregent, Interest; by the monstrous doctrines, that 'whatever is profitable is right', that 'the end sanctifies the means', and that 'human actions ought to be free', they dissolve the bonds of society.[48]

Jacobin doctrine, in its promise of unstrenuous gratification and of individual interest banishing the rigours of law and society, offers a corrupted reconstruction of pastoral in the realm of politics.

Each of West's novels witnesses a progressive elaboration on this negative reading of pastoral. *Advantages of Education* suggests that excessive tenderness leagued with a credulous faith in 'arcadian scenes of felicity' destroys domestic peace.[49] More problematically, since pastoralism speaks both to the prevalence of fashion and the class emulation upon which it was seen to depend, there exists the danger of its extension beyond the middle class:

Suppose for one instant [Prudentia comments] that the rage for idleness (I beg pardon, I mean refinement; I always mistake those words) should spread to the next order in society, and our housemaids and cooks, weary of their dirty occupations, should grow as refined as their young ladies. The industrious mother cannot perform all the domestic affairs herself; and as we do not live in Utopia, but in a country, where exertion must precede enjoyment, our elegant girls must be either useful or starve.[50]

As this passage suggests, the attack on pastoral is predicated on its openness to the claims of universal leisure advanced by radical thinkers. In the world of 'common sense', 'exertion must precede enjoyment', and enjoyment must be keyed to social status.

By a series of deft moves, West manages to implicate aristocratic codes in this Jacobin valorization of leisure. In this way, she undercuts the opposition between the two political extremes and advances her claim for the special moral status of the enterprising middle class. In *Advantages of Education*, the villain Stanley, actually Sir Henry Neville in disguise, exploits pastoral rhetoric in his efforts to seduce Maria, whom he dubs the 'village nymph':[51] 'The lover, who had a few *aristocratic* notions (I use that word to prove my knowledge of modern politics) seemed to think it impossible that [Maria's mother] should object [to the seduction], when acquainted with his rank and character.'[52] Prudentia's ironic evocation of the radical vocabulary in this context develops from her conviction that men are limited in their relations with women either

[48] Ibid. ii. 273.   [49] *Advantages*, ii. 235.   [50] Ibid. i. 34.   [51] Ibid. 130.   [52] Ibid. 158.

to protection or predation. Jacobins and aristocrats, in the political sphere, achieve coherence with pastoral in the literary, and with romantic rhetoric in the discursive spheres, by virtue of their shared willingness to negate distinction in the pursuit of self-interest. Reader and writer are, in turn, drawn into this complex by the suggestion that formulaic sentimentalism encourages rote responses; the value of interpretation, conversely, hinges on the difficulties involved in exercising meticulous judgement. Marianne, in *A Gossip's Story*, thus stands at once as a figure for the pastoral character, writer, and reader:

> Marianne had now an additional employment, besides playing upon her harp, reading pastoral poetry, walking in the woods by moonlight, and listening to distant water-falls. She kept a journal of the events of the day, and every morning dispatched two sheets of paper, closely written, to her beloved Eliza. If any sceptical critic should censure this as a violation of probability . . . I shall pity his ignorance, and refer him to the productions of many of my contemporaries; where he may be convinced, that sentiment is to the full as ductile as gold, and when beaten thin will cover as incalculable an extent of surface.[53]

Self-referential writing, in its eliciting of shallow emotion from the reader, participates in the debilitating effects of leisure, formally represented in these novels under the sign of pastoral.

West's reading of pastoral thus allows the conflation of gender, genre, and the politically specious. Countermanding its exclusion from the grace of labour are the georgic values West ascribes to the heroines of her first two novels. The classical associations of the georgic with work as a particular form of 'masculine activity' distinguish it from the alignment of both pastoral with leisure and epic with war and heroism. In the eighteenth century it was '*the* characteristic . . . cultural mode, essentially related to other such characteristic phenomena as the country house and the landed estate'.[54] West's particular interest in the problematic status of women's enterprise encourages the assimilation of this masculine and aristocratic genre to the rhetoric of the female and the middle class. Her novels retain the conventional emphasis on the civilizing and reconstructive powers of georgic, but locate these within the domestic sphere by representing georgic industriousness most often as a product of mundane accidents of financial failure. While war is not then causally prior to the reforging of order, the resonances of the classical tradition encourage the reader to understand domestic reconstruction in relation to the threat of revolutionary France and of civil war.

[53] *Gossip*, i. 225–6.
[54] John Murdoch, 'The Landscape of Labour: Transformations of the Georgic', in Kenneth R. Johnston, Gilbert Chaitin, Karen Hanson, and Herbert Marks (eds.), *Romantic Revolutions: Criticism and Theory* (Bloomington, Ind., 1990), 181, 189.

The imminence of this danger and the vigilance it demands typically emerge through contrast with the irresponsible idealization elicited by pastoral. When Louisa's father loses his money, the pair are forced to retire to the Lancashire estate left to her by her grandfather 'as a supply for pin-money'.[55] Characteristically, Marianne congratulates her sister on the prospect of living in a cottage, since 'that name suggested every thing that was pastoral and charming'.[56] In fact, the 'most enthusiastick imagination could hardly associate pastoral ideas with the neglected wilderness of Seatondell, could suppose it peopled by Naids [*sic*] and Dryads, or fancy that Pan ever awoke its echoes with his tabor and pipe, while Cynthia and her maids of honour danced cotillions'.[57] West's deflation of pastoral rhetoric, with its unseemly and factitious conjunction of nymphs and cotillions, underscores by contrast the substantial virtues ascribed to Louisa's programme of georgic enterprise: 'We shall find [she informs her father] both health and amusement in improving our farm in summer, and in winter books and musick will afford a never-failing resource from chagrin'.[58] The significant and adult world of georgic here displaces the illusory and childish realm of pastoral. In their complementary alignments with conservatism and radicalism, West's adaptations of the classical genres inform the progressive social model which her fiction advances.

The actual tilling of the soil at Seatondell, of course, is effected by a 'party of labourers'.[59] Louisa's georgic exercises exchange literal for supervisory labour in order to confirm the intransigent distinction of tenant from property-owner: 'Accustomed to oeconomick attentions, she knew how to husband her bounty, and by adding to it her personal services, to render a trifle valuable. She visited the sick, consoled the afflicted, instructed the ignorant, and reproved the idle'.[60] This feminized and class-specific interpretation of georgic may seem at first to assign to Louisa a merely local function. But her investment of the labour of 'personal services' gives a value to her husbandry that is associated throughout West's works with efficacious social control. Active intercession in the lives of the poor through charity allows the rod of correction to be applied to the 'ignorant' and the 'idle'. If her father 'stimulated the industry of thousands' through his 'mercantile pursuits', Louisa's more intimate connection with labour achieves complementary results. Georgic's meliorating capacity thus affects the social registers above and

---

[55] *Gossip*, ii. 48.   [56] Ibid. 40.   [57] Ibid. 48.   [58] Ibid. 52–3.
[59] Ibid. 55. This division of labour according to class reveals an entirely characteristic distinction between West's adaptation of georgic and those of earlier eighteenth-century novelists. Arthur Young's *Emmera* (1767), for instance, typically represents the possibility of social regeneration through the active farming of both husband and wife.
[60] *Gossip*, ii. 62.

below the middle class with which West primarily associates it, becoming the conduit through which the reform of both the licentious rich and the idle poor is attempted.

A Tale of the Times more rigorously defends georgic industry by elaborating on the supervisory relation of women to the rural poor, their correlatives in class terms. Yet it finally disallows the redemptive power of labour to its heroine, Geraldine, Lady Monteith, condemning her instead to a flattened and reductive variation on Clarissa's death following rape. The failure of georgic here reflects a fundamental division within the novel itself, a division that follows from West's attention in the second volume to the destructive machinations of the arch-revolutionary (and highly derivative) villain, Fitzosborne. The first volume focuses on the conventionally paired West heroines, rendered less schematically than in earlier works since both are actively virtuous[61]— though Lucy, who is the less wealthy of the two, has the edge of 'superior energy' of mind.[62] The more privileged Geraldine, 'like Pygmalion, became deeply enamoured with the creature of her own imagination',[63] Monteith, whom she marries despite his intellectual and moral inferiority to her. In the first four happy years of their marriage she dedicates herself to improving her husband's Scottish estate on which she intends to build a 'neat little village' inhabited by those tenants who 'seem to fulfil their duties with marked propriety'. Her role she imagines in terms conventionally deemed paternalistic, but which West's novels rewrite as the province of women: 'I will frequently visit them; I will be their legislator, their instructor, their physician, and their friend. They shall look up to me with gratitude, and my own heart shall enjoy the pure recompense of conscious beneficence.'[64] Such appropriation of male virtue is made necessary by Monteith's feckless inattention to the realities of dissension, an inattention linked to his dangerously feudal notions of the necessary distance between master and labourer. He regards Geraldine's project as a leisurely diversion, a way to 'amuse' herself when she has 'no other employment', and stipulates only that she install 'no manufactories in my neighbourhood.—All our family hate the very name of them.—They only encourage a horde of idle insolent vagrants, who fly in your face upon every occasion.'[65]

Geraldine's grasp of political relations is, in this instance at least, considerably more complex than her husband's. While he insists that

---

[61] For analysis of the paired-sisters motif, see Patricia Meyer Spacks, 'Sisters', in Mary Anne Schofield and Cecilia Macheski (eds.), *Fetter'd or Free?: British Women Novelists, 1670–1815* (Athens, Ohio, 1986), 136–151, and Eleanor Ty, 'Jane West's Feminine Ideal of the 1790s', *1650–1850, Ideas, Aesthetics, and Inquiries in the Early Modern Era*, 1 (1993), 1–19.
[62] *Tale*, i. 105.   [63] Ibid. 115.   [64] Ibid. ii. 10.   [65] Ibid. 18.

women and children be 'fed at the castle gate', she understands the social dynamics of obligation: 'No, let them eat the bread of industry, and enjoy those delights which the active exertion of our native energies always inspires.' Such 'provident benevolence' will ensure that they 'will long need the protecting care of their benefactor, and consequently cannot affect an insolent independence of his bounty'.[66] The social utility of labour expressed generically here through georgic once again acquires additional force through the contrasting associations of pastoral. Geraldine's nemesis, Fitzosborne, embodies the seemingly contrary but equally pernicious attributes of Jacobin and aristocrat, linked as in *Advantages of Education* and *A Gossip's Story* under the sign of pastoral. While Monteith's failures are those of a man profoundly bored by 'every scheme not immediately connected with his own pleasures',[67] Fitzosborne embodies the active power of evil, directed by the 'covert war which he waged, not merely against the chastity, but also against the principles of his victims'.[68] As with Lovelace, Fitzosborne's intelligence and lack of a coherent identity (in both figured as protean changeableness) fuel his capacity to exploit the telling weaknesses of others. Countering Arabella's comment (quoted earlier) that the poor should be shot like worn-out horses in order that she not be offended by the sight of them, Fitzosborne, alert to Geraldine's presence, but at this point misreading the latter's charity as the product of copy-book idealization, declaims on the beauties of 'those obscure cots, the chosen abodes of innocence and virtue'. To this, she responds in turn:

My long residence in retirement allows me positively to counteract the popular notion, that the country is the seat of Arcadian happiness and purity, though much may be done to ameliorate the condition of the lower classes of society; and I am convinced, that residing among them is one of the more probable means of effecting that important design.[69]

But even as West invests Geraldine's sentiments with all the positive resonances of georgic industry and suggests that women are peculiarly fitted to the supervisory control of the extended household, she is bound for reasons of both politics and gender to punish Geraldine and her husband. In West's earlier novels, the combination of wealth and unhappiness characteristic of the less successful of the paired heroines is made

---

[66] Ibid. 19–20.   [67] Ibid. 22.   [68] Ibid. 153.
[69] Ibid. 128–9. This argument has a long-standing place in conservative novels, as evidenced by Fielding's comment in *Joseph Andrews* on Lady Booby's arrival in the country; she was greeted by the 'Acclamations of the Poor, who were rejoiced to see their Patroness returned after so long an Absence, during which time all her Rents had been drafted to *London*, without a Shilling being spent among them, which tended not a little to their utter impoverishing' (Henry Fielding, *Joseph Andrews*, ed. Martin C. Battestin (Middletown, Conn., 1967), 277). Prudentia aligns her writing with the 'simple elegance and rational amusement' of 'Addison, Goldsmith, and Fielding', which she distinguishes from

to correspond to private failures of generosity or inner strength. Here the pathos of the heroine's fate depends on the virtual absence of such personal weakness. Geraldine is '[a]dorned with every natural and acquired accomplishment; "chaste as the icicle on Dian's temple"; attached to her husband; the fondest of mothers; domestic, prudent, and religious'. Yet with all of these attributes, she, nevertheless, must fall. Active virtue alone is insufficient to withstand the 'covert assault'[70] prepared by the devious Fitzosborne. And her intemperate husband, prey to aristocratic vices and so lacking the attentiveness characteristic of genuine 'manliness', fails to repulse the danger.

While *A Tale of the Times* is not an allegory, the anti-Jacobin tethering of politics to sexuality invites us to consider character as an index to larger cultural preoccupations. The conservative programme of the 1790s held to two imperfectly meshed paradigms of femaleness generated by the 'culture of sensibility': woman is both a physical being susceptible to masculine appropriation and an agent of the civilizing values of domesticity that are a product of her moral acuteness. Geraldine's integrity and, more especially, her identification with the distinctive national virtues exemplified by georgic encourage our reading her, in the light of the second of these paradigms, as a figure for Britain itself. But her openness to the blandishments of the insinuating radical Fitzosborne points to the shadowy presence of the first paradigm and implicitly argues the need for Britons' continued vigilance, for resistance to any influence imported from France, for strong government. The merging of sexual and political discourses here under the sign of woman and the implication that such merging figures Britain's vulnerability to French radicalism also make compelling the need to gender politics in definitively masculine terms. The 'manliness' which the anti-Jacobins construe nationalistically both marks out the preserve of politics as masculine and sanctions the representative function of the chaste woman as symbol of the integrity and security of the state.

The conclusion to *A Tale of the Times* draws generously on these conservative standards. In the narrator's retrospective survey of Geraldine's rape and death, only a 'latent spark of vanity' can be isolated as their possible cause. But even this is sufficient, we are told, in the absence of a husband's 'firm judgment, the manly tenderness, which should guide and direct this attracting woman through the thorny maze of public life'

---

the 'high-sounding phrases and inconceivable wonders, signifying nothing' (*Tale*, ii. 164) of contemporary novelists. Her treatment of the issue of residence, however, is explicitly attentive to the potential threat of the poor in ways that mark her difference from those she claims as models.

[70] *Tale*, ii. 149.

to guarantee her destruction.[71] The lack of protective manliness allows the 'pestilent notions'[72] inherent in revolutionary rhetoric to mimic the course of infectious disease; the 'attracting' host, the undefiled body of the woman, tempts the Jacobin villain to sully and pollute. 'Manliness' alone stands as a barrier between the achievement of domestic felicity, with its public expression as '*amor patriae*', and the forces destructive of 'our religion, our morals, our government'.[73] If women represent what is best in any culture, they also, and more importantly, may become the vessel through which that culture is corrupted.

III

West's commitment to the commonplace stands, in her own view, as the source of the insight that enables both narratorial omniscience and political acuteness—the complementary spheres of the textual and actual worlds. Attention to 'real life' and not to the 'Utopian geography of many modern novelists'[74] allows the confirmation and hence preservation of this densely textured quotidian vision with its powerful impulse toward conformity. Through the resolute ordinariness of her narratorial voice, of her sense of the reader, and of her didacticism, West draws into conjunction public and private. By a parallel logic, the extraordinary or exceptional is vilified, both in its philosophical form of the 'scepticism [which] owes most of its adherents . . . to the pride of human reason, and the love of singularity' and its authorial one of the 'singularity' courted by successful writers, 'those huge Leviathans [who] toss and sport as they please in the great deeps of literature'.[75] She, in contrast, identifies her efforts as writer and polemicist not with the insouciant freedom assumed by 'modern novelists', but with the obligation of the 'lesser fry [to] submit to some precautions, or endure the harder alternative of annihilation. Our morose taskmasters . . . impose upon us the hard laws of having a beginning, a middle, and an end'[76]—the same 'hard laws' of the 'narrative way' which links 'the muse of history and the muse of fiction'. Such emphasis on discipline and commitment in relation to her own authorial efforts locates them within the moral imperatives that govern georgic. The framing of writer and audience within this context alerts us to the wider implications of the politics of reading that West painstakingly constructs in all three novels. The decade in which they appeared was marked by a succession of near famine years that provoked, from one side of the political spectrum, calls for revolutionary change and, from

---

[71] Ibid. iii. 278–9. [72] Ibid. 372. [73] Ibid. 388.
[74] *Gossip*, ii. 96. [75] *Tale*, iii. 62; i. 99. [76] Ibid. i. 99

the other, the anti-Utopian prescriptions of such authors as Thomas Malthus. For West, the georgic mode, with its urging of unremitting labour, its acceptance of necessary pain, and its promise of political stability after great upheaval, served as both a literary and a political paradigm for the relation of 'common life' to history that her novels represent.

5 Edgeworth's Stern Father: Escaping Thomas Day, 1795–1801

MARILYN BUTLER

In the pleasant valley of Ashton there lived an elderly woman of the name of Preston; she had a small neat cottage, and there was not a weed to be seen in her garden. It was upon her garden that she chiefly depended for support: it consisted of strawberry beds, and one small border for flowers. The pinks and roses she tied up in nice nosegays, and sent either to Clifton or Bristol to be sold; as to her strawberries, she did not send them to market, because it was the custom for numbers of people to come from Clifton, in the summer time, to eat strawberries and cream at the gardens in Ashton.[1]

The opening paragraph of the first story of Maria Edgeworth's *The Parent's Assistant* (1796) tells its intended readers, who are children, not just where the widow Preston lives, but how she makes her living: the efficient style in which she runs her small market garden, and the well-heeled city customers for whom she grows her expensive, fragile, pretty things—strawberries, pinks, and roses. Most eighteenth-century stories for children were based on fable and fairy-tale, and likely to use the conventional appeal of a land of perpetual summer, along with the sensuous pleasures of sight, smell, and taste. Parents might notice that this one also opens into the contemporary world. Bristol's wealth and more particularly the wealth of the prosperous suburb of Clifton has bred its own support-system in the surrounding countryside. The strawberries are even part of a new leisure industry, a brand of middle-class down-market tourism which draws Bristolians out into the countryside on fine weekends to eat strawberry teas.

In the second paragraph, however, the serpent has visited the garden. The widow Preston's pleasant world is threatened with ruin, for a winter of sickness and, worse, of medicines means that she is two guineas short of meeting her rent, and must sell the old horse on which her small business depends. This is the crisis which launches her only son Jem on the tale's action, his project of earning the money needed to save the horse and their livelihood.

---

[1] 'Lazy Lawrence' (1796); from *The Parent's Assistant or Stories for Children* (6 vols.; rev. and enlarged 3rd edn., London, 1800), i. 3.

Together these two paragraphs mark their writer as henceforth something more than a specialized educationalist and her father's junior partner. Jem's experiences in the micro-world belong to the macro-world, knowledgeably redefined as the market place. What is more, the story is an experience: a child's sudden first challenge to act an adult role. While all works of the imagination enlarge children's sense of the community to which they belong, Edgeworth seems to capture the freshness of intellectual discovery.

She was born in 1768 (not 1767, as nineteenth-century sources say), making her seven years older than Austen. She had three prolific decades, after beginning her publishing career in 1792, to Austen's one, begun in 1811; perhaps twelve novels and substantial novellas of (to say the least) intelligence and originality, to Austen's great six. Unlike most writers of either sex in the period, she had a thorough training—in the specialized but fast-growing field of writing for children. At 14 she translated Mme de Genlis's Rousseauistic, pedagogic *Adèle et Théodore*, but publication of her version was pre-empted by a rival translation. Soon her growing band of stepbrothers and sisters needed educational materials: in 1787 she wrote a story for and about children, 'The Bracelets', and her first collection for children at the beginning-reader stage, *Dog Trusty and Other Stories*, appeared in 1792. The volume ushers in her major decade as an educational writer, centred on the important treatise, *Practical Education* (1798), which R. L. and Maria Edgeworth authored jointly. Her father's name also appears with hers on the volumes of instructive dialogues for children of about 4 to 14, collectively called 'Early Lessons' (1801, 1812, 1825), and designed for parents who followed the Edgeworthian system for teaching children at home.

The pedagogic dialogues are deft and, for their genre, natural, but more unmistakably instrumental than Maria Edgeworth's solo stories for children (of which 'Lazy Lawrence', in the volume *The Parent's Assistant*, is one), for adolescents (the series of so-called *Moral Tales* (1801)), and for literate but simply educated 'new readers' (*Popular Tales* (1804)). These three collections contain true creative writing, and reveal a youthful author going through the crucial early moves of mastering her medium, yet distancing herself from its previous masters. Above all this meant coming to terms with Thomas Day, who was both a disciple of Rousseau and a key educational mentor for Edgeworth herself.

Most of the better-known women's writing careers of Edgeworth's lifetime emerged from such well-defined social groupings, professionally based and generally linked by a correspondence network. Barbauld and Opie belonged to the widening circle of East Anglian Dissent; Wollstonecraft, Inchbald, and Robinson to professional literary London; Baillie,

Hamilton, later Brunton and Ferrier, to Scottish university circles. Edgeworth's unusually wide corresponding circle touched, interestingly, on all these women-friendly circles, once she was established. She corresponded in time with Barbauld, Inchbald (and Joseph Johnson, doyen of London literary publishers), Baillie, Hamilton, and one of the most thoroughgoing of women networkers, Helen Stewart, the second wife of the moral philosopher Dugald Stewart of Edinburgh.[2]

More to the point, Edgeworth as a child had to learn to rely on her father's impressive intellectual network when he and her immediate family let her down. After her mother died in childbirth when she was 5, her father hurried home from France—and Maria, his second child and eldest daughter, could not recognize him. R. L. Edgeworth left at once, to court and speedily to marry Honora Sneyd, whom he already loved passionately. They formed a partnership which was intellectual as well as physical. Honora may have initiated much of the avant-garde pedagogic system that became the family's corporate trade mark; she certainly introduced to Edgeworthstown the new, companionate republican marriage, which had the effect of imposing a severe code of discipline on her husband's children by his first marriage. Maria Edgeworth proved so troublesome by the age of 7, usually it seems to Honora, that she was sent away from Edgeworthstown to English boarding-schools. It was a classic case of daughter/(step)mother friction, as both battled not merely for the father's love and attention, but for access to the knowledgeable pursuits to which he held the key.

For seven impressionable years, Maria Edgeworth was not always able to go home even in the holidays: she was even more neglected before and after her stepmother died, in 1780, of tuberculosis. In these crises, her father asked two old friends and fellow-members of the Lunar Society of Birmingham—Erasmus Darwin, the doctor, scientist, educationalist, and poet, and Thomas Day, the educationalist and moralist—to keep an eye on her; her closest contact with Day, in the summer of 1781, was as we shall see at a particularly distressing time for Maria Edgeworth. Then from 1782 she was able to live at home for a decade in Ireland, under a gentler regime created by Elizabeth Sneyd, Honora's sister and R. L. Edgeworth's third wife. At this point Maria Edgeworth was in touch with Day, Darwin, and her father's Lunar Society friends only through their books or their correspondence with her father. But the Edgeworths as a family renewed friendships in the English Midlands a decade later, when in the early 1790s they spent a year and a half at Clifton, near Bristol, for Lovell Edgeworth, Honora's surviving child, to be treated in

---

[2] Dugald Stewart (1753–1828), his wife Helen, and his son Col. Matthew Stewart corresponded with Edgeworthstown from 1803 into the 1830s.

his turn for tuberculosis. At this time, the threshold of Maria Edge-worth's career as a publishing writer, she worked with her father on a volume of his memoirs, a project which required both father and daughter to review the last three decades with what was, for both, autobiographical intensity. It is because her career as author began in these circumstances that it is Day, not Edgeworth, who psychologically became Maria Edgeworth's bad literary father.

Edgeworth is one of many eighteenth- and nineteenth-century women writers now identified as having had problematic relationships with their fathers: Burney, More, Staël, Barrett Browning (and, less often cited, Austen and George Eliot) are others. The existence of such a relationship is often disliked in modern times because it suggests emotional or intel-lectual dependence on the male; but, as Elizabeth Kowaleski-Wallace honestly admits, the *problem* here may well be that of the modern critic, not the original writer. Kowaleski-Wallace observes that modern aca-demic feminists feel particularly bound to resist women who 'were "their fathers' daughters" ', an attachment which she proceeds to gloss as male identification, or 'patriarchal complicity', on the daughter's part: 'If feminist study has been characterized by the search for foremothers, women with whom we can identify and to whom we can turn for inspiration, what kind of a model is a "daddy's girl"?'[3]

Where modern women value strong female models, earlier women may have felt a need for sympathetic mentors, intellectual nurturers who were, perforce, more often the father. In Edgeworth's childhood experi-ence, as we have seen, life with father at home represented both emo-tional security and access to knowledge. Later her 'father-love' is often hard to separate from the intellectual discipleship many clever young women practise, and, arguably, most ambitious writers. If self-empower-ment is the underlying motive, male identification as such may not follow. Edgeworth's father did in time (that is, after Honora's death) share his knowledge with his eldest daughter, gave her the life of the mind she craved for, and rewarded her achievement with a special place in the family at his right hand—the mother's or eldest son's usual place. All the same, he was not the only family member who rewarded her in this way. Nor did those few creative works she specifically associated with him amount to as much, either in bulk or quality, as the writings she wrote with and read to the Ruxton women, or her domestic circle of adults and children.[4]

---

[3] Elizabeth Kowaleski-Wallace, *Their Fathers' Daughters* (New York, 1991), pp. ix, vii.
[4] Evidence from family correspondence regarding the contributions of different family members to Edgeworth's novels is surveyed in M. Butler, *Maria Edgeworth: A Literary Biography* (Oxford, 1972), chs. V, VI.

Her *œuvre* is large and complex; different people nurtured its various parts. The educational projects were grounded in the previous generation, and never narrowly R. L. Edgeworth's; quite apart from Honora's contribution, which in fact placed the mother at the centre of the enterprise, this work in the broad tradition of Locke and Rousseau was nothing if not teamwork, with Day, Darwin, and Priestley within the circle, Barbauld and de Genlis outside it, all playing a part. Edgeworth's adult fiction is by no means a simple continuation, but in some sense coterie, anti-child, a bid for authorial independence; some of her stepbrothers and sisters at times express resentment of the novels on which she increasingly concentrated after 1800, and perhaps the feminized, companionable, secretive adult network she established in letters to the Ruxtons.[5]

After the work of John Pococke and others, it comes as no surprise to name the special enabling factor in the late eighteenth-century domesticated production of writing as, essentially, a form of republicanism. But this cultural manifestation, which straddles the public and the private sphere, and has no necessary connection with affairs of state, hardly feels the same phenomenon as what modern historians of ideas designate the main line of state-centred political theory from Machiavelli to Burke. There was a second kind of republicanism, impressionistic, popular, yet also (according to Patrice Higonnet, following Habermas) 'transcendental',[6] by which middle-class people opened their lives to a civic dimension. They learnt it from (for example) Smith's *Theory of Moral Sentiments* (1754), Hume's *Essays*, the more private writings of Rousseau (*Émile, Julie*, the *Confessions* and the *Reveries of a Solitary Walker*), and John Millar's *Origin of the Distinction of Ranks* (1771).[7] The writings of late-Enlightenment women allude pervasively to a notional republic, in effect the neighbourhood, then 'society', and the more vaguely perceived economic and political worlds, which formed the outer concentric rings round any family group. In the technically sophisticated sentimental novel, women characters, women readers, and women writers deploy a new language, of sympathy, sociability, ethics, which in fiction or dumbshow repeatedly infiltrates society and thus pretends to bring the hitherto male sphere under feminine rule. The standard denouements of these novels—achieved by the benevolence of the rich and the gratitude of the poor—are also the signs of a new, unsettling campaign to preach social interdependence and to elicit

[5] Ibid. 179–80.
[6] Patrice Higonnet, *TLS*, no. 4714, 6 Aug. 1993, p. 5.
[7] See Jane Rendall, *The Origins of Modern Feminism: Women in Britain, France and the United States, 1780–1860* (London, 1985), 7–65, and especially her discussion (pp. 25–8) of John Millar, *Origin of the Distinction of Ranks* (London, 1771, rev. 1779).

mutual respect: to get prosperous readers to know and live Rousseau's social contract.

Where the home was represented, the education it offered became crucial. A wise, virtuous couple would devote themselves to their children's moral instruction. The republic must first be imagined; such imaginings required new mentalities; a dynamic vision of family life emerged, which late-Enlightenment women writers helped shape. Yet Rousseau's most ardent contemporary disciple in England was a man, Thomas Day—who emerged, in most respects, as the most eloquent exponent of a new *métier*, the child's guide to transcendental republicanism. His *Sandford and Merton* establishes a dialogue between an adult and a child as at once the pre-condition and the essence of the new domestic republican ethos. Parental teaching will breed future leaders derived not from the aristocratic model—historically, a soldier—but from a farmer, such as the Roman Cincinnatus, who was ready for the call when the republic needed him.

Unhappily for many women republicans, the pedagogue in *Sandford and Merton* is a man, the clergyman Mr Barlow. In all Day's long story compilation, which ranges across many cultures and ages, he finds not a single example of a wise woman, or exemplary instructress. Day was as firmly against women's citizenship of this republic as Rousseau, or for that matter Plato, could have been. In his adoption of the civic Rousseau—a construction that makes most use of the two *Discourses* (1750, 1752), the *Social Contract* (1762) itself, and the pedagogic treatise *Émile* (1762)—he accepts Rousseau's argument in *Émile* that women do not participate in the public sphere and, because modern girls' education is trivializing and corrupting, that they should have less rather than more instruction than at present. Day avoids, admittedly, the regrettably French scheme Rousseau dreams up for Sophie in *Émile*, a training in feminine arts which will make her delightful to Émile. Instead he recommends a firm grounding in morals and religion, plus the housewifely, managerial skills, appropriate to farmers' wives, that Hannah More, Elizabeth Hamilton, and others adapted more sympathetically for women's use in the early nineteenth century.[8]

The relationship between Day's work and Wollstonecraft's or More's is interesting, but between his and Edgeworth's it is also personal, emotional, and conflicted. Published in three volumes in 1783, 1786, and 1789, *Sandford and Merton* had special significance at Edgeworthstown

---

[8] A more detailed examination of women's domestic duties and, in effect, styles of management is given in early nineteenth-century conduct books and in two influential novels, Elizabeth Hamilton, *Cottagers of Glenburnie* (London, 1808), and Hannah More, *Coelebs in Search of a Wife* (London, 1808).

because it was originally designed as a short contribution to the 'Harry and Lucy' series of dialogues for children planned by R. L. and Honora Edgeworth in the late 1770s. In any case, Day was a man with strong links, indeed entanglements, with different key members of the Edgeworth family circle. R. L. Edgeworth and Day first met in 1765 when Day was a 17-year-old Oxford undergraduate, and Edgeworth an unhappy husband and father of 21. Between 1765 and 1772 Day proposed marriage to no fewer than three Edgeworth women: R. L. Edgeworth's sister Margaret, afterwards Ruxton; Honora Sneyd, later Edgeworth's second wife; and Elizabeth Sneyd, still later his third, or in the 1780s current, wife. The first two at least turned him down because they did not share his preference for a life of simple farming, which bore particularly rigorously on his wife. In addition to the warm personal friendship between the two men, there are barely acknowledged but deep ideological differences of principle and life-style between the Day and Edgeworth households, which Maria became uncomfortably aware of during the summer of 1781, when Day temporarily took charge of her.

A year after Honora's death from tuberculosis, R. L. Edgeworth was still unable to secure the church's permission to marry her sister Elizabeth; he remained besides in deep mourning, and there was no settled home in which to house his children. In Maria's school summer holidays she had to go to the remote farmhouse at Annesley in a heathy part of Surrey, in which Day had at last established the ménage of his dreams. He had only recently (1778) married Esther Milnes, wealthy and serious-minded, the first woman he addressed with the philosophy and idealism to give up her harpsichord and servants, while Day gradually gave away his fortune.

At 13, desperately anxious after six years to settle in her own home, Maria Edgeworth must have found the eccentric household at Annesley comfortless and strict. She arrived in July with a painful eye complaint, which doctors thought threatened her sight. Day insisted on dosing her with Bishop Berkeley's favourite remedy, tar-water. He also instructed her; but where R. L. Edgeworth sometimes managed to write encouragingly, asking to see her writing, Day's restrictive principles about women's education and pursuits remained unshaken. When at last the following year Maria Edgeworth was able to go home to Edgeworthstown, to a feminist-republican life-style in which reading and writing were daily fare for both sexes, Thomas Day's disapproval of the Edgeworth policy followed her, in letters logically addressed to her father rather than to her. Though his best work was appearing from 1783 as hers began, and was to prove the most pervasive literary influence on her early writing, she was never in a position to write to him directly about it, nor indeed does she discuss Day's work openly elsewhere. It is only the reader of her children's stories and early novels, reconsidering the texts in their ideological and biographical context, who notices at last how eloquent they are in relation to this second, sterner father. Following in the footsteps of three commanding women of her parents' generation, she in her style refuses him too—by using his work to carve out a place in the republic for herself, and showing child readers how they may do the same.

Day died in September 1789, when a colt he had been taming by his own kindly method threw and killed him. R. L. Edgeworth resolved to write a memoir of his friend in the manner of Rousseau's *Confessions*. Though appropriate in principle, the experiment fails in practice, since the internalized narration throws light on Edgeworth rather than on Day; it was, partly for that reason, abandoned as a book primarily about Day, to become instead the substance of the first volume of Edgeworth's posthumously published *Memoir* of himself (1820). Like Edgeworth's other early acquaintances, Day appears there at intervals as a phantasmagorical figure, forever in mourning for lost women or for something unexplained. Disconnected, disturbing, this is avant-garde, surreal writing, more Buñuel than Rousseau. The supercargo of grief seems to be R. L. Edgeworth's own, as, retelling his best friend's life, he is drawn also to his own, and Honora's, turbulent and passionate early years.

Maria Edgeworth as her father's amanuensis probably helped him with this odd book, covering incidents which had helped shape her childhood. At about the same time she certainly helped him with lessons for his and Elizabeth's six children, who needed instruction and amusement when the family lived for eighteen months in lodgings at Clifton, near Bristol, in 1792–3. It was here at Clifton that Maria Edgeworth first drafted, for oral telling, the children's stories which established her reputation, and released her from Thomas Day's taboo. Altogether six of her subsequent works could scarcely have been written without Day: *Letters for Literary Ladies* (1795), *Parent's Assistant* (1796), *Practical Education* (1798), the 'Harry and Lucy' series (from 1801), 'Forester', one of the *Moral Tales* (1801), and *Belinda* (1801). The more pedagogic ones need not concern us here; in fact, though from their inception associated with Day, they also departed from the un-bookish Rousseauistic model, and adopted instead the syllabus, first worked out at Warrington Academy, which the chemist and educationalist Joseph Priestley promoted from the 1760s.[9] In advocating that girls as well as boys should follow this modern curriculum, tilted away from the traditional Classics (and theology)

[9] Joseph Priestley, *Essay on a Course of Liberal Education* (London, 1768).

towards practical science (chemistry and mechanics), the Edgeworth father–daughter partnership puts on record, volume by volume, a programmatic rejection of the Rousseau–Day exclusion of girls from modern knowledge, and the most comprehensive available plan for home-educating parents to follow with all their children.

Letters for Literary Ladies deserves brief attention, if only because it has been reprinted in modern times, and thus is more available for teaching than most of Edgeworth's corpus. Appearing when it does, and beginning with a version of a letter from Day to R. L. Edgeworth objecting to female authorship, it looks like the manifesto of a silenced author, even a silenced generation. But the volume is too slight for this portentous role, and the gentlemanly exchange of letters too pompous. The novelette which makes up the volume's middle section, 'Letters from Julia and Caroline', dully tries to prove that an educated woman is less likely to be seduced than an ignorant one. Only the last part, 'An Essay on the Noble Science of Justification', a lampoon of a silly woman's style of argument, has much individuality or life. Edgeworth works through her differences with Day mechanically, before doing it imaginatively.

Instead of replying to Day the man, she replied to his great book, *Sandford and Merton*; her opening counter-statement in their dialogue is her own master-work in children's fiction, *The Parent's Assistant*. The Day volume announces its debt to the Socratic dialogue in many ways: by foregrounding dialogues between an adult and child, for example, or between its boy protagonists, Harry Sandford, a farmer's son, and Tommy Merton, the son of a rich owner of West Indian plantations. It also opposes two cultural ideals, life-styles, or ideologies. In the end Day seems most concerned to compare the primitive world, in which the essential human individual and citizen first emerged, with an advanced society based on property. Modern conditions allow the rich to exploit and domineer over the poor, who become yet more wretched, while the corrupted, effeminate upper orders are hardly healthy or happy. Harry, the modern Cincinnatus or honest man, is brave, truthful, and active, while the younger Tommy, though imaginative and naturally generous, is easily swayed by his own vanity, or by the snobbery of his rich friends. Within a highly episodic narrative, well adapted to family reading, the two boys typically encounter a member of the lower orders (a grateful negro, impoverished Highlander, or beggar), even an animal, and do right (Harry) or wrong (Tommy) by them. Inset stories rework the same motifs, from ancient Sparta to the woods of modern America, and from Lebanon to Kamchatka. Day has an eye for the Crusoe-like tale of human ingenuity and endurance, of a kind which might have appeared in a newspaper. He tells, impressively, how three stranded Russian sailors survived for six years without weapons or equipment on ice-bound Spitzbergen, and how a group of women and children, buried by an avalanche in an Alpine barn, kept themselves alive for more than five weeks with the help of two milk-yielding goats.[10]

Edgeworth's stories are, by contrast, economical, fictional, and self-contained. Other obvious models, La Fontaine and especially Marmontel, write about naïve worlds with conscious elegance: Edgeworth's openings and her dialogue conjure up this polished French style, and so implicitly depart from Day's deliberate effect of spontaneity or even ruggedness. All the same, she also employs two favourite protagonists: the spoilt boy or girl easily tempted into extravagance or showing-off (such as Rosalind in 'The Purple Jar', and Hal in 'Waste Not, Want Not'), or the sturdy poor child (Jem in 'Lazy Lawrence', Simple Susan in the tale of that name), each of whom manages to make enough money to see the family through a crisis. In *The Parent's Assistant* as a whole (both the 1796 volume, and the three-volume 1800 edition), spoilt brats and little entrepreneurs pretty well balance one another. Thus Edgeworth's collection repeats, without saying so, the cross-class dialogue of *Sandford and Merton*.

It is at first disconcerting to find that Edgeworth's beautifully delineated village worlds and troubled small children are not simply her own invention, but variations on Day's. Young Jem Preston, 10-year-old hero of 'Lazy Lawrence', is another Harry Sandford, with the same health, energy, enterprise, and warmth of heart. In her version, at least, we get to these characteristics not by having them pointed out (often, in Day, by the pedagogue Mr Barlow), but by observing the child's affection for the elderly horse Lightfoot, or by seeing him play cricket enthusiastically after work. Jem's foil, the Lazy Lawrence of the tale's title, combines the worst features of Tommy Merton with the actions of 'The Ill-Natured Boy', in the most Hogarthian of Day's inset stories. Edgeworth's Lawrence is just like Day's Boy in being the spoilt son of an alehouse-keeper, who pays off his child with six pence as he heads off for a drinking session.[11] But Lawrence also seems a real personality, and as much victim as villain: a rather lonely lack-lustre pre-adolescent, something of a depressive, and possibly obese (since he spends all his pocket money on sweets), a child easily induced by older boys to steal the money which Jem earns.

Day's social philosophy draws substance from French physiocrats and from Adam Smith. He sees agriculture as the paradigmatic economic activity: hence the heroic status of the working farmer, as opposed to the idle rich, the parasitical great proprietor or, morally worst of all, the

[10] Thomas Day, *Sandford and Merton* (3 vols.; London, 1783–9), i. 103–19; ii. 84–93.
[11] Ibid. i. 143–4.

plantation-owner. But we never learn quite enough about Harry the individual boy to clinch Day's leap from general principle to particular example. It comes as something of a surprise when the rich slave-owner Mr Merton requires his son to humble himself before the farmer's son: 'That little boy has the noblest mind that ever adorned a human being; nor shall I ever be happy till I see my son . . . entreating forgiveness.'[12]

Edgeworth builds up her child heroes by engaging them naturalistically in the trading and servicing activity of their immediate neighbourhood: the finding, cultivation, development, or making, and afterwards the selling, of small, intriguing objects with consumer-appeal, of a kind that both adults and children respond to. Jem, brought up on a market garden, already grasps how the laws of supply and demand operate between wealthy people and the trading class. He shows unusual flair and also perseverance in collecting saleable objects—crystals, fossils, shells—but also an eager disposition that makes adults plausibly willing to help him out. Jem has found a lady prepared to be his benefactor—the *deus ex machina* who rules the world of so much Georgian fiction—though she exacts a sound twelve-hour day weeding her garden, for which she pays Jem the going rate for child labour. One day, while he is diligently at work weeding her borders and carrying her pot plants, Jem gets mud on the floor because there is no mat at the garden door into the house. He resolves to make her a mat by plaiting heath-plants together (the salvation of a poor man in the second of Day's inset stories[13]). His first venture into craft does not come easy:

What toil, what time, what pains did it cost him . . . Two hours he worked before he went to bed. All his play hours the next day he spent at his mat; which, in all, made five hours of fruitless attempts—The sixth, however, repaid him for the labours of the other five; he conquered his grand difficulty of fastening the heath substantially together, and at length completely finished a mat, which far surpassed his most sanguine expectations. He was extremely happy—sung, danced round it—whistled—looked at it again and again, and could hardly leave off looking at it when it was time to go to bed.[14]

There is an underlying similarity to Harry's achievements; the difference, which her humorous tone draws attention to, lies in the humdrum object of all this heroic effort, and in Jem's childish way of expressing his pleasure. Above all, the story is told through the boy's own desire for the pretty things he collects, and pride at having made an object of value. Edgeworth does not only represent characters who are producers and consumers, she shows how they think and feel in these roles.

[12] Ibid. iii. 185.
[13] 'The Gentleman and the Basket-Maker', in ibid. i. 43–51.
[14] 'Lazy Lawrence', i. 38–9.

If Jem is one of the most engaging of Edgeworth's child protagonists, Maurice the gardener's son in 'Forgive and Forget' (1796) is at least his equal for rapport with the things his labour produces. Again, the entry into this crucial relationship, of manufacturer with product, is mapped out with as much care as the novelist bestows on the early stages of a love-affair—and may even be slily parodic of that familiar topic of romance. Maurice has been sent to a shop to buy common seeds, but while waiting he meets an irascible stranger from remote parts: a classic opening in oriental tales. At first the stranger seems minded to do Maurice harm, for no reason, but when Maurice does him a favour he becomes his good angel:

The seedman looked out all the seeds that Maurice wanted, and packed them up in paper: he was folding up some painted-ladypease, when, from a door at the back of the shop, there came in a square, rough-faced man, who exclaimed, the moment he came in, 'Are the seeds I ordered ready?—The wind's fair—they ought to have been aboard yesterday. And my china jar, is it packed up and directed?—where is it?' . . .
'Immediately, sir, as soon as I have done up the parcel for this little boy.'
'What signifies the parcel for this little boy? he can wait, and I cannot—wind and tide wait for no man. Here, my good lad, take your parcel, and sheer off,' said the impatient man; and, as he spoke, he took up the parcel of seeds from the counter . . . all the seeds fell out upon the floor, whilst Maurice in vain held his hands to catch them.

As Maurice kneels on the shop floor, picking up his seeds, he sees that the captain's foot is entangled in some packthread hanging down from the shelf on which the china jar is standing. He seizes the captain's leg:

'Stay! stand still, sir . . . or you will break your china jar.'

The man stood still [and] looked . . . 'I am really very much obliged to you, my little fellow,' said he; 'you have saved my jar, which I would not have broken for ten guineas . . . it is for my wife, and I've brought it safe from abroad many a league . . . this was returning good for evil. . . . Be so kind,' continued he, turning to the shopman, 'as to reach down that china jar for me?'
The shopman lifted down the jar very carefully, and the captain took off the cover, and pulled out some tulip roots . . . 'Here are a couple of tulip roots for you; and if you take care of them, I'll promise you that you will have the finest tulips in England in your little garden. These tulips were given to me by a Dutch merchant, who told me, that they were some of the rarest and finest in Holland. They will prosper with you, I'm sure, wind and weather permitting.'[15]

---

[15] 'Forgive and Forget', in *The Parent's Assistant*, v. 194–9.

By saving the beautiful, fragile jar, Maurice earns a reward which looks at first sight as humdrum as the seeds by which he and his father make their living, but in the commercial system, in which luxuries are often rarities imported from remote places, an exotic variety serves Maurice and his father as the treasure traditional to folk-tale. What is naturally English—gardening—can be raised to an altogether higher dimension, all the more readily because labouring with the soil is the traditional sign of the employment of the poor, while gardening with discrimination—for example, introducing an exotic new species— has become a tasteful, distinguishing activity of the well-to-do, and of their children.[16] Gardening embodies new-republican egalitarian idealism, subtly eliding with the lust to possess what is beautiful and unique. In yet another deft touch, the dull root which will become an exotic tulip serves as a metaphor for Maurice's life, which by his virtue and labour promises to open out into wealth, ease, or unspecified opportunity.

In her many borrowings from Day, Edgeworth changes his register in ways which seem consistent overall. On class, for example, she may seem at first sight to provide so much more specific detail (of her characters' incomes, or lack of income, and precise social level) that she toughens, even democratizes, Day's abstracted, rich-man's republicanism. Her protagonists include girls, whereas his of course do not, and children much more socially disadvantaged than Jem. In Edgeworth's 'The Orphans', the death of Mary's widowed mother, an Irish seamstress, leaves her at 12 to bring up her younger brother and two sisters in the only refuge she can find for them, the roofed corner of a ruined Irish castle. Paul and his little sister Anne, in the 'Basket-Woman', are the orphaned children of a beggar, who have been taken in by a very poor old woman, another seamstress: 'Grandmother', as they call her, cannot afford a blanket to cover her in winter. Franklin in 'The False Key' is the son of a ne'er-do-well, and has been brought up as a charity-boy by a member of the Bristol Philanthropic Society. At 13 he is set to earn his own living as a kitchen boy in the household of a wealthy lady living in Queen's Square, Bristol—a hostile environment, anticipating *Oliver Twist*, and an unusually harsh setting for Edgeworth to offer child readers. In fact this is a rare literary route for a children's author to take at this time, in a genre aimed at middle-class book-buyers. These Bristol servants' quarters make a true underworld, a sealed-off domain ruled by bickering petty despots, the cook and the butler. It takes luck and of course good judgement for a poor boy to prosper under a hierarchy which makes it

---

[16] For gardening as a child's activity, see the Edgeworth story 'Frank', in *Early Lessons* (London, 1801), and ch. 1, 'Toys', *Practical Education* (London, 1798), i. 20–1.

normal practice to pilfer food and drink, and to cover up by throwing suspicion on someone weaker.

But by positing social confrontation along what can only be class lines, between the amoral rich, and the more conscientious middling order, or between upwardly mobile plantation-owners and morally responsible Tory farmer-squires, Day makes well-articulated, timely political points, which must have given his book cogency in an era of great class tension. Political radicalism embraces for Day both the middle-class critique of aristocratic profligacy, and the Tory critique of commercial-class greed. By comparison, when she individualizes her young entrepreneurs, studies their feelings, views their careers as personal experience, Edgeworth exhibits the limitations as well as the strengths of miniaturization: it puts general issues to one side.

On gender, however, she is the more trenchant. In her mature tales for adults, Edgeworth's inventive, counter-stereotypical characterization effectively rebuts Day's negative portrayal of them. Though the simplicity and brevity of the children's tale only rarely allow sustained character-development, she goes into the motives of her child entrepreneurs with some care. They are not out to 'better themselves' in the world, nor desirous of accumulating capital, nor, what is often Day's apparent assumption, virtuous simply because their social utility makes them so. Instead her children have short-term goals, typically a family crisis, so that their motivation approaches the traditional, religiously sanctioned ones of family bonding, friendship, or loving thy neighbour as thyself. When money is made or saved, it goes to others; even when spent, it is commonly offered as a gift.

In fact gift-giving, as a ritual form of social exchange and proof of moral worth, is central not only to Edgeworth's mature novels of social life, but to the children's tales, where it already takes subtle, satisfying forms. Even more than coins, gifts serve as key symbols of sociability itself, but they are seldom sentimentalized. In 'The Bracelets' (written 1787), Edgeworth's earliest story to survive into a published collection, schoolgirls are coolly observed competing with one another, partly through present-giving, to buy friendship and popularity. Laura in 'The Birthday Present' gives money as an act of charity, Rosamond in the same story squanders it on a foolish fragile basket—with the good intention, but not the effect, of pleasing her cousin. Gifts are only a form of currency, and sometimes too dear, or less credit-worthy than their cash equivalent. Susan Price, the most heroic of Edgeworth's child protagonists, learns this hard lesson when she has to give away her mother's present, a pet lamb.

Susan, about three years older than Jem, needs to earn a larger sum of money—nine guineas, without which her father, a small farmer, will be drafted into the army. She begins, unlike Jem, with something of her own, two pets with a market value—a pretty guinea-hen and the plump lamb, Daisy, who follows Susan about. In a far more complex way than Jem's fossils and mats, the hen and the lamb work throughout as the story's real currency—at once tokens of love or of status, and cash. The guinea-hen, for instance, strays into the next-door garden belonging to the litigious lawyer Case, whose grasping, socially ambitious daughter Barbara, once Susan's friend, impounds it, and tries to sell it back at an exorbitantly high price, before presenting it as a gift to the local gentry family in order to curry favour. Meanwhile lawyer Case has discovered that the new Squire likes roast lamb for his dinner. By playing on Susan's anxiety over her sick mother and drafted father, he meanly contrives to use her remaining pet to advance his own career:

'Yes, but you have a lamb,' said the hard-hearted attorney.

'My poor little lamb!' said Susan, 'but what good can that do?'

'What good can any lamb do?—is not lamb good to eat? Why do you look so pale, girl? Are not sheep killed every day, and don't you eat mutton? Is your lamb better than any body else's, think you?' . . .

'It feeds out of my hand, it follows me about; I have always taken care of it, my mother gave it to me.'

'Well, say no more about it then, if you love your lamb better than your father and your mother both, keep it, and good morning to you.'

'Stay, oh stay!' cried Susan, catching the skirt of his coat with an eager trembling hand;—'a whole week, did you say? My mother may get better in that time.—No, I do not love my lamb half so well.' The struggle of her mind ceased, and with a placid countenance and calm voice, 'Take the lamb,' said she.

'Where is it?' said the attorney.

'Grazing in the meadow, by the river side.'

'It must be brought up before nightfall for the butcher, remember.'

'I shall not forget it,' said Susan, steadily. But as soon as her persecutor turned his back and quitted the house, she sat down, and hid her face in her hands.[17]

A heroine out of pastoral as well as the sentimental tale, Susan is obliged, unusually, to acknowledge the lamb's market value as dead meat. Of all Edgeworth's counters of exchange, in her trader's world of production and consumption, this is one of the most resonant and longest-remembered by nineteenth-century readers. It is, of course, yet another literary convention, used with aplomb. The sacrificial animal, meekly gazing up at his murderer, is one of the most affecting of all literary emblems of oppressed innocence or social and ritualized

---

[17] 'Simple Susan', in *The Parent's Assistant*, ii. 107–8.

savagery: 'Pleas'd to the last, he crops the flowery food, I And licks the hand just rais'd to shed his blood.'[18] In *Sandford and Merton*, both Harry and his classical *alter ego* Strephon, from one of the inset stories, narrowly escape seeing a pet lamb butchered. As with so many of her borrowings, Edgeworth retains the traditional moral value of the device, while asking her readers to think anew about its possible applications in a modern commercial economy. Jane Austen may understandably have 'Simple Susan' at the back of her mind when in *Mansfield Park* she gives another Susan Price, and her older sister Fanny, the neo-republican roles of exemplary 'simple' characters, agents of a transcendental reformation.

While Maria Edgeworth was at Bristol, creating her best children's stories for oral delivery to her little brothers and sisters, Day's young disciple, the chemist, doctor, educationalist, and moralist Thomas Beddoes, was taking Day's place in the family circle. In 1793 Beddoes, partly on Edgeworth's advice, moved from lecturing in chemistry at Oxford to medical practice at Clifton; the following year he married Maria Edgeworth's sister nearest in age, Anna, who thereafter lived at Clifton and moved in its scientific and literary circles.

Maria Edgeworth, her father, and her third stepmother, the former Frances Beaufort, returned to Clifton in 1799, to encounter the young Humphry Davy, his famous experiments with nitrous oxide or laughing gas, and a Beddoes who was preparing to extend his intellectual range to the analysis of a society sick of consumerism.[19] Back at Edgeworthstown, Maria Edgeworth incorporated unmistakable features of both Day and Beddoes in delineating two fictional critics of society. The more obvious caricature is the late-adolescent student drop-out Forester, hero of the first and most substantial of her *Moral Tales* (1801). Sent to Edinburgh to complete his education (like Beddoes in real life in 1784), Forester admires the academic chemist and physiologist with whom he boards, Dr Campbell (as Beddoes admired the leading chemist Joseph Black), but precipitately leaves the house rather than submit to polite conventions such as dancing and clean shoes. Instead he tries to live by his fundamentalist principles, first by working for a commercial gardener, then as a printer's compositor. Forester's picaresque misadventures exploit Day's reluctant, ill-fated attempts to learn to dance, in order to win Elizabeth

---

[18] Pope, *Essay on Man*, i. 83–4.
[19] For Beddoes's later works in natural philosophy, *Hygeia: or Essays Moral and Medical, on the Causes affecting the Personal State of our Middling and Affluent Classes* (3 vols.; Bristol, 1802–3), and *A Manual of Health* (London, 1806), books which are part general medicine, part social criticism, see Roy Porter, *Doctor of Society: Thomas Beddoes and the Sick Trade in Late-Enlightenment England* (London, 1992), esp. chs. 4 and 5.

Sneyd, and Beddoes's slovenly appearance, 'repulsive' manners, and incurable habit of railing at the glitterati.[20]

More overtly sympathetic, less obviously a portrait, two leading male characters of Edgeworth's first full-scale novel, *Belinda* (1801), the hero Clarence Hervey and his friend Dr X——, exhibit between them the social nonconformity and pedagogic severity affected at times by Rousseau, Day, and Beddoes. Dr X—— in *Belinda* is in himself anything but ridiculous, and indeed also serves as a complement to the surgeon–novelist Dr John Moore, author of the widely admired satirical 'anatomy', *Zeluco* (1789). But X——has more particular plot functions, to guide and slowly to re-educate the gifted but erratic Hervey, whose eccentricities include the training of an *ingénue* to be his future wife, and to reform a woman Hervey greatly admires, the fashionable Lady Delacour. The novel's middle chapters are taken up with the doctor's diagnosis and cure of Lady Delacour, so that readers are led to expect a conventional outcome, the victory of a male sage over a transgressive woman. But Edgeworth in fact withholds this triumph. The contest between the two is resolved less predictably.

Believing she has breast cancer, Lady Delacour will take advice only from a woman servant and a male quack (a behaviour-pattern which Beddoes afterwards held typical of aristocratic effeminacy).[21] Dr X—— soon spots that she is ill, and later urges her to put herself in the hands of the best-qualified professional, a surgeon who can perform the mastectomy that may be needed. At the technical level Dr X——has reason on his side, but he does not consider the whole woman. Lady Delacour rules in her own house, dominating her dull husband, and in the fashionable world she has achieved much the same ascendancy. To submit to physical mutilation, regulated moreover by two men, the domestic despot and the professional one, is also to abdicate from a rare position of power:

'So it is the doctor's opinion, that I shall inevitably destroy myself, if, from a vain hope of secrecy, I put myself into ignorant hands? These are his own words, are they? . . . I must beg you to recollect, that I am neither a child nor a fool; that I am come to years of discretion, and that I am not now in the delirium of a fever; consequently there can be no pretence for *managing* me. In this particular I must insist upon managing myself. I have confidence in the skill of the person whom I shall employ. Dr X——, very likely, would have none, because the man may not have a diploma for killing or curing in form. That is nothing to the purpose. It is I that am to undergo the operation. It is *my* health, *my* life, that is risked;

[20] See Butler, *Maria Edgeworth*, 109–10.
[21] See Porter's resumé of the arguments advanced in *Hygeia* and the *Manual of Health* concerning fashionable folly and gullibility (*Doctor of Society*, 63–80).

and if I am satisfied, that is enough. Secrecy, as I told you before, is my first object.'

'And cannot you', said Belinda, 'depend with more security upon the honour of a surgeon who is at the head of his profession, and who has a high reputation at stake, than upon a vague promise of secrecy from some obscure quack, who has no reputation to lose?'

'No,' said lady Delacour: 'I tell you, my dear, that I cannot depend upon any of these 'honourable men'. I have taken means to satisfy myself on this point: their honour and foolish delicacy would not allow them to perform such an operation for a wife, without the knowledge, privity, consent, &c. &c. &c. of her husband. Now lord Delacour's knowing the thing is quite out of the question.'[22]

Somewhat disingenuously, Edgeworth works a compromise: Lady De-lacour does submit to an examination by a surgeon, who finds no operation is necessary. But if here Lady Delacour is seen reluctantly retreating, she advances again in the later stages of the novel, when it is her strength of mind and defiance of convention that releases Clarence from his theory-led engagement to Virginia, and upholds Belinda in pulling out of her imminent marriage to a rich young West Indian, Vincent. Lady Delacour's firm approval of an action normally con-sidered scandalously wayward is a final reminder that from the novel's early chapters Belinda has accepted guidance from 'the most dissipated viscountess in town'. Though Lady Delacour significantly associates her views with those of Dr X——on the point of principle, her way of wording her congratulations has an assertiveness especially her own:

I give you infinite credit for your *civil courage*, as Dr X——calls it: military courage . . . may be had for sixpence a day. But civil courage, such as enabled the princess Parizade, in the Arabian Tales, to go straight up the hill to her object, though the magical multitude of advising and abusive voices continually called to her to turn back, is one of the rarest qualities in man or woman, and not to be had for love, money, or admiration.[23]

Lady Delacour's high regard for admiration—that is, for seeming admirable—is what is striking here. Aristocratic virtue is socially oriented: display, surface, matter more than say a good conscience or sincerity of feeling, both of which rate high in the protestant-bourgeois system of values. Like Henry James's women of fashion, Lady Delacour is both meretricious and superb. She threatens and eventually oversets the Rousseauistic hypothesis, that aristocracy is effeminate, degenerate. Though women certainly rule in most of Edgeworth's panoramas of high

[22] *Belinda* (1801), in Maria Edgeworth, *Tales, and Miscellaneous Pieces* (14 vols.; London, 1825), ii. 225–6.
[23] Ibid. iii. 281.

life, of which *Belinda* is the first, they usually do so on the basis of their personal distinction. Just as her children's tales imagine worlds of a child's desires, so her fashionable tales reimagine society as a sphere of women's empowerment.

Belinda remains, importantly, a middle-class novel. In its accurate delineation of the world of things and its inter-class tensions it is one of the paradigmatic novels of the early nineteenth century. The figure of the writer–scientist–moralist Dr X——, situated within the frame of the picture and drawing in the eye, suggests a classically positioned portrait-of-the-artist. He 'is' Edgeworth herself in many of her attitudes, as he is Thomas Day and Thomas Beddoes, the censurers of effeminacy. All the same, Edgeworth has made sure that Lady Delacour talks X——down, and that the novel's clinching remarks on womanly strength are hers, not his. As Lady Delacour theatrically brings down the curtain on an arresting denouement, she signals victory in Edgeworth's twenty-year campaign to escape the regimen of Thomas Day.

PART TWO

Marginal Texts

6 'I was a kind of an Historian': The Productions of History in Defoe's Colonel Jack

KATHERINE A. ARMSTRONG

Since all texts, fictional and non-fictional, are equally shaped by their historical circumstances, it would be nonsensical to describe *Colonel Jack* (1722)[1] as one of Defoe's most historical novels. Certainly *Colonel Jack* is, of Defoe's best-known novels, one of those most packed with historical detail—the reason, perhaps, for its relative critical neglect in the twentieth century by comparison with, say, *Robinson Crusoe* or *Moll Flanders*, and perhaps for the recent slight rise in its critical fortunes[2]— but we are justified in describing it as a historical novel less by its supposed generic identity than by its thematic investigation of history as both the producer and production of the individual.

In this chapter I shall argue that in *Colonel Jack* Defoe offers two competing models of the relationship between society and the individual, or history and historical persons. The first, a more conventional and simplistic model in which the individual is a victim of historical and social forces beyond his or her control, is finally overtaken by the second, which acknowledges the contribution of the individual to the course of history. Although Jack would like the reader to subscribe to the first model, since this would absolve him of responsibility for his many crimes and deceits, his narrative none the less reveals his agency, that is to say, his direct role in the creation of his times. But Defoe does not replace the first model with one equally mechanistic. Ultimately *Colonel Jack* proposes that historical epochs and those who live through them are mutually determined. I shall first consider Defoe's enlightened presentation of his hero as the product of social deprivation in childhood and early adulthood, then his exposure of this hero's attempts to disown responsibility for his conduct, and lastly the still more enlightened recognition, implicit in the text, that history is simultaneously produced by, and

---

[1] [Daniel Defoe], *The History and remarkable Life of the truly Honourable Colonel Jacque, vulgarly call'd Colonel Jack* . . . (London, 1722). All subsequent references are to the World's Classics *Colonel Jack*, ed. Samuel Holt Monk, with a new introduction by David Roberts (Oxford, 1989).
[2] Paula Backscheider discusses *Colonel Jack* at length in both her critical study, *Daniel Defoe: Ambition and Innovation* (Lexington, Ky., 1986), and her biography, *Daniel Defoe: His Life* (Baltimore, 1989).

producer of, individual people. As we shall see, all three approaches to history—whether as a source or consequence of human errors or both—are used to support Defoe's objections to Catholicism, Jacobitism, and the ascendancy of France, and to reflect his concern with certain social evils: inadequate state education; childhood poverty; institutional brutality, in England, Scotland, and the English colonies.

On the most straightforward level *Colonel Jack* is intended as an attack on certain social abuses. Defoe exonerates his protagonist at least in part for crimes which are shown to be the direct consequences of his acute need. In lamenting the absence of state provisions for the care and education of orphans the preface establishes a precedent for the hero's subsequent presentation of his crimes as the result of neglect. Jack's 'editor' gives official sanction to the rationale the hero will invariably offer for his behaviour, the preface's formal diction ('*If he had come into the World with the Advantage of Education, and been well instructed how to improve the generous Principles he had in him, what a Man might he not have been*' (p. 1)), articulating exactly the same opinion which Jack puts so colloquially: 'As for your humble Servant, Colonel *Jack*, he was a poor unhappy tractable Dog, willing enough, and capable too, to learn any thing, if he had had any but the Devil for his School-Master' (p. 6). Necessity as the motive for crime is first mentioned in the preface,[3] but it soon becomes almost a refrain in Jack's narrative, applied not only to his own case (e.g. p. 156) but to that of others, such as the cultivated gentleman who is forced to turn highwayman and narrowly misses the gallows (p. 161), or the impoverished gentlewoman who may be starved into prostitution (p. 232).

According to the preface, the answer to ridding England of its swollen population of juvenile offenders is an overhaul of the state education system ('*publick Schools, and Charities*' (p. 1)),[4] since a decent education would obviate the need for children to commit crimes. Although Jack's tone is often informal, as in the passage quoted above, he too can be serious and explicit in urging solutions to certain social and ethical problems. Bald appeals for an expansion of the transportation system punctuate the first half of the narrative. The hero's passionate belief in the colonies as the antidote to both poverty and crime is voiced over and over again during his first sojourn in Virginia. Criminals would be honest

[3] For Defoe on the subject of necessity, see Maximillian E. Novak, *Defoe and the Nature of Man* (London, 1963), ch. 3.
[4] An account of the charity schools controversy as it relates to *Colonel Jack* is given by David Blewett in *Defoe's Art of Fiction: Robinson Crusoe, Moll Flanders, Colonel Jack and Roxana* (Toronto, 1979), 102–4.

if only they were skilled enough to find legitimate employment: the theme is recurrent in Jack's account of his years as a bonded servant and is finally summarized schematically as one of a number of listed items which attest to the value of transportation (pp. 152–3). His demonstrations of the benefits of using reason rather than violence in the management of slaves are similarly repetitive. Just in case the reader has missed the point of the several anecdotes illustrating the effectiveness of extending mercy towards slaves, Jack concludes his digression with a justificatory recapitulation of his arguments and ends: 'I HAVE dwelt the longer upon it, that if possible Posterity might be perswaded to try gentler Methods with those miserable Creatures, and to use them with Humanity' (pp. 149–50). And like the 'editor' in the preface, Jack presents juvenile crime as the responsibility of a society which hands unwanted children over to an unregulated body of private nurses and which does not trouble itself about enforcing the law of parish relief: the connection between thieving and childhood neglect is made at intervals throughout the account of his growing-up.

As well as through these formal statements by the editor and the narrator, Defoe is able to infer the necessity for social and penal reforms through delicately pointed parallels and correspondences which underpin Jack's narrative. Parallels and correspondences are, of course, characteristic of Defoe's fiction and are associated particularly with *Robinson Crusoe*, in which the 'concurrence of days'[5] in the hero's life serves to remind him of Providence's guiding hand. In *Colonel Jack*, too, the occurrence of parallels and coincidental correspondences can suggest that the author is keeping a watchful eye on the workings of fate or Providence. For example, the hero returns in middle age to the scenes of his childhood, as though unable to shake off the ill deeds of his youth. He grew up in the squalid neighbourhood of Ratcliffe Highway (p. 8), a place synonymous with crime and dereliction, and when he goes back to London as a prosperous merchant his origins catch up with him in the shape of a beautiful young woman who lives 'near *Ratcliff* or rather *Stepney*' (p. 238). Equally ironic is the fact that when Jack goes to London after his military campaigning he lives in 'a narrow Court not much unlike *Three King Court* in *Lombard Street*' (p. 186), a direction which will remind an attentive reader that Jack's first serious crime in boyhood involved a hasty exit from Lombard Street via Three King Court (p. 21). Sometimes the reader seems more alert than Jack to such recurrences; he does not recognize his first wife when he finds her labouring as a transport on his plantation, but the reference his manager

---

[5] Daniel Defoe, *The Life and Adventures of Robinson Crusoe*, ed. Angus Ross (Harmondsworth, 1965), 143.

makes to her reputed 'fifteen Hundred Pound' marriage portion (p. 253) should have prompted Jack to recall the bitter quarrels years earlier between himself and his wife over the '1500 *l.*' (p. 194) which had been insufficient to maintain her gambling habit. Jack might also have reflected on the irony that he is cuckolded by a man whose occupation as sea-captain is identical to that of Jack's wife's first husband (pp. 235, 240). Some of Defoe's parallels and correspondences function emblematically: the disturbing image of the gallows, for example, recurs dozens of times in the novel, from the opening page to almost the last (it is the fear of hanging as a traitor which sends Jack off to Cuba). The gallows are omnipresent in the text: a minor character (destined to hang) is called '*Wry-Neck*' (p. 9); the hero's friend Will (who will also hang) wounds a gardener in the neck (p. 81); Jack's 'Tutor' (p. 169) has endured the same terrifying visions of the 'Gibbet' (p. 164) as Jack himself.

The aesthetic and thematic unity suggested by these examples is borne out in the larger structure of the novel. Parallels and correspondences are used to promote Defoe's solutions to social problems, most importantly to reinforce Jack's plea for the erring individual as the product of flawed social institutions and practices. The juxtaposition of Jack's life as a pickpocket with his life as a plantation overseer might at first sight seem to indicate Defoe's propensity for narratives in which disparate subjects are loosely, even arbitrarily, connected through the adventures of a fictional individual. *Moll Flanders*, written in the same year as *Colonel Jack*, is a like blend of criminal biography and propaganda on behalf of transportation. Yet Jack draws attention explicitly to the ethical implications of his sudden elevation from criminal to law-enforcer: 'This part turn'd the very blood within my Veins, and I could not think of it with any temper; that I, who was but Yesterday a Servant or Slave like them, and under the Authority of the same Lash, should lift up my Hand to the Cruel Work, which was my Terror but the Day before' (pp. 127–8). The long discussion of corporal punishment on the plantations which follows is not a digression nor an attempt by Defoe to cram as much didactic material as possible into his novel. Rather it bears a direct relationship to the preceding English section of the narrative in which Defoe was similarly preoccupied with transgression and correction. Just as the story of Jack's boyhood exposes the brutality and inefficacy of conventional forms of punishment in England, especially the corporal punishment of young offenders, so the story of his years as an overseer is used to censure the colonial practice of whipping slaves. Jack's first traumatic experience as a child is not the death of his only adult protector, a misfortune he greets with equanimity, but his witnessing of his foster-brother's whipping at Bridewell, a sight which 'frighted [him] almost to Death' (p. 12). When Jack subsequently thinks he has lost all his money, his reaction recalls the scene at Bridewell: 'I came away in dispair, crying, and roaring like a little Boy that had been whip'd' (p. 25). Faced with the possibility of arrest at one point, Jack cannot rid himself of the image of his brother's cruel whipping (p. 28), a fear which Will exploits in order to silence his accomplice's objections to what they have done (p. 30). Many years later Jack's foster-brother, Captain Jack, is awed by the spectacle of two criminals being scourged in the streets of Edinburgh by the public hangman, since it inevitably reminds him 'of what he had suffer'd, when he was but a Boy; at the famous place, call'd *Bridewell*' (p. 100). Given the potency of whipping as an image of agony and shame in the text, it is hardly surprising to find Jack taking considerable satisfaction one day in caning his wife's lover 'till he roar'd out like a Boy soundly whipt' (p. 243). Though appalled by the threat of Bridewell, Jack was not, however, permanently deterred by it from crime. His experiences as a thief are interspersed with horrified references to his likely fate, but he continues to steal anyway, while his foster-brother, Captain Jack, seems hardened rather than subdued by his beating.

In the context of so much concern with whipping as both a valueless punishment and an inhumane one, Jack's attempts to reform coercive methods on his Virginian plantation can be seen in two ways. On the one hand, they are an implicit critique of the English penal code, and, on the other, they are supported by Jack's earlier first-hand testimony to the inutility of whipping child criminals. As he keeps pointing out, he was a potential victim of the official whip himself, first as a boy and then as a bonded servant. He knows that the fear of corporal punishment brutalizes rather than reforms.

In order to make the connection clear between Bridewell and the 'Place where the Servants were usually Corrected [on the plantation]' (p. 130), Defoe provides numerous reminders that English criminals and Black slaves are, in terms of their legal and social status, one and the same. Dressed in his overseer's garb and furnished with a mount and a scourge, Jack is barely distinguishable from an English country gentleman whose dominion over animals seems inextricably linked to his authority over the poor: 'when I entered upon my Office, I had a Horse given me, and a long Horse-whip, like what we call in *England* a Hunting-whip; the Horse was to ride up and down all over the Plantation to see the Servants and *Negroes* did their Work' (p. 127).

England is constantly evoked in the discussion of plantation beatings, the practice of whipping slaves being associated with the English colonists above all others. Jack hastens to absolve his countrymen from the charge that they are inherently tyrannical and cruel (p. 128), but the identification of the English with whipping is later admitted first by the planter (p. 145) and secondly when Jack alludes to the dreadful conditions of slaves in Barbados and Jamaica (p. 149), both of which were English colonies in the late-seventeenth and early eighteenth centuries. There is, too, a telling pun in the planter's question to Jack: 'did you really intend to Whip the poor *Negro* twice a Day, for four Days together; *that is to say*, to Whip him to Death, for that would have been the *English* of it, and the End of it' (p. 132). Jack echoes him by citing a national proverb which bears out the hard-line approach to crime of the English; there are, Jack concedes, a few incorrigible villains, though he would argue only a very few, either among Blacks or Europeans, despite the '*English* Proverb; *that if you save a Thief from the Gallows, he shall be the first to Cut your Throat*' (p. 145). The analogy between the planter or overseer in Virginia and the officials who pursue and chastise English criminals is revealed not only by Jack's revulsion against whipping ('I am incapable of being an Executioner, having been an Offender myself' (p. 133)) but also by his instinctive perception of his master as a judge who will listen to his defence (p. 129) as the Justice did in Stepney years before. And the terms in which Jack describes the most recalcitrant slaves are, not surprisingly, strongly reminiscent of the terms in which he previously described his recidivist foster-brother, Captain Jack. The 'Negroes' are characterized by 'Brutallity' and an 'obstinate Temper'; by 'Rage' and 'Cruelty' (p. 128). Captain Jack, too, was 'brutish, bloody, and cruel in his Disposition' (p. 5). Captain Jack, like the exceptional slave, was unteachable, and when Jack promises his employer that within a very short time only the odd unruly boy will require physical punishment—'a few Boys who were incapable of the Impressions, that good Usuage would have made' (p. 147)—the reader knows that the hero has in mind his own childhood and the 'sensible Impressions made upon [him] . . . by the severe Usage of the Captain' (p. 13). It is impossible to ignore the implications of Jack's radical reply to the planter's appeal to custom as the justification for whipping slaves. Jack's language betrays that he is thinking about his mother country, not just the colonies: 'There are it may be Publick and *National* Mistakes and Errors in Conduct, and this is One' (p. 135; emphasis added).

It is evident that Defoe is sincere in his objections to physical punishment both within the English penal system and on colonial plantations, and that he draws implicit parallels between the two. He is equally passionate in reviling the wholesale abandonment by the state of foundling children, whose natural innocence is inevitably corrupted by poverty, and to remedy this social and moral evil he proposes a huge expansion of the transportation system for convicts and a restructuring of state education. Yet *Colonel Jack* is more than a thinly fictionalized blueprint for certain reforms, and only the least sophisticated reader could accept uncritically the hero's estimation of himself as a pitiable victim of social injustices who bears no blame for his life of thievery and fraud. As well as an indictment of late seventeenth-century English and colonial institutions, *Colonel Jack* is a portrait of a criminal who, try as he might, cannot evade the charges levelled at him of greed, deceit, and self-delusion. To the initial proposition embodied in the text—that crime is environmentally conditioned, and the individual merely the victim of irresistible social and historical pressures—Defoe juxtaposes a less forgiving but more complex view of his hero as both innocent and liar, as both perverted by his upbringing yet deliberately and persistently dishonest. As pickpocket, footpad, deserter, mercenary, Jacobite, and smuggler, Jack bears the imprint of his upbringing among criminals and rebels; but he is also unmistakably responsible himself for the social and political evils which undermine the state. The desire to distance himself from the moral implications of his actions is present throughout his narrative and ultimately helps to underscore the fundamental dishonesty of his character.

It cannot be overlooked that for all his many confessions of past wrongdoings Jack repeatedly finds excuses for himself, seeing some mitigation in his having been surrounded by temptations. In describing the moment in boyhood when he finally surrendered to the arguments of the experienced pickpocket his language becomes sub-Miltonic: 'WELL, upon the perswasions of this Lad, I walk'd out with him, a poor innocent Boy, and (as I remember, my very Thoughts perfectly well) I had no Evil in my Intentions; I had never stolen any thing in my Life . . . but the subtile Tempter baited his Hook for me' (p. 19). They are almost the same words he will use to describe his seduction by the first woman he marries: 'I began to be ensnared, I knew not how, or to what End; and was on a sudden so embarrass'd in my Thoughts about her, that like a Charm she had me always in her Circle; if she had not been one of the subtilest Women on Earth, she could never have brought me to have given myself the least Trouble about her' (p. 187). Even when he assaults his second wife he justifies himself ('you must consider me now in the Circumstances of a Man enrag'd' (p. 230)), while his involvement in the Jacobite uprising of 1715 is the fault of a '*Romish* Priest' whose provocative talk 'gave [Jack] no rest' (p. 264). And his participation in the lucrative illegal trade with New Spain is presented as the only natural and just response to unreasonable Spanish protectionism and barbarity (p. 287).

What these examples collectively imply is an ironic discrepancy in moral terms between the author and his hero; and the many reproaches Jack aims at a callous society which does not feed, clothe, or educate its children are problematized by Jack's precocious ability to make capital from his misfortunes. He is not a mere victim of social abuses or historical conditions: he is at times accountable for such evils himself. In a moment I shall explore the issue of Jack as an agent of history as opposed to its passive subject (or, alternatively, as a constituent of the society in which he lives rather than merely a product of it), but I shall first indicate ways in which Defoe encourages us to distrust his hero's self-portrait as a helpless innocent led by poverty into crime.

For one thing, Jack as a very young boy shows remarkable ingenuity in extracting the sympathy and even admiration of the authority figures who catch him out in criminal acts. As he says, he 'had a natural Talent of Talking' (p. 7) which manages to convince at least one gentleman— though wrongly—of his fundamental honesty (p. 38).[6] Later, in Virginia, he will talk himself out of bondage (pp. 122–5). For another thing, Jack is conspicuously lacking in loyalty to anyone or anything with the exception of himself. On the way back to England he loses some goods to a French privateer, but his interest in privateering as a novel method of legal theft far outweighs his concern for his personal effects, and he spares little thought for the English merchants whose livelihood is under threat from the predatory vessels of the French (p. 180). We are not, therefore, surprised to find him later passing through Ghent as an unconcerned sightseer when his countrymen are fighting in King William's war against the Spanish, nor when he later fights for William's rival, Louis XIV, against the Austrians in Italy. His indifference to England's national interest at these junctures prepares the ground for his greater acts of treason during the Jacobite uprisings of 1708 and 1715.

Despite these instances of his mercenary concern for self over king and country Jack reveals what amounts to an obsession with his supposed status as a gentleman, and reacts violently to perceived slurs on his honour. He develops an aversion to swearing when he learns it is ungentlemanly, and, although he does not actually use his sword very often, he frequently threatens to challenge sexual rivals to duel with him. As he would have it, he was born a gentleman and this is the explanation and justification of all his misdemeanours: they are the consequence of his ambition. Yet the reader begins to suspect that for Defoe the concept

[6] Equally artful would seem to be the condition in which Jack and Will return a stolen pocketbook to a callous gentleman at the Exchange. The description of the book suggests a conscious attempt by the boys to imitate amateur thieves (as opposed to the professionals they really are): it is 'wrapt up in a Dirty peice of a Colour'd Handkerchief, as black as the Street could make it; and Seal'd with a piece of sorry Wax, and the Impression of a Farthing for a Seal' (p. 53).

of the gentleman is deeply ironic in the context of his hero's life. Can an illegitimate child who is quickly dispatched to a nurse seriously claim gentle birth? Though Jack believes passionately in the moral superiority of gentlemen (e.g. pp. 60, 62, 155), gentlemen feature repeatedly in this novel as seducers and libertines (e.g. pp. 6, 201, 224, 241, 249), and 'gentleman' is a cant term for thief in the London underworld in which Jack grows up. Though he hesitates to accept the definition of a gentleman offered by the pickpocket, Will, Jack refers quite naturally to his fellow-robbers as 'Gentlemen Rogues' (p. 69), and does not seem to notice that their much-vaunted code of honour among thieves is in fact rarely adhered to.[7]

While it has been shown that it is dangerous to place too much weight on Defoe's title-pages[8]—the title-page of the first edition of *Colonel Jack*, for example, is evidently designed as an advertisement of the book rather than as an accurate description of its contents—we may wonder whether anything is meant by the rather specious-sounding address of 'Truly Honourable' with which the title-page introduces the hero. Were Jack an earl, a viscount, a baron, a lord mayor, or a lord provost, he would be the *Right* Honourable, but 'Right Honourable Colonel' is a solecism and 'truly honourable' equally dubious. It anticipates the hero's slightly absurd insistence on his status throughout his narrative and also his high-flown outburst of gratitude to George I when the Jacobite rebels are for the most part pardoned. There Jack will refer to himself as a 'Man of Honour', a claim which can scarcely avoid prompting a smile in the light of his recent subversive activities.

In the rest of this chapter I shall examine the alternative model of the history-making process with which Defoe challenges his hero's portrayal of himself as both outside society and, therefore, innocent, and yet the child of his times, contaminated by contemporary evils. For Defoe the relationship between history, society, and individuals is a materialist one in which men and women both constitute and are constituted by their times. They cannot deny their part in shaping their society any more than society at large can deny producing citizens who reflect the general evils of poverty, violence, and political unrest. As we come to see, Jack is not so much alienated from his times as an exemplification of them. His narrative serves to demonstrate the links between the proliferating thefts and assaults on the streets of London and the political crime of

---

[7] Like Blewett in *Defoe's Art of Fiction* (p. 94), I disagree with Michael Shinagel's uncritical view of Jack's gentlemanly aspirations in *Defoe and Middle-Class Gentility* (Cambridge, Mass., 1968).

[8] See Rodney M. Baine, 'The Evidence from Defoe's Title Pages', *Studies in Bibliography*, 5 (1972), 185–91.

Jacobitism: both are manifestations of the instability which reduced England to anarchy in the mid-seventeenth century and which continued to threaten the country after the Protestant accession. In 1722, when *Colonel Jack* was published, the Jacobite threat seemed as acute as ever, the uprising of 1715 led by the Earl of Mar having demonstrated that there remained significant and potentially destabilizing opposition to the Hanoverian line. And the late 1710s and early 1720s were years of widespread alarm about perceived rises in crime, alarm which a year after the publication of *Colonel Jack* would produce Robert Walpole's notoriously repressive Waltham Black Act (1723), and a drastic increase in the number of capital offences.[9]

Close attention to the political and religious allusions in Jack's narrative reveals his affinity with many of the figures and movements which Defoe, as a lifelong apologist for the Revolution Settlement of 1688–9, considered inimical to England's peace. Jack's birth can be dated as roughly contemporaneous with James II's avowal of Catholicism in 1672, and the passing of the Test Act in 1673,[10] since he says he was not yet 10 years old when his nurse's husband died in the sinking of the *Gloucester* in 1682. This ship was carrying the Duke of York—later James II—when it foundered, and reminds the reader of James's unconstitutional resumption of the naval command in 1684.[11] Moreover, James's role in the *Gloucester* affair was highly controversial; Gilbert Burnet's *History of his own Time* (1715), for example, represents James as being much to blame for the incident.[12] Reinforcing Jack's infant associations with the Catholic king is his nurse's slur on one of the heroes of English Protestants in the seventeenth century, the Duke of Monmouth. The nurse assures Jack that she has 'known Colonels come to be Lords, and Generals, tho' they were Bas——ds at first' (p. 5). Monmouth, Charles II's illegitimate son, was a focus for the hopes of anti-Jacobites, Defoe included, and his father was rumoured not to be Charles after all, but Colonel Robert Sidney.[13] It seems unlikely that the nurse could be alluding to the Duke of Berwick (1670–1734), the illegitimate son of James II who was brought up as a Catholic in France, since this

[9] Backscheider discusses Defoe's many writings on crime between 1718 and 1721 in *Daniel Defoe: His Life*, ch. 18.
[10] The Test Act required all holders of crown, civil, or military office to take communion in the Church of England and was therefore prejudicial to Dissenters, though some Dissenters were inclined to obey the letter rather than the spirit of the law.
[11] See Maurice Ashley (*James II* (London, 1977), 74) for James's official appointment to the commission of Lord High Admiral in 1661, his resignation following the Test Act in 1673 (p. 98), and his effective resumption of the post in May 1684 (p. 150).
[12] Gilbert Burnet, *History of his own Time*, abridged by Thomas Stackhouse with an introduction by David Allen (London, 1906; repr. London, 1991), 190.
[13] See George Roberts, *The Life, Progresses and Rebellion of James, Duke of Monmouth* (2 vols.; London, 1844), i. 3.

would involve her in a glaring anachronism. But Defoe may have meant to remind his readers in 1722 of Berwick's Jacobite credentials: he fought for his father in Ireland from 1689 to 1691 and, through great generalship of the French and Spanish troops at Almansa in 1707, established the throne of Philip of Spain.[14]

Jack's upbringing in this fervently Jacobite household is partnered by his habit of listening to old soldiers and sailors reminiscing about their days in the French army. France was, of course, England's rival both in the late seventeenth century and in the 1720s, when Defoe wrote *Colonel Jack*. The veterans recall the taking of Maastricht in 1673, a victory for the besieging Duke of Monmouth which won him a colonelcy from Louis XIV and which confirms the nurse's sardonic assurances that illegitimacy is no barrier to a meteoric career. Jack thrills to all these romantic stories, and by the time he is 14 he has learnt the names of all the ships in the navy, then, of course, under the Duke of York's command.

That Defoe wishes to associate Jack not only with the extremist Jacobites but with the high Tories generally is indicated by the sumptuous costume in which the hero dresses when he wants to deceive a Quaker clerk who has kept some money for him. Jack invents a name for his supposed employer, 'Sir *Jonathan Loxham*' of '*Somersetshire*' (p. 76) and, like his showy green and pink livery, this suggests his attraction to the country party of knights and squires. The password of the gang to which Jack belongs, 'GOOD TOWER STANDARD', evokes an image of defiance against the state, and it seems appropriate that when the fosterbrother Captain Jack is beaten for his part in the kidnapping trade his punishment is administered by Sir William Turner, a prominent Protestant who lost his office under James II.[15] Captain Jack is as much associated with Jacobitism as the colonel, for we can assume that when he fought in Ireland in around 1690 (pp. 103–4) he was supporting James at the Battle of the Boyne.

Given his early links with Jacobitism, it comes as no surprise that the adult Jack swears loyalty to 'his Catholick Majesty', King Philip of Spain, when threatened by imprisonment in Havana (p. 279), or that he calls on the services of a '*Romish* Priest' to marry him and Moggy in what amounts to a priest's hole (p. 249). (Later this priest encourages Jack to join the Jacobites at Preston.) At one point, fearing Spanish privateers on the voyage from Virginia to London, Jack adopts Spanish colours for his merchant vessel and gives it the highly Catholic-sounding name of '*Nuestra Segniora de la Val de Grace*' (p. 284).

[14] See Charles Petrie, *The Marshall Duke of Berwick: The Picture of an Age* (London, 1953).
[15] Turner is identified by Samuel Holt Monk in the notes to the World's Classics edition, p. 312.

Despite the hero's gestures (often self-interested and insincere) towards the Jacobites and the Catholic Church, the religious and political foundations of Defoe's novel are Protestant, Dissenting, and anti-Stuart. The preface evinces a concern for the future of (nonconformist) charity schools, and places a Puritan emphasis on Jack's story as a 'Parable' (p. 2). A Puritan tendency to allegorize[16] is also illustrated by the preface's offering of the narrative as *'a delightful Field for the Reader to wander in; a Garden where he may gather wholesome and medicinal Plants'* (p. 2). Within the main narrative there are several hints that Dissenting Protestantism is the source of moral and spiritual truth. As a child Jack receives sympathy and practical help from a clerk whose speech (e.g. p. 33) reveals him to be a Quaker, and in adulthood a reformed highwayman encourages him to try the Puritan practice of Bibliomancy (p. 169) and to read the Scriptures (p. 171). When Jack reviews his wicked life at the very end of the novel, he acknowledges that his only sources of spiritual guidance have been this 'Tutor' and also some 'sober religious Company' he encountered in Scotland, presumably Presbyterians like those Defoe befriended in his visits to Scotland in the 1700s.[17] Jack offers his life story as one conducive to his reader's 'moral and religious Improvement' (p. 307), recalling more orthodox, exemplary, Puritan autobiographies, and declares that at last he has learnt, 'as *Job* says, *to abhor my self in Dust and Ashes*' (p. 308).

In characterizing the political, religious, and social conditions which have produced his hero, Defoe shows how and why Jack, the petty thief with delusions of grandeur, eventually becomes a threat to national security, pro-French, pro-Catholic, and pro-Stuart. The bitter divisions left by the Civil War and the Restoration have left their mark on those who grew up in a climate of political and social turmoil and religious intolerance. Jack's impetuousness and volatility reflect an aspect of early eighteenth-century politics which many writers from Swift and Pope to Defoe deplored: its polarization. Defoe wrote eloquently against putting party interests above those of country,[18] a vice to which he regarded Jacobites as especially prone. The wider consequences of Jack's careless disregard for his country's interests begin to manifest themselves when he

[16] That allegory is a particular feature of Puritan discourse is argued by both Edwin B. Benjamin in 'Symbolic Elements in *Robinson Crusoe*', *Philological Quarterly*, 30 (1951), 206–11, and J. Paul Hunter in *The Reluctant Pilgrim: Defoe's Emblematic Method and Quest for Form in 'Robinson Crusoe'* (Baltimore, 1966).

[17] See Backscheider, *Daniel Defoe: His Life*, 217.

[18] In *An Appeal to Honour and Justice* [1715], for example, Defoe writes, with deep irony, that 'It is many Years that I have profess'd my self an Enemy to all Precipitations in Publick Administrations; and often I have attempted to shew, that hot Councils have ever been distructive to those who have made use of them: Indeed they have not always been a Disadvantage to the Nation, as in King James II's Reign, where as I have often said in Print, his Precipitation was the Safety of us all; and if he had proceeded temperately and politickly, we had been undone, *Felix quen faciunt*' (p. 5).

makes his first voyage from Virginia, fired with ambitions to see the world. He has already expressed a suspicious enthusiasm for the martial French king who has taken on the whole of Europe (p. 172), and when his ship is captured he is remarkably quick to collaborate with the enemy. When he gets back to London, he sees no stigma in adopting a French identity; in fact he declares he is 'infinitely fond of having every Body take me for a *Frenchman*' (p. 186). It will not be long before he is enlisting with the French in Italy, and when he tires of this campaign he says he 'pretended a great deal of Zeal' (p. 222) for the Old Pretender, James Stuart, and went back to England to raise supporters for him.

Colonel Jack is far more than an entertaining portrait of a plausible rogue; its aim is to demonstrate the connections between dishonest individuals and 'Publick and National Mistakes and Errors in Conduct' (p. 135). Jack typifies his times: he is the inevitable product of a society divided by economic inequities and political factions. In adulthood he perpetuates the conditions which undermine his country's stability—and that of Europe—by conspiring directly and indirectly against his monarch. He has no conception of what is meant by duty, loyalty, or self-sacrifice, and his career is one of endless deceits. Numerous historical allusions in his narrative—to James II, the continental wars, and the Jacobite opposition to the Glorious Revolution and the Protestant Settlement—remind the reader of England's tempestuous recent past, suggesting that *Colonel Jack* goes beyond an indictment merely of Jacobitism to characterize the late seventeenth and early eighteenth centuries as a period of general disorder and dissimulation in both public and private life.

What Defoe offers with *Colonel Jack* is not just a historical novel, therefore, but a demonstration of how history is made. He rejects the tendency of individuals to deny their social and political instrumentality, viewing such denials as morally evasive. He depicts a world in which every action has its consequences, from the negligent administration of parish relief (a problem as urgent in 1722 as it had been in the 1680s) to the crimes of the wretchedest pickpocket. As a child Jack is appalled by the devastation caused by his petty thefts—his victims lose irreplaceable documents along with their small change—and, when he claims years later to have played key roles in European battles or to have engineered the Preston rebellion practically single-handedly, Defoe is showing not only how vain his hero is but also the genuine importance of the individual in determining the course of history. The connection between the individual as both product of history and its producer is made most suggestively when Jack describes his childhood fondness for listening to old men's stories, stories which boast of daring exploits in the service of the French king, and comments that 'I was a kind of an Historian' (p. 11). Making history and being made by it are impossible to distinguish here. Paradoxically, the personal ambition which makes Jack careless of his fellow human beings is what binds him to them and to his historical moment, for it proves that he is the product of that careless and divided society in the first place, even as he perpetuates its history of conflict and betrayal.

7 Master and Servant: Social Mobility and the Ironic Exchange of Roles in Swift's Directions to Servants

SHIRSHENDU CHAKRABARTI

I

Swift's *Directions to Servants* remains a curiously neglected or under-rated work: critics in the past have usually regarded this unfinished piece as a straightforward, meticulously observed exposure of menial parasitism and duplicity. They have either dismissed it on grounds of its 'low' material, its flatness and triviality, or expressed revulsion at the copious and gratuitous documentation of nastiness that stifles its comic potential. For Swift, however, the work was the fruit of compilation and consideration over several years. In a letter of August 1731 he made clear his involvement with 'two great works in hand' (*Polite Conversation* and the *Directions*):

one to reduce the whole politeness wit, humor & style of England into a short System for the use of all persons of quality, and particularly the Maids of Honor: the other is of almost equal importance; I may call it the whole duty of servants, in about twenty several Stations from the Steward & waiting woman down to the Scullion & Pantry boy.[1]

Of late, some critics have begun to recognize the importance of the *Directions*, its depth and complexity making it an integral part of Swift's *œuvre*. Irvin Ehrenpreis, for instance, has interpreted it as an ironic commentary on *The Whole Duty of Man*. Swift's initial, tentative title, 'the whole duty of servants', is an evidently sardonic parallel. The *Directions* can indeed be seen as a parody of advice-books in the tradition of Fleury's *Devoirs des maîtres et des domestiques* (1688).[2] Ehrenpreis refers also to *The Refin'd Courtier* by N.W. (1663), which is a

---

[1] *The Correspondence of Jonathan Swift*, ed. Harold Williams (5 vols.; Oxford, 1963–5), iii. 493.
[2] Irvin Ehrenpreis, *Swift: The Man, his Works, and the Age* (3 vols.; Cambridge, Mass., 1962–83), iii. 834–5.

version of the *Galateo* of Giovanni della Casa (1558): 'The instructions
for servants in this book are often reversed by Swift's persona in *Directions to Servants.*'³ This typically Swiftian exercise in comic inversion is,
of course, inseparable from what Ehrenpreis identifies as the unique
sociological interest lying in the mock recommendation of precisely those
faults of servants which were constantly complained of at that time.⁴
David Nokes's psychoanalytical analysis of the work as a handbook of
domestic guerrilla warfare or an anarchists' handbook compiled by the
chief of police needs to be grounded on this social reality.⁵ If we do that,
the servants widely practising roguery, cheating, and insubordination
become thereby the instruments of a radical reorganization of the master–servant relationship in the eighteenth century.

In view of the changing relations between the ruling and the serving
classes in the eighteenth century, the ancient lineage and persistent appeal
of advice-books for servants, I suggest, make Swift's satire on them
historically prescient. Like Machiavelli in *The Prince*, he chooses the
vantage-point of actual practice in order to expose from within the
bookish obsolescence of concepts and categories. Ehrenpreis himself
arrives at an intuitive recognition of the subversive possibilities of the
Directions: 'In final effect the piece is sometimes obsessional; one has a
disquieting sense that Swift is competing with the servants.'⁶ My chapter
attempts to probe this 'obsessional' quality and 'disquieting sense' in the
perilous context of unprecedented social mobility. Swift makes master
and servant barely distinguishable from each other as part of his comic
search for identity through the erasure of familiar hierarchical margins.

II

Swift's attitude towards his servants was often harsh, demanding, irascible, even suspicious; nevertheless, his domestic justice was indubitable.
While insisting on good work, he treated and paid his servants well,
regularly providing them with meals at the Deanery on top of board
wages. His deep attachment to his model servant, Saunders McGee, is
evident in his anxiety at McGee's impending and untimely death: 'the
best servant in the world dying in the house, which quite disconcerts
me. . . . I know few greater losses in life.' The quaintness of the sentiment
does not detract from its sincerity, which was further demonstrated in the
gentleman's funeral Swift arranged for McGee. He put up a tablet in his
own cathedral with an inscription in which he referred to himself as

---

³ Ibid. 835 n. 1.   ⁴ Ibid. 835.
⁵ David Nokes, *Jonathan Swift, a Hypocrite Reversed* (Oxford, 1985), 402–3.
⁶ Ehrenpreis, *Swift*, iii. 835.

McGee's 'grateful friend and master'. According to Delaney, Swift was subsequently persuaded by 'a gentleman more distinguished for vanity than wisdom' to omit the words 'friend and'. This is probably an allusion to Dr Sheridan.[7]

Snobbish vanity of Dr Sheridan's variety is perhaps symptomatic of a changing attitude to servants not unrelated to the increasing dominance of the *parvenu* and the *arriviste*. Such vanity is thus exposed in the *Directions* as a disguised expression of fear at the formidable competitor rising from below. In *Gulliver's Travels*, we may recall, the ambition of the Lilliputian courtier is described as a peculiar combination of obsequiousness and aspiration, of creeping and leaping. In both his political journalism and his larger satirical work, Swift consistently diagnoses the *malaise* as the corrupting effect of money. In the Augustan perception of early capitalism, it is the disruptive and dislocating influence of money that is often condemned in contrast to a stable social order rooted in relationships based on land. No wonder, then, that the *Directions* abounds in instructions for extracting 'vails' and 'perquisites', and its immediate social background is not Swift's household in Dublin but the bourgeois metropolis, the London establishment of a married couple with children.

Here, as we proceed through the entire repertoire of menial deception, Swift almost imperceptibly erases the hierarchical distinction of the roles of master and servant. The ironic parallel—Swift's stylistic answer to social instability and the relativity of values—becomes inescapable by the time we reach the directions to the footman. If deception dominates the inventive mischief of the servant, it colours the master's attitude of condescension to a humble companion, a chaplain, a tutor, or a dependent cousin at table.[8] In Swift's scheme, the source of deception is not only in the human mind, in its proneness to self-delusion, but also in human nature, in man's infinite capacity for deceiving others: he is a fraud by nature with an inborn perverse delight in mischief. The *Directions* exposes this in the domestic sphere, in the manner in which master and servant, mistress and maid, exploit each other. The irony deepens when we realize that deception practised by both master and servant is ultimately an expression of self-deception. Deception and self-deception play in a minor key the darker and deeper themes of destruction and self-destruction, since the dinner-table presents a daily social ritual emblematic of the traditionally ordered patriarchal household. The order is further subverted when the servants—the butler and the footman in this

---

[7] Ibid. iii. 323.

[8] *Directions to Servants*, in *The Prose Works of Jonathan Swift*, ed. Herbert Davis *et al.* (14 vols.; Oxford, 1939–68), xiii. 18.

case—reveal an insidious affinity with their master and act in collusion with him by being the quickest to discern the sneering attitude and to emulate it.[9] There may be a trace here of Swift's lifelong sense of insecurity, despite proximity to the ruling classes. Did he encounter at Moore Park a somewhat similar indifference?

The footman, the fine gentleman of the servant family with whom all the maids are in love, is obviously the below-stairs version of the fawning but ambitious courtier. Not only does he contrive to conceal his actual identity in public and suggest social parity with the master and mistress, but the master himself, by implication, is such a courtier. The ironic interchangeability of their roles is driven home succinctly with typical capricious force: 'You are sometimes a Pattern of Dress to your Master, and sometimes he is so to you.'[10] The parallel is worked out properly. Waiting at table gives the footman knowledge of the world, of men and manners, and a reserved seat at the theatre entitles him to be a wit and critic. He is advised to sneeze or cough on the plate he carries under his arm to prevent spraying the gentlefolk at the table; this is then compared to the similar practice of gentlemen and ladies with a hat or handkerchief. When we learn that footmen become the delight of nine ladies out of ten and the envy of ninety-nine beaux out of a hundred because of the oaths, songs, and new-fangled words that they pick up, we are left to wonder which way the ironic edge cuts.

The parallel between master and servant is extended to the relationship between mistress and maid. When we are told that the master of the house may probably like the latter, although she was not half as handsome as the lady, at once a relationship of mutual exploitation is set up, for she is expertly advised to manipulate the master financially. The master's son is bound to be a common rake or a fool and the daughter appears to be a moronic receptacle for the 'romantic' fantasies that the maid pours into her. Here again, a typically levelling and degrading relationship is insinuated between the amorous fancies of the daughter and the maid's encounters in St James's Park, infamous for prostitution. Between the lady and the maid, there is a collusion in 'gallantry'; the latter is advised to encourage the mistress's paramours who are liberal with their money, but admonished to be patient if the former chooses a handsome footman as her lover—for, we are assured, this is not a singular humour but a very natural appetite. Moreover, it 'is still the safest of all home Intrigues, and was formerly the least suspected, until of late Years it hath grown more Common'.[11] Both above stairs and below, the household becomes the centre of subversion.

---

[9] Ibid.   [10] Ibid. 33.   [11] Ibid. 59.

Despite the scurvy treatment that they often receive, the footmen or gentlemen in livery manage to fulfil their courtier-like ambitions of rising in the social scale. This is why the world of the master and that of the servant are subtly linked through the stairs. The stairs intended to keep the two worlds apart actually connect them and therefore become a simple but powerful metaphor for movement up and down, for the equivocal nature of social mobility. When a certain Court-lady admires superficial, mincing manners as politeness in her footman—'the Gracefulness with which he tript before her Chair, and put his Hair under his Hat, that she made him many Advances'[12]—politeness itself is punished along with the aspiring footman. No wonder that he moves from behind her coach to sit beside her in it as her husband, reminding us of the marriage between the Laputan lady and her footman in *Gulliver's Travels*. Similarly, pert and saucy behaviour, though attended with dangers of caning and kicking at times, at last helps footmen to change from livery to a pair of colours. It is thus not a coincidence that, in the summer of 1731, the two manuscripts that Swift had carried to the country retreat were *Directions to Servants* and *Polite Conversation*, for they constitute the recto and verso of Swift's imagination grappling with the crisis of social instability in his time.

The footman's rise to prestige and respectability almost inevitably overreaches into ruin and collapse. His movement up perennially borders upon, strays into, the movement down. For example, he teaches the Court-lady he had married to drink brandy, whereupon she drank herself to death and he fell to the status of a journeyman 'maltster'. The footman-courtier's slippery prosperity can pull him down from the highest to the lowest station of life in an instant and he can become in no time a 'skipkennel' turned out of place. Since to grow old in the footman's office is the greatest indignity, he is located on Swift's ironic knife-edge between hopes of favour and preferment or the prospect of crime leading to the gallows.

III

The de-vitalization of polite culture (of which *Polite Conversation* is a remarkable verbal record) and the energetic infiltration from below is, of course, a part of the inexorable emergence of the bourgeoisie as the dominant social group, and certainly satire on it goes as far back as to Rabelais and Montaigne.[13] In the eighteenth century, however, a point of

[12] Ibid. 42.
[13] See Quentin Skinner, *The Foundations of Modern Political Thought* (2 vols.; Cambridge, 1978), i. 258.

crisis and polarization is reached and the old ideological assimilation of servants within a patriarchal, familial set-up is disrupted. Master and servant become equally insecure, equally suspicious and exploitative of each other. In the *Directions*, the servant is often encouraged to get his wages raised by systematically cheating and occasionally threatening to leave service for a supposedly better prospect. But the master is not the only one afraid of instability; the servant must keep excuses ready to stay on should his devious bargaining prove to be unsuccessful. Dr Sheridan's sense of uneasiness at the coupling of 'friend and master' is borne out by the attempt to segregate and marginalize the servants of a household. As Carol Flynn has noted, the serving class, long considered part of the little family of the greater household, each servant being an integral member subject to reciprocal accommodation, was being put in a new place back stairs, out of sight.[14]

But in fact, in being pushed out of sight, the servant acquired a new power of ideological subversion: in Swift's *Directions*, *de facto* control of the household is in the hands of the servants. Nevertheless, the ruling classes continue to adopt a condescending and sanctimonious tone towards servants. Lord Orrery's disapproval of the *Directions* suggests this clearly: 'A man of SWIFT's exalted genius ought constantly to have soared into higher regions. He ought to have looked upon persons of inferior abilities as children whom nature had appointed him to instruct, encourage, and improve.'[15] Orrery's sense of pity may look forward to the rising ethic of sentiment initiating the vogue for charity. But, without lapsing into a sentimental or benevolist attitude towards poverty and crime—an attitude that amounts to ideological mystification—Swift makes the poor an obtrusively visible sign of social and economic upheaval. Whether in the *Tale* or *The Mechanical Operation of the Spirit* or *Gulliver's Travels* or *A Modest Proposal*, brutalized and criminalized poverty serves as an indictment of the ruling classes. The disruptive demotic energies that it signifies become available for close scrutiny, particularly in the master–servant relationship as anatomized in the *Directions*.

We may pause to glance at typical attitudes of masters to servants. Stephen Copley has noted 'a fear of social insubordination, which is usually countered by demands for increasingly rigorous measures of social control'.[16] The advocacy of charity, especially charity schools for educating the poor, only appears to present a contrast to the stance of

---

[14] Carol Houlihan Flynn, *The Body in Swift and Defoe* (Cambridge Studies in Eighteenth-Century Literature and Thought, 5; Cambridge, 1990), 168.

[15] Quoted in ibid. 162.

[16] *Literature and the Social Order in Eighteenth-Century England*, ed. Stephen Copley (London, 1984), 132.

censorious severity. But together they constitute the usual combination of repression and indulgence so effective in consolidating political power. Sentimental humanitarianism in its premiss of moral hauteur—charity as the instrument for the reformation of manners and morals of the poor— is actually the obverse of the cynical authoritarianism, say, of Mandeville. For Mandeville, humane and charitable enthusiasm is misplaced in matters of economic organization, and the poor in any case are not accessible to moral improvement. Defending the necessity for poor servants and therefore of the cultivation or education of a servile mentality among them,[17] he attacks the growing popularity of charitable institutions: 'Charity, when it is too extensive, seldom fails of promoting Sloth and Idleness, and is good for little in the commonwealth but to breed Drones and destroy Industry.'[18]

Mandeville's astringency finds an echo in the views of Defoe. Defoe emphasizes stern control in response to change and unrest: increasing the wages of servants becomes a futile and dangerous measure of appeasement, for the raise inevitably makes them idle and insolent. Commenting on the cunning of the servant cheating his master, Defoe adopts the tone of injured moral piety so common among the ruling classes of the time. Gratitude, as the usual argument goes, is not a natural principle among the common people, and higher wages not only make the poor insolent, idle, and rebellious but destroy their moral fibre as well: they give up those values of thrift, diligence, and timid prudence that actually constitute the so-called Protestant work-ethic underpinning the emerging capitalist system. From such a point of view, the possibility of crime becomes endemic in society: under a stop of trade, the servants wander, starve, beg, steal, and are hanged, and in a glut of trade, they become saucy, lazy, and debauched.[19]

In Fielding's legal writings, however, the acknowledgement of all-pervasive instability redeems a moralistic attitude to poverty and crime that seems callous by our modern standards. Fielding accepts the liberty of people to be as wicked and as profligate as their superiors:

Thus while the Nobleman will emulate the Grandeur of a Prince; and the Gentleman will aspire to the proper State of the Nobleman; the Tradesman steps from behind his Counter into the vacant Place of the Gentleman. Nor doth the Confusion end here: It reaches the very Dregs of the People, who aspiring still to a Degree beyond that which belongs to them, and not being able by the Fruits of honest Labour to support the State which they affect, they disdain the Wages to

[17] Bernard Mandeville, *The Fable of the Bees* (1714–25), in *Literature*, ed. Copley, 140–2.
[18] Ibid., in *Literature*, ed. Copley, 138.
[19] Daniel Defoe, 'Letter IV', *The Great Law of Subordination Consider'd* (1724), in *Literature*, ed. Copley, 143–9.

which their Industry would intitle them; and abandoning themselves to Idleness, the more simple and poor-spirited betake themselves to a State of Starving and Beggary, while those of more Art and Courage become Thieves, Sharpers and Robbers.[20]

While Swift in *Gulliver's Travels* makes use of the humanist vocabulary of luxury and venality in order to denounce expanding capitalism and its impact on human relations, Oliver Goldsmith would later find nothing more ridiculous than the pride and luxury of the middling class of people in London. He mocks their eager desire of being seen in a sphere far above their capacities and circumstances.[21]

   At first sight, Swift's attitude to his servants seems remarkably similar—we have only to look at his draconian 'Laws for the Dean's Servants' (1733). In the sermon 'Causes of the Wretched Condition of Ireland' Swift vehemently defends the common complaints of masters against servants and emphasizes the relationship between poverty and crime. But more than that of the others, Swift's interest is always in the causes and origins of criminalized poverty and the role of the governing classes. Talking of the strolling beggars, Swift first unequivocally accuses the ruling classes for their gross neglect and misgovernment and only then blames those poor for bringing ruin on themselves by their own vices like sloth, drink, luxury, imprudence, and extravagance. He identifies the root of the evil in pride and vanity of social aspiration: citizens and shopkeepers decay 'by their expensive Pride and Vanity, affecting to educate and dress their Children above their Abilities, or the State of Life they ought to expect'.[22] This same conservatism acquires a curiously radical edge to it when Swift holds the landlords and masters responsible for dereliction of duty and his sense of impotent anger at them finds expression later in the devastating irony of *A Modest Proposal*. If servants fail in their duties, their masters are equally, indeed more, at fault. In the sermon 'On Mutual Subjection', Swift writes that since 'no Man can be a Prince without Subjects, nor a Master without Servants, nor a Father without Children', the servant owes obedience, diligence, and faithfulness to his master and has a just demand for protection, maintenance, and gentle treatment.[23]

[20] Henry Fielding, 'An Enquiry into the Causes of the Late Increase in Robbers' (1751), in *Literature*, ed. Copley, 185.
[21] Oliver Goldsmith, *The Bee* (1759), in *Literature*, ed. Copley, 51.
[22] 'Causes of the Wretched Condition of Ireland', in *Works of Swift*, ix. 205–6.
[23] 'On Mutual Subjection', in ibid. 144.

IV

It is this hierarchical balance between master and servant that is disrupted by the so-called financial revolution in England. The ironic exchange of roles between master and servant is not unrelated to Swift's perception of the fluctuations of the new money-based economy. The wealth of the nation which 'used to be reckoned by the Value of Land, is now computed by the Rise and Fall of Stocks'.[24] The growth of credit, speculation, and stock-jobbing acquired the contingent force of Fortuna as defined by Machiavelli, and generated an epistemology of fantasy, as J. G. A. Pocock has put it.[25] The individual in this situation, calculating about the objects of his own desires, was no longer identical with the individual of civic-humanist discourse which continued to dominate conservative ideology in the eighteenth century. The individual of rational egoist theory could appeal to no paradigm of virtue comparable to that in an agrarian past.[26] The *Directions* is planned and executed in such a way that the bond between master and servant becomes one of obsessive financial computation, viability, and profitability. Swift's own habits of keeping accounts and pruning expenditure bear testimony to this compelling force of calculation.

In such a situation of crisis, the tendency is to espouse either the ideology of the master or the cause of the servant. But Swift steers clear of both these limited certainties and thereby achieves a deeper fidelity to social mobility that he represents habitually as the interchangeability of opposites. It would be not only anachronistic but discordant with his entire vision to expect from him traces of sentimental piety in his portrayal of life below stairs. He scrupulously inspected the waiters' habits at meals, and at Quilca he was driven to anger and amusement at the misrule of the Sheridan household which was corrupting his own servants.[27]

This characteristically divided response might have sprung from the deep-seated antithetical drives of the preacher and the jester in his nature. In fact, Swift highlights the robust vitality and resourcefulness of the servants with such gusto and detail as to suggest almost a vicarious participation in the roguery. On the other hand, the obsessively exhaustive catalogue of servants' tricks suggests an attitude of imperious astringency. But clearly the master in the *Directions* lacks in both moral and

---

[24] 'The Examiner', in ibid. iii. 6.
[25] J. G. A. Pocock, 'Early Modern Capitalism—the Augustan Perception', in Eugene Kamenka and R. S. Neale (eds.), *Feudalism, Capitalism and Beyond* (London, 1975), 76.
[26] Ibid. 81.
[27] 'The Blunders, Deficiencies, Distresses, and Misfortunes of Quilca', in *Works of Swift*, v. 219-21.

effective authority. Thus, the simultaneous uneasiness at and enjoyment of misrule seem to spring from the complex matrix of jeopardized identity in a world of collapsing values and verities—for, we must not forget, neither master nor servant is secure in his traditional station any more. In the *Directions* we have, therefore, a vivid picture of unanchored oscillation between the point of view and interest of the master and that of the servant: like Gulliver, the reader is divested of an authentic social or moral identity. No wonder that Swift chooses to speak in the voice of the footman who has left service: 'I have a true Veneration for your Office, because I had once the Honour to be one of your Order, which I foolishly left by demeaning myself with accepting an Employment in the custom-house.'[28] The footman–narrator's mimicry of mincing politeness is a betrayal of the obsequious ambition that he typifies. His avowed aim in writing the directions is to help the servants come to better fortunes. The low-born pursuit of respectability through the acquisition of wealth involves the concealment of identity. Since the footman could rise to the position of master and fall to the status of a 'skipkennel', both master and servant become tainted by loss of social identity and moral authenticity. The situation is further complicated by Swift's familiar logical inversion of social rank and effective power. By birth the master may be superior in status but the sources of his power have become precarious, while the servant is low born but seems to hold the master in his clutches. The reader's sense of identity is caught in a cleft stick between these two alternatives. It is this same technique of transfer and exchange, half-playful, more than half-serious, that places Gulliver and the reader in a state of perplexity and despair between Yahoo (bestiality in human shape) and Houyhnhnm (rationality in animal form).

The relationship between imperilled identity and social mobility is, of course, anticipated in Restoration literature. For instance, in Etherege's play, *The Man of Mode*, Dorimant's sense of psychological instability is surely not unrelated to the phenomenon of servants emulating their superiors. In Dryden's *Absalom and Achitophel*, the slippery uncertainties of language and value appear to stem from the ideological apparatus of emerging bourgeois society. The first Earl of Shaftesbury or the Duke of Buckingham is made to join cause with upstart aspirants like Slingsby Bethel and Titus Oates: the traditional differences between high and low are blurred. Similarly, Dryden suggests that Charles II's concubines control him from a position of social inferiority: 'like slaves his bed they did ascend.'[29] But what serves as background to Restoration literature becomes the foreground in the *Directions*.

[28] *Directions*, in ibid. xiii. 42.
[29] *The Poems and Fables of John Dryden*, ed. James Kinsley (Oxford, 1970), 190.

The prospect of assimilation into bourgeois society through marriage offered to the obedient and diligent servant formed an important element of the master's ideology. The hypocrisy involved in such inducement to submission is satirized by Swift through the perilous prosperity of the footman and the exposure of unscrupulous scheming on the part of servant aspirants. It is not a coincidence that Samuel Richardson's treatise *Apprentice's Vade Mecum*, published in 1734, is more or less contemporary with Swift's *Directions*. The prohibitions laid down by Richardson are a series of admonitions couched in prudential terms written from the point of view of the master, summing up his patriarchal relationship with the apprentice. But, as I have tried to show, the patriarchal relationship was being rendered increasingly obsolete by the power of money, and actually the prohibitions disguise a feeling of threat to authority. The apprentices were a bunch of unruly adolescents constantly running after sex, drink, gambling, and the theatre as modes of rebellion. As Ronald Paulson has noted shrewdly, their jokes aimed at the master (a surrogate father) or his wife were based on hatred of his power but concentrated on his wealth or bourgeois sensibility. Many of these turned on the fantasy of marrying the master's daughter or widow and thereby assuming paternal control of the shop. The verbal joke thus bordered upon and overlapped with verbal threat. As a deterrent to rebellion and an incentive to conformity, Richardson offers the polar opposites of Dick Whittington and George Barnwell: one became the Lord Mayor while the other was driven to ruin and the gallows.

Swift's originality in the *Directions* lies in making these two ideals and trajectories capriciously interchangeable, thereby rendering dubious the very virtues considered necessary for servile aspiration. His method finds an interesting parallel in Hogarth's treatment of the same issue in his twelve plates on *Industry and Idleness*. We have here the familiar alternatives: the laudable career of apprentice Francis Goodchild who ends up marrying the master's daughter and the lamentable fate of the slothful Tom Idle. As Paulson puts it, despite the simple design of contrast, Hogarth's manipulation of the general and the subtle reader led to an ironic undermining or undercutting around the fringes of primary difference. In the last pair of plates, the two apprentices stationed on the left and the right become nearly indistinguishable. Goodchild has moved leftwards into exactly the same space as that of the criminal Idle whom he condemned to death in Plate 10.[30] Such an ironic exchange between respectability and criminality, such a reduction of the two as arbitrary, contingent categories, becomes to some extent the basis of Gay's satire in

[30] Ronald Paulson, *Popular and Polite Art in the Age of Hogarth and Fielding* (Notre Dame, Ind., 1979), 9–11.

The Beggar's Opera as well: 'it is difficult to determine whether (in the fashionable Vices) the fine Gentlemen imitate the Gentlemen of the Road, or the Gentlemen of the Road the fine Gentlemen.'[31] But in Hogarth and Gay, the irony is ultimately moored in an intimacy between artist and viewer or reader that keeps the two perspectives, polite and popular, distinct. By contrast, Swift's irony in the *Directions*, and indeed elsewhere, obliterates distinctions of meaning and precipitates us towards meaninglessness.

The dehumanized squalor and violent, anarchic potential of poverty is often expressed by Swift through the ugly, famished, diseased bodies of the poor. In the *Directions* as well as in what Roger Lonsdale calls the unpoetic intensity of his poetry,[32] oppressive physical presence and functions have a subversive and disorientating effect. Compulsively drawn towards the body, Swift is simultaneously repelled by it. Carole Fabricant has stressed Swift's strong sense of identification with the poor. In Dublin streets, he had become the 'King of the Mob' of which he nevertheless remained distrustful.[33] Such a seeming inconsistency stems from the insecure ambivalence of his social status. A spokesman for the Country opposition to Walpole, he was at the same time not averse to investing in stocks and bonds. The source of his insecurity among the élite may be traced back to psychology; but, aided by social instability and the fear of anarchy, it enabled him to cut through the peace of the Augustans to dramatize the subversion of authority.

The *Directions* is thus crucial to Swift's larger struggle with a ruptured world-view. Among other things the quarrel between the Ancients and the Moderns was a version of the conflict between a civic-humanist, aristocratic culture of *politesse*, on the one hand, and bourgeois mobility and demotic unrest, on the other. Swift repeatedly exposes the subtly corrosive kinship underlying the opposition between the two, between master and servant. This strategy juxtaposes the conceptual stability and decorum of the age with a complementary, declassicized view from below: Lonsdale's new anthology of eighteenth-century verse is a clinching affirmation of the necessity for such a revision of perspective.

Historians are divided among themselves about a stabilized or destabilized view of Augustan England. J. H. Plumb's seminal work on the growth of political stability in Augustan England has been challenged by the equally seminal work of historians like E. P. Thompson, and the debate remains unresolved. Some recent historians, J. G. A. Pocock in

---

[31] John Gay, *The Beggar's Opera*, ed. Peter Elfed Lewis (Edinburgh, 1973), 112.
[32] *The New Oxford Book of Eighteenth-Century Verse*, ed. Roger Lonsdale (Oxford, 1984), p. xxxiii.
[33] Carole Fabricant, *Swift's Landscape* (Baltimore, 1982), 244.

particular, have recognized the role of classical political ideas in the Augustan perception of social and economic dislocation.[34] But in the literature and art of the period we often come across an inclusive fidelity spanning the view from above as well as from below. This is perhaps the peculiar prerogative of art to capture the 'totality of concrete, practical, and undivided life'.[35] In Swift, inclusiveness is stamped with the polite-demotic opposition and the suspicious and subversive mutuality that obtains between them. There is thus an aesthetic justice in his pitting the master against the servant, in their competitive and strangely oscillating roles. In fact, Augustan neo-classicism or epigonic classicism may be profitably seen as a formal tool for representing this bifocal vision of reality involving the collusive confrontation of polite and demotic. It is used to create a sustained effect of heterogeneity and conflict instead of a serene homogeneity. The *Directions* is able to hold together contradictory responses of gaiety and revulsion, even fear, by virtue of the unseen presence of the classicist canons of polite culture. Similarly, an unremitting fidelity to the disturbing immediacy of the real world spills over into zany fantasy, phantasmagoria. Such an aesthetic unevenness becomes achievable paradoxically because of the peculiar status and function of classicism in our revised view of the Augustan age.

V

Master and servant in the *Directions* perform a domestic variation on the iterative motif of interchangeable opposites in Swift's work. Since these overlapping margins always involve a hierarchical dualism—spirit and flesh or reason and the passions—the master–servant relationship could well be seen as a paradigm of it. Thus, the *Directions* deserves to be brought from the periphery of the Swift canon to its centre. The contraries of rise and fall in the footman's career serve as a barrier to the realization of identity. Gulliver's experience suggests a similar absence of proportion: deprived of the knowledge of his usual or right size, he is tossed between midget and giant by his fluctuating self-estimate. Similarly, in the *Tale*, the mind of man 'naturally sallies out into both extreams of High and Low, of Good and Evil', but then 'having soared out of his own Reach and Sight, not well perceiving how near the frontiers of Height and Depth, border upon each other', it falls into the lowest bottom of things. Man's conception of God is inevitably accompanied by

[34] See e.g. J. H. Plumb, *Growth of Political Stability in England 1675–1725* (Harmondsworth, 1977); E. P. Thompson, *The Making of the English Working Class* (London, 1963) and *Whigs and Hunters: The Origin of the Black Act* (New York, 1975); J. G. A. Pocock, *Politics, Language and Time* (London, 1972).

[35] Arnold Hauser, *The Sociology of Art*, trans. Kenneth J. Northcott (London, 1982), 4.

fear of the Devil, for the imagination lifted up very high must be equally terrified of the precipice below.[36] In *The Mechanical Operation*, as soon as the soul is raised beyond and above matter, the contraries of divine 'inspiration' and diabolic 'possession' are found to border upon each other.[37]

In exposing the self-deceptive and self-destructive character of all aspiration, including obsequious aspiration in the *Directions*, Swift ultimately seems to attack the Renaissance picture of the innate and indeterminate mobility of the mind or soul perpetually yearning for union with higher and nobler forms of life. The picture itself is part of the legacy of Neoplatonism to the Renaissance image of man, assuming and advocating for the progress of the soul the mastery of the spirit over flesh or reason over the passions. Swift's perception of social disruption prompts him to subvert this relationship of hierarchical subordination, suggesting in its place one of unresolved competition and mutual domination. At first sight, his antagonistic affiliation to Neoplatonism may seem farfetched: we are more likely to apply Neoplatonism as a tool to analyse the poetry of Donne than the work of Swift. But the iterative variations on the fundamental dichotomy of flesh and spirit in a fluid context of mutual exchange suggest a consistently satiric and revaluative relationship with the entire Platonic tradition.

The justification for satire is to be found in the strange outcome of Neoplatonism in the life of European man. As J. H. Randall has put it, the Neoplatonic goal of forsaking the flesh for the higher things of the spirit resulted no doubt in visions of ecstatic rapture and bliss, but it also gave rise to hypocrisy and concealment.[38] Hence this competitive dualism and its resultant obscuration of self-knowledge and identity invited the ironic ridicule of Renaissance sceptics like Rabelais, Montaigne, and their followers. Theriophily or the mock-praise of beast over man—subversion here again—was a direct expression of this critique. In Swift's treatment, master (spirit) and servant (flesh) exchange roles at random. He plays on this theme obsessively and there is a perpetual game of leap-frog between the contraries.

Master and servant also correspond to the hierarchical division of superior and inferior organs and faculties in the traditional physiological schema. Thus, in the *Tale*, the madness of one monarch is caused by unrequited lust which pushes the semen through the spinal duct into the brain, while, in the case of another, the circulating vapour—parodying the Neoplatonic mobility of the spirit, an intermediary linking soul and

---

[36] *Tale*, in *Works of Swift*, i. 99–100.
[37] *The Mechanical Operation*, in ibid. 174–5.
[38] J. H. Randall, *The Making of the Modern Mind* (rev. edn., Boston, 1940), 46–9.

body—moving from the superior to the inferior faculties, concludes in a fistula at the anus.[39] The physiological explanation in *The Mechanical Operation* stresses reversibility: 'the Spinal Marrow, being nothing else but a Continuation of the Brain, must needs create a very free Communication between the Superior Faculties and those below.'[40] Similarly, in the *Tale*, we are told, 'if there be a Protuberancy of Parts in the *Superiour* Region of the Body, as in the *Ears* and *Nose*, there must be a Parity also in the *Inferior*'.[41] Madness, which in Swift is the aspiration and over-reaching of the mind in any form, proceeds from vapours ascending from the lower faculties to overshadow the brain.[42] In *The Mechanical Operation* Swift highlights with comic gusto the subversive force of the lower parts of man: 'Lovers, for the sake of Celestial Converse, are but another sort of *Platonicks* who pretend to see Stars and Heaven in Ladies Eyes, and to look or think no lower; but the same *Pit* is provided for both.' Their fate is parallel to that of the philosopher, 'who, while his Thoughts and Eyes were fixed upon the *Constellations*, found himself seduced by his *lower Parts* into a Ditch'.[43] The spiritual ecstasies and visions of religion are reduced to a species of auto-erotic arousal and collapse.

Superior and inferior or higher and lower find in *Directions to Servants* their proper theatrical representation in life above and below stairs. The stage metaphor is suggested by Swift's preoccupation with man's performance, offering an Augustan ironic extension of the Humanist metaphor for man's role in the universe: an 'actor' involved in disguise and make-believe engaged in the plastic intensity of self-expression. As if the organization of the servants' society is not hint enough for us to grasp its allegorical power, Swift occasionally establishes more overtly a nexus between higher and lower. For instance, the lameness of chairs is explained philosophically with the help of 'two Causes, which are observed to make the greatest Revolutions in States and Empires; I mean, Love and War'.[44] Here again, the chair is found to serve equally for quarrels and amours which link together the pursuits of the higher and lower worlds.

The picture of the native anarchy of the mind, derived ultimately from Renaissance scepticism, may be seen as the psychological equivalent of social instability. Its overreaching restlessness matches the perilous status of the master *vis-à-vis* the servant, and its self-subversive tendency corresponds to the master's loss of authenticity and moral authority. No wonder Houyhnhnm society (or Lilliput before its degeneration or, for

[39] *Tale*, in Works of Swift, i. 104.
[40] *The Mechanical Operation*, in ibid. 188.
[41] *Tale*, in ibid. 129.
[42] Ibid. 105.
[43] *The Mechanical Operation*, in ibid. 189–90.
[44] *Directions*, in ibid. xiii. 10.

that matter, Brobdingnag) is free from the mobility of classes: it is dominated by an inflexible, static hierarchy. The psychological equivalent of the body as metaphor is constituted by the creatural-biological energies of man. Here again, biologically disoriented as his thought was, Swift never tires of acknowledging within the larger complex of his style the sheer force of such drives from 'below'. It is thus significant that, in the *Directions*, the servants' duplicity and rebellion find expression through food, drink, and sex. Their strategies are almost entirely directed at the acquisition of ready money, food, drink, and furtive sex. However, these instinctual drives, subversive as they are of the meagre and dubious authority of the master, do not provide a healthy outlet unequivocally endorsed by Swift. On the contrary, they become mere aids to the obsequious rise of a parasite to power. By implication, soul becomes footman, a lackey to flesh. Perhaps this is why Swift's imagination revolves in the closed circuit of seat, chair, table, theatre, stairs (for obsequious and furtive climbing). Indeed, the stairs may be viewed as a debased travesty of the ladder or hierarchy of being in Platonic thought, reducing the carefully graded, unbroken link of reciprocity between the highest and lowest forms of life to chaotic mobility.

Swift's destructive use of the legacy of dualism thus challenges the Platonic dialectic which was an instrument of definition, distinction, demarcation, and synthesis on a higher plane. The schematism of interchangeable opposites systematically closes all escape routes to transcendence and goads us towards the meaninglessness of things. Stylistically, however, Swift's hospitable comic mode, accommodating within it an entire range of registers from rollicking fun to savage bitterness, becomes the bond and copula of a disintegrating universe. His world explodes with laughter, as otherwise it would fall apart. In a world where all the meaning is what we put into it, laughter is the ultimate principle of self-preservation, the supremely human means of affirming one's identity unsubmerged by the ceaselessly encroaching meaninglessness of things. That is the essence of artistic form, too, constantly creating meaning, redeeming the native formlessness of matter. In the *Directions*, he is unable to side with either the master or the servant and is caught up in a paralysed crisis of identity. But it is in the exhaustively acute observation and documentation of menial roguery and bourgeois uncertainties that Swift forges an instrument of triumph over his bafflement and despair. Relentlessly traversing the embittered comic journey of descent, collapse, and degeneration, his style thereby becomes a vivid confirmation of the mind's power of ascent and renewal.

8 Boswell at Work: The Revision and Publication of The Journal of a Tour to the Hebrides

IAN McGOWAN

What a treasure would it be if we could have Virgil's own copy of his works, and see the corrections which he made. Yet Warburton has obliged us with several variations in Pope's poetry; and while we are entertained by comparing them with the text, we have an opportunity of being at the same time convinced that correction is not always for the better.

Boswell, *Hypochondriack*, 27 (1779)[1]

The minute changes made in their compositions by eminent authors are always a matter of both curiosity & instruction to literary men, however trifling and unimportant they may appear to blockheads.

Malone[2]

Boswell's *Tour to the Hebrides* caused a contemporary sensation, and has remained popular with the general reader, inspiring dramatizations and several modern imitations. In its own time, it was overtaken by the *Life of Johnson*, which has continued to hold the greater critical attention; but the *Tour* retains its place for the student of biography and literary representation as Boswell's breakthrough in technique. Only in this century, however, has it been possible to document in detail the working processes and the consciousness of his art. This chapter discusses how Boswell prepared for publication his contemporary account of his tour in Scotland with Samuel Johnson; its reshaping in response to a specific situation; and the beginning of his literary collaboration with Edmond Malone. It is based on the large body of material preserved in Boswell's archive.[3]

[1] *Boswell's Column*, ed. Margery Bailey (London, 1951), 159.
[2] Quoted by Helen Gardner, *The Composition of 'Four Quartets'* (London, 1978), 3.
[3] On the archive, see David Buchanan, *The Treasure of Auchinleck: The Story of the Boswell Papers* (London, 1975); Frederick A. Pottle, *Pride and Negligence: The History of the Boswell Papers* (New York, 1982); and Marion S. Pottle, Claude Colleer Abbott, Frederick A. Pottle, *Catalogue of the Papers of James Boswell at Yale University* (3 vols.; Edinburgh, 1993). Boswell's journals are catalogued under J; letters from him, L; other Boswell MSS, M; letters received, C; printed matter, P. These catalogue numbers are used in the main text. Quotations from unpublished MSS and proofs

Shortly after they met in 1763, Johnson expressed what Boswell called a 'very romantick fancy' that they might visit the Hebrides together, as he had been 'highly pleased' with Martin Martin's account, given him by his bookseller father. A decade of persistence by Boswell paid off when Johnson arrived in Edinburgh on 14 August 1773 for a visit which took them up the east coast of Scotland, across to Skye, Mull, and other islands, to Inveraray, to Boswell's home at Auchinleck, and back to Edinburgh, from which Johnson set out for London on 22 November. Between August and November Boswell contributed seven brief reports to the *Caledonian Mercury* and one to the *London Chronicle*; in January 1774 he drew on these for an article in the *London Magazine*, of which he was part owner. Having fathered the tour itself, he became midwife to Johnson's account, based on his 'book of remarks' kept on the tour and on his letters to the Thrales. Johnson's *Journey to the Western Islands of Scotland* appeared on 18 January 1775, when Boswell received the book in sheets, in thirteen franked packets from the author. Johnson himself quickly passed through the ensuing controversy over his attitude to Scottish culture, especially Ossian, while Boswell saw himself as both Johnson's defender and custodian of their original experience: he wrote eleven pages of 'Remarks'[4] on Johnson's book, mainly minor corrections of fact and some stylistic comments.

Boswell had kept notes on Johnson's stay in Edinburgh of 14–17 August 1773 (J 32), and had himself during their journey kept a journal (J 33) in three notebooks, supplemented by some loose sheets of paper, written up to 22 October 1773. There survive 318 leaves of the journal: damp has affected legibility in some places, and carried away many fragments, especially of margins; in the worst cases, less than half the page survives. This manuscript, in Boswell's typical round, easy hand, and unparagraphed, now bears deletions made when it was lent to friends; the extensive revisions made for publication; instructions to the printer; marks of the press-signatures. Boswell had brief notes down to 5 November, and journal for 10–11 November (J 33.1). These, plus miscellaneous documents and letters, were what joined his archives at the end of the tour, and would serve in 1785, with a few intermediate recollections, as the basis of his own book.

During 1775 a favoured few, including Mrs Thrale, had been allowed to read Boswell's manuscript journal. In March, he met Reynolds:

appear by permission of the Editorial Committee of the Boswell Papers, to which and to the late Professor Pottle I am indebted for access to extensive materials; I have occasionally preferred an alternative reading in published letters.

[4] The Adam–Hyde unique copy is in the hand of Boswell's clerk, John Lawrie, with one note in Boswell's hand and a cover endorsement by Malone; a facsimile follows p. 44 of *The R. B. Adam Library relating to Dr. Samuel Johnson and his Era* (4 vols.; London, 1929–30), ii.

I had a very pleasing reception from Sir Joshua, and read him some passages of my journal on the tour with Mr. Johnson, and he said, 'It is more entertaining than his.' As Mr. Johnson and I came along in the hackney-coach, he advised me not to show my journal to anybody, but bid me draw out of it what I thought might be published, and he would look it over. This he did upon my telling him that I was asked to publish; but he did not seem desirous that my little bark should 'pursue the triumph and partake the gale'.[5]

As the manuscript shows, he made some additions from memory in 1779 and 1780, several pages in 1781, and a 'good deal' in August 1782, bringing the journal down to the part-entry for 26 October 1773. From some twenty words of contemporary notes—mainly listing places visited—he was able to write thirty-seven manuscript pages recreating in detail many events and conversations, including Johnson's whisky-drinking, dicta on Goldsmith, Pope, and others, and a brilliant account of their visit to the Duke of Argyll's Castle at Inveraray combining circumstantiality with an awareness of the tensions there. And all this with a care to indicate where he cannot remember the precise words of conversation: '(I am glad to find that I remember so many particulars after the lapse of almost seven years. My Journal cannot have the same freshness and fullness when written now as when written recently after the scenes recorded. But I hope I shall preserve some valuable remains or fragments.)'[6] He also had available to him copies of letters written and received by him in 1773, together with copies of such Johnsonian documents as the poems composed: here Boswell was fulfilling his role as Johnson's 'custos rotulorum'.

Most of Boswell's original manuscript journal has now been published. It shows his skill in executing and recording his experiment on Johnson in an alien environment; and is part of both his biographical and autobiographical projects, with his usual sharp observation of personality and dramatic detailing of conversation. Largely written during the tour, it was occasionally posted several days in arrears, with violations of chronology: he records details of Prince Charles Edward collected at Raasay some pages before he records arriving there. His concern for precision and fullness led him to regret that 'what is written falls greatly short of the quantity of thought. A page of my Journal is like a cake of portable soup. A little may be diffused into a considerable portion.'[7] (Johnson, who praised its style, also sustained his aim at amplitude.) Boswell's observations testify to his accuracy and assiduity, but interest

[5] *Boswell: The Ominous Years 1774–1776*, ed. Charles Ryskamp and Frederick A. Pottle (London, 1963), 101–2.
[6] *Boswell's Journal of a Tour to the Hebrides*, ed. Frederick A. Pottle and Charles H. Bennett (London, 1963), 346.
[7] Ibid. 165.

most when they offer a distinctive human challenge; people rather than places were his forte: 'I find I can do nothing in the way of description of any visible object whatever. Whether it is owing to my not seeing with accuracy, or to my not having the use of words fitted to such sort of description, I cannot say.'[8] With little taste for rural beauties, he dutifully piles up facts about the romantic scenes or wild coastlines: 'A landscape or view of any kind is defective, in my opinion, without some human figures to give it animation.'[9]

The journal has material of some value concerning the 1745 rising, of which Boswell later intended to write a history; more prominently, it charts the tension between accepting the Hanoverian succession and his sometimes comic nostalgia for the days of the Stuarts, the old feudal ways, and his family connection with Robert the Bruce. His recurrent religious strain culminates in his resolutions at the cathedral on Iona, and his 'serious joy' in hearing himself read aloud a sermon of his favourite divine, Dr Ogden. He is fearful of ghosts, uneasy about witches, dreams of family deaths; he seeks out stories of the 'second-sight'—highlanders' ability to see the future, or actions taking place elsewhere. Such was the raw material in his 'archive' concerning the 1773 tour.

Johnson died on 13 December 1784, while Boswell was in Edinburgh. Within days the London newspapers were reporting biographies in preparation; Cooke's Life was published on the 27th. In a virtually guaranteed market for more ambitious works, Boswell was publicly touted as a leading candidate. By 18 December he had been approached by the firm of Dilly, friends since the youthful triumph of his book on Corsica, 'in the true spirit of the trade wanting to know if I could have an octavo volume of 400 pages of his conversations ready by February'.[10] Boswell replied that he intended to publish in the spring 'my tour with Dr. Johnson, a good Prelude to my large Work his Life'.[11] He felt self-doubt over the immense labour of research and composition; he also knew that his Life could draw on the earliest memoirs. While the Johnsoniana in his journal archive gave him unrivalled resources, he needed to find a method. It was natural, therefore, to propose a 'Prelude' in the account of the self-contained episode for which he had full, unique materials that could quickly make a book to satisfy immediate public curiosity and stake his claim amongst the biographers. Reports based on this decision appeared in the St James's Chronicle, published by Henry Baldwin, who was a partner with Boswell, Edward Dilly, and others in

[8] Ibid. 220.   [9] Ibid. 331.
[10] Boswell: The Applause of the Jury 1782–1785, ed. Irma S. Lustig and Frederick A. Pottle (London, 1981), 272.
[11] Register of Letters, quoted in Yale Catalogue at M 128.

the *London Magazine*, and was at this time inviting Boswell to take a share in the *Chronicle*. Baldwin supported a campaign by George Steevens to promote Boswell over rival biographers such as Sir John Hawkins.

In Edinburgh, meanwhile, Boswell found himself unable to 'apply to the writing out' of the *Tour*, but was reassured by friends, including Hugh Blair, that his journal could be printed 'with little variation':[12] at the end of February he decided to go to London for this purpose, and try at the age of 45 to transfer his flagging career to the English bar. Sir William Forbes, who had read his manuscript, anticipated an account 'upon a plan totally different from that printed by Dr Johnson as it relates less to descriptions of the Country than to accounts of conversations in which the Dr. bore always a considerable share'.[13] Boswell arrived in London on 30 March, but spent most of April deep in its turbulent pleasures, and much of May on writing a political pamphlet, a *Letter to the People of Scotland*.

On 29 April Boswell dined with Edmond Malone, an acquaintance but not a close friend: 'Most agreeable day. Sat with him till two in morning, full of bar scheme, and encouraged.'[14] The following day found Boswell 'In almost all forenoon writing *Tour*. Dined Solicitor-General. But a dull day, yet content. Then Dilly's; with Baldwin and fixed printing *Tour*. "You must *feed* the press." '[15] After publication of his pamphlet, Boswell got down to concentrated work on the *Tour*: 'In all day in night-gown and wrote *Hebrides*' (28 May).[16] This point also marked the beginning of the detailed help of Malone, a fastidious scholar, who valued Johnson's memory and Boswell's passion for authenticity: their association was to last as long as Boswell's subsequent literary career. Even while printing his *Shakespeare*, Malone was with Boswell some two days out of three from July until the *Tour* appeared in early October. Boswell recognizes his importance in a letter to Bishop Thomas Barnard in Ireland (1 July); Boswell was frequently at Baldwin's printing house, occasionally at Dilly's shop, but he says:

The printing goes on more slowly than I supposed it would, for a reason that both I and my Readers will certainly not regret—My *Journal* is revised by Mr. Malone, who I really think is the best critick of our age; and he not only winnows it from the chaff which in the hurry of immediate collection could not

---

[12] *Applause*, ed. Lustig and Pottle, 276–7.
[13] Forbes to Bennet Langton, 21 Jan. 1785, MS Yale, C 1274.
[14] On their relationship, see the Introduction in *The Correspondence of James Boswell with David Garrick, Edmund Burke, and Edmond Malone* (hereafter *Correspondence*) (London, 1986), 165–85.
[15] *Applause*, ed. Lustig and Pottle, 288.
[16] Ibid. 302.

but be in it, but suggests little elegant variations which though they do not alter the sense, add much grace to the expression.[17]

Boswell's intention was to use as far as possible his original materials as the printer's copy. As the first seven pages of J 33 and most of J 32 were too fragmentary, he wrote a general introduction leading into new copy based on those, incorporating copies of letters and such portions of the original record as could stand here without extensive rewriting. After page 45 of the new copy, J 33 became the basic unit round which everything else was built, running from page 8 through page 641, where he had stopped in 1773, to page 677, where he had finished writing up in 1782. For the end of the book he wrote fresh copy based on memory, his *Caledonian Mercury* notes, and the Edinburgh Journal (J 33.1), part incorporated direct; here, too, he took in various letters. Boswell generally expanded his text on the original manuscript where possible; virtually every page of the journal is covered in deletions, interlineations, and marginal additions; the three bound notebooks were torn apart. Where extensive revision and wholly new material required extra space, he deleted and directed the printer to a series of 'papers apart' with the additional copy. The archive now preserves, in addition to the original journals and notes, substantial bodies of new copy and notes by Boswell and Malone, correspondence about the preparation of the text, and an almost complete set of proofs, including the cancels.[18]

Boswell had collected anecdotes of 1745–6, and solicited an account of Prince Charles's escape. Exercised about the designation of that person, he wrote to the King: 'Your Majesty having convinced me by your enquiries at the levée that my *Journal of a Tour to the Hebrides* is not beneath the notice of my Sovereign, I with all humility presume to consult the King himself on a point of delicacy as to which the King alone can satisfy me' (6 June). The King's failure to reply to Boswell's proposals brought on him another personal interview on 15 June, recorded with unconscious comedy in the journal: (Boswell) ' "Pretender" may be a *parliamentary* expression, but it is not a *gentlemanly* expression; and, Sir, allow me to inform you that I am his cousin in the seventh degree.' Little wonder that when Boswell next went to Court, on 24 June, the King 'only asked about what time I should be in the North this year. (A hint this.) I said, "Not till what I am engaged in be finished." '[19]

[17] *The Correspondence of James Boswell with Certain Members of The Club*, ed. Charles N. Fifer (London, 1976), 196.
[18] The resulting groups of manuscripts and other relevant papers are listed in the Appendix to this chapter.
[19] For their exchanges and the note added to the *Tour*, see *Applause*, ed. Lustig and Pottle, 307–13; *Boswell's Life of Johnson together with Boswell's Journal of a Tour to the Hebrides*, ed. G. B. Hill, rev. L. F. Powell (6 vols.; Oxford, 1934–64), v. 531–2, 185–6.

Boswell and Malone now had to work intensively to revise the long manuscript because Baldwin's men were making progress and several times apparently ran out of copy. On folio 11ᵛ of his new copy, M 132, Boswell notes, 'Here is to come in a paragraph which shall be sent tomorrow'; but the corresponding proof, page 11, was printed without it, and the subsequent insertion involved shifting type over several pages. The *Tour* was principally set by the 'accurate, obliging' Loder; Malone reported that Selfe, the corrector of the press, 'had a great deal of the trouble and the merit in decyphering the MS.; for in all difficulties Loder applied to him'.[20] We cannot always assign responsibility for the changes between the original manuscript and the first edition, as Boswell and Malone were normally both present and kept no record of their discussion. But the mechanics of revision for the second edition were supervised in London by Malone, as Boswell had returned to Scotland: they exchanged by letter detailed proposals for revision and comments on them. We have, however, for the first edition one paper[21] in which Malone comments on Boswell's drafts, including revised journal, fresh copy, and papers apart: these are our first test of his influence on the minutiae of style. Some of his emendations of awkward phrases are accepted, some not; on Boswell's recollection of Johnson's remark about a house in 'disrepair', Malone doubted 'whether Dr. J. used this word—because, I believe, it does not exist'. Boswell accepted the suggestion of 'decay'; also the change from 'I insisted to scottify' to 'on scottifying'. Of 'sixteen cattel grazing', Malone thought: 'this is not quite right. It strikes my ear that when any particular *number* is specified, it is better to say "beasts".' In fact it became 'head of black cattel'.

Malone had more than a dozen suggestions and queries relating to the portion of journal before him. He caught several Scotticisms: 'muir' for 'moor'; 'box bed' for 'press-bed'; 'worthy-like' ('I don't know what it means & therefore know not how to supply its place'); he noted where Boswell had forgotten to add a comment on Johnson's Latin translation of Dryden. Some of the original expressions he found too strong: 'rebuked' Boswell changed to 'remonstrated to'; for 'violent quarrel' Malone proposed 'warm altercation', but Boswell compromised on 'violent altercation'. Many of Malone's comments show what Boswell could expect from the average British reader, on whom the Scottish words and customs would jar: 'after "as to prescription of murder"—shd you not add "in Scotland". We have no such rule in the English Law.' Most of Malone's suggestions were accepted, and some of Boswell's own modified; but the grateful author was also capable of overriding advice, and

[20] Malone to JB, 5 Nov. 1785, *Correspondence*, 268.
[21] Malone to JB, between 3 and 10 June 1785, C 1888.1, *Correspondence*, 189–93.

made further changes in the proofs. One suggestion elicited an important policy statement. At page 29 Boswell had very briefly noted Johnson's remarks on Homer. Malone proposed an expansion of these; but Boswell, while recognizing a problem, was unwilling to change his original record; he compromised by quoting in a note the opinion of 'One of the best criticks of our age' but also defended his text:

Brevis esse laboro, obscurus fio. Yet as I have resolved that *the very Journal which Dr. Johnson read*, shall be presented to the publick, I will not expand the text in any considerable degree, though I may occasionally supply a word to complete the sense, as I fill up the blanks of abbreviation in the writing; neither of which can be said to change the genuine Journal.[22]

Boswell changed his mind about a similar passage originally printed in italics, between swelled rules, between the entries for 18 and 19 August: its eventual removal involved the cancellation of E3–4, with inconvenience to the printer.

My Journal begins in an octavo paper book, the day on which we left Edinburgh. It was read from that day by Dr. Johnson. At first it is imperfectly kept, so that the matter is now in part supplied from memory, and the expression filled up and corrected. It gradually grows more perfect, and by-and-by will be found to be verbatim as printed, with only small insertions of words, and omissions of passages not fit for publication. I once thought of writing it anew; but Sir Joseph Banks, Sir Joshua Reynolds, and other friends, thought it would be better to give the genuine transcript of what passed at the time, and add notes to explain or enlarge. A great part of its value is its authenticity, and its having passed the ordeal of Dr. Johnson himself.[23]

Taken as a whole, Malone's notes and Boswell's reactions concerning these two portions of copy show that Boswell remained his own man: Malone's more fastidious stylistic proposals follow general lines already adopted in Boswell's revision. At this point Boswell still thought that no extensive rewriting would be called for; on 10 June, sending Malone pages 59 to 82 of his journal, he writes: 'I think the little Original Book will do surprisingly.'[24]

Printing was hot on the heels of revision. At the beginning of May, Boswell had his copy 'fairly put to the press'—apparently the copy for signature B and perhaps some of C; Malone's notes of early June cover material in D–H; by 1 July Boswell had sent Barnard seven printed sheets, as far as H; on 3 August he sent I–T, and benefited in his Errata from Barnard's correction of a slip in Latin. By late August, Malone was writing:

[22] *Life*, v. 78 n. 5.
[23] *Tour* proofs, pp. 54–5, Yale Collection, P 84.
[24] *Correspondence*, 193.

I enclose the Revise of Aa, which is now to be *for press*; but you had best take a last look at it. You have also the new proof, Bb . . . The description of *Col* [an island], you may remember, I had some apprehensions about, on account of the great number of small particulars, and *short* paragraphs. I have endeavoured to remedy the latter, by running sometimes two into one . . .[25]

This is done in the surviving proof of Bb, while two sets survive of Aa, both marked almost entirely in Malone's hand, with a third called for. After a joint session of revising manuscript copy, Malone probably took the principal share in seeing it through the press. (The *Tour* Dedication blandly thanks him for having 'obligingly taken the trouble to peruse the original manuscript'.) Notes on the proofs show that Boswell went to the printing-house to revise them, but some thirty technical directions to the printer are mainly in Malone's hand: he is particularly concerned with problems of page layout after extensive proof changes; he instructs how many lines are to be transferred to another page and how spacing can prevent awkward effects being apparent. He is always aware of the practical difficulties caused by squeezing in extra matter by closer setting, but cares too about the effect of the visual display on the reader. He knows how verse should be set out, how different type sizes, italics, capitals, should be used to mark names, signatures, quotations, and so on. When parts such as the narrative account of Prince Charles are to be set off, he repeatedly demonstrates the exact length and shape the rules are to be. Boswell was not ignorant of printing techniques, but here and in the printing of the *Life* he relies heavily on Malone's experience and technical knowledge. (The retention of many divergences from the manuscript suggests the absence of careful reading against copy: Johnson, for instance, was originally recorded as having called David Mallet 'the prettiest drest poppet', but in print, after at least two sets of proofs for signature O, it appears as 'puppet'.)

The end was now clearly in sight. Looking to his title-page, Boswell had written to the Keeper of the Lyon records in Edinburgh for a drawing of his crest, the hooded hawk; eventually he was supplied by his lawyer cousin Robert Boswell with a design originally made for Lord Auchinleck. Boswell's idea of a copper engraving would have required a separate working in a rolling press; Malone therefore had the crest cut on a wood block, to be dropped into the type; on 7 September Boswell paid five shillings for the cutting.[26] His hardest labour was over by the first week of September, although he continued to make insertions in proof. Having taken his farewell of the King at the levée on 21 September ('tomorrow is *coronation* day with me too'), with publication announced

[25] Malone to JB, *Correspondence*, 198.
[26] Malone to JB, 26 Aug. 1785, *Correspondence*, 199.

for 1 October, he prepared to return to Scotland. He paid Loder two guineas 'extra', presumably for the additional bother over the proofs; and gave the warehouseman 2s. 6d.; he was later to discover that Selfe was also entitled to a gratuity from a 'Gentleman Author'. The list of thirty-eight intended recipients of presentation copies is headed by the King.

The published work is tighter than the original manuscript: Boswell retained the structure of the journal, writing under date lines, with introduction and conclusion added to give a narrative frame which emphasizes the potential conflict between the Scots and the 'John Bull . . . true-born Englishman' and finally stresses the success of the venture, thus throwing into relief Boswell's social skill in 'handling' Johnson and his literary skill in writing him up. He chose to adapt his material for this trial run and holding operation for the *Life*: especially in the second half, when he realized how much he was printing, he cut his topography heavily (all of the dozen principal rearrangements are of this sort except Lord Macdonald's failures as host, and the separate accounts of Prince Charles). Out too went some material critical of others, or in doubtful taste such as Johnson on 'little-houses' (lavatories). The *Tour* remains, however, a very indiscreet book: unwelcome remarks still hit home to their subjects. As autobiography becomes memoir, although the author is sometimes comically to the fore, Boswell does cut much personal material such as his own 'hypochondria' (melancholy); his love of a dram in the morning; his superstitions, fear of ghosts, and melancholy imaginings. Leading characteristics of Boswell's journals generally are his belief in the value of the precise, documented detail, and a dramatic presentation of situation, with dialogue. The published *Tour* retains these, although, in the search for elegance which Malone encouraged, Boswell sometimes substitutes a generalization, or formalizes his language: faced with a remark about his social initiative, for instance, he originally wrote: 'Let me value my forwardness.' In revision, he pompously proposes to 'offer a short defence of that propensity in my disposition, to which this gentleman alluded'.[27] Although he had as a young man won a European reputation for his book on Corsica, reviewers had picked up stylistic faults, especially Scotticisms, cut from the second and third editions: like many of his race, class, and profession, he was painfully aware that his written style would be judged by southern English norms; hence the value of the keen eye of Malone, ironically, an Irishman. In the present case, he encouraged Boswell in the basic decision to keep the journal structure and dramatic presentation, and this was surely correct.

[27] *Tour*, 176; *Life*, v. 216.

We may feel that Malone encouraged rewriting which, if it helped reshape and clarify Boswell's material and toned down his tendency to literary indecent exposure, also lost something of his spontaneous best. Malone's advice during the writing of the *Life* is relevant: 'take care of colloquialisms and vulgarisms of all sorts. Condense as much as possible, always preserving perspicuity and do not imagine the *only* defect of stile, is repetition of words.'[28] If on the whole Boswell is extremely faithful to his record of Johnson's *ipsissima verba*, in addition to fresh recollections there are occasional slight rearrangements. The selection—playing up circumstances in which Johnson appears to advantage, and playing down or suppressing less endearing qualities, such as his repeated rudeness to and about their Scottish hosts, or his 'taking off' Lady Macdonald—continuously directs the reader's response. In this extensive reconstruction of the portrait of Johnson for public consumption, the central figure is not essentially changed, but his fascinating roughness is partly rubbed away. However, as Boswell quickly discovered, his frankness ran well in advance of contemporary taste, and the *Tour* exposed both subject and author to ridicule and hostility. The published book, then, has a greater sense of form and theme, while preserving the journal's openness to experience; few of the regretted anecdotes could reasonably have stood without further hurting the living. The revision shows an ability to control response and heighten effect by presentation of context, vivid detail, and direct speech; but if Boswell is a first-rate stylist in his journals, his public prose can dissipate his observation in pomposity.

It was not inevitable that Boswell should present his material in journal form, albeit heavily edited. When subsequent revision showed the inaccuracy of the italic passage quoted above, defining the relationship between original journal and book, he had to cancel E3–4. The material sent to the printer for the opening section of the book, M 132, contains several pages which appear to be an attempt to 'write it anew', presumably no later than early May, by which time Malone was available to confirm his original decision.

In M 132 there are two leaves, four written pages, three of them numbered in its page sequence 39, 40, 44; and the verso of 44 which is strictly a 'paper apart' to the main journal. They therefore fall at three different points in the final text; but the physical evidence, the continuity, and the catchwords show that they once constituted a distinct section, or rather—since the sense is incomplete at beginning and end, and they bear an earlier numbering—that they are the surviving fragment of an earlier draft. Part of this draft is based on the sketchy opening pages of the main

[28] Malone to JB, 23 Dec. 1790, *Correspondence*, 387.

journal, J 33, in places now seriously damaged, but whose text in note form can with some confidence be reconstructed from later versions. The draft is solidly based on Boswell's first record, whose natural plain style of simple sentences shows through; but even before Malone's arrival on the scene we find minor examples of revision towards greater verbal elegance and a directed view of Johnson. More importantly, the page now numbered 44 and its verso show a radically different treatment of Boswell's journal material. The original journal, J 33, and the printed version in the *Tour*, both go into detail about the journey through Fife and up the east coast, together with their stay in St Andrews; this included pages of Johnson's conversation ranging over religious beliefs, legal etiquette, literary property, and some excellent anecdotes. Boswell's initial treatment cuts almost all of this and drops the date-lines characteristic of his journal. Instead, he employs the centred heading 'St. Andrews' and begins: 'After what Mr. Johnson has said of St. Andrews which while he formerly talked of going to Scotland was allways a capital object, I can say little. I must not however omit to make my grateful acknowledgements to the Professours . . .'[29] In dropping his best material, Boswell was attempting a version which might emulate Johnson's *Journey*, a work distinguished not by narration of particular events but by broad reflection induced by his observation. Johnson had risen well to the challenge at St Andrews of 'the uneasy remembrance of an university declining, a college alienated, and a church profaned and hastening to the ground'.[30] Attempting a non-journal account, but realizing that he could not compete with these fine pages, Boswell wrote what was frankly little more than a supplement[31] to them, consisting primarily of defences of Johnson's behaviour in the tour. Cutting much detail, he then jumps to his next centred heading, 'Lawrence-Kirk', and offers anecdotes.[32]

This fragment attempts a compromise between the racy style and detail of Boswell's own journal, and the dignified style and reflective subject-matter presented under topographic heads in Johnson's *Journey*. He quickly realized that this was to neglect his own essential genius; but the concept had not been absurd: we too easily forget the authorial experience of his successful *Corsica*, based partly on existing sources, and partly on his own experiences, written up as continuous narrative, to

[29] MS Yale, M 132, p. 44.
[30] Samuel Johnson, *A Journey to the Western Islands of Scotland* (London, 1775), 14.
[31] He had used this word in letters to Temple, 4 Apr. and 10 May 1775: *Letters of James Boswell*, ed. C. B. Tinker (2 vols.; Oxford, 1924), i. 218, 222.
[32] E. Matthew Goyette ('Boswell's Changing Conceptions of his "Journal of a Tour to the Hebrides"', *Papers of the Bibliographical Society of America*, 73 (1979), 305–14) fails to persuade that this draft dates from 1775 or is to be identified with JB's 'Remarks' on Johnson's *Journey*, which have survived (n. 4 above).

focus on another Boswellian hero, General Paoli. As he accepted Dilly's commission on Johnson's death, he remarked: 'I wished I could write now as when I wrote my *Account of Corsica*.'[33] We can only partly know the circumstances under which the *Tour* first draft was abandoned: Banks and Reynolds gave their opinions, Malone no doubt confirmed them. By early May, at any rate, he was back on track.

The dramatic later history of the *Tour* is briefly sketched. Publication created a sensation: it was widely reviewed, serialized in magazines, satirized in the Rowlandson–Collings cartoons. In newspaper controversies Boswell had to defend his accuracy or taste: a dozen or so people particularly felt attacked, betrayed, or misrepresented; Boswell lost several friends and had to face the possible loss of his life. He learnt that in much of what we now value—the dramatic vividness and the revelation of private conversations—he had run ahead of the literary world. For the most part, however, he enjoyed the editorial support of the press: many of the newspapers were run by his friends, and we know from autumn correspondence that Malone intervened pseudonymously.

Boswell was cheered by a letter from Charles Dilly within a week of publication, giving encouraging details about the book trade's subscriptions: 'a few took as many as 50 Copies each.' Malone confirmed that 1,000 copies would be gone by the end of the week: as he and Boswell knew, the controversies, and the insertion of news items and inventions, kept the book in the public eye, and contributed to sales. Even the unpaid serialization, Dilly believed, helped 'the fate of all Books—particularly when the Editors of News Papers are fair enough to acknowledge from whence they take the Paragraphs'. Dilly was already hoping that Malone could 'prune the Volume & have it ready for a second Edition by the Conclusion of this Month'.[34] The revision was in fact to take three months, and was partly to be conducted via the mails while Boswell was in Auchinleck; Malone reported that Dilly was urging Baldwin to 'get through *five* sheets a week' (the book was of course being reset), but Malone felt that that would be 'utterly impossible on my part', and supposed '4 sheets a week is the most we can do'.[35]

Two major disputes ran through autumn 1785. Boswell had recorded Johnson's brusque dismissal of the advocate A. F. Tytler, who had defended *Fingal* as genuine though he could not read Gaelic. He virtually accused Boswell of lying about his express permission to print the story, and demanded its suppression. In long negotiations involving Malone,

---

[33] *Applause*, ed. Lustig and Pottle, 272.
[34] Dilly to JB, 5 Oct. 1785, MS Yale, C 1049; Malone to JB, 5 Oct., *Correspondence*, 200 and n. 3. 1,500 copies were printed of the first edition; 1,000 of the second; and probably 1,500 of the third (*Correspondence*, 236, 289). Each cost 6s. in boards.
[35] Malone to JB, 19 Oct. 1785, *Correspondence*, 227.

Professor Dugald Stewart, and others, they agreed that there had been misunderstanding somewhere and that Tytler's *name* should be suppressed; but Boswell's honour had been impugned, and he in turn exacted an apology from Tytler.[36] He had meanwhile become more seriously embroiled with Lord Macdonald, the former Sir Alexander, criticism of whom had already been toned down in the first edition, notably by the M4 cancel, although many readers correctly identified the anonymous butt of various remarks. In London on 27 November, having already decided to soften the text still further, Boswell received 'a most shocking, abusive letter from Lord M. which I thought made it indispensable for me to fight him'.[37] This appallingly written letter accuses Boswell of lying, forgery, and treachery to Johnson in 'your mass of fabricated Apothegms, which bubble upon the surface of an heated imagination'.[38] Regretting the hurt but defending his method and his honour, Boswell demanded that Macdonald withdraw his offensive expressions and provided John Courtenay with a formal challenge to a duel. Fortunately, Macdonald gave the required concessions, and the second edition softened the three main paragraphs in dispute. Boswell inserted the blind poet Dr Blacklock's letter of complaint as an Appendix to the second edition, together with a defence of his contemporary record. With these obvious changes, and much detailed revision, the second edition of the *Tour*, complete with Boswell's crest now engraved at a cost of 10s. 6d., was published on 24 December. Before leaving for Edinburgh, Boswell added to his will a codicil entrusting to Malone, a casual acquaintance only eight months before, his Johnsonian papers and many volumes of his own journal.

A major source of information about Malone's contribution, specifically about revision for the second edition, is the long self-contained correspondence in autumn 1785,[39] which confirms deductions about the earlier revision, and shows that the final readings result from detailed discussion and conscious choice, with proposals originating on both sides. Malone is chiefly concerned with obscurities, Scotticisms, and

---

[36] Claire Lamont ('James Boswell and Alexander Fraser Tytler: I. A Note on an Alteration in the Second Edition of Boswell's "Journal of a Tour to the Hebrides", 1785', *Bibliotheck*, 6 (1971), 1–8) prints an extract from Tytler's Commonplace Book and quotes a number of the letters; but Tytler's self-satisfaction requires to be balanced by consultation of the unpublished Boswellian archive (*Yale Catalogue*, i. 371–2).

[37] *Boswell: The English Experiment 1785–1789*, ed. Irma S. Lustig and Frederick A. Pottle (London, 1986), 9.

[38] For full documentation, see *The Private Papers of James Boswell from Malahide Castle* (18 vols.; Mount Vernon, NY, 1928–34), xvi. 221 ff. The affair is summarized in *Yale Catalogue*, i. 207–8. (In Jane Austen's 'Love and Friendship', Letters 12–13, the 'heavy' father is the 'malevolent and contemptible' Macdonald of Macdonald-Hall.)

[39] *Correspondence*, 200–79.

verbal awkwardness; Boswell normally accepts his suggestions on minor points of style. His own observations are more idiosyncratic, including a concern with 'teutonick original' spellings. Malone passed on suggestions from many friends, including Reynolds, Bennet Langton, Isaac Reed, and John Courtenay; Reynolds's intervention led to a renewed discussion of Johnson's 'convulsive contractions'. Several people objecting to the account of Burke's wit, Malone wrote a long, resolutely anonymous footnote. (Boswell later sent a copy of this edition to Burke, with a letter explaining the origin of the note; but Burke's unenthusiastic reply is easily understood.[40]) On the whole, this reworking shows Malone's interest in clarity, propriety, and stylistic elegance; Boswell is rarely stubborn except in changes of personal or family concern, or where the integrity of his original record might be threatened. It is now clear that the persistent interpretation of the 250 annotations in Malone's hand in the Adam–Hyde copy of the first edition as representing the principal source of emendations is quite wrong.[41]

The controversy over the *Tour* continued after publication of the second edition: Malone wrote a pseudonymous defence in the *Gentleman's Magazine*; 'Peter Pindar's' *Poetical and Congratulatory Epistle to James Boswell* ridiculed his passion for minutiae, and falsely reported his altering the second edition in response to Macdonald's threats (Rowlandson caricatured a terrified Boswell tearing out pages at sword point). A letter to the press and an addition to the third edition refuted this report; but by then the mud had stuck. Some six months after the *Tour*'s first publication, Boswell could reasonably have thought his troubles were over. In fact, he was on the brink of a major quarrel with the former Mrs Thrale, a rival for the Johnson market.[42] The *Tour* quoted Johnson as saying of Mrs Montagu's *Essay on Shakespeare* that 'neither I, nor Beauclerk, nor Mrs Thrale, could get through it'. Feeling embarrassed and threatened, Mrs Thrale attacked Boswell in her *Anecdotes*, then printing, and proclaimed her admiration of Mrs Montagu's *Essay*; as Malone pointed out, the *Anecdotes* reveal malice against Boswell, who, with Malone and Courtenay, wrote a hard-hitting attack which was widely circulated in the press and became a note in his third edition: he had accurately recorded Johnson; and Johnson and Mrs Thrale herself had both read the manuscript journal without objection. He also attacked her in anonymous newspaper verses as 'The wife of honest Thrale

---

[40] *Life*, v. 32–4; JB to Burke, 20 Dec. 1785, Burke to JB, 4 Jan. 1786, *Correspondence*, 147–50.
[41] The classic statement is by R. W. Chapman in his edition of the *Journey* and the *Tour* (Oxford, 1924), pp. xviii–xix.
[42] See Mary Hyde, *The Impossible Friendship: Boswell and Mrs. Thrale* (Cambridge, Mass., 1972); *Life*, v. 245–6.

the brewer'; they were joint victims in Pindar's *Bozzy and Piozzi*, comic poems, and gross caricatures. At least these 'enlivened the demand for the book. It was now out of print. I went to Baldwin's to hasten the third edition.'[43] That edition contains in the Advertisement and in some new notes yet another defence of his novel methods and his preservation of Johnson's memory. It appeared on 10 October 1786, and marks the end of Boswell's continuous interest in the book. There was subsequent bother in 1786–7 with Archibald Douglas, who resented the reporting of Johnson's 'witty attack on his *filiation*' concerning the famous Douglas inheritance dispute; and as late as 1789 Boswell was still occasionally having to justify his text or note apprehensions that in the forthcoming *Life* he would repeat some of his indiscretions.

Publication of the *Life* in 1791 allowed Dilly to market some copies of the third edition of the *Tour* by issuing them with a map of the route, which could also be bought separately for 6*d*. But they must have gone slowly: Dilly was still advertising as late as 1799. By then, its commercial value was small, as we see finally in a letter from Dilly to Forbes, one of the executors, the year after Boswell's death:

The demand for the Tour to the Highlands is decreasing and I believe there hath not been a Dozen Copies sold thro' the present Year—and the Books in hand 430 cannot be sold but as remainders.

Mr Boswell [that is, the brother David] is acquainted that many Books when the demand is over will produce no more than Waste Paper—I have set the Tours at one shilling—[44]

[43] *English Experiment*, ed. Lustig and Pottle, 69.
[44] Dilly to Forbes, 24 Aug. 1796: MS National Library of Scotland Acc. 4796.

APPENDIX: THE BOSWELL ARCHIVE

(A) M 132, pp. i–v: copy for Title-page, Dedication, Epigraph; Boswell's instructions to the printer for the first half-sheet.
pp. 1–45: new copy for the opening section.
pp. 678–739: new copy for the closing section, the pagination following from J 33.
pp. *i–*ii: copy for Errata and Advertisement.

(B) M 133: 'Papers apart'; the relevant portion (many folios being lost) runs to 161 written sides of different sizes, often fragmentary, and includes copy for the escape of Prince Charles in 1745; also original documents.

(C) Boswell's correspondence with Malone, Thomas Barnard, James Cummyng, Robert Boswell, Hugh Blair, Lord Hailes, James Hill, relating to the making of the first edition.

C 1931: Malone's annotated transcript of six passages not in the *Tour* or extant Journal.

C 1888.1: Malone's suggestions on Boswell's copy M 132, pp. 35–40, and J 33, pp. 25–8.

M 131: Boswell's list of intended recipients of presentation copies.

(D) P 84: Proof sheets or revises for all signatures of first edition of *Tour* except F; B is incomplete. Further proofs of title-page, O, P, R, Z, Aa. The cancels—C2, C7, E3, E4, M4—are preserved in three states, including the cancellanda and replacement copy.

9 At the Boundaries of Fiction: Samuel Paterson's Another Traveller!

KATHERINE S. H. TURNER

For some 200 years, the 'imitations' of Sterne's *A Sentimental Journey* which fill the 'minor fiction' pages of bibliographies have been subject to critical denigration. J. C. T. Oates, the indefatigable bibliographer of Sterneana, reports that 'an extensive course of reading in works such as these cannot but reduce the brain to the consistency of damp flannel'.[1] Such judgements often derive from the application of critical standards appropriate for fiction, but inappropriate for travel narratives, for *A Sentimental Journey* and its many imitators were reviewed—and indeed written—less as novels than as works occupying the ambiguous territory between fiction and first-person travelogue. Reviewing *A Sentimental Journey* in the *Monthly Review*, Ralph Griffiths remarks that 'Of all the productions of the press, none are so eagerly received by us Reviewers, and other people who stay at home and mind our business, as the *writings of travellers*.'[2] This rather surprising description of Sterne's work testifies to the critical problems posed by the emergence of a genre which was commercially and critically successful, yet which defied generic categorization. These problems have largely continued into modern critical treatments—indeed, neglect—of such works.

This chapter will examine one of the most successful of the denigrated 'imitators' of *A Sentimental Journey*: by exploring the closely related issues of genre and originality, and placing these within a historical framework, new light is thrown on the social and political importance of the 'sentimental' travel narrative.

Within the evolving critical parameters of travel literature in the mid-eighteenth century, apparent literary naïvety in the transcription of observations and personal responses was taken as evidence of the 'truth' of a travelogue: more powerful evidence, in fact, than simple facts, which might easily have been copied from a guidebook. The deceptive 'immediacy' of *A Sentimental Journey* accorded with such standards, and in turn had a strongly enabling influence on many writers who might never otherwise have ventured into print. The eighteenth-century reviews,

[1] J. C. T. Oates, *Shandyism and Sentiment, 1760–1800* (Cambridge, 1968), 15.
[2] *Monthly Review*, 38 (1768), 174 (emphasis added).

especially the liberal-minded *Monthly Review*, are reluctant simply to condemn the so-called 'imitators' of Sterne. While sometimes acknowledging the low literary standards of such texts, reviewers accord praise on moral and political grounds to even the most 'minor' accounts of European journeys; and the text examined in this chapter, Samuel Paterson's *Another Traveller!*, was hailed by the *Monthly* and *Critical* Reviews as a literary and moral *tour de force*.

Samuel Paterson (1728–1802) was a 'well-known and justly-celebrated Bookseller and Auctioneer', who 'constantly failed in business, as he always preferred reading to selling books'.³ He began his career as a bookseller, and published *Poems on Several Occasions* by Charlotte Lennox (then Ramsay) in 1747. He was described by Samuel Johnson, who stood as godfather for his son (also called Samuel), as 'a man for whom I have long had a kindness'.⁴ Perhaps Johnson and Paterson collaborated in supporting Lennox; according to Nichols, 'Honest Sam Paterson used to boast that he had the honour of first introducing her to the publick.'⁵ Failing at bookselling, he set up as an auctioneer, book-buyer, and pioneer of bibliographical cataloguing. In 1768 and 1769, under the pseudonym of 'Coriat Junior', he produced a playful two-volume travelogue entitled *Another Traveller! Or Cursory Remarks and Tritical Observations made upon a Journey through Part of the Netherlands In the latter End of the Year 1766*, which ran to a second edition in 1782.⁶ Paterson's earliest biographers describe *Another Traveller!* as 'the result' of a book-buying 'tour through Holland and Flanders' (much as *A Sentimental Journey* is loosely derived from Sterne's own travels), and they write respectfully of Paterson's literary abilities. John Nichols describes him as 'a writer of some consideration', and in 1788 he was included in a *Catalogue of Five Hundred Celebrated Authors of Great Britain, Now Living*.⁷ Chalmers describes Paterson as 'of philanthropic looks, sonorous voice, and unassuming and polite manners. His moral character was eminent, and unexceptionable, in every sense of the word'.⁸ An obituary notice by 'a friend', T. Mortimer, in the *European*

---

³ Henry Richard Tedder, in *Dictionary of National Biography*, xv. 468; John Nichols, *Literary Anecdotes of the Eighteenth Century* (9 vols.; London, 1812–15), iii. 438. See ibid. iii. 438–40 for a biographical account and iii. 733–6 for an account of Paterson's bibliographical achievements.

⁴ *Boswell's Life of Johnson*, ed. G. B. Hill and L. F. Powell (6 vols.; Oxford, 1934–64), iii. 90.

⁵ Nichols, *Literary Anecdotes*, iii. 200.

⁶ The second edition of *Another Traveller!* in 1782 was renamed *An Entertaining Journey to the Netherlands* (London, 3 vols.).

⁷ Nichols, *Literary Anecdotes*, iii. 736. In addition to *Another Traveller!*, Paterson published a collection of miscellaneous essays entitled *Joineriana, or the Book of Scraps* (2 vols.; London, 1772), and polemics against ecclesiastical and legal corruption.

⁸ Alexander Chalmers, *The General Biographical Dictionary* (32 vols.; London, 1812–17), xxiv. 188.

Magazine for 1802 notes that 'Mr. Paterson was a miscellaneous writer of various little tracts, having for their subject public utility, sound policy, and moral admonition'.⁹ As we shall see, these public-spirited qualities are prominent in Paterson's travelogue, and were commended by the reviewers. Paterson's moral earnestness, but more especially his apparent plagiarism of Sterne, seems to have provoked the disdain of his biographer in the *Dictionary of National Biography*, who pronounces that his 'original works' were 'not remarkable', and describes *Another Traveller!* as 'sentimental travels in the manner of Sterne, of very poor quality'.¹⁰

In fact, Paterson's text is one of the most readable and apparently 'authentic' sentimental travelogues of the 1760s or 1770s. Coriat Junior journeys by land, sea, and canal from London to Antwerp and its environs. He invariably makes use of public transport, whether this be coach or barge, and thereby encounters a rich variety of fellow-travellers, English and foreign. Descriptions of the towns and cathedrals where he alights, and accounts of his personal encounters (with charitable monks and beautiful nuns in particular), are interwoven with dramatized dialogues and reflections:

My intention is to diversify this short travel as much as possible—to make it narrative, descriptive and sometimes allegorical—always with a little meaning and seldom without a moral. . . . the very moment I discover that I have nothing to say, I shall lay down my pen—I have no opinion of forcing, under the notion of assisting nature, and, from my soul! I abominate Dr. *Slop*'s forceps!¹¹

Coriat Junior describes particular inns and innkeepers, bookshops and booksellers, cathedrals and friars, simultaneously paying tribute to kindly hosts and providing helpful information for future travellers. These descriptive sections are balanced with more eccentric passages of fictive dialogue and meditation.

The style of *Another Traveller!* is consciously Shandean, with much use of dashes, exclamations, and white space, and much discussion of the mechanics of writing, publishing, and reading. Its textual self-awareness may owe something to Paterson's bookselling background as well as to his reading of Sterne. In a chapter entitled 'Which as it relates chiefly to the Author, cannot be very interesting to the Reader', Coriat Junior engages in dialogue with a hostile reader, who exclaims 'A Book of travels quotha!—I believe nobody ever saw such a book of travels!—a

⁹ *European Magazine*, 42 (1802), 428. For similar assessments, see also *Gentleman's Magazine*, 72 (1802), 1074–5 (obituary); Nichols, *Literary Anecdotes*, iii. 438–40, 733–6; *Dictionary of National Biography*, xv. 467–8.
¹⁰ *Dictionary of National Biography*, xv. 468.
¹¹ *Another Traveller!*, i. 174.

book of wanderings rather—interserted with whimsical digressions and unseasonable reflections'.[12]

Another Traveller! self-consciously stretches the stylistic conventions of travel literature. The traditional epistolary or journal form of the travel narrative is abandoned by both Paterson and Sterne, who adopt instead a more fragmentary approach; chapters materialize out of apparently 'immediate' observations and associationist digression. This method permits a sometimes chaotic intermingling of reflections—on authorship, sentiment, prejudice, religion, charity, and political morality—within the journey framework. It also offers a broader social and moral scope than would be possible within the rigorous linearity of traditional travel narrative. Coriat Junior's hostile reader objects to this corruption of the genre: 'If a man has a mind to indulge serious reflections, let him write a book on purpose.' But Coriat's reply makes clear that the very oddity of the text enables its morally educative thrust: 'Yes, as you say—and then he will be pretty sure that nobody will read them—I tell you mine are just in the right place—for here many may stumble upon them, who never dreamt of any such thing.'[13] Paterson reclaims the traditionally educative function of travel literature for sentimental ends. As we shall see, Coriat Junior's 'serious reflections' and reformatory impulses are more precise than Sterne's broader professed design in *A Sentimental Journey* of 'teach[ing] us to love the world and our fellow creatures better than we do'.[14] Or, put another way, we can see in *Another Traveller!* a more anxious and outspoken intelligence than Sterne's, engaging more explicitly with the problems of inequity and intolerance brought into focus by foreign travel. Less titillating and evasive than *A Sentimental Journey*, Paterson's text in many ways has greater historical and political significance.

The title-page to volume one of *Another Traveller!* bears the date 1767.[15] This is mendacious. The text was not published until 1768, and appeared after the publication of *A Sentimental Journey* earlier in the same year; but Paterson was clearly keen to establish his originality by claiming an earlier publication date. Given the increasing tendency at this time to stigmatize the derivative and celebrate the original, Paterson's claims to prior publication are not perhaps surprising; nor, indeed, are they finally verifiable. Yet the way in which he presses his claims is not merely amusing; it also reveals the extent to which originality was seen

[12] Ibid. 150.   [13] Ibid. 152.
[14] Letter to Mrs William James, 12 Nov. 1767, in Lewis P. Curtis (ed.), *Letters of Laurence Sterne* (Oxford, 1935), 401.
[15] Volume one was published in two separate parts, and *Another Traveller!* is therefore sometimes recorded as a three-volume work; but the pagination is continuous within the two parts of volume one.

as an index of moral and social virtue as well as literary value; and, indeed, suggests that 'originality' was a rather unstable term in this context.

Within the text, Coriat Junior's denial of plagiarism is winsomely dramatized in a chapter of dialogue with his bookseller Joseph Johnson, who anxiously enquires after the progress of the manuscript. Johnson is especially worried by an advertisement he reads out from the *St James's Chronicle*:

'Speedily will be published—*A sentimental journey*, by Mr. YORICK'
Good!—I am heartily glad of it!—for then we shall have something worth reading!—How can this affect us, but with delight?
  'Are you not abashed?—And will not malicious folks say?'—
Let them say what they will—for after him, and a thousand worse, ANOTHER TRAVELLER will still be read!—There is room enough in this big world for him and me too—Shadows fill no place—Mr. YORICK will be read for his wit—I must be read for my cause.[16]

Here, Coriat Junior admits to being a 'shadow' of Yorick (whether the Yorick of *Tristram Shandy* or of *A Sentimental Journey* is unclear), in terms of wit and literary delightfulness. Yet the point of the dialogue is to protest innocence of mere imitation. The distinction between Yorick's 'wit' and Coriat Junior's 'cause' suggests a moral extension of Sterne's stylistic innovation; as we shall see, it is this aspect of sentimental journeying which *Another Traveller!* develops.

For all the playfulness of this passage, the question was important enough to prompt Paterson to publish, in 1769, a formal protestation of his absolute originality, *An Appeal to the Candid and Spirited Authors of the Critical Review, against Ignorance, Malevolence and Detraction*. In this pamphlet, booksellers' affidavits are invoked to prove that *Another Traveller!* 'is so far from being a copy, or imitation of the aforesaid SENTIMENTAL JOURNEY of the aforesaid inimitable Yorick, that it was several months antecedent to the said SENTIMENTAL JOURNEY of the said Yorick, in our hands, and in the hands of the printer'.[17] While the *Critical Review* supports Paterson's claims, pronouncing that he 'owes nothing to the last printed volume of Yorick's Sentimental Journey', the *Monthly*'s reviewer is more sceptical. He points out that the 'very ample specimens of [Sterne's] *peculiar manner of travelling*, in his later Volumes of Tristram Shandy, published long enough before either the *Sentimental Journey*,' or Mr. Coriat's performance', could have furnished Paterson with a model for Shandean travels.[18] Paterson himself, in the Preface to

---

[16]   *Another Traveller!*, i. 443.
[17]   See *Critical Review*, 28 (1769), 387.
[18]   Ibid. 28 (1769), 387; *Monthly Review*, 40 (1769), 167.

Another Traveller!, admits the influence of *Tristram Shandy*: he jestingly apologizes for daring to publish 'a couple of *Shandean* duodecimos'. He also explains that 'travelling is the mode, and that it is no less the mode to print travels', as if to claim for himself the original integration of two fashionable modes of writing into the genre of Shandean travelogue.[19]

The *Monthly*'s point about the probable influence on Paterson of the satiric travel sections of *Tristram Shandy* is acute; but, strangely, it evades the question of whether *A Sentimental Journey* or *Another Traveller!* is the more 'original' text. This unconcern may seem curious to a modern critic or bibliographer, for whom the value of a literary work, especially a work of 'fiction' (for as such is *Another Traveller!* generally classified), resides almost entirely in its 'originality'.[20] As Paterson's somewhat contradictory claims and concessions suggest, however, the central issue is not, for the author or reviewer in the eighteenth century, one of creative uniqueness. Part of the reason for this lies in the related and sometimes confused issues of genre and narrative singularity, to which we now turn.

By the middle of the century, the first-person travel narrative was becoming increasingly affective, anecdotal, and introspective, rather than documentary. This is particularly the case with accounts of Europe, where the itinerary had become so familiar, to readers and travellers alike, that a text could only claim attention through novelties of style and authorial singularity. Paradoxically, the scope—indeed, demand—for stylistic novelty was coming to subsume the rigorously empirical foundations of travel-writing. Boundaries between documentary fact and descriptive fiction were becoming more fluid, and Paterson's text is paradigmatic of this shift. Ralph Griffiths's review of the first volume of *Another Traveller!* provides a sense of these developments: significantly, Sterne by no means has a monopoly over the genre, within the framework which Griffiths provides:

Sentimental Travels seem now to be coming into vogue; and, indeed, we shall rejoice to see a final period put to those dull details of post stages, and churches, and picture-catalogues, with which books of travels have heretofore chiefly abounded . . .
The sprightly, the humorous, the sentimental Yorick, was the first who had sense and taste enough to quit the beaten pack-horse path; and the ingenious

[19] *Another Traveller!*, i, pp. vii–viii.
[20] The *New Cambridge Bibliography of English Literature 1660–1800* (Cambridge, 1971), 1002, classifies *Another Traveller!* as 'minor fiction', and as an 'Imitation of Sterne, Sentimental journey' (yet unquestioningly accepts 1767 as the date of publication). More recently, James Raven includes *Another Traveller!* in his bibliography of *British Fiction 1750–1770: A Chronological Check-List of Prose Fiction Printed in Britain and Ireland* (London, 1987), but categorizes it as a 'miscellaneous work' (pp. 292, 309, 330).

author of the present travels has the good fortune to follow him at no despicable rate. There have been many imitators of that celebrated original; but none who, in our opinion, have caught so much of his manner and spirit as Mr. Coriat Junior . . .[21]

At this stage in the proliferation of sentimental travels, the individuality of any one work written in the new mode is less important than the inherent value of the sentimental approach.

This value is social as well as literary: the 'books of travels' which Ralph Griffiths thankfully sees as becoming outmoded include not only guidebooks but also the languid productions of aristocratic Grand Tourists. The change which Griffiths perceives in literary fashion reflects the rapid increase in middle-class European tourism after the 1763 Peace of Paris, an increase which challenged the cultural exclusiveness of the aristocratic Grand Tour. Through their literary and actual invasion of the European arena, the 'middling sort' expand the scope of their claim to centrality in public life and national affairs.

For all the lofty cultural ideals of the gentleman's Grand Tour, the institution was widely perceived as a means of exporting unsavoury adolescent rites of passage, bringing Britain into disrepute through their drunken debauchery. Moreover, Grand Tourists, whether adolescent or mature, tended to offset their courtly cosmopolitanism with broad contempt for the superstitious Catholic excesses of the foreign peasantry and clerisy. Sentimental travellers deliberately distinguish themselves from these patterns of behaviour.

Repeatedly in discussions of aristocratic degeneracy abroad, Grand Tourists are represented not as individuals but as an unthinking herd. Coriat Junior in Brussels encounters a 'crew of noisy Englishmen' intent on laughing at Catholicism, drinking copiously, and whoring enthusiastically: 'Englishmen are always at home—hark! they begin to roar already.'[22] This impression of bestial anonymity is one reason why travel-writers, sentimental or otherwise, are keen to establish a distinctive narrative character. They thereby distinguish themselves from what Smollett describes as 'a number of raw boys, whom Britain seemed to have poured forth on purpose to bring her national character into contempt'.[23]

The concept of 'national character' is an important one. To an almost tiresome degree, travel and other writers in the eighteenth century enjoy formulating national stereotypes for the European countries which they

[21] *Monthly Review*, 39 (1768), 434–5.
[22] *Another Traveller!*, i. 236.
[23] Tobias Smollett, *Travels through France and Italy* (London, 1766), ed. Frank Felsenstein (Oxford, 1979), letter XXIX, p. 251.

visit. The French are frivolous, the Italians deceitful, the Germans stolid. Or, as Coriat Junior laments, 'most of my countrymen . . . set out with prejudices against the natives they are going to visit—they know their characters before-hand—a Frenchman, is a puppy; an Italian, a cheat; a German, a pedant; and a Dutchman, a brute'.[24]

Within this stereotyping framework, the insular English, by contrast, resist definition. Smollett's account in *The Present State of All Nations* (1768–9) is typical (one finds such arguments in almost every travelogue and review of the period). Having tentatively suggested that bluntness and honesty to some extent constitute the 'national character' of the English, he notes that their 'conversation' is 'extremely irregular':

Such variation will always be found in a people like the English, endued with sensibility, whose spirits are affected by the sudden changes of an irregular climate: for the same reason, they will be as variable in their tempers, whimsical, capricious, and inconstant. . . . The whimsical disposition of these islanders appears in very strange singularities . . .[25]

A badly behaved Grand Tourist in *Another Traveller!* invokes the contempt of his Flemish host, who 'thanks heaven that he was not born an *Englishman*, if all are of the same turbulent disposition'.[26]

Some years earlier, in his essay 'Of National Characters' (1748), David Hume had rejected the argument from the 'physical' cause of climate, positing instead what he describes as a 'moral' cause, which is in fact political. He attributes the 'wonderful Mixture of Manners and Character', for which 'the *English* are the most remarkable of any People, that perhaps ever were in the World', to the unique 'Mixture of Monarchy, Aristocracy, and Democracy' in England's government. Hume stresses the liberating effect of such a mixed form of government on private disposition:

And the great Liberty and Independency, which they enjoy, allows every one to display the Manners, which are peculiar to him. Hence the *English*, of any People in the Universe, have the least of a national Character; unless this very Singularity be made their national Character.[27]

Again, versions of this argument are ubiquitous in eighteenth-century travel-writings. Within the framework of English liberty, enshrined in the British constitution, individuals are free to develop the eccentricity or 'singularity' for which they were becoming celebrated in Europe.[28]

[24] *Another Traveller!*, i. 161.
[25] Tobias Smollett, *The Present State of All Nations* (8 vols.; London, 1768–9), ii. 215.
[26] *Another Traveller!*, i. 189–90.
[27] David Hume, *Essays, Moral and Political* (London, 1748), 278–9.
[28] See e.g. *Letters describing the Character and Customs of the English and French Nations* (London, 1726), published anonymously by a Frenchman, Béat Louis de Muralt, where it is remarked

Being English meant being beyond the scope of national stereotyping. This was something one did to other countries. Even Sterne, whose text ostensibly seeks to discredit xenophobia, asserts English singularity and thus superiority:

should it ever be the case of the English, in the progress of their refinements, to arrive at the same polish which distinguishes the French, if we did not lose the *politesse de cœur*, which inclines men more to human actions, than courteous ones—we should at least lose that distinct variety and originality of character, which distinguishes them, not only from each other, but from all the world besides.[29]

The movement of this passage, from the implicit claim to superior English virtue, to the more neutral claim of English singularity, is deceptive, since the claim of greater humanity is never revoked.

From the middle of the eighteenth century, more and more travel-writers, from the humblest sentimental variety to the most erudite, present a distinctive, even eccentric narrative character. Not only does this make for a more novel and marketable text; it also testifies to the liberty provided by the British political constitution for an infinite variety of individual, psychological constitutions. Travelogues, even those now considered minor and trivial, received extensive coverage in the encyclopaedic volumes of the *Monthly* and *Critical* Reviews. The range and variety of travel-accounts, even if the places they described were well documented by this stage, amounted to a gallery of narrative individuals, who testified, in their multiplicity, to that British freedom of expression which evinced a wider political liberty.

Moreover, personal distinctiveness identifies the writer as a character *not* defined primarily by his or her national character or prejudice. His or her views are therefore to be trusted as unbiased accounts of 'abroad'. Such accounts are frequently described, by their authors and reviewers, as 'candid'. Candour, a ubiquitous term in the reviewing world of the later eighteenth century, is especially relevant to travel-writing and its reception in this period. The unprejudiced traveller's attitude towards the countries through which he or she travels finds a parallel, ideally, in the attitude of critic or reader towards the author. This attitude is frequently described as 'candid', and is constantly invoked by authors and reviewers. The *New English Dictionary* in 1757 defines 'candour' as 'favourableness of judging of others', and the *Complete English Dictionary* in

that 'The Characters in *France* are general, and comprehend an entire Order or Rank of People; but in *England*, where every one lives according to his Fancy, the Poet can hardly find any thing but particular Characters, which are very numerous, and can never produce any great Effect' (p. 20).

[29] Laurence Sterne, *A Sentimental Journey through France and Italy by Mr Yorick* (1768), ed. Gardner D. Stout jun. (Berkeley, Calif., 1967), 231–2.

1765 offers 'a temper of mind unsoured by envy and unseduced by prejudice'. Johnson's *Dictionary* in 1755 glosses 'candid' as 'without malice; without deceit; fair; open; ingenuous', and cites a couplet from Pope's 'Essay on Criticism' which nicely sums up the critical and personal sympathies denoted by the term:

> A candid judge will read each piece of wit
> With the same spirit that its authour writ.[30]

As William Empson and Donald Davie have both demonstrated, 'candour' before the late 1770s did not carry the implications of either hypocrisy or radicalism which it acquired in the final decades of the eighteenth century.[31] Moreover, according to Davie, 'candour' in the late 1760s and earlier was 'equivalent indeed to the theological and especially dissenting virtue of Christian *charity*'. Intriguingly, charity is perhaps the chief preoccupation of Paterson's text, and his theological as well as social position is in some senses dissentient.[32]

'Candour' at this time was also associated with *political* virtue and claims to citizenship. Cicero's speech, 'In Toga Candida', described in Middleton's *Life of Cicero* (1741) as a 'most severe invective on the flagitious lives and practices of his two competitors', is the *locus classicus* of the politically virtuous resonances of candour.[33] These associations are invoked by Hume in the same essay ('Of National Characters'), where he remarks that 'Candour, Bravery, and Love of Liberty, form'd the Character of the ancient *Romans*; as Subtilty, Cowardice, and a Slavish Disposition do that of the modern'.[34] The ancient Roman character, along with political liberty, has implicitly been transferred to modern Britain; to mid-eighteenth-century readers familiar with works such as Addison's 'A Letter from Italy' (1703), Thomson's 'Liberty' (1735–8), and Gray's 'The Progress of Poesy' (1757)—to name only the best-known treatments of this theme—this transference of political character had attained the status of belief.

---

[30] The couplet is in fact misquoted from 'An Essay on Criticism', ll. 233–4, and should read:

> A perfect Judge will *read* each Work of Wit
> With the same Spirit that its Author *writ*.

[31] I owe this point to Isabel Rivers. See William Empson, 'Sensible and Candid', in *The Structure of Complex Words* (1951; repr. London, 1985), 306–10; and Donald Davie, 'An Episode in the History of Candor', in *Dissentient Voice: Enlightenment and Christian Dissent* (Notre Dame, Ind., 1982), 83–93.

[32] *Another Traveller!* was published by John Payne and Joseph Johnson. Johnson was to become the doyen of Dissenting publishing in the 1780s and 1790s.

[33] I owe this point to David Omissi; Conyers Middleton, *The History of the Life of Marcus Tullius Cicero* (2 vols.; London, 1741), i. 142.

[34] 'Of National Characters', in *Essays, Moral and Political* (1748), 277.

Not only is candour a desirable quality in every traveller, and therefore a *communal* characteristic: it also involves a frank narrative self-projection or 'sincerity', and thus contributes to *singularity*, which is often explicitly opposed to communal prejudice. Coriat Junior wrestles with this difficult nexus of ideas:

> *I beg leave then to proceed in my own way*—and tho' it is become so much the fashion among my countrymen of late to decry foreign customs and manners, and to cry up whatever is of *British* growth, whether right, or wrong; I shall nevertheless take the liberty so far to differ from them, as to commend whatever in my judgment has appeared commendable, without dread of the forfeiture of my allegiance . . .
>
> By such candid proceeding I flatter myself it is not impossible but that I may be able with reason to remove the illiberal prejudices of some of my readers, and to laugh away the childish notions of others.[35]

Here, as elsewhere, Coriat Junior detaches himself from complacent British prejudice; yet his claims to candour and tolerance constitute a claim to virtuous British citizenship, the value of which is never seriously challenged. The issue is not that of international relations; instead, *Another Traveller!* interrogates the moral structure of British society.

Much of *Another Traveller!* is devoted to comparative descriptions of civil systems of law, order, religion, and morality, with implicit reference to the British state of affairs, and, often, suggestions for improvement therein. Coriat Junior thus asserts a moral guardianship over his nation. Here, his fictive persona is significant. The playful allusion to Thomas Coryate, the early seventeenth-century author of *Coryats Crudities, Hastily Gobbled up in Five Moneths Travells* (1611), is expanded by Coriat Junior into a celebration of his namesake's 'modesty and humility', as well as his satiric wit. We are also informed that 'Tom possest one part of *Falstaffe*'s character in a very eminent degree; and if he was not over witty himself, he was the true cause *that wit was in other men*'.[36] The comparison with Falstaff reinforces the symbiotic relationship between English singularity and typicality which 'Coriat Junior' and 'Yorick' also signify: like Sterne's Yorick, Coriat is at once an individual and a fragment of shared English culture. He is fictive, but not realistic, and can thus stand, paradoxically, as a *representative* of English *singularity*; in other words, as England's moral spokesman.

The *European Magazine*'s obituary describes the subjects of Paterson's writings as 'public utility, sound policy, and moral admonition'.[37] Reviews of *Another Traveller!* likewise appreciated Paterson's role as monitor.

[35] *Another Traveller!*, i. 32–3.
[36] *Monthly Review*, 39 (1768), 435–6; *Another Traveller!*, i. 113.
[37] *European Magazine*, 42 (1802), 428.

The *Critical Review* approvingly notes the absence of Shandean obscenity: more expansively, Ralph Griffiths in the *Monthly Review* candidly admits that 'we do not think the present Traveller equal to Yorick, in any respect, except'—and it is a large exception—'in the solidity of his Judgment, the chastity of his pen, and the moral cast of his observations'.[38]

Coriat Junior's reflections on public and private virtue do not exist in a political vacuum; they embody a challenge, or at least a rebuke, to the moral government of England. Central to the political positioning of *Another Traveller!* is a satirical chapter entitled 'An Apology for Wooden Shoes'.[39] In this chapter, Paterson discusses the value and significance of clogs, those potent symbols of continental despotism and misery which were particularly ubiquitous in xenophobic satirical prints of the period. In a charged refocusing of satiric attack, Paterson chooses to celebrate the practical value of clogs in inclement continental weather: 'Humanity pleads strongly in their favour.' Indeed, clogs are far preferable to the bare-footed oppression evident 'in the northern part of this loved island, where property is so partially divided that all are lords, or beggars; shoes are almost as scarce as parishes'.[40]

This manœuvre places Paterson in an oppositional position, given the still potent association of Scottish oppression, centred on the figures of Bute, Mansfield, and other politically powerful Scots at court, with the perceived absolutist pretensions of George III. Jeremy Black has suggested that the political resonances of Scottophobia after 1760 channelled xenophobic feeling away from the Continent.[41] This is a generalization to which many exceptions can be found: xenophobic travel narratives continued to be produced. But the notion of refocusing is an important one. Smollett, as a Scot and an active supporter of Bute, attempts to restore the earlier focus: his *Travels through France and Italy* (1766) notoriously reinforce Francophobia, perhaps deliberately to counter the shifting of public contempt from France to Scotland.

The Whiggish *Monthly Review* reprints the entire chapter attacking Scottish corruption.[42] It is worth remembering in this context that Johnson, in his interview with George III, characterized the 'authours' of the *Monthly Review* as 'enemies to the Church', and 'for pulling down all establishments', whereas the 'Critical Reviewers are for supporting the constitution, both in church and state'.[43]

---

[38] *Critical Review*, 26 (1768), 354; *Monthly Review*, 39 (1768), 435.
[39] *Another Traveller!*, i. 360–6.   [40] Ibid. 364–5.
[41] Jeremy Black, 'Tourism and Cultural Challenge: The Changing Scene of the Eighteenth Century', in John McVeagh (ed.), *All Before Them, 1660–1780* (London, 1989), 185–202.
[42] *Monthly Review*, 39 (1768), 446–8.
[43] *Boswell's Life of Johnson*, ii. 40; iii. 32. See also Derek Roper, 'The Politics of the *Critical Review*, 1756–1817', *Durham University Journal*, NS 22 (1961), 117–22.

Paterson's text is not, in fact, levelling in the exaggerated sense which Johnson's remarks on the *Monthly Review*'s Whiggishness might suggest. But it does display a more blatant concern with social and political issues than does the subtly evasive *Sentimental Journey*. As we have seen, the chapter on wooden shoes provides a high-political critique of Britain: at other times, Coriat Junior similarly rewrites traditional attacks on Catholicism to provide an ironic questioning of British social practices. For example, a horror-struck description of mystical 'human sacrifices' performed by an 'arch-priest' upon an 'unhappy victim', and reviled as 'the effects of ENTHUSIASM!', is in fact prompted by a glimpse of a public gallows, and develops into a general attack on the practice of hanging, with its 'strange notions of Heaven's wrath and Heaven's relenting!'[44]

A Sentimental Journey has provoked the disdain of Marxist critics for its evasiveness and alleged hypocrisy: Sterne explores 'Liberty' and its oppressors in terms which refer subtly to Wilkes's persecution, yet stops short of any democratic programme, conceding to 'the roughest peasant' only 'a portion . . . sometimes' of sensibility.[45] Critical disapproval of Sterne's politics has tainted by association the works of his so-called 'imitators'. But to berate eighteenth-century middle-class writers— among whom Samuel Paterson would be included—for not being democrats or revolutionaries gives insufficient weight to the challenge offered by the 'middling sort' to the cultural and political hegemony of the ruling aristocracy. During the 1760s the commercial press became an important arena for public discussion, and 'an instrument of social ferment' as well as social control.[46] Although less overtly, literary journalism (as Johnson realized) and literary texts themselves performed this function, mediating the gap between rulers and ruled on the limited terms available.

Samuel Paterson seems aware of just how (for all the vaunted liberty of British public life) limited these terms are: yet *Another Traveller!* derives much of its narrative dynamic from Coriat Junior's commitment if not to revolution, then at least to social fermentation. There is a curious tension in the text between engagement and defeatism. Coriat Junior can be pessimistic not only about the efficacy of his own writing, but, more broadly, about the possibilities for political reform within English society. Indeed, his focus on the need for a revision of social morality is related to a sense of the limitations of merely political freedoms. In Brussels, Coriat Junior argues with an acquaintance, Monsieur Neron,

[44] *Another Traveller!*, i. 200–2.
[45] Sterne, *A Sentimental Journey*, 278–9. On the political resonances of 'Liberty' in *A Sentimental Journey*, see Carol Kay, *Political Constructions: Defoe, Richardson, and Sterne in Relation to Hobbes, Hume, and Burke* (Ithaca, NY, 1988), 242–3, 246–63.
[46] See Lance Bertelson, *The Nonsense Club: Literature and Popular Culture, 1749–1764* (Oxford, 1986), 4–5, 155.

about the much-vaunted value of British liberty: 'I look upon *England*, sir, said I, to be the only land of liberty and free intelligence—"Hum" said monsieur *Neron*.'[47] Coriat's enthusiasm for the multiplicity of British journalism, factions, and parties ('party is the life-blood of liberty') meets with astonishment. Monsieur Neron prefers the party-less stability of Dutch government, which permits a steady maintenance of public order, morality, and welfare, and is horrified at Coriat's account of the 'unlicenced lictors' and scandalmongers of the British press—'O monstrous!—such inhuman jesters would not be suffered to live in any other country!—if this is liberty, long may you enjoy it'.[48] This passage is characteristic of *Another Traveller!*: the dialogue form, and Coriat Junior's semi-fictive narrative persona, permit a fluid, sometimes daring clash of opinions, the outcome of which is not so much a conclusion as an acknowledgement of complexity and relativity.

In the second volume, a chapter of 'incoherent Remarks, inconclusive Conclusions . . . bestowed by certain misjudging Spirits upon the Author and his Book' dramatizes six critical voices who attack the earlier volume's preoccupation with Roman Catholic charity and benevolence, a preoccupation which highlights by comparison British failures in philanthropy. Again, this multiplicity of voices is typical of *Another Traveller!*, and creates a broader sense of community, whether amicable or quarrelsome, engaging in vigorous debate. ' "This new-fangled author, this romancing traveller, or travelling romancer, said one, must certainly be a papist in disguise!" '; another pronounces Coriat Junior ' "a downright bloody papist" '; and another skilfully drawn coffee-house caviller inveighs against the unpatriotic tendencies of *Another Traveller!*:

after all that he has seen, has he ever met with any country like OLD ENGLAND, I should be glad to know?—I'm sure I never have, nor any man breathing I believe.—Curse him! and his *Allons donc!*—he has hinder'd me from reading the account of the great cock-match.—Here, boy! bring me the *Gazetteer* and another dish of coffee![49]

Coriat Junior is filled with despondency at his imagined reception, concluding that

> *Truths wou'd you teach, or save a sinking land,*
> *All fear, none aid you, and few understand.*

Six examples, and all fairly produced—wou'd you have any more, reader?—'tis unnecessary—and if the book should chance to meet with five hundred

---

[47] *Another Traveller!*, i. 266.
[48] Ibid. 268, 273. [49] Ibid. ii. 33–7.

readers—(let me whisper you)—four hundred and fifty of them, at least, will be of the misjudging feather.[50]

Coriat Junior creates for himself and his reader a beleaguered, morally sensitive community, which finds a literary counterpart in the under-valued and liminal genre of his narrative. This manœuvre invokes the moral determinism inherent in sensibility, which presents the sentimental hero(ine) as painfully subject to the abuse of the irredeemably non-sentimental herd (Mackenzie's *Man of Feeling* represents perhaps the quintessence of such vulnerability and its associated pessimism). Board-ing the ship for Ostend, Coriat Junior and his companion stand politely back, only to find that every other passenger presses forward, 'and my companion and I were fain to lay, the one upon a bulk, the other upon the cabin floor'. This upsetting experience prompts the following reflec-tion:

Such are the disadvantages which the modest man frequently labours under, to which the impudent is an utter stranger—the forward and bold constantly avail themselves of the backwardness of the humble and modest, turn their punctilios into jests, and, in short, reap every advantage at their expence, save one—arising from a certain sensibility, which as they can never feel, so it is impossible to make them comprehend.[51]

Whereas the fictional *Man of Feeling* finally expires at the realization of his sensitive isolation, Coriat Junior, being only semi-fictional and thus cut off from the more extreme possibilities of fictional isola-tion, is borne more cheerfully along on his journey. The isolation of the sentimental traveller is turned to more positive, and more political, effect:

You are to understand that I am a plain citizen of the great world; not a gay fellow of the little one—a common pilgrim in the beaten track; not a courtly passenger in the bye path:—an humble tenant of the wide forest and the open field; not a lord of the lawn, the grove, and the terras; who carefully shuns the din and plash of the populace, and studiously avoids interfering with the lot of those beneath him; lest, by degrees, he should be insensibly wrought upon, to contemplate the nothingness of his own.[52]

This is a crucial passage. Within the world of European travel literature, it redefines the cosmopolitan universality usually claimed by the aristo-cratic Grand Tourist, and appropriates the term to describe the universal benevolence of the 'plain citizen'. Elsewhere, Coriat Junior actually

---

[50] Ibid. ii. 48. The couplet is from Pope, *Essay on Man*, iv. 265–6.
[51] *Another Traveller!*, i. 29.
[52] Ibid. ii. 167–8.

describes himself as a 'well-meaning cosmopolite', distinguished by philanthropy, not by classical or courtly culture and connections.[53] Thus, the sentimental benevolence of the middling sort is placed at the centre of national life, determining even international conduct. The question of genre is important here: the 'foreign-ness' of the traveller's experience, and the wide scope of his benevolence, pushes the boundaries of sympathy to their furthest extent. The theatrics of sentimental fiction are displaced by a more relentless documentary confrontation with issues of social inequity.

The political dimensions of sensibility are probed by its exercise abroad. On one level, the spectacle of foreign poverty and misery convinces the traveller of the superiority of the British constitution more powerfully and reassuringly than can any such spectacles at home. But this easy equation between bad government and widespread poverty can prove troubling. Yorick, trying to evade charity towards the monk at Calais, remarks that 'the unfortunate of our own country, surely, have the first rights; and I have left thousands in distress upon our own shore'.[54] This statement is of course complicated by Yorick's dubious motives, but its impact is still powerful.

In *Another Traveller!* Coriat as first-person narrator is imbued with none of the sexual or moral ambiguities of motive which characterize Yorick; he is whole-heartedly philanthropic, and candidly aware of the shortcomings of British society in comparison with the generally well-regulated legal and charitable affairs of the Netherlands (whether Catholic or Protestant). As we have seen, Coriat Junior is also well aware that such candour, or freedom from national prejudice, renders him liable to accusations of disloyalty and popery; yet he is stalwartly open-minded, and subsumes questions of religious difference into a sympathetic universality:

rail at the believer, wrapt up in a particular-fashioned habit, as long as we like, we can never strike him of something that lies under it—That by which so many good people are daily benefitted, must needs be praise-worthy—and, indeed, to which, as to articles of faith, we must subscribe whether we will, or no.[55]

The 'offices, or acts of mercy' built into the daily pattern of monastic life are presented as a moral paradigm for society in general, and for the sympathetic traveller in particular, promoting general welfare and individual self-definition: 'For to contemplate the condition of others, are the only means by which I shall arrive at the knowledge of myself.'[56]

---

[53] Ibid. i. 321. [54] Sterne, *A Sentimental Journey*, 73.
[55] *Another Traveller!*, i. 318. [56] Ibid. i. 330–3.

To complicate the issue further, Coriat Junior, with his energetic ability to examine both sides of any question, is not so un-English as to be unaware of the evident shortcomings of the Roman Catholic faith: its superstition, irrationality, and, most affecting of all, its anti-social cloistering of beautiful young women better suited to a life of marriage and motherhood. As we have seen, *Another Traveller!* presents few issues as straightforward, and stresses the difficulty of reform. Paterson's text is significant, rather, because it shows us an extremely 'ordinary' citizen of the middling sort engaging with a complex set of political, social, and moral issues which the wave of European travel literature in the 1760s was thrusting into the public consciousness, at a time when domestic issues of political justice and freedom were also powerfully in the public eye. Without providing easy answers ('Let observation point out the evil, and wisdom plan the remedy'[57]), Coriat Junior, merely by engaging with the issues he raises, is staking his claim, and that of his class, to a central position in public life. Quite apart from the imaginative vigour of *Another Traveller!* and its vivid rendering of eighteenth-century literary life and travel, Paterson's text demands our attention. The 'foreign-ness' of Coriat Junior's sentimental journey, and the thoroughgoing social and political curiosity of its eccentric narrator, provide a dynamic sense of cultural relativity. Paradoxically, the generically liminal status of *Another Traveller!* has been a major cause of its critical neglect; yet this very indeterminacy creates its imaginative and polemical energy.

[57] Ibid. i. 280.

10 'Oral Tradition': The Evolution of an Eighteenth-Century Concept

Nicholas Hudson

'Oral tradition' is now established as a familiar and authoritative concept of literary and ethnographic scholarship. To us, it is perfectly plausible that cultures without writing can have a well-developed heritage of poetry, customs, and laws. For most scholars in the Renaissance and seventeenth century, however, it was absurd to suggest that any substantial body of knowledge or literature could be preserved without the use of letters. While the term 'tradition' did have an embryonic form in works of Catholic theologians, who used it to describe the unwritten doctrines of the Church, there was, as yet, no clear conception of how 'orality' could serve as a reliable foundation for an organized society and a cultural legacy.

'Oral tradition', in a recognizably modern form, is a coinage of the eighteenth century. Yet even in the eighteenth century this concept was controversial and its acceptance slow and uncertain. Two major landmarks in the ultimate acceptance of oral tradition as a legitimate scholarly idea are works that remain relatively neglected in our time, despite their immense historical significance. These are James Macpherson's *Poems of Ossian* and Robert Wood's *Essay on the Original Genius and Writings of Homer*, both published in the 1760s. Macpherson and Wood made bold claims for the powers of oral tradition — claims that were hotly disputed by major intellectual figures of the time. Their ideas none the less signalled a new willingness to believe that pre-literate peoples are not merely lawless savages, but can possess a valuable cultural and artistic heritage. It is the purpose of this chapter to trace the various intellectual currents that made possible this new understanding of oral tradition.

European society was itself predominantly oral until the sixteenth century, when a steep rise in literacy and the dissemination of printed books began to revolutionize Western thought and culture. Given the proximity of Renaissance Europeans to their traditional roots, it might be assumed that they would be acutely aware of the oral world being transformed by Gutenberg's invention. In fact, 'oral tradition' was almost never used in this era to describe non-literate cultures or the legends and stories passed down through generations by word of mouth. That this modern idea of oral tradition developed only slowly should not surprise us. Major social changes, taking place over many decades, are often easier to discern in retrospect. And, as Marshall McLuhan noted, our consciousness of media often lags well behind the pace of technological change: European intellectuals achieved a clear perception of 'orality' only after their own world had been engulfed in print.[1] Habituated to a world filled with books, Europeans recognized the profound chasm that separated their forms of language and thought from those of non-literate peoples.

Significantly, the first use of the term 'oral tradition' was not to describe bardic poetry or the customs of non-literate people. Rather, this was originally a theological expression. Catholic theologians of the Renaissance developed the concept of an 'unwritten' tradition, preserved by the Church, and of equal authority to the written Word of the Bible. The notion of an unwritten legacy of doctrines was, as George H. Tavard has indicated, an innovation specifically of fifteenth-century thinkers like Thomas Netter, and not of theologians in some earlier era: 'Neither the Fathers nor the medieval theologians believed that elements of the Apostles' doctrine had been transmitted orally from generation to generation.'[2] The so-called '*dual-source* theory of doctrine', which maintained that truths of Christianity came down through both the Bible and oral tradition, became a central dogma of the Counter-Reformation, and was upheld in an early session of the Council of Trent in 1546.[3] The Protestant rejoinder was '*sola Scriptura*', the so-called 'formal principle' of the Lutheran Reformation. Luther's teaching was that the written word of God was the fountainhead of religious knowledge, and that all other doctrines had authority only in so far as they were consonant with the Bible.[4]

During the sixteenth and seventeenth centuries, the term 'tradition' or 'oral tradition' was used almost entirely in this theological context. According to the *Le Grand Dictionnaire de l'Académie Française* (1694), for example, '*Tradition* . . . se dit principlement dans les matières de religion.'[5] Moreover, the theological idea of oral tradition bears only a partial similarity to our modern literary or ethnographic concept. The

[1] See Marshall McLuhan, *The Gutenberg Galaxy* (Toronto, 1962), 130.

[2] George H. Tavard, *Holy Writ or Holy Church: The Crisis of Faith of the Protestant Reformation* (New York, 1959), 56.

[3] See *Canons and Decrees of the Council of Trent*, trans. H. J. Schroeder, OP (Rockford, Ill., 1978), 4th session (8 Apr. 1546), 17.

[4] For discussion of this conflict in Christian thought of the Reformation, see Timothy George, *Theology of the Reformers* (Nashville, Tenn., 1988), 79–86; Alister E. McGrath, *Reformation Thought: An Introduction* (Oxford, 1988), 95–110.

[5] *Le Grand Dictionnaire de l'Académie Française* (2nd impression, Paris, 1695; facs. repr. Geneva, 1968). See also the definitions of 'tradition' in Edward Phillips, *The New World of English Words* (London, 1658), and John Kersey's *Dictionarium Anglo-Britannicum* (London, 1708).

theological term, as Thomas White explained in his defence of this doctrine in 1654, was properly defined as an 'Oral, or mental tradition'. White called this tradition 'mental' because he considered it to be more than a set of verbal formulations. It was engrained in the thought of all Catholics, 'a living word written in their Breasts, which governs all their actions relating to religion'.[6] White acknowledged that the unwritten directions of Christ and his disciples had not been preserved word for word. But the fundamental *meaning* of their words had been sustained by the traditions of Catholicism. 'Oral tradition' referred to 'a sense delivered not in set words, but settled in the Auditors' hearts, by hundreds of different expressions explicating the same meaning'.[7] Unlike modern scholars of oral tradition, therefore, White placed no importance on repeated epithets, standard phrases, or any other verbal devices.[8] He thought of oral tradition as a legacy of beliefs and practices that depended in no essential way on language. And he made no claim that this form of transmission was possible outside the special conditions that existed in the Church.

At least in insisting on the existence of their own unwritten heritage of doctrine and ritual, Catholic theologians laid the groundwork for later, secularized notions of oral tradition. As for Protestants of the seventeenth century, they poured scorn on the belief that any substantial legacy of knowledge could be preserved orally. In the words of John Tillotson, noted Anglican scholar and future Archbishop of Canterbury, 'we deny, That the Doctrine of Christian Religion could with any probable security have been conveyed down to us by the way of Oral Tradition'.[9] Protestants could appeal convincingly to what Edward Stillingfleet called 'the notorious uncertainty of meer Tradition'. 'I say, notorious,' declared Stillingfleet, 'because there never was any Tryal made of it, but it failed, even when it had the greatest Advantages.'[10] Reports from the New World, as Stillingfleet well knew, revealed that many peoples were without any system of writing except pictographs or other rudimentary forms of inscription. The almost universal impression of these pre-literate people—conveyed by both Protestant and Catholic travellers to the New World—was that they were ignorant barbarians, lost in a timeless fog of superstition and dream-like fables of the past. 'Letters are a thing so necessary to men', observed Francisco López de

---

[6] Thomas White, *An Apology for Rushworth's Dialogues* (Paris, 1654), 135.

[7] Ibid. 81.

[8] See Milman Parry, *The Traditional Epithet in Homer* (1928), in *The Making of Homeric Verse: The Collected Papers of Milman Parry*, ed. Adam Parry (Oxford, 1971), 1–190; Walter J. Ong, *Orality and Literacy* (London, 1982), 34.

[9] John Tillotson, *The Rule of Faith* (London, 1666), 38. Tillotson was replying to White and to a later work by John Sergeant, *Sure-footing in Christianity, or Rational Discourses on the Rule of Faith* (London, 1665).

[10] Edward Stillingfleet, *Scripture and Tradition Compared* (London, 1688), 23.

Gómara in his account of the Spanish conquest, 'that without them they are like true beasts.'[11] Without writing, agreed Samuel Purchas in his famous collection of travels, people are 'Brutish, Sauage, Barbarbous'. They had no history, laws, government or even 'society' of any kind.[12]

It cannot be said that these authors held anything approaching our idea of oral tradition. Nevertheless, in the background of these sceptical assessments of non-literate peoples were political and intellectual developments that would ultimately lead to a better appreciation of how history, social codes, and customs could be preserved without writing. As J. G. A. Pocock has shown, Puritans of the Civil War era commonly evoked the authority of an unwritten tradition of English customs and law—the 'Ancient Constitution'—to legitimize their own claims to power against the written laws of the king.[13] On the Continent, Protestant scholars such as Hugo Grotius and Samuel Pufendorf delineated the principles of an unwritten 'natural law' governing the conduct of nations and giving force to the mandates of statutory law.[14] Neither the 'Ancient Constitution' nor 'natural law' constitute versions of oral tradition: they were advanced by seventeenth-century scholars solely as forms of knowledge that supported or supplemented the written codes of a literate society. Nevertheless, as more Europeans accepted the notion that unwritten beliefs played a fundamental role in their own civilized world, they became more inclined to re-evaluate the assumption that non-literate peoples were utterly lawless and without history.

In the early eighteenth century, this re-evaluation gave rise to the idea of the 'noble savage'. This Enlightenment image of uncivilized innocence and wisdom implied some important doubts about the necessity of written language to maintain morality and law. In a fictionalized dialogue with a Huron chief named 'Adario', published in 1705, the Baron de Lahontan portrayed the native Americans as living efficiently and happily without writing. The Hurons are 'Natural Philosophers' living in virtue, and endowed with 'a perfect Mechanism' of 'Laws, Judges, and

---

[11] 'Vne chose si necessaire aux hômes que sans icelles il sont côme vraies bestes' (Francisco López de Gómara, *Histoire géneralle des Indes occidentales & terres neuues* (1554), trans. M. Fumée (Paris, 1569), ch. 114, fo. Kk2ᵛ).

[12] Samuel Purchas, *Purchas his Pilgrimes* (4 vols.; London, 1625), i. 176. On the importance of writing and literacy as marks of the superiority of Europeans to pre-literate peoples in the New World, see Michael Harbsmeier, 'Writing and the Other: Travellers' Literacy or Towards an Archeology of Orality', in Karen Schousboe and Morgens Trolle Larsen (eds.), *Literacy and Society* (Copenhagen, 1989), 197–228; Stephen Greenblatt, *Marvellous Possessions: The Wonder of the New World* (Chicago, 1991), 9–12.

[13] See J. G. A. Pocock, *The Ancient Constitution and the Feudal Law: A Study of English Historical Thought in the Seventeenth Century* (Cambridge, 1957); *The Machiavellian Moment: Florentine Political Thought and the Atlantic Republican Tradition* (Princeton, NJ, 1975), 333–60.

[14] See Hugo Grotius, *De jure belli ac pacis libri tres* (Paris, 1625); Samuel Pufendorf, *De jure naturae et gentium libri octo* (London, 1672).

Priests'.[15] When offered a lesson in writing, the noble Adario is disdainful. Had not writing introduced many of the corruptions of European society, including useless disputes, vanity, pernicious doctrines, and licentious *billets doux*? 'O! that cursed Writing;' exclaims the chief, 'that pernicious Invention of the *Europeans* . . . Calculated not for the Instruction but for the Perplexing of Men's Minds.'[16] In Lahontan's narrative, an unlettered society, governed by the unwritten laws of nature, is presented as an innocent alternative to European corruption.

Such was also the view of pre-literate nations adopted for satiric purposes by Swift in *Gulliver's Travels* (1726). In part 4 of the *Travels* we discover that the wise and peaceful Houyhnhnms 'have no Letters, and consequently, their Knowledge is all traditional'. These rational horses are not debilitated by their lack of writing because—happily free of the European pestilence of wars, lawyers, doctors, politicians, and scandalmongers—they have very little 'history' that needs to be recorded: 'there happening few Events of any Moment among a People so well united, naturally disposed to every Virtue, wholly governed by Reason, and cut off from all Commerce with other Nations; the historical Part is easily preserved without burthening their Memories.'[17] In Swift's work, therefore, the reliance of Europeans on writing reveals the proliferation of 'unnatural' needs and corrupt institutions in their allegedly 'advanced' society. Indeed, as Terry J. Castle has pointed out, the absurdity of the nations visited by Gulliver seems directly proportionate to their dependence on books and written documents.[18]

But did Lahontan and Swift intend to delineate the characteristics of an 'oral tradition'? Not really. Their primary purpose was satiric rather than ethnographic: they set out mischievously to upset European vanity, which was spurred by the assumption that literacy exemplified the superiority of Europeans over the native peoples of the New World. Such satiric rebuttals to European pride none the less mark an important shift in attitudes towards pre-literate peoples. Europeans of the early eighteenth century were more prepared than ever before to examine oral means of transmission as legitimate alternatives to written records.

An outstanding work in the development of this new ethnographic idea of 'oral tradition' was *Mœurs des sauvages amériquains* (1724), by Joseph François Lafitau. A Jesuit missionary who lived between 1712 and 1718 with the Mohawk, one of the Iroquois Five Nations, Lafitau shared the view of most previous commentators that oral tradition was

---

[15] Louis Armand de Lom d'Acre, Baron de Lahontan, *Voyages*, ed. Stephen Leacock (Ottawa, 1932), 218.
[16] Ibid. 333. [17] Jonathan Swift, *Gulliver's Travels* (Oxford, 1965), ch. 9, p. 273.
[18] See Terry J. Castle, 'Why the Houyhnhnms don't Write: Swift, Satire, and the Fear of the Text', *Essays in Literature*, 7 (1980), 31–44.

an extremely inefficient means of preserving history. Nevertheless, he dispelled the image of pre-literate peoples as lawless barbarians without government, organized religion, or arts. While the Iroquois have 'no letters', he observed in his account of native society, 'they have, however, a kind of sacred tradition which they are careful to conserve'.[19] He went on later to describe the importance of oral tradition in native government, and in the maintenance of common values and collective beliefs:

> It is affairs of state which carry off the principal attention . . . they are always occupied, among themselves, in reflecting on all that happens, in observing and deliberating endlessly over the least events, shaping the young people for business, teaching them the style of their councils, the oral tradition which they conserve of their country's history, of their ancestors' virtue and keeping alive in them that martial spirit which assures their tranquillity during peace and their superiority during war.[20]

In his observations on Iroquois life, Lafitau was able to add greatly to the knowledge of how oral cultures work. He noted how no single person or group was solely in charge of keeping alive the tribal beliefs and history, but that all participated by means of dancing, 'pantomime', and other communal ceremonies. Ritual, he perceived, played a central role in their lives, for everything from victory at war to 'the hair cutting and naming of a child' was accompanied by some sort of feast and celebration.[21]

Lafitau's grounding in the doctrinal concept of oral tradition, as propounded in Catholic theology, clearly influenced this description of how ritual and communal practice could form the basis for a workable system of laws and beliefs. Moreover, this missionary was among the earliest authors to present an image of life in oral cultures that would profoundly influence European ideas about literary history: the Iroquois, he testified, were particularly distinguished for their stirring and impassioned eloquence. He found classical precedents for the eloquence of native orators at their assemblies. Their speeches did not 'consist of long harangues, composed on the model of Demosthenes or Cicero', he mused; 'the Iroquois, like the Lacedaemonians, wish a quick and concise discourse. Their style is, however, full of figures of speech and quite metaphorical; it is varied according to the different nature of business.'[22] Such comparisons between native eloquence and the highest achievements of European oratory became thoroughly conventional in later descriptions of native American life. According to the Abbé Raynal, in his *Histoire philosophique et politique des établissemens et du commerce des Européens dans*

---

[19] Joseph François Lafitau, *Customs of the American Indians*, trans. William N. Fenton and Elizabeth L. Moore (2 vols.; Toronto, 1974–7), i. 81.
[20] Ibid. 308.   [21] See ibid. 325.   [22] Ibid. 298.

les deux Indes (1770), even the ordinary language of native Americans was bold and figurative in the style of the epic:

Their metaphors were bolder and more familiar to them in common conversation, than they are even in epic poetry in the European languages. Their speeches in public assemblies, especially, were full of images, energy, and pathos. No Greek or Roman orator ever spoke, perhaps, with more strength and sublimity than one of their chiefs.[23]

This tendency to 'classicize' American native peoples, who were increasingly imagined as latter-day Greeks and Romans, reflects their generally more sympathetic treatment by European travellers and historians of the eighteenth century. It also reveals the changing understanding of the classical ages. More and more scholars were willing to acknowledge that the father of the epic, Homer himself, may well have owed his vigorous language to the relatively primitive state of his own society. In *An Enquiry into the Life and Writings of Homer* (1735), a popular book both in Britain and on the Continent, Thomas Blackwell argued that Homer's Greece was just entering the first stages of civilization, when the language retained much of 'its *Original, amazing, metaphorical* Tincture'.[24] That Homer may even have been *illiterate* is, significantly, not mentioned by Blackwell. This was still an egregious proposition to make about the founder of the Western literary tradition. Nevertheless, yet another piece had been added to the emerging picture of ancient literature and oral cultures. A rising generation of authors, nurtured on accounts of the fiery eloquence of native speakers, were increasingly willing to speculate that oral tradition could give rise to literature of outstanding merit.

Prominent in this generation was a young Highlander named James Macpherson, who was a student in the early 1750s at Marischal College in Aberdeen, where Thomas Blackwell was Principal. After leaving Aberdeen, Macpherson came under the influence of Scottish scholars who were expounding the 'primitivist' thesis that pre-literate cultures were fertile ground for the growth of impassioned, 'epic' language. This was a position taken, for instance, by the Edinburgh rhetorician and man of letters Hugh Blair, among the most enthusiastic supporters of Macpherson's project to collect and translate fragments of ancient Highland verse. 'An American chief, at this day,' declared Blair, 'harangues at the head of his tribe, in a more bold metaphorical style, than a modern European would adventure to use in an Epic poem.'[25] Surrounded by

[23] Guillaume-Thomas-François Raynal, *A Philosophical and Political History of the Settlements and Trade of the Europeans in the East and West Indies* (3 vols.; Glasgow, 1811), iii. 79.
[24] Thomas Blackwell, *An Enquiry into the Life and Writings of Homer* (London, 1735), 46.
[25] Hugh Blair, *A Critical Dissertation on the Poems of Ossian* (London, 1763), 2.

such sentiments and urged on by the Scottish literati, Macpherson produced a landmark in the history of the developing concept of oral
tradition, *The Poems of Ossian* (1762–3).

According to Macpherson, these were the translated works of the
third-century Highland bard Ossian, including the epics *Fingal* and
Temora. In his initial statements, he claimed that they had been transmitted down the centuries largely by oral tradition.[26] It was daring and
controversial to claim that so much material could have been preserved
in this way. Indeed, as we will consider, even Macpherson and his allies
retreated from this position in the face of doubts raised by his prodigious
adversary, Samuel Johnson. Their wavering reveals the continuing
doubts of authors—even those sympathetic to oral tradition—about the
possibility of substantial literature emerging before the dawn of literacy.

Macpherson described the primarily *oral* basis of the Highlands poetic
tradition in his 'Dissertation concerning the Antiquity, &c. of the Poems
of Ossian the Son of Fingal', which prefaced the epic *Fingal* (1762). 'The
use of letters was not known in the North of Europe till long after the
institution of the bards,' he wrote; 'the records of the families of their
patrons, their own, and more ancient poems were handed down by
tradition.'[27] How could these bards remember so much? Macpherson,
not knowing the mnemonic use of epithets and other formulae, argued
that the harmony and cadence of ancient Celtic verse made it easy to
remember:

Each verse was so connected with those which preceded or followed it, that if one
line had been remembered in a stanza, it was almost impossible to forget the rest.
The cadences followed in so natural a gradation, and the words were so adapted
to the common turn of voice, after it is raised to a certain key, that it was almost
impossible, from a similarity of sound, to substitute one word for another.[28]

The Ossian poems, he contended, were not only outstanding works of
literature, but provided an accurate account of history in third-century
Scotland. He harshly criticized those who consider 'every thing, that is
not committed to writing, fabulous'.[29]

Macpherson was not claiming that these bards had been responsible
for preserving the Ossian poems even down to the present age. According
to his notes to *Temora* (1763), the bards became 'extinct after they
became a nuisance'.[30] Ejected from the noble homes where they origin-

---

[26] Macpherson's 'translations' certainly had some basis in the actual oral tradition of Scotland, as
pointed out by Fiona J. Stafford, *The Sublime Savage: A Study of James Macpherson and the Poems
of Ossian* (Edinburgh, 1988), 13–14.

[27] James Macpherson, *Fingal, an Ancient Epic Poem in Six Books* (London, 1762), p. xii.

[28] Ibid. [29] Ibid., p. xiii.

[30] James Macpherson, *Temora, an Ancient Epic Poem* (London, 1763), 113 n.

ally resided, the bards wandered the Highlands, contriving supernatural fables to amuse the vulgar, and adding their own corrupt additions to the compositions of Ossian. Among Macpherson's major challenges as an editor, he said, was to purify the poems of Ossian from the dross of interpolations by later bards. He sought these poems among ordinary Highlanders, none of whom knew all of Ossian's poetry, but could repeat fragments. Macpherson reassembled the fragments into their original form, guided by his intuition for 'the spirit of Ossian'.[31]

Macpherson's 'oral tradition' was, therefore, handed down by a whole culture of story-telling, not by any single group. In this way, it corresponded roughly to the Catholic idea of an oral tradition carried on by the whole body of believers, or to what Lafitau had observed about the transmission of Iroquois customs and beliefs by the entire tribe. But was this defence of the oral tradition of the Highlands acceptable to Macpherson's contemporaries? Even Macpherson, in fact, seemed finally to have doubts about the bold claims made in the preface to *Fingal*. A year later, in his opening 'Dissertation' on *Temora*, Macpherson evinced a scepticism with unwritten histories that seems similar, at first sight, to the scepticism of his critics. 'The Romans give the first and, indeed, the only authentic accounts of the northern nations,' he declared. 'Destitute of the use of letters, they themselves had no means of transmitting their history to posterity.'[32] This appears to be in direct contradiction to his statements in *Fingal*, where he defended the reliability of an oral tradition. But Macpherson went on to make an exception for the Highland traditions. Oral tradition could only be continuous and reliable, he argued, when a people was isolated from all 'intermixture' with foreigners. Such was the case with the inhabitants of the wild regions of northern Britain. Shielded from the corrupting influence of foreign stories and language, 'the ancient traditional accounts of the genuine origin of the Scots have been handed down without interruption'.[33]

But others, even some sympathetic Scots, were less willing to exempt the Ossian poems from their general distrust of oral tradition. Any mention of the Highland tradition was conspicuously absent from William Robertson's general rejection of unwritten histories in *The History of America* (1770). 'From the experience of all nations,' wrote this

[31] Ibid. 144 n. [32] Ibid., p. ii.
[33] Ibid., p. xxxiii. It is possible that Macpherson had some ulterior motive to argue that the oral traditions of the Highland could be relied on while others could not. He seems to have been particularly concerned to discredit the oral traditions of the Irish. According to these legends, not only the Ossian legends, but the whole Highland people derived from Eire. In the 'Dissertation' on *Temora*, therefore, Macpherson alluded with great asperity to the 'monstrous' fables of the Irish bards. Only the Highland legends, he insisted, could be trusted (see ibid., p. xxxiv). Macpherson's views on this and other subjects may have been influenced by Dr John Macpherson, a minister on the Isle of Skye, whom the editor of Ossian visited and whose knowledge of Celtic antiquities he greatly respected.

170 Nicholas Hudson

Scottish historian, referring explicitly to the Aztecs, 'it is manifest, that the memory of past transactions can neither be long preserved, nor be transmitted with any fidelity, by tradition.'[34] And the greatest sceptical philosopher of the century, David Hume, finally surrendered to his doubts about the authenticity of the Ossian poems. Hume had sought diligently for proof of the antiquity of the works translated by Macpherson. But in an unpublished work on the Ossian poems written sometime after 1775, he acknowledged that the claim for the transmission of two third-century epics by oral tradition contradicted the only reliable measure of truth—human experience: 'will any man pretend to bring testimony to prove, that above twenty thousand verses have been transmitted, by tradition and memory, during more than fifteen hundred years; that is, above fifty generations, according to the ordinary course of nature?' In Hume's opinion, the Highlanders not only lacked the means to transmit poetry over the centuries, but were insufficiently civilized to produce epic poetry. They were a people 'who, during twelve centuries, at least, of that period, had no writing, no alphabet; and who, even in the other three centuries, made very little use of that imperfect alphabet for any purpose'. He went on immediately to comment on 'the imperfections of government' among the ancient Caledonians, their 'internal hostility', and the primitive state of their agriculture.[35]

If Le Bon David finally rejected the possibility of whole epics passing down through an oral tradition, one can hardly be surprised by the incredulity of Samuel Johnson, who shared much of Hume's sceptical outlook but none of his loyalty to Scots. Johnson's famous charge in *Journey to the Western Isles of Scotland* (1775) that Macpherson had merely forged the Ossian poems has been ascribed by some modern commentators to little more than an irrational hatred of everything Scottish. But Johnson's case against Macpherson was grounded on a major premiss in his linguistic thought—the very premiss that motivated his monumental labour of the 1755 *Dictionary of the English Language*. Consistent with the positions outlined in his *Dictionary* and elsewhere, Johnson denied that language and literature could achieve any level of refinement before the introduction of letters.[36] The very language of the Ossian poems showed that they were the product of a modern, *literate* culture.

[34] William Robertson, *The History of America* (11th edn., London, 1818), iii. 277.

[35] David Hume, 'Of The Authenticity of Ossian's Poems', in *Philosophical Works*, ed. T. H. Green and T. H. Grose (4 vols.; London, 1882–6; facs. repr. Scientia Verlag Aalen, 1964), iv. 428. On Hume's changing views on the authenticity of the Ossian poems, see Ernest Campbell Mossner, *The Forgotten Hume: Le Bon David* (New York, 1943), 82–102; David Raynor, 'Ossian and Hume', in Howard Gaskill (ed.), *Ossian Revisited* (Edinburgh, 1991), 147–63.

[36] See Johnson's Preface to *A Dictionary of the English Language*, where he describes the 'wild and barbarous jargon' that existed while words 'were unfixed by any visible signs' (in *Samuel Johnson*, ed. Donald Greene (Oxford, 1984), 308).

Absolutely central to Johnson's case against the authenticity of the *Poems of Ossian*, therefore, was his controversial assertion that 'Earse never was a written language'.[37] Having no written form, he contended, Scots Gaelic could not have been the language of an epic or of any substantial poetry, beyond popular ballads. He called Welsh and Irish 'cultivated tongues' because they had achieved a standardized orthography—precisely what he had aimed to establish for English by means of his *Dictionary*. Indeed, 'the Welsh, two hundred years ago, insulted their English neighbours for the instability of their orthography'. Scots Gaelic or 'Earse', on the other hand, 'merely floated in the breath of the people'. For this reason, it could 'receive little improvement'.[38] The orality that Blair and others of the 'primitivist' school thought so advantageous to the poetic power of language was treated by Johnson as its major limitation.

Macpherson's work, as I have argued, stands as a landmark in the developing concept of oral tradition. And Johnson's critique of Macpherson, despite its dross of anti-Scottish prejudice, represents an important and early description of the beneficial effects of 'literacy' on language. Strongly anticipating the work of modern scholars of literacy, such as Jack Goody, Johnson analysed how literacy facilitates the improvement of language towards a form suitable to modern poetry and *belles-lettres*: writing makes the spoken form of language available for analysis and comparison; it gives speakers an understanding of how their tongue has changed and improved over the centuries; it fosters a class of teachers and intellectuals who compete for the most striking manner of expression.[39] For all these reasons, argued Johnson, the kind of poetic language found in Macpherson's 'translations' of Ossian could not possibly have existed in an oral culture, such as he believed the third-century Highlands to be.[40]

In his assumption that great poetry is produced only by literate cultures, Johnson was wrong: we now know that oral cultures can produce—and are even especially suited to produce—the kind of ritualistic, sensual language admired by modern literate people as 'poetic'. But Johnson was essentially correct in pointing to writing and literacy as major factors in the cultivation of modern forms of expression. Johnson and Macpherson, despite their intense antagonism, were in fact partners

---

[37] Samuel Johnson, *A Journey to the Western Isles of Scotland*, ed. Mary Lascelles, vol. ix of *The Yale Edition of the Works of Samuel Johnson* (New Haven, Conn., 1971), 114.

[38] Ibid. 115.

[39] See ibid. 115–16. Johnson's analysis of the effects of literacy on the development of language is comparable with that of Jack Goody in *The Domestication of the Savage Mind* (Cambridge, 1977), 44.

[40] Johnson's observation that the language of Macpherson's poems bore the marks of a modern, literate style was corroborated by Hume, who deemed that 'this Erse poetry has an insipid correctness, and regularity, and uniformity, which betrays a man without genius, that has been acquainted with the productions of civilised nations' (*Philosophical Works*, iv. 417).

in defining the difference between 'oral' and 'literate' language. Macpherson delineated the possibility of a poetic tradition passing down through a whole culture, where every individual was an agent in that tradition, and where the basic content of the poetry was preserved by the mnemonic resources of verse. Johnson described the ways in which writing releases language from the particular 'occasion' of its utterance, facilitating its refinement in literate culture.

As the champion of literacy in this debate, Johnson still had the intellectual prejudices of his time on his side. The Scottish antiquarians who rose to Macpherson's defence were deeply insulted by the allegation that Highland culture had been illiterate until the eighteenth century. Illiteracy remained, even as it generally remains today, a cultural stigma of blackest hue, a shameful badge of ignorance and barbarity. Thus, Johnson's charges precipitated a shift of focus away from the issue of oral tradition, and towards the question of whether Ossian's culture possessed writing. Macpherson's advocates did not entirely abandon the case for the reliability of oral tradition. In a book-length reply to Johnson's *Journey to the Western Isles of Scotland*, Donald M'Nicol tried to show why tradition was 'not of that vague and uncertain nature which Dr. *Johnson* represents it to be'.[41] But in M'Nicol's work, as in a later defence of Macpherson by John Clark, the new priority was to prove that the third-century Highlanders *were* literate. Aiming to make ancient Scotland look more like Augustan Rome, and less like the wilds of Canada, M'Nicol and Clark argued that the Highlanders preserved their poetic heritage in *both* oral recitations and written records. The bards were not unlettered 'savages', like the American chiefs, but highly educated literati who had trained in bardic academies.[42]

This new focus on the *literate* heritage of Scotland was intended, in part, to legitimize Macpherson's belated claim to possess a chestful of written fragments of Ossian's poetry. Macpherson's allies also seemed uncomfortable with the prospect of defending the fidelity of an oral tradition. This prospect remained daunting to authors still imbued with their culture's distrust of unwritten traditions. In Johnson's view, however, the Scots were strategically unwise in insisting that Ossian's works had been preserved in writing as well as song. 'If [Macpherson] had not talked unskilfully of *manuscripts*,' he observed in 1775, 'he might have fought with oral tradition much longer.'[43] Johnson was, of course, being snide: he meant that Macpherson could have continued his subterfuge

[41] Donald M'Nicol, *Remarks on Dr. Samuel Johnson's Journey to the Hebrides* (London, 1779), 223–4.

[42] See ibid. 362–3; John Clark, *An Answer to Mr. Shaw's Inquiry* (Edinburgh, 1781), 26–8.

[43] James Boswell, *Life of Johnson*, ed. G. B. Hill, rev. L. F. Powell (6 vols.; Oxford, 1934–64), iii. 310.

longer if he had not created the difficulty of producing non-existent documents. Yet Johnson's statement also signals an important change in the intellectual climate of the time. Even the Great Cham, redoubtable champion of literacy, was acknowledging that oral tradition was at least an *arguable* notion.[44] Macpherson's *Poems of Ossian* appeared right at the time when this concept was widely entering critical and historical discourse outside theological literature. For, by 1775, the case had been strongly made that Homer, the first and greatest of epic poets, belonged to an 'oral tradition'.

This was the position advanced by the English traveller and antiquarian Robert Wood in *An Essay on the Original Genius and Writings of Homer*, written in 1767 and published in 1769. Wood's claim was not entirely unprecedented. Even in classical times, the possibility that Homer was illiterate had been brandished as a shocking riposte to the hegemony of Greek values and institutions. In *Against Apion*, a first-century attack on the alleged slanders of the Greeks against the Jews, Flavius Josephus alleged that the much-vaunted Homer did not even know his letters, an invention that the backward Greeks adopted only slowly.[45] This portrait of an illiterate Homer, so insulting to the dignity of ancient literature, was recirculated by the 'Moderns' during the *querelle des ancients et modernes* of the late seventeenth and early eighteenth centuries.[46] In the *Scienza nuova*, Vico implied that Homer was ignorant at least of alphabetical writing (though his heroic world widely used emblems and hieroglyphics).[47] Rousseau questioned Homer's literacy in his *Essai sur l'origine des langues*, which was probably composed in the late 1750s.[48] But no one before Wood had constructed a detailed case for

---

[44] In his *Dictionary*, Johnson recognized the non-theological significance of the word 'tradition' to mean any oral transmission of ideas: 'The act or practice of delivering accounts from mouth to mouth without written memorials; communication from age to age.' His illustrations for this definition were none the less both theological—from works by Hooker and Milton. Moreover, the citation from Milton categorically rejects belief in the faithful transmission of Christian doctrine without writing.

[45] See Flavius Josephus, *Against Apion*, in *Works*, trans. William Whiston (Baltimore, 1839), bk. 1, ch. 2, p. 580.

[46] On iconoclastic views of Homer during the *querelle*, see J. A. Davison, 'The Homeric Question', in Alan J. B. Wace and Frank H. Stubbings (eds.), *A Companion to Homer* (London, 1962), 242–4; Kristi Simonsuuri, *Homer's Original Genius: Eighteenth-Century Notions of the Early Greek Epic* (Cambridge, 1979), 19–45.

[47] See *The New Science of Giambattista Vico*, trans. Thomas Goddard Bergin and Max Harold Fisch (Ithaca, NY, 1948), bk. 3, 'Discovery of the True Homer'. In a recent article, Patrick H. Hutton argues that Vico 'prepared the way for historical inquiry into collective mentalities, collective memory, historical psychology, and oral tradition' ('The Problem of Oral Tradition in Vico's Historical Scholarship', *Journal of the History of Ideas*, 53 (1992), 3–23). While there is merit in Hutton's thesis, it is complicated by the problem that Vico did not believe that ancient society was ever entirely 'oral', for he believed that the original language of ancient peoples was 'mute'—that is, consisting of heroic emblems.

[48] See Jean-Jacques Rousseau, *Essay on the Origin of Languages*, ch. 6, in *On the Origin of Language*, trans. John H. Moran and Alexander Gode (Chicago, 1966), 23–4.

Homer's 'orality', or had proposed that this poet had even derived some *advantage* from being a part of a pre-literate world.

Wood thus has a strong claim to originality. Yet it is no accident that his work appeared at this point in history. Many of his arguments were inspired by the same intellectual trends that we have seen building in eighteenth-century thought. He mentioned Macpherson's *Poems of Ossian* as important evidence that oral traditions had spawned worthy literature in many parts of the world. 'The ingenious editor of Fingal', in his view, was a kind of latter-day Pisistratus, who had collected 'curious fragments of ancient tradition' and reduced them to an orderliness required by the 'taste and judgement' of a modern, literate age.[49] He was also clearly acquainted with eighteenth-century accounts of pre-literate societies in the New World. These reports convinced Wood that nations suffered far less from their lack of alphabetical writing than some travellers had assumed in the early years of exploration and conquest in the Americas. Wood denied that literacy was a mark or prerequisite of 'civilization': 'the Mexicans,' he remarked, 'though a civilised people, had no alphabet.'[50] It did seem 'very striking', as Wood admitted, that Homer could 'acquire, retain, and communicate, all he knew, without the aid of letters'. But the capacity of oral transmission had been underrated: 'upon comparing the fidelity of oral tradition, and the powers of memory, with the Poet's knowledge, we find the first two much greater and the latter much less, than we are apt to imagine.'[51] The oral traditions of Mexico and 'the bards and fileas' of Ireland proved that the history of a people could be preserved quite faithfully without letters.[52] The ancient world so comprehensively described by Homer showed a high level of organization before the introduction of writing. It revealed that 'legislation was considerably advanced before the written laws were in use'.[53] Indeed, as Wood reminded his readers, many *English* legislators were illiterate only a century before.[54]

Much as eighteenth-century travellers had found order and nobility in oral societies of the Americas, Wood showed how the similarly remote world of Homer also functioned without letters. It was a world filled with ritual and speech-making, where a sacrifice or priestly chant took the place of a written treaty or memorial inscription.[55] It was also a world where language was fiery and metaphoric, just as at tribal assemblies in the New World. In Homer's time, he argued, 'speaking and singing would differ little'. 'The simple tones of Nature' would have been stronger, for language had not yet been enervated by 'the cold and

---

[49] Robert Wood, *An Essay on the Original Genius and Writings of Homer* (London, 1824), 169.
[50] Ibid. 153.   [51] Ibid. 157.   [52] Ibid. 158.
[53] Ibid. 157.   [54] Ibid. 151.   [55] See ibid. 153.

languid circumlocution' of 'artificial language' in literate society.[56]
According to Wood, language had been more musical and expressive
near its primitive origins—a view widely taken in previous decades by
philosophers such as Condillac and Rousseau.[57] Most important to
Wood was that Homer derived his knowledge not from books, but from
the real world. The great merit of the Homeric epics, in his view, lay in
the accuracy and detail of Homer's observations on the ancient world—
not in his learning or his grandeur, but in his power of *mimesis*.[58]

Initial reactions to Wood in Britain were dominated by a mixture of
scorn and indifference. Neither Johnson nor any of the participants in the
Ossian controversy so much as mentioned Wood's *Essay*, despite its
professed relevance to Macpherson's rediscovery of the 'Homer of the
Highlands'. But Wood's ideas were taken very seriously on the Continent, particularly in Germany. Two of the greatest German classicists of
the generation, G. A. Heyne and F. A. Wolf, applauded Wood's 'brilliant
audacity' in arguing for Homer's orality.[59] In *Prolegomena ad Homerum*
(1795) Wolf acknowledged that the Englishman had inspired his own
position, set forth in Teutonic detail and depth, that Homer belonged to
an oral tradition. With Wolf's stamp of approval, 'oral tradition' finally
became something more than an eccentric and slightly whimsical proposition. It achieved the status of a respectable, weighty (though still
controversial) tenet of philological and ethnographic scholarship. It was
Wolf's *Prolegomena* that set the tone for Homeric scholarship in the
nineteenth century. In the coming decades, classicists propounded the
view not only that the author of the *Iliad* belonged to an oral tradition,
but that 'Homer' was really only the name given to the whole legion of
bards who sang the old stories in the pre-literate ages of Greece.[60]

Neither Wood nor Wolf went quite this far. In other ways, as well, their
idea of oral tradition fell short of our modern understanding of this term.
Perhaps most important, no eighteenth-century scholar discerned the
importance of stock epithets and other verbal formulas in allowing the
bard to improvise variations on traditional stories in metrical verse. This
integral device in oral transmission would remain obscure until Milman
Parry's investigation of Serbo-Croat heroic verse early in our century. To
the ears of Macpherson or Wood, the 'orality' of ancient language
was signalled by its impassioned, figurative, and disconnected quality,

[56] Ibid. 171–2.
[57] See Étienne Bonnot, Abbé de Condillac, *Essay on the Origin of Human Knowledge* (1746), pt. 2,
sect. 1, ch. 3; Rousseau, *Essay on the Origin of Languages*, ch. 4.
[58] See Wood, *Essay*, 179 and *passim*.
[59] F. A. Wolf, *Prolegomena to Homer*, trans. James E. G. Zetzel (Princeton, NJ, 1985), 71. On
Heyne, see Zetzel's introduction, 14.
[60] See Davison, 'The Homeric Question', 245–65.

untempered by the sobering effects of literate culture. Stock epithets merely contributed to the grander sound of poetic language favoured by speakers at a more 'primitive' level of linguistic development. Nevertheless, these eighteenth-century scholars did apprehend the mnemonic importance of verse in general. And it was Macpherson and Wood, though so widely neglected in modern scholarship, who planted the seed that ultimately flowered into our modern concept of 'oral tradition'.

As I have argued, this seed germinated and ultimately flourished because it was planted in an intellectual culture that had become increasingly receptive to the possibility of organized societies and great poetry without the knowledge of letters. The key juncture in this process was the transferral of the concept of oral tradition from a theological to an ethnographic context, as exemplified by Lafitau's 1724 *Mœurs des sauvages amériquains.* Acceptance of the idea that oral tradition could serve as the basis of a highly organized society was bolstered by the concept of the 'noble savage', which entered strongly into European *belles-lettres* of the early eighteenth century. At a slightly later period, 'primitivist' theories in critical and rhetorical scholarship inspired the search for epic poetry in oral or largely oral societies. The history of 'oral tradition' thus exemplifies how new ideas can enter the discourse of a culture through a slow and tentative process influenced by numerous, interconnected fields of research. In the age of print, European literati gained a much clearer perception of an oral world that now seemed both immensely alien and endlessly intriguing.

11 *Sir Joshua's French Revolution*

RICHARD WENDORF

For more than four years, from 1786 to 1790, the Royal Academy failed to appoint a new Professor of Perspective, and Sir Joshua Reynolds, as the Academy's long-time President, argued that this vacancy had not only disrupted the institution's programme of instruction, but had become a public embarrassment to its members. Save an 'Infant Academy', he told his fellow Academicians, 'from the disgracefull appearance of expiring with the decrepitude of neglected old age'.[1] Reynolds was an old man himself at the time. A year earlier, having lost the sight of one eye and fearful of losing sight in the other, he had virtually abandoned his practice as a painter, completing a few commissions but rarely engaging in new ones. His retirement, however, was not without drama and incident, for he had been immersed for some time in a battle of wills at the Academy, in whose affairs he remained keenly interested. In the winter of 1789–90 he proposed that an Italian architect, Giuseppe Bonomi, be elected an Associate, an Academician, and subsequently the Academy's Professor of Perspective.

Much to Reynolds's surprise, his colleagues opposed their President's recommendations with both warmth and tenacity, and the ageing painter found himself—for the first time in his professional career—thwarted by what he soon came to believe was a hostile, impolite, and disloyal group of followers. His fellow Academicians did not like the fact that Bonomi was a foreigner, nor that Sir Joshua had proposed him as a favour to one of his own patrons, the Earl of Aylesford. They therefore elected a number of associates before finally turning to Bonomi (for whom Reynolds himself cast the deciding vote); and when, at a subsequent meeting, they refused to promote the Italian to full status as an Academician, and behaved in what Reynolds believed was an insolent fashion, the President resigned both from the chair and from the Academy itself.

Reynolds's actions—and those of his colleagues—quickly filled the pages of London's newspapers and pamphlets, with fierce partisanship on either side. For his part, the retired President consulted with his closest

---

[1] Frederick Whiley Hilles, *The Literary Career of Sir Joshua Reynolds* (Cambridge, 1936; repr. Hamden, Conn., 1967), 254. Unless otherwise indicated, all references to Reynolds's 'Apologia' are to this edition. I have, however, revised Hilles's method of transcribing. The words in square brackets are emendations; words in angled brackets were deleted in the manuscript.

friends and wrote his own heated vindication of his conduct at the Academy. He called it his 'Apologia', his 'Justification in the matter of Bonomi and the resignation of the Presidt's Chair',[2] but he neither completed nor published it, instead setting it aside after his colleagues, in a conciliatory mood and supported by the intercession of the King, beseeched him to resume his former duties and contrived a way for him to return to Somerset House while also saving face. He complied with their request, and died in office two years later.

Although the incident itself and the pamphlet war it generated held the attention of London society for several weeks, the Bonomi affair has been largely neglected by Reynolds's modern commentators. This fracas at the Royal Academy is unlikely to draw the attention of many art historians because it is a personal and institutional dispute not directly related to actual paintings; but even those interested in the relationship between individual works of art and the context in which they are created have been noticeably silent. Reynolds's biographers seem to be faintly embarrassed by the incident; the historians of the Royal Academy tend to treat it as yet another internecine quarrel in the early years of a fledgling institution.[3] Even Frederick Hilles, who carefully edited the 'Apologia' in 1936 (it has never been critically examined since then), remarked that it is 'worth reading, if only to illustrate Sir Joshua's state of mind at the time'.[4] Hilles reminds us of Edmond Malone's remark that Reynolds suffered 'little from disappointments, or what others would have thought mortifications',[5] and thus the painter's response to the treatment he received at the Royal Academy in the early months of 1790 marks an exception, in Hilles's eyes, to his normally acquiescent behaviour. This is surely true, and the incident marks—as I shall argue—the final, ironic chapter in a personal history that was otherwise characterized by a uniformity of easy, congenial behaviour (what was called both complaisance and complacency during Reynolds's lifetime). But there is much more at stake here as well, for the Bonomi affair reveals deep-seated fissures in the artistic, social, and political life of Britain during the final decade of the eighteenth century.

[2] Ibid. 249.
[3] See e.g. Sidney C. Hutchinson, *The History of the Royal Academy 1768–1968* (London, 1968), 69–70, who characterizes the affair as another 'pin-prick for Reynolds'. William Sandby (*The History of the Royal Academy of Arts from its Foundation in 1768 to the Present Time* (London, 1862), i. 167) took the matter more seriously but misjudged the underlying forces: 'That such a trifling circumstance should have estranged one so eminent in his art, and so revered by his brethren, would indeed have been a disaster to the rising Academy, and it is greatly to the credit of the Council that they immediately took measures for bringing about a reconciliation between them and the President.'
[4] Hilles, *Literary Career*, 176.
[5] Ibid.

The literal cause of the dispute was noted by James Northcote, who tells us that 'a spirit of resistance appeared' when Reynolds exerted his influence on behalf of Bonomi's election to a full Academicianship, 'owing, I believe, to some misconception, or to some informality on the part of Sir Joshua, in producing some drawings of Bonomi's'.[6] The question of *how* a candidate should best present his credentials for the Professorship had in fact been raised several months earlier by another Associate, Edward Edwards, who demanded permission to deliver a probationary lecture to be judged by five people, one of them not drawn from the Academy itself.[7] In response to this request, the Council ruled on 11 December that 'whoever is a Candidate to be an Academician, for the purpose of being hereafter Professor of Perspective: must produce a Drawing.—& inform Mr. Edwards, that there will be an Election for an Academician, on ye 10th. of Feby. next'.[8] Edwards refused to submit to this ruling, and Reynolds was therefore confident of Bonomi's chances for election when he presented the architect's drawings at the crucial meeting of the General Assembly two months later.

The minutes of the 10 February meeting are exceedingly brief, but they are accompanied by a folded note that has been inserted in the Academy's records at this point; it is in Reynolds's hand, and provides a relatively dispassionate view of the turbulent proceedings:

The Prest. open'd the business of the meeting, that it was to choose an Academician in the room of Mr. Meyer[,] that he need not repeat what he had so often said at former meetings, the necessity of filling up the place of Professor of Perspective which had been so long vacant to the great disgrace of the Academy. Mr. Bonomi as they all knew had been many Years a candidate for that place. And as the Academicians had at last taken this business up by Electing him an Associate for this very purpose, His drawings now were on the table for their inspection.—And as his rival Mr. Edwards appear'd to have declin'd the contest from his not sending a specimen, He hoped the Question before them would be, Ay. or No—was he, or was he not qualified for the office.——

Mr. Tyler demanded by whose authority the drawings were sent to the Academy.—

The President answer'd, by mine

Mr. Tyler then moved that those Drawings should be put out of the room,— this motion was seconded by Mr. Banks.

The Question being then put.—was carried by a great majority.——

The President afterwards endeavoured to explain, but being refused a hearing—he immediately proceeded to the Election &c &c.

---

[6] James Northcote, *The Life of Sir Joshua Reynolds* (2 vols.; 2nd edn., London, 1819), ii. 252.
[7] Council Minutes, 11 Dec. 1789.
[8] Ibid.

Fuseli received nineteen votes, Bonomi eight, Humphry two, Edwards and Bourgeois one each. In the run-off, Fuseli received twenty-one votes to Bonomi's nine and was duly elected an Academician.

Contrary to what Northcote writes, Reynolds was neither informal nor working under a 'misconception' when he introduced poor Bonomi's drawings to the General Assembly: he knew precisely what he was doing, and he shepherded the architect's candidacy just as carefully here as he had when Bonomi was elected an Associate. We know, for instance, that he wrote to a fellow Council member, John Bacon, in January, chastising him for declaring that he would vote for Edwards whether or not a drawing was produced: 'This report I have treated with the contempt such a Calumny deserves.'⁹ But the drawings, after all, are not the real issue, which centres on William Tyler's question ('by whose authority'?) and on Sir Joshua's answer: 'by mine'. Tyler and Banks are not merely questioning *whose* authority, but authority itself; and Reynolds, who has the authority of the Council's edict behind him, answers with a personal response—the kind of assurance that his colleagues had long trusted and accepted—rather than with a more accurate, institutional one.

Four weeks later, after an intense period of public sniping and private negotiation, the General Assembly passed Thomas Sandby's motion that

The President had acted in conformity with the intention of the Council, in directing Mr. Bonomi to send a Drawing or Drawings, to the General Meeting, to evince his being qualified for the Office of Professor of Perspective.

But the General Meeting not having been informed of this new regulation of the Council, nor having consented to it, (as the Laws of the Academy direct) The generality of the Assembly judged their introduction irregular, and consequently Voted for their being withdrawn.

Face was thus saved on both sides, and a committee was appointed to accompany Reynolds back to Somerset House, his 'declared objection to resuming the Chair being now done away'.¹⁰ This is true so far as it goes, but just as important to the aggrieved Reynolds was the *behaviour* of his antagonists during the preceding month. By refusing to bow, by refusing to defer even to the preliminary intercession of the King, Reynolds carefully defined the terms in which he would return and in which his integrity would be protected. At the same time, it was essential to Reynolds that his former colleagues apologize for the impoliteness and lack of deference with which he had been treated, and Northcote's account of the deliberations that took place in the early days of March

⁹ *Letters of Sir Joshua Reynolds*, ed. Frederick Whiley Hilles (Cambridge, 1929; repr. New York, 1976), 192.
¹⁰ General Assembly Minutes, 3 Mar. 1790.

almost suggests a meeting between a benign monarch and his wayward subjects:

They had an interview with him at his house in Leicester Square, and were received with great politeness; and every mark of respect was expressed by those who had hitherto been deemed least cordial to the interests of the President. . . . [Reynolds], after a handsome declaration of his gratitude for this honourable proceeding towards him, consented to resume the chair, and the whole of the delegates were invited to dine with him, in order to convince them that he returned to his office with sentiments of the most cordial amity.[11]

Both this scene of mutual liberality and the barebones account of the fateful meeting of the General Assembly in February are far removed from Reynolds's actual responses to the treatment he received at Somerset House. He wrote twice, heatedly, to Sir William Chambers, the Academy's treasurer and principal founder, in an attempt to justify both his resignation and his decision not to withdraw it.[12] At the same time, he drafted his vehement and sometimes inchoate 'Apologia', which reads radically differently from his polished, more even-tempered writings. Here, in a remarkable moment-by-moment rendering of how the meeting proceeded, Reynolds provides a clear picture of his apprehensions and responses. He tells us that he lost his confidence the minute he arrived at the Academy: 'A greater number than ever appeard[.] I suspected that this number was not in my favor . . . Instead of the members as usual stra[g]gling about the room, they were allready seated in perfect order and with the most profound silence.'[13] He searched for the candidates' drawings, and 'at last spyed those of Mr. Bonomi thrust in the darkest corner at the farthest end of the room'.[14] When Reynolds asked the Secretary, John Richards, to show the drawings to the assembly, Richards at first pretended not to hear the President. After a second request he rose and

in a sluggish manner walked to the other end of the room (passing the drawings) rung the bell and then stood with his folded arms in the middle of the room; Observing this extraordinary conduct of the Secretary, ⟨I found he had joined the Party which I considered as a rebellion in him⟩.[15]

Richards refused to touch the drawings himself, instead ringing a bell for the servant, who would have to 'mount that long flight of steps in order to move two drawings from one side of the room to the other'.[16] It was an act, Reynolds remarks, that revealed the 'rude spirit and gross manners of this cabal'.[17]

---

[11] Northcote, *Life*, ii. 259.   [12] Reynolds, *Letters*, 194–9.   [13] Hilles, *Literary Career*, 262.
[14] Ibid.   [15] Ibid.   [16] Ibid.   [17] Ibid.

Against Reynolds's restrained description of the events that followed—the dispassionate commentary left in the Minutes Book—we can place the personal account he included in the 'Apologia'.

As soon as the prst. sat down, ⟨Mr. Tyler⟩ an academician who is & has been long considered as the spokesman of the party demanded ⟨in a peremptory tone⟩ who ordered those drawings to be sent to the academy. The president answerd it was by his order. He asked a second time in a still more peremptory tone. The president said I did. I move that they be sent out or turned out of the room. Does any one second this motion—Mr. Barry rose with great indignation No says he Nobody can be found so lost to all shame as to dare to second so infamous a Motion. Drawings that would do honour to the greatest Academy that ever existed in the world &c. ⟨he said much more with great vehemence.⟩ Mr. Banks with great quietness seconded the motion On the shew of hands a great majority appeared for their expulsion The President then rose to explain to them the propriety of Mr. Bonomi's drawings being there, to oppose Mr. Edwards['s] which were expected and ordered by the Council but he was interrupted from various quarters that the business was over, they would hear no explanation, that it was irregular Mr. Copley said to talk upon business that was past & determin'd. The Prest. acquiesced and they proc[e]eded in the Election.[18]

It was, in short, a world turned upside down for the ageing President of the Academy: large numbers, ominous silence, feigned deafness, bad manners, collusion, and open rebellion. To everyone's astonishment, even James Barry rose to Reynolds's defence. As an anonymous pamphleteer remarked, 'He, who had formerly, with his fist clenched in the very face of the President, threatened him with a personal assault when his measures were right, now seemed disposed to offer the same insult to any one who should dare to oppose them, when they were wrong.'[19]

Reynolds's chief antagonist in this and other disputes at the Academy was Sir William Chambers. It was Chambers who framed the argument against Bonomi's election to the Professorship, and it was to Chambers that Reynolds gave the two heated letters he addressed to his fellow Academicians. In a sentence crossed out in the 'Apologia' he wrote, 'Sir Wm. little thinks that he is guilty of high treason against the Institution.'[20] Reynolds clearly did, and the language of the 'Apologia' is therefore heavily steeped in the discourses of warfare, rebellion, and political economy. Much of the President's rhetoric attempts to capture the conniving, virulent, and irrational behaviour of his antagonists. In arguing that an ingenious Associate (Edwards) could provide lectures on

[18] Ibid. 264–5.
[19] *Observations on the Present State of the Royal Academy: With Characters of Living Painters. By An Old Artist* (London, 1790), 8–9.
[20] Royal Academy MS Rey/3/90ᵛ (previously unpublished).

perspective in lieu of a Professor, and in employing 'the plural number (we)', Chambers reveals the fact that 'he had enlisted himselfe under the banner of this resolute partizan Mr. Tyler who had courage to dare anything, to brow-beat the President in his Chair'.[21] William Tyler is always the 'daring' man or the 'impudent bold man'.[22] Reynolds (as we have seen) discovers that the Secretary, Richards, '⟨had joined the Party which I considered as a rebellion in him⟩'.[23] Edwards's friends represent '⟨the whole Cabal Party the existence of which is so much to be lamented⟩'; they are 'turbulent Spirits' who would move 'heaven & earth' to foil the President's plans.[24] Such a successful rebellion, he adds, '⟨loses its name and is stampt with the sanction of lawful reformation or revolution⟩'.[25]

Even men as distinguished as West have been 'incited by a few of the most inconsiderable members who perhaps had no other object at first in view than to elevate themselves into some consequence in the Academy conscious of their own nothingness out of it'.[26] This is a jibe at the architect Tyler (among others), whose profession is similarly disparaged when Reynolds, in his conclusion, denigrates 'Men who have been used to lay[ing] down the law in Alehouses to Masons & Bricklayers [who then] presume to interfere in a higher station where he has crept in by mere accident'.[27] Reynolds's vehemence is so high-pitched in the closing pages of the manuscript that his incomplete sentences flow into each other:

To venture myself with a set of men the majority of which either from weakness or malevolence ar[e] so ready to be led away and enlist under the banner of ⟨what ever⟩ be led to wherever impudent boldness will undertake to direct them I cannot act with such a majority and that majority encreasing every [?day;] the Elections are already in their hands and I am sorry to see so much timidity where I expected more firmness . . . I did not quit my station because I could not persuade the Aca[demicians to] defend the garrison to the last and dye in the breach even after Sir Wm. Chamb[ers] had deserted the defence and and [*sic*] had joined in the attack ⟨but by their junction they were so insultingly⟩ triumphant insolent.[28]

And so on, until the 'Apologia' finally, mercifully breaks off.

We do not know with whom—if anyone—Reynolds shared these drafts, although it is clear that the painter spoke with warmth to the

[21] Hilles, *Literary Career*, 260. Cf. Derek Hudson, *Sir Joshua Reynolds: A Personal Study* (London, 1958), 219–20, who quotes from a contemporary poem in which Chambers is guilty of 'mischievous browing'.
[22] Hilles, *Literary Career*, 260; RA MS Rey/3/93.
[23] Hilles, *Literary Career*, 262.
[24] Ibid. 256 (cf. p. 262); RA MS Rey/3/93.
[25] Hilles, *Literary Career*, 266.
[26] Ibid. [27] Ibid. 276. [28] Ibid. 275.

friends who visited him in Leicester Square once he had resigned his post. He asked Bonomi if he could keep one of the fateful drawings so that he could display it as a 'full vindication' of the work he had recommended. In a letter to the architect, he apologized for having been the cause of so much needless trouble and remarked that he could not persuade himself 'any longer to rank with such beings'.[29] Years later Bonomi would recall that Reynolds said to him, 'pointing to the Hackney Coachman in Leicester Square, "*I would sooner belong to a club of such people as these than to that body.*" '[30]

When the crisis had passed, however, one of his nieces recorded him as being in 'high spirits' as he prepared to resume the chair:

> they had all acknowledged themselves wrong. He told me he would rather have declined accepting it again, as he feels himself getting old: but it was impossible after the concessions they had made him. Indeed he has reason to feel himself in spirits from the honour he gains by this affair, for all the kingdom have been interested about him, and that his resignation would be a public loss. The King has behaved very handsomely to my uncle: at first in expressing his wish that he should not resign; and on Wednesday at the levée, when my uncle's message was delivered to him (I think by Lord Heathfield), whether he had his Majesty's permission to take his seat again, the King bid him 'tell Sir Joshua that it was his most earnest wish that he should do so'.[31]

By December, when he delivered his final discourse to the Academy, he was prepared to be generous indeed. Although he argued that none of the professorships 'should be ever left unfilled', he began by belittling the disputes of the previous winter: 'Among men united in the same body, and engaged in the same pursuit, along with permanent friendship occasional differences will arise.' But these 'little contentions' will not be noticed by others, and 'they ought certainly to be lost amongst ourselves, in mutual esteem for talents and acquirements'. Every controversy ought to be 'sunk in our zeal for the perfection of our common Art'.[32]

And so the controversy *has* sunk, and in reviving it I am interested not simply in placing Reynolds's behaviour within the context of complacency—the art of pleasing—in which it clearly (if incongruously) fits, but in situating it in contemporary political discourse as well. The central

[29] Reynolds, *Letters*, 193.
[30] *The Diary of Benjamin Robert Haydon*, ed. Willard Bissell Pope (5 vols.; Cambridge, Mass., 1963), iv. 573. Earlier, in 1826, Haydon noted that 'The party that expelled Reynolds & brought the Academy into contempt is dead & powerless. This party I attacked & successfully. Young men of talent have been admitted, & the whole state & condition are improved' (iii. 90).
[31] Robert Charles Leslie and Tom Taylor, *Life and Times of Sir Joshua Reynolds: With Notices of Some of his Cotemporaries* (2 vols.; London, 1865), ii. 585–6.
[32] *Discourses on Art*, ed. Robert R. Wark (1959; 2nd edn., New Haven, Conn., 1975), 266, 265.

issue, as I have suggested, is one of authority; and the major concern of Reynolds's contentious colleagues is whether the President has, in his own words, engaged in 'overbearing tyrannical conduct' or presented the 'appearance of a dictatorial style'. It is interesting to note, for example, how often the lexicon of authority and tyranny is invoked by both Reynolds's friends and foes. In his *Testimonies to the Genius and Memory of Sir Joshua Reynolds*, published the year Reynolds died, Samuel Felton collected a number of poetical tributes that had appeared in the popular press. We thus find the poet 'Fresnoy' exclaiming:

> To thee, the Monarch of the finest art,
> That charms the eye, and captivates the heart,
> Both sexes kneel, all women and all men.[33]

Another anonymous writer contemplates the Orphic head of Reynolds, affixed to a palette, floating down the Thames to Somerset House, where a pack of artists contends 'to possess its brains'.[34]

In his *Farewell Odes*, Peter Pindar alludes both to Reynolds's pre-eminence among contemporary painters and the consequent envy of his peers,[35] and this is the thematic focus of a long-winded defence of Reynolds that appeared immediately after he resigned from the Academy. The author, Edward Jerningham, depicts a 'wild Faction' only too eager to 'Insult the Father of the modern school':

> Oh, and is all forgot?—The sons rebel,
> And, Regan-like, their hallow'd fire expel.
> Cou'd not his faculties, so meekly borne,
> Arrest the hand that fix'd the rankling thorn?

Mixing his metaphors even more strongly, Jerningham asks us to

> Mark, mark the period, when the children stung
> The parent's feelings with their serpent tongue;
> It was while dimness veil'd the pow'rs of sight,
> And ting'd all nature with the gloom of night.[36]

---

[33] Samuel Felton, *Testimonies to the Genius and Memory of Sir Joshua Reynolds* (London, 1792), 75.

[34] Ibid. 78. Cf. a similar speculation in one of the newspapers after Reynolds resigned: 'Sir Joshua's vacant chair, we suppose, will be cut into pieces by the students, to have some relic of their ingenious President; as the students in painting in Antwerp did by that of Rubens, after his decease.' Quoted by Felton, ibid. 87. For other accounts in the press, see Hudson, *Sir Joshua Reynolds*, 219 and Hilles, *Literary Career*, 175.

[35] Felton, *Testimonies*, 81. In 1785 Pindar defended Reynolds from the machinations of his colleagues at the Academy by attacking Sir William Chambers: 'Though *thou* 'midst dulness mayst be pleased to shine, | Reynolds shall ne'er sit cheek by jowl with swine' (Leslie and Taylor, *Life and Times*, ii. 473).

[36] Felton, *Testimonies*, 86–7.

Reynolds appears in the poem, in swift succession, as King Lear, Christ, and Milton (if not God himself), and the Shakespearian analogy was quickly taken up by one of Reynolds's antagonists, the anonymous author of the *Observations on the Present State of the Royal Academy*, which was hurriedly printed in the spring of 1790 in an attempt to prevent Reynolds from returning to the chair. The self-proclaimed 'Old Artist' who is responsible for the pamphlet notes that, although Jerningham likened Reynolds to King Lear, the difference between the two is obvious: Lear withdrew after he had given everything to his daughters, whereas Reynolds withdrew because he could not keep everything to himself.[37]

Reynolds's associate is both clever and tireless in his defence of the Assembly's actions. We learn from him that the ageing President expected 'a continuance of that subservient disposition among the Academicians, which he had long been accustomed to receive from them'.[38] But honourable men could not be expected to behave in a subservient fashion when their leader failed to speak truthfully with them: Reynolds is (unfairly) accused of incorrectly stating that Edwards had declined to be a candidate; he had no 'justifiable authority to make such a declaration'. In doing so, the President, he argues,

was guilty of a deception, as a public character, presiding in the Academy, which, I trust, he could never have brought himself to practice in his private capacity.—Indeed, he had been so long in the habit of dictating from his gilded chair, and had been so continually flattered by the submission of those over whom he presided.[39]

In Reynolds's second letter addressed to Chambers, moreover, he is seen to insult his colleagues by letting it appear that he 'quitted the Presidency of the Academy, because he could no longer be the tyrant of it'.[40] During that Presidency, 'the love of power,—the thirst of rule,—and a dictatorial spirit have been evident, from the beginning of his administration to the close of it'.[41] His resignation, this critic continues, will turn out to be advantageous to the Academy because selfish 'patronage, caprice, and ambition' will be removed. Just as important, he argues, 'the natural equality of power which belongs to the society at large, [will no longer] be swallowed by one overbearing and tyrannical individual'.[42]

These are arguably exaggerated complaints, but they are far less heated than Reynolds's own response in the 'Apologia', and they clearly and coherently present the perspective of those who did not flourish under this President's reign (Fuseli was suspected of having 'a considerable

---

[37] *Observations*, 11.   [38] Ibid. 4.   [39] Ibid. 6–7.
[40] Ibid. 9.   [41] Ibid. 17.   [42] Ibid. 18–19.

hand in composing the pamphlet').⁴³ One of the most intriguing features
of the argument elaborated here is the observation that, in polite society—in the world beyond the Academy—Sir Joshua's interpretation of
the Bonomi affair will undoubtedly be accepted. Like so many other
contemporary commentators, this author explains how the fledgling
painter became a part of the society he depicted; but this time the
narrative is not even grudgingly admiring of its subject. Because of

his elegant mode of living,—his general information, with the candour in which
he knows how to clothe his opinions, and the amiable manners he can, at any
time, assume,—as well as from his courtly disposition to pay all due respect to
persons in superior station, he most certainly contrived to move in a sphere of
society in which no Painter was seen to accompany him.

Because he is known in society only as a talented artist and 'as a man of
the most mild and pleasing demeanour', his friends in the great world
have no difficulty in supporting his reputation and cause. And thus, as a
consequence, 'The tricks of his pencil,—the prejudice of his criticism, and
his over-bearing love of power, are not known, or at least believed
among them'.⁴⁴ Edward Gibbon came to the same conclusion in a letter
to his friend: 'I hear you have had a quarrel with your Academicians.
Fools as they are! for such is tyranny of character, that no one will believe
your enemies can be in the right.'⁴⁵ Tyranny of character (for Gibbon)
was tyranny of appearances—of reputation—for at least one of Reynolds's colleagues. The lifelong practice of complacency had become a
protective envelope even when Reynolds behaved in what appeared to be
a very different fashion at the Royal Academy.

The language of tyranny, rebellion, and abdication that we find in
Reynolds's writings and in those of his contemporaries is anything but
exceptional; it can be found throughout most eighteenth-century discourse, which had inherited and domesticated the vocabulary of Shakespeare, Milton, Dryden, and Pope. Reynolds makes an explicit connection
in his 'Apologia', however, between his own unapostasized state and
Milton's vision of a world of fallen angels:

no doubt appearances are against the Pr[esident]. He cannot reasonably expect such
perfect confidence from the world in his favour—[that] like Uriel he <only is>

faithful found
Amongst the faithless faithful only He
Amongst innumerable false.⁴⁶

---

⁴³ Stephen Gwynn, *Memorials of an Eighteenth-Century Painter (James Northcote)* (London, 1898),
217.
⁴⁴ *Observations*, 10–11.
⁴⁵ *The Letters of Edward Gibbon*, ed. J. E. Norton (3 vols.; London, 1956), no. 761 (iii. 194).
⁴⁶ Hilles, *Literary Career*, 267.

Reynolds's memory of the closing passage in Book V of *Paradise Lost* is not precisely accurate—and he is obviously thinking of Abdiel rather than Uriel—but the analogy poignantly reflects the painter's sense of alienation as well as self-righteousness. It can therefore hardly be a coincidence that, as Reynolds came to the close of his final discourse to the Academy on 10 December, Edmund Burke immediately rose, took the painter by the hand, and quoted the following lines from the opening of Book VIII:

> The Angel ended, and in *Adam's* Ear
> So charming left his voice, that he a while
> Thought him still speaking, still stood fix't to hear.[47]

Reynolds had intended 'that the last words which I should pronounce in this Academy, and from this place, might be the name of—MICHAEL ANGELO',[48] but his gesture was countered by that of Burke, whose clever analogy named Reynolds himself as—Raphael.

It could be argued that Reynolds was in good company as either of Milton's angels, and it is clear that he saw both Burke and himself in Abdiel's role, for the following August he published a mezzotint from his best portrait of Burke, with Milton's lines describing his unfallen angel appended beneath it.[49]

It is likely that, if Reynolds shared his 'Apologia' with anyone, he did so with Burke, whose counsel he sought more often than ever following the death of Johnson in 1784. We know that Reynolds and Burke were frequently together in 1789 and 1790; we know, moreover, that Burke shared his work with his long-time friend as he drafted his reflections on the French Revolution. The shared Miltonic allusions link Reynolds and Burke together in an intriguing way in 1790, but they also point to a much stronger bond between the two men, one that was political—cultural in the broadest sense of the term—as well as personal.

In twice invoking the allusion to Abdiel, Reynolds clearly saw both himself and his friend as outcasts: one from the Royal Academy, which had been established by the King; the other, as a Whig, from the ministry that currently directed the King's government. Both men, moreover, shared the same response to the political changes that were buffeting France and that had sent strong reverberations throughout England. And both writers therefore employ what Albert O. Hirschman has recently

---

[47] Leslie and Taylor, *Life and Times*, ii. 594; cf. William T. Whitley, *Artists and their Friends in England 1700–1799* (2 vols.; London, 1928), ii. 134–5.

[48] *Discourses*, ed. Wark, 282.

[49] Hilles, *Literary Career*, 183, whose source is Sir James Prior, *Life of Burke* (2 vols.; London, 1826), ii. 163.

called 'the rhetoric of reaction', a strategy by which the status quo is defended against what are perceived to be radical and dangerous agents of change. Much of Reynolds's reaction to the dispute at the Royal Academy in 1790 was influenced by his sense of the broader changes that were threatening both French and English society; and thus the Bonomi affair might best be seen as a reflection or re-enactment in miniature of the political tumult that had engulfed France and still posed dangers within England. Burke entitled his book, after all, *Reflections on the Revolution in France, and on the Proceedings in Certain Societies in London Relative to that Event*,[50] and it was largely through his friend's eyes that Reynolds interpreted these disturbing events.

As early as 1778 Johnson in fact complained that Reynolds was unduly influenced by Burke in his political views: 'Reynolds is too much under Fox and Burke at present,' he told Boswell. 'He is under the *Fox star* and the *Irish constellation*. He is always under some planet.'[51] Boswell might have countered by noting that both he and Reynolds were primarily of Johnson's school, and that Johnson did not easily countenance what he considered laxity in his friends' political views. Northcote was more even-handed, noting that both men were under great obligations to each other.[52] But even Northcote was easily misled by Reynolds's response *in society* to the French Revolution, claiming that the painter did not mingle in the political debates at the Club in 1789, instead preserving 'the same friendly tenor of conduct and suavity of manners to his associates there, that he exercised towards all men in private life: for politics never amused him nor ever employed his thoughts a moment'.[53]

Others knew better. Boswell had written to Reynolds about his convictions as bluntly as he possibly could in 1784: 'I know your political principles, and indeed your settled system of thinking upon civil society and subordination, to be according to my own heart.'[54] And thus, when Charles James Fox's niece, Caroline, burst out 'into glorification of the Revolution' during a dinner conversation with Reynolds at Holland House, she was, in her own words, 'grievously chilled and checked by her neighbour's cautious and unsympathetic tone'.[55] Malone, who was as

[50] Edmund Burke, *Reflections on the Revolution in France, and on the Proceedings in Certain Societies in London Relative to that Event*, in *The Writings and Speeches of Edmund Burke*, viii. *The French Revolution 1790–1794*, ed. L. G. Mitchell (Oxford, 1989). Burke's preliminary title began 'Reflections on Certain Proceedings of the Revolution Society'; see James T. Boulton, *The Language of Politics in the Age of Wilkes and Burke* (London, 1963), 77.
[51] *Boswell's Life of Johnson*, ed. George Birkbeck Hill and rev. L. F. Powell (6 vols.; Oxford, 1934–64), iii. 261.
[52] Gwynn, *Memorials*, 236.
[53] Northcote, *Life*, ii. 249–50.
[54] *Letters of James Boswell*, ed. Chauncey Brewster Tinker (2 vols.; Oxford, 1924), ii. 319.
[55] Leslie and Taylor, *Life and Times*, ii. 544 n.

vehement in his denunciation of the French as Burke himself, praises his friend for 'the rectitude of his judgment concerning those pernicious doctrines' that fuelled the Revolution.[56] Reynolds 'was lavish in his encomiums' on the *Reflections*, 'never weary of expressing his admiration of the profound sagacity which saw, in their embryo state, *all the evils with which this country was threatened by that tremendous convulsion*' (emphasis added).[57] Reynolds well knew how eagerly 'all the wild and erroneous principles of government' the revolutionaries were attempting to establish in France 'would be cherished and enforced by those turbulent and unruly spirits among us, whom *no King could govern, nor no God could please*'.[58] The allusion to 'Absalom and Achitophel' is Reynolds's own, for Malone tells us that, long before the *Reflections* were published, Reynolds frequently 'avowed his contempt of those "Adam-wits", who set at nought the accumulated wisdom of ages, and on all occasions are desirous of beginning the world anew'.[59] Although Reynolds's voice is filtered through Malone's own virulence here, both the language and the sentiments are consonant with the apologist who would lament, a few months later, that 'The whole Fabric the work of years was shaken to its very foundation and all its glory tarnishd'.[60]

Reynolds visited the Burkes at Beaconsfield in July and then in mid-October 1789, just a few weeks before Burke would write his famous first letter to Depont concerning 'the astonishing scene now displayed in France'.[61] Burke showed part of the *Reflections* to Reynolds and a small handful of other friends early in 1790; one of them, Sir Philip Francis, conveyed his strictures to Burke on 19 February, and it is clear from their correspondence that Burke was circulating a substantial section of the book in both manuscript and proof sheets, including the famous set piece on Marie Antoinette.[62] It is this important passage, perhaps above all others, that would strike the deepest chord in Reynolds: not the theatrical handling of the mob's invasion of the royal palace at Versailles, necessarily, but the moral Burke drew from this event when he concluded that 'the age of chivalry is gone' and with it the principles of 'subordination' and 'obedience' that had their origin in this ancient code.[63]

[56] Ibid.   [57] Ibid.   [58] Ibid.
[59] *The Works of Sir Joshua Reynolds, Knt.*, ed. Edmond Malone (2 vols.; London, 1797), i, pp. lvi–lvii.
[60] Hilles, *Literary Career*, 276. Malone's invocation of 'turbulent . . . spirits', moreover, is an exact harbinger (or echo) of a phrase in the 'Apologia' (RA MS Rey/3/93).
[61] *The Correspondence of Edmund Burke*, vi, eds. Alfred Cobban and Robert A. Smith (Cambridge, 1967), 41.
[62] Prior, *Life of Burke*, ii. 110; Burke, *Correspondence*, vi. 85–92; Boulton, *The Language of Politics*, 75–82. It is worth noting that Burke's and Fox's opposing parliamentary speeches on the Revolution were delivered in February as well; see Burke, *Correspondence*, vi. 81–2.
[63] Burke, *Writings*, viii. 127.

'Are all orders, ranks, and distinctions to be confounded?' Burke asked in another famous outburst earlier in the *Reflections*.[64] The 'mixed system of opinion and sentiment' based on 'the antient chivalry' has, 'without confounding ranks', produced 'a noble equality, and handed it down through all the gradations of social life'.

It was this opinion which mitigated kings into companions, and raised private men to be fellows with kings. Without force, or opposition, it subdued the fierceness of pride and power; it obliged sovereigns to submit to the soft collar of social esteem, compelled stern authority to submit to elegance, and gave a domination vanquisher of laws, to be subdued by manners.[65]

Burke's discourse on a vanishing social economy in Europe—a discourse based on 'manners' in the broadest sense of the word—bears a striking resemblance to Joseph Addison's description of the virtues of 'complaisance', which appeared in the *Guardian* in 1713. Complaisance, he wrote,

renders a Superior amiable, an Equal agreeable, and an Inferior acceptable. It smooths Distinction . . . produces Good-nature and mutual Benevolence, encourages the Timorous, sooths the Turbulent, humanises the Fierce and distinguishes a Society of Civilised Persons from a Confusion of Savages. In a word, Complaisance is a Virtue that blends all Orders of Men together in a Friendly Intercourse of Words and Actions.[66]

The principles of chivalry, Burke argued, also harmonize 'the different shades of life'; they incorporate into politics 'the sentiments which beautify and soften private society'.[67] Such virtues, such sentiments, may depend upon all 'the pleasing illusions' that make power gentle and obedience liberal, as Burke puts it, but they are nevertheless essential to the maintenance of civilized society. 'There ought to be a system of manners in every nation which a well-formed mind would be disposed to relish,' Burke concludes. 'To make us love our country, our country ought to be lovely.'[68]

Burke acknowledges that the line of demarcation signalling 'where obedience ought to end and resistance must begin is faint, obscure, and not easily definable'. Revolutions should not be determined by single acts or events; governments must be 'abused and deranged indeed' before their subjects may act; and, whether one's cause is right or wrong, 'a revolution will be the very last resource of the thinking and the good'.[69] Burke is therefore adamant in his portrayal of a stable, unchanging England founded on native prejudice and 'our sullen resistance to

[64] Ibid. 105.   [65] Ibid. 127.
[66] *The Guardian*, ed. John Calhoun Stephens (Lexington, Ky., 1982), no. 162 (p. 528).
[67] Burke, *Writings*, viii. 128.   [68] Ibid. 129.   [69] Ibid. 81.

innovation'.[70] We have not materially changed in four hundred years, he argues: 'we still feel within us, and we cherish and cultivate, those inbred sentiments which are the faithful guardians, the active monitors of our duty, the true supporters of all liberal and manly morals.'[71] Burke's essential conservatism—'A disposition to preserve, and an ability to improve, taken together, would be my standard of a statesman. Every thing else is vulgar in the conception, perilous in the execution'[72]—leads him to embrace gradual, even 'imperceptible' growth.[73] To preserve *and* to reform is quite different from what has been proposed by those whose motive it is 'to destroy an old scheme of things, because it is an old one'.[74] Like Reynolds, Burke invokes what Hirschman defines as 'the perversity thesis': the argument that any 'purposive action to improve some feature of the political, social, or economic order only serves to exacerbate the condition one wishes to remedy'.[75] The 'work of ages' cannot be reformed in a few months, Burke writes,[76] although it may well be destroyed.

The contours of Burke's famous defence can thus be read as a gloss on Reynolds's experience at the Royal Academy and his reactions to it in February and March of 1790, but it would presumably be more accurate to say that Burke's own discourse set the broader terms for the painter's response. In the *Reflections* Reynolds would have heard his friend cautioning against '*new* power in *new* persons' and speculating that 'Those who quit their proper character, to assume what does not belong to them, are, for the greater part, ignorant both of the character they leave, and of the character they assume'.[77] Surely this is advice that Reynolds would have kept in mind when, in the 'Apologia', he decried an antagonist (Tyler) who presumed 'to interfere in a higher station where he has crept in by mere accident'.[78] In the *Reflections* Reynolds would have read of insidious 'cabals', a 'gang of usurpers', traitors, bold and faithless men, rash and ignorant counsel, 'Turbulent, discontented men', daring and violent men who teach 'servile, licentious, and abandoned insolence'.[79] He would have seen his friend describe the treacherous breeding-ground of academies and clubs in both France and England, and would have heard him support the integrity of the English constitution with precisely the same metaphorical insistence on the wholeness of this

[70] For Reynolds on prejudice, see Hilles, *Literary Career*, 136, 157–8. John Barrell (*The Political Theory of Painting from Reynolds to Hazlitt: 'The Body of the Public'* (New Haven, Conn., 1986), 146) suggests that Reynolds may anticipate Burke here, and later notes (p. 159), as I do below, the relationship between the *Reflections* and Reynolds's 'ironic discourse'.
[71] Burke, *Writings*, viii. 137.   [72] Ibid. 206.   [73] Ibid. 217.   [74] Ibid. 138.
[75] Albert O. Hirschman, *The Rhetoric of Reaction: Perversity, Futility, Jeopardy* (Cambridge, Mass., 1991), 7; for his analysis of Burke, see esp. p. 15.
[76] Burke, *Writings*, viii. 217.   [77] Ibid. 59, 62.   [78] Hilles, *Literary Career*, 276.
[79] See Burke, *Writings*, viii. 61, 64, 89, 90, 97, 138, and *passim*.

edifice or 'fabric' that he would adopt in his own defence of the Royal Academy's constitution.[80] For Reynolds, as for Burke, 'historically sanctioned practices are to be cherished for something apart from themselves', as David Bromwich has recently noted: 'The value they represent, and in the name of which he defends them, is *order*.'[81]

It is possible that Reynolds began to frame his own thoughts on the revolution in France. Hilles discovered that on the back of his niece Mary Palmer's fair copy of the fifteenth discourse Reynolds had written the gist of an argument concerning the downfall of the *ancien régime*: the Bourbons, he wrote, cultivated arts that added splendour to the nation but they neglected more fundamental trades that would support the French economy. The French may have placed too great an emphasis on ornament, Reynolds writes, 'but does it follow that a total revolution is necessary', 'that because we have given ourselves up too much to the ornaments of life, we will now have none at all'?[82] This was already an established principle in Reynolds's mind, one that he had adumbrated in the seventh discourse, in which he warned that 'he who neglects the cultivation of those ornaments, acts contrary to nature and reason'.[83] In the final discourse itself, Reynolds boasted that 'it is no small satisfaction to be assured that I have, in no part of [my lectures], lent my assistance to foster *newly-hatched unfledged* opinions'.[84] One of the principal objects of his addresses has been to ensure that 'the young Artist' is not seduced from the right path by following 'what, at first view, he may think the light of Reason'.[85]

This distrust of showy appearances, of facile novelty, is also at the heart of Reynolds's final commentary on the French Revolution, his so-called 'ironic discourse'. Like his remarks on the fall of the *ancien régime*, this unfinished and long-unpublished essay was written on the verso of the fair copy of his final discourse,[86] and both in physical format and in its

---

[80] See ibid. 72, 85–6, 118–19, 143, 176, 216, and 292. Both Boulton (*The Language of Politics*, 111–12) and F. P. Lock (*Burke's Reflections on the Revolution in France* (London, 1985), 128) draw attention to the importance of this metaphor in Burke's thought.

[81] David Bromwich, *A Choice of Inheritance: Self and Community from Edmund Burke to Robert Frost* (Cambridge, Mass., 1989), 54. Cf. Boulton, *The Language of Politics*, 105–9, and J. G. A. Pocock's edition of Burke's *Reflections* (Indianapolis, 1987), p. xliv: 'Burke's central doctrine is that the social order antedates the human intellect and sets the moral and practical conditions under which both theory and practice must be carried on.'

[82] Hilles, *Literary Career*, 188–9.

[83] Reynolds, *Discourses*, 135; Reynolds repeats this argument in 'Apologia': see Hilles, *Literary Career*, 255.

[84] Reynolds, *Discourses*, 269.   [85] Ibid. 270.

[86] Reynolds wrote part of it on the back of a letter to the *Gentleman's Magazine* that was published in July 1791, thus enabling us to date it fairly accurately; see *Portraits by Sir Joshua Reynolds*, ed. Frederick W. Hilles (London, 1952), 124. David Bindman (*The Shadow of the Guillotine: Britain and the French Revolution* (London, 1989), 67) includes the ironic discourse in his extensive survey of artistic responses to the French Revolution in England.

ironic argument it should be seen as a substantiation of Burke's dictum in the *Reflections* that 'To make everything the reverse of what they have seen is quite as easy as to destroy'.[87] Indeed, for Reynolds as well as for Burke, to reverse *is* to destroy.

Reynolds's 'sixteenth' discourse, which his friends persuaded him could 'bring up the rear of his last volume',[88] may itself be ironic, but the painter's introduction, written in the third person, is as straightforward as it can be. Here we learn that Reynolds's experiment in fact owes its origin to a conversation on Burke's *Reflections*, a book that he enthusiastically admired 'both in regard to the doctrine which it contained, and the eloquence in which that doctrine was conveyed'.[89] The conversation turning to 'the power which is lodged in majorities', Sir Joshua argued that, in politics as well as in art, matters should be determined by the learned few rather than 'the ignorant majority'. The tree of knowledge, after all, 'does not grow upon a new made, slender soil'—a favourite Burkian metaphor—'but is fastened by strong roots to ancient rocks, and is the slow growth of ages'. Learning may be more widely diffused than before, but this 'smattering of knowledge' does not qualify people to 'set up for legislators' in either politics or the arts: 'Few people reach the summit from which they look down on the rest of mankind.'[90] To be a politician, Reynolds adds, is 'as much a trade or profession as his own'; like a true taste in art, the science of politics is acquired by study and labour.[91]

These principles and suppositions, to which Reynolds and his friends so easily and firmly adhere, are nevertheless felt to be out of step with the views of those whom the painter variously calls the majority, the vulgar, the ignorant; and in a playful, malicious moment he therefore speculates on what it would be like to produce a lecture that would actually 'come home to the bosoms of the ignorant (which are always the majority)'. Such a set of ironic pronouncements would be thought to contain more 'sound doctrine' than what Reynolds normally delivers in the Academy; 'proceeding *ex cathedra*' from the President's chair, such a discourse 'would probably so poison the minds of the students as might eventually keep back the harvest of arts which we expect from the nation, perhaps for fifty years'.[92] If Reynolds (like Burke) argued on behalf of prejudice in the fifteenth discourse, for example, he would simply reverse his argument in its successor: 'But shall we in these enlightened times tamely adopt and inherit their ignorant prejudices? No! Let us examine everything by the standard of our own reason, renounce all prejudices for the

[87] Burke, *Writings*, viii. 216.   [88] Reynolds, *Portraits*, 130.
[89] Ibid. 127.   [90] Ibid. 128.   [91] Ibid. 130.   [92] Ibid.

reputed wisdom of others.'[93] And if, in the fifteenth discourse, Reynolds drew his students' attention to the firm ground on which 'the fabrick of our Art is built',[94] the absurdity of his ironic vision, he trusted, would reinforce his views in the sixteenth:

Destroy every trace that remains of ancient taste. Let us pull the whole fabric down at once, root it up even to its foundation. Let us begin the art again upon this solid ground of nature and reason. The world will then see what naked art is, in its uneducated, unprejudiced, unadulterated state.[95]

These are the sentiments—and this is the language—in which, in the 'Apologia', Reynolds had already cast the voices of Chambers and Richards, Tyler and Banks.

Reynolds's first editor and biographer, Edmond Malone, decided not to include the ironic discourse in his friend's collected works, and it remained among Boswell's papers, unpublished and unknown, until 1952. One cannot help but wonder how William Blake would have annotated it, considering that it already represented an ironic and contradictory marginal gloss no less acidulous than Blake's own (although with quite different intentions and effects). The ironic discourse's vehemence and élitism—indeed, its self-complacency—should be compared to the much more generous remarks Reynolds made at a dinner party at Topham Beauclerk's in April 1775. According to Boswell, Reynolds said that 'the more artificial wants we could make to be gratified, the greater our happiness. That this was the advantage of civilized society. He said he saw in this nation all the symptoms of a great and flourishing state: magnificence, elegance, plenty; everybody living better than formerly.'[96] The following fifteen years, however, have clearly brought significant changes. The gratification of 'artificial wants' has led, in France at least, to the fatal neglect of fundamental needs;[97] and the benignity, the egalitarianism, of Reynolds's optimistic view has been quenched by forces, resistance, opposition that he can no longer entirely control. If the majority were still living better in 1790, in Reynolds's eyes they were behaving worse.

At one point, Boswell, into whose hands many of Reynolds's papers fell, clearly intended to write a proper life of his friend; he collected material, and he drafted a few preliminary biographical sketches.[98] It was generally assumed that Boswell abandoned his scheme because he was not familiar enough with the painter's profession, and there is probably

[93] Ibid. 136–8.   [94] Reynolds, *Discourses*, 269.   [95] Ibid. 140–2.
[96] *Boswell: The Ominous Years 1774–1776*, ed. Charles Ryskamp and Frederick A. Pottle (London, 1963), 140.
[97] Hilles, *Literary Career*, 188–9.   [98] See Reynolds, *Portraits*, 12–24.

some truth in this. But Boswell had learnt a great deal in writing his life of Johnson, and it appears that he doubted whether Reynolds would make a proper biographical subject. Following Reynolds's death in 1792, he wrote that 'Sir Joshua was indeed a man of pleasing and various conversation, but he had not those prominent features which can be seized like Johnson's'. Although Boswell had been able to gather various anecdotes concerning him, he confessed that 'I doubt much whether I could write a life of him.'[99] Boswell's dilemma lay precisely in his friend's virtues, amiability, and success. The easy affability and gentle manners that had characterized Reynolds both socially and professionally throughout his career would ironically work against him within a biographical narrative. Reynolds's complaisance, his art of pleasing, his very blandness (to adopt Goldsmith's word): everything that was prized by his friend posed problems to his biographer. It was also a life without real drama—except, of course, for the Bonomi affair—and here Boswell also found himself stymied, for he told Joseph Farington that in publishing a life of Reynolds he would probably offend his niece, Mary Palmer (now Lady Inchiquin), since he believed that Reynolds was actually to blame in his quarrel at the Royal Academy.[100]

The Bonomi affair therefore represents, among other things, Sir Joshua's French Revolution: the point at which a distinguished public figure, someone who had endeavoured to elevate the status of the arts within English culture, found himself betrayed, abandoned, attacked, deposed by the very people it had been his obligation to nurture and protect. He argued along institutional lines, attempting to separate himself personally from the presidential chair in which he sat; but he could not see that he had, in a sense, *become* the establishment, that his own inflexibility and sense of self-worth posed inherent dangers to an academy designed to train new generations of artists.

Partially blind, almost totally deaf, deprived of the principal activity that had given his life meaning, he became, like his ironic discourse, a counter-example to so much that he had personally or professionally embodied. The issues embedded in his resignation remind us of how intricately the career of one painter intersects with the life of artistic institutions, with contemporary political discourse and historical events, and with the shifting social formations in which both private individuals

[99] Ibid. 19–20.
[100] *The Diary of Joseph Farington*, ed. Kenneth Garlick and Angus Macintyre (12 vols.; New Haven, Conn.: Yale University Press for the Paul Mellon Centre for Studies in British Art, 1978–83), ii. 319. Boswell was, however, sympathetic to his friend's plight. He wrote that Reynolds was 'shamefully used by a junto of the Academicians', and following Reynolds's death he was aware of the troublesome nature of his 'democratic' colleagues at the Royal Academy. See *Boswell: The Great Biographer 1787–1795*, ed. Marlies K. Danziger and Frank Brady (New York, 1989), 43, 267.

and public entities are grounded. Reynolds's confrontation with his fellow Academicians provides a full and complicated example, moreover, of what Patricia Crown has recently characterized as the essential dialectic of eighteenth-century art, which she describes 'as a series of ruptures with tradition and the establishment's attempts to suppress what were perceived as artistic insurrections'.[101]

---

[101] Patricia Crown, 'This is not a Conclusion', *Eighteenth-Century Studies*, 25 (1991–2), 618.

12 'Great as he is in his own good opinion': The Bounty Mutiny and Lieutenant Bligh's Construction of Self

K. A. REIMANN

Speculation concerning the factors that instigated the mutiny aboard HMS the *Bounty* in 1789 has imbued the incident with an importance that far exceeds its contextual historic significance. In cold historical terms, the *Bounty* mutiny can be categorized as a minor incident, 'infinitely less ominous than that on HM frigate *Hermione* in 1797, when the crew hacked the captain to pieces, killed nine other officers, and delivered the ship over to the enemy'.[1] Yet for two hundred years it has been the events of the *Bounty* mutiny that have been periodically re-enacted to express contemporary interpretations of the actors and the significance of their actions, while other eighteenth-century mutinies— among them the great rebellions at Spithead and the Nore in 1797—have been largely disregarded. These *Bounty* re-enactments have employed populist forms of expression to reach the largest audience possible. They range from the four films back through several fictionalized novels[2] to a late eighteenth-century pantomime and a series of political pamphlets that argued Fletcher Christian's case. Through these rewritings the story has achieved something like a mythical status. It is not the incident itself, but the way in which the *Bounty* mutiny was originally written into the public consciousness that has generated the continuing interest.

One of the most dynamic elements of this myth is the problematical nature of William Bligh's character—did Bligh himself instigate the act of mutiny? This is a question that remains unanswerable in the context of the known actions that took place on the morning of 28 April 1789. That Bligh himself generated the controversy concerning the assignation of blame after the mutiny is an issue that has been little investigated. Bligh's *A Narrative of the Mutiny on Board H.M.S. Bounty* (1790) and *A Voyage to the South Sea* (1792) are two survivor texts of the eighteenth

[1] As cited in Terry Coleman's review 'Bligh and Good Things on a Voyage into Higher Tosh', *Guardian*, 6 Feb. 1993.
[2] Most notably Nordoff's and Hall's *Mutiny* trilogy, but also Owen Rutter's *Cain's Birthday*. See also n. 27 for eighteenth-century publications.

century. Their periodic reissue in popular Everyman and Penguin editions attests to continuing public interest for reasons that have yet to be defined. I would suggest that a factor in their enduring popularity is the frustrating sense that they are texts that do not tell the audience the story that they want to know. The elements in the mutiny that have subsequently come to be regarded as of interest were remote from Bligh's agenda in writing these publications.

The mutiny was an event that revealed its importance only through Bligh's texts and through the public reaction that those texts provoked. Before his return to England, the *Bounty*'s Master, John Fryer, one of the men who did not mutiny against Bligh, had resigned himself to the likelihood that 'the People in England will hear of our misfortunes and forget them before we get home'.[3] He penned this line in a private letter to his wife on the basis of his experience of the events of the mutiny, in the expectation that the mutiny, like the savage attack on the officers aboard the *Hermione*, would be reported in a few paragraphs in the newspapers and journals of the day, and then disappear.[4] It was only after Fryer read Bligh's published version of the events that he was moved from private resignation to public argument. Fryer found Bligh's *Narrative of the Mutiny* so objectionable that he was spurred to write a narrative of his own, attacking what Bligh had done in his text.

The mystery of the mutiny, as one modern scholar has put it, encourages the ongoing production of 'various historical fictions'[5] rather than a concrete interpretation of 'hard facts'. But it was Bligh's original publications that spurred production of these re-evaluative accounts; it was Bligh himself who provoked the controversy. It is to Bligh's works, therefore, that a reader must return to gain an understanding of why the mutiny continues to excite interest.

James Cook's Third Voyage

When William Bligh revised his log-book account of the *Bounty* voyage for publication, his attitude towards text was anything but neutral. Naval officers of this period were sensitive to the power of text to shape

---

[3] John Fryer in a letter to his wife from Batavia (1789), quoted by Owen Rutter, Introduction, in *The Voyage of the Bounty's launch as related in William Bligh's Despatch to the Admiralty and the Journal of John Fryer*, ed. Owen Rutter (London, 1934), 17.

[4] The initial reporting of the incident in the *Gentleman's Magazine* reflects a similar assessment of the event's importance. In the issue in which the story first made its appearance (*Gentleman's Magazine*, 60 (1790), 463: 'Port News') it had to compete with the rather more lengthy account of the 'next memorable Occurrence', the 'Disaster that befell His Majesty's ship *Guardian*'. Ship disasters, it seems, were too prevalent an occurrence to be of more than passing interest, as the one-paragraph account of the *Hermione*'s brutal mutiny (*Gentleman's Magazine*, 67 (1797), 1062–3) suggests.

[5] Greg Dening suggests in his *Mr. Bligh's Bad Language* (London, 1992) that the 'various historical fictions' of the *Bounty* mutiny perform a useful function by teaching a 'patently presentist, relativist

lives and careers, but Bligh's experience of the way a text could be transformed for publication was particular and direct. At the time of Cook's first voyage in the late 1760s, the Admiralty was exercising strict control over the published narratives of official voyages of discovery. Aggressive competition with the French for new territory in the Pacific basin during this period meant that publication of such discoveries had political importance, not least in justifying imperial policy in these waters. A single official account would be published by order of the Lord Commissioners of the Admiralty. This expedient would ensure not only that the English discoveries got on record, but that the means by which such discoveries had been effected would go on record. Certain officers could receive public commendation; the actions of others could be eliminated. The accepted course for accomplishing this purpose was to commission a competent writer to edit the captain's journal, smoothing out nautical turns of phrase and repressing evidence of inhumane misconduct.[6]

When Cook returned from his second voyage in 1775, the controls were still in place, but overt hostilities against the French were temporarily suspended. Pursuant to Admiralty instructions, Cook had confiscated from 'the officers and petty officers the log-books and journals they had kept; which were . . . sealed up for the inspection of the Admiralty',[7] but the political reasons behind this confiscation were considerably diminished. The second voyage had achieved little in the way of positive discovery (Cook had established that there was no southern continent to balance the northern land mass). As there was less political pressure to be guarded about the true nature of the voyage, Cook was trusted to produce his own narrative. That the Admiralty continued to impose restraints on alternative narratives at this time seems to have been less a measure to control the political content of the narrative than a token of respect to Cook, to allow him to reap a further financial reward from his endeavour. Returns from the sales of the best-selling *A Voyage Towards the South Pole and Round the World* (1777) netted Cook a handsome profit without putting the Admiralty out of pocket. Indeed, a significant

notion of history . . . [showing] how obviously the films fail to cope with either the differences between the present and the past or with the differences between cultures' (pp. 366–7).

[6] John Hawkesworth was commissioned to write up the voyages of those who had preceded Cook in the Pacific Basin, as well as Cook's first voyage. Cook, at least, was dissatisfied with Hawkesworth's publication, though he had consented to (what were then considered) emendations of his nonjudgemental descriptions of the natives' view of sexuality as disassociated with sin. See Lynne Withey, *Voyages of Discovery* (London, 1987), 168–72.

[7] The potentially lucrative nature of these journals is perhaps best exemplified by the sailor on this voyage who concealed his journal by interlining it in his Bible. Though Cook reports that such journals 'were so badly written that no one could read them', at least one made it into print. See James Cook, *Voyage Towards the South Pole and Round the World* (2 vols.; London, 1777), ii. 287.

factor in retaining the controls for the publication of Cook's third voyage (1784) seems to have been to enable Cook's widow material support. Here William Bligh enters the scene.

Bligh had sailed with James Cook as sailing-master aboard the *Resolution* on Cook's final voyage in the years 1776–9. Bligh made a substantial contribution to those aspects of the voyage that proved a success, particularly the discovery of the Sandwich Islands and the charting of the north-west Pacific. His reward for so doing was formally acknowledged by the eighth share he received from the proceeds of the official account of the voyage. The first edition of *A Voyage to the Pacific Ocean* (three large volumes priced £4 14s. 6d.) sold out in three days. Second and third editions were printed to meet the popular demand.[8] Enthusiasm for Cook went to extremes: two popular engravings showed his apotheosis, the eighteenth-century naval officer rising triumphantly into the clouds in full dress uniform and wig. In the aftermath of his death, many who had sailed under his command scrambled to make the most of the reflected glory of the fallen martyr of the Enlightenment.

The recognition accorded to Bligh's contributions within *A Voyage to the Pacific Ocean* was not commensurate with the financial reward he received from the publication. The third volume, drafted by James King (who had assumed partial command of the expedition after the deaths of Cook and a second commanding officer), made little mention of the role Bligh had played in re-establishing order after the catastrophe of Cook's murder. The survey work Bligh had undertaken with Cook went entirely uncredited, Bligh's charts being identified on the title-pages of all three volumes as having been taken from 'the original drawings of Lieutenant Henry Roberts'. These omissions and inaccuracies could be described as products of 'neglect';[9] Bligh himself viewed them as deliberate—almost malicious—belittlement. He peppered his copy of Cook's *Voyage* with angry comments on King and on John Douglas.[10]

Bligh's marginalia have been used as a historical source to untangle the confused circumstances of Cook's death;[11] more usefully for my purposes, these notes reveal Bligh the reader in critical mode, angrily comparing passages of Cook's journal with the text as it had been edited for

---

[8] Withey, *Voyages of Discovery*, 404.

[9] As in Milton Rugoff's essay on Bligh, in William Bligh, *A Voyage to the South Sea . . . and An Account of the Mutiny on Board H.M.S. Bounty* (New York, 1961; repr. 1989), 221.

[10] Douglas had prepared the first two volumes of the *Voyage to the Pacific Ocean* from the journal Cook had kept until the day of his murder (James Cook and Captain James King, *A Voyage to the Pacific Ocean* (3 vols.; London, 1784)). William Bligh's copy has been housed by the Admiralty Library (now the MOD Library) since the early nineteenth century (ref. MODWL Sb170). All references to Bligh's marginalia are to the page numbers in the MOD Library's copy of the *Voyage*.

[11] See e.g. Rupert Gould's piece in the *Mariner's Mirror*, 14/4 (1928), 371–85, at 378, in which a version of Bligh's notes was first published. See also n. 16 below.

publication. The focus of his criticism is what Bligh saw as King's self-serving and overtly partial editorship.

Certain passages in the third volume of *A Voyage to the Pacific Ocean* cast James King as Cook's heir apparent. King introduces an anecdote in which several principal chiefs at the Sandwich Islands 'waited upon Captain Cook, whose son they supposed I was, with a formal request that I be left behind',[12] with the following obsequious flourish: 'I hope I may be permitted to relate a trifling occurrence in which I was principally concerned.' The word 'trifling' is obviously not intended at its face value—the incident is important to King in establishing his implied relationship with Cook. In the overall context of the narrative, this implied kinship claim is a successful piece of writing. It adds pathos to the harrowing scenes describing King's attempts to recover Cook's body from the Sandwich Islanders. Even as the account invites fresh outrage at the pathetic recovery of Cook's feet, or of the meat of his upper torso, King reports manfully that 'the consequent return of the natives to their former friendly discourses with us, are strong proofs that they neither meant nor apprehended any change of conduct'.[13] King recalls the reader to Cook's celebrated sympathies towards the natives. At the same time, as attempts were being made to recover piece after forlorn piece of Cook's dismembered corpse, King writes of himself as attempting to re-establish relations with the natives. Through King's actions, the text suggests, the spirit of Cook lives on.

Though King's writing coheres as an affecting account of the events, Bligh's marginalia make it plain that he regarded these passages of emotively heightened humanity as 'Hypocritical'. He offers alternative interpretations of the action to support this view, accusing King of backwardness and sloth. King's claims of feeling towards Cook are reduced by Bligh's commentary to acts of pure self-service: 'C[ook's] death was no more attended to in the course of a few days than if he n[ever?] existed.'[14] Bligh's marginalia make it clear that he views King's account as blatant self-promotion rather than as respectful celebration of Cook's profound humanity and vision. This is most bluntly stated in the episode in which Lieutenant Phillips, a man whose actions King went out of his way to commend, is characterized by Bligh as 'a great Croney of C. Kings, and he has taken care not to forget'.[15] Phillips, Bligh claims, 'never was of any real service the whole Voyage'. Preferment in these published accounts was intimately connected with the issue of who would be awarded prestigious future commands in the Pacific, and this seems to have been the primary resentment riding behind Bligh's angry

[12] Cook and King, *A Voyage to the Pacific Ocean*, iii. 30.
[13] Ibid. 37.   [14] Bligh, in MODWL Sb170 iii. 59.   [15] Bligh, in ibid. 53.

reading of King's account. A series of passages are marked as significant with little other comment than 'Not in Capt. Cook'. Gould (who first published this marginalia in 1928) takes this as evidence that Bligh is 'fully alive' to the fact that Cook's journal was extensively edited for publication, but the passages thus singled out have a repeated theme: the passages noxious to Bligh all concern the future exploration of the Pacific, the definition of future arenas of discovery, and their implicit suggestion of the appropriateness of King and his cronies in defining and fulfilling these roles, just as King had been appointed to take over Cook's role as narrator of the official *Voyage* account.[16] 'Of what number this newly-discovered Archipelago consists, must be left for future investigation', King writes.[17] 'Not in Cook,' states Bligh. Who will be promoted to the command of such 'future investigations'? In Bligh's eyes the account is tantamount to an unseemly act of manœuvring to secure future commands or preferment (both King and his 'croney' Phillips received promotions on their return from the voyage, while Bligh had been passed over). Bligh swings between crude sarcasm—'A pretty old Womans story' and 'charming humane Speech'—and explicit denunciation. King writes: 'I shall now leave [Cook's] memory to the gratitude and admiration of posterity; accepting, with a melancholy satisfaction, the honour, which the loss of him hath procured me, of seeing my name joined with his.'[18] To which Bligh notes, 'An honour he has no right to, as that should be with Capt Gore who commanded & brought the Ships home.'

Bligh's unremitting rejection of King's right to join his name honourably with Cook's is problematical. Whether or not King was the total layabout coward Bligh characterized him to be is incidental: Bligh's inability to acknowledge him as anything other than such a character is not. King and Gore had shared the command and brought the ships home; King and Bligh (and others) shared in the sale profits of the *Voyage to the Pacific*. Bligh failed to acknowledge the sharing of these rewards, focusing only on moments of disappointment. Bligh's jealousy concerning the assignment of credit and blame would come to be the

---

[16] These passages have a confused record. Gould does not record them, but his notations ignore several latitude corrections in Bligh's hand. A. C. F. David, in his further notes on the passages (*Mariner's Mirror*, 67/1 (1981), 102) writes of Bligh's 'hydrographical notations' on several of the charts, but does not specify which of the marks he believes to be Bligh's. Two cases are catalogued by an unidentified nineteenth-century hand on the flyleaf of vol. i (i. 130; ii. 220), the remainder have only recently been noted by myself (i. 4; ii. a3ᵛ, 189, 194, 195, 221, 532). These side-lined passages have little overt 'historical' significance, and have perhaps on this account been disregarded. Their authenticity is implicit in notations made by Gould and David (as revealed by a cross-reference to all the notes previously ascribed to Bligh), but it is to be regretted that such marking of the text was not registered earlier, as it has little by way of a 'signature' hand to affirm its authenticity.

[17] Cook and King, *A Voyage to the Pacific Ocean*, ii. 221.

[18] Ibid. iii. 52.

distinguishing hallmark of his relations with officers of equal or inferior rank, both in his service as a naval officer and as a writer.

For the moment, Bligh, denied posterity in the official account of one of the most prestigious voyages of the century, wrote with rancour about the sweet advantages of gaining control of the text. The lesson he had chosen to learn from King would deeply influence his attempts to produce accounts of his own voyages.

Bligh's Construction of Self

Interpretations of the *Bounty* mutiny have commonly constructed the incident as a clash between the personalities of Bligh and Christian.[19] Such a reading would have been particularly offensive to Bligh. He would have found it offensive not because he did not see the event in stark terms of right and wrong, but because his works do not concede to Christian any of the stature such a counterpart relationship implies.

Bligh's accounts were in no way studied reports of the actions of the men who had usurped his command. Neither the *Narrative of the Mutiny on Board H.M.S. Bounty* of 1790 nor the longer *Voyage to the South Sea* of 1792 offers detailed speculations as to what these men might have hoped to accomplish by mutinying. Indeed, those manuscript passages from Bligh's log-books that addressed these issues survive almost verbatim in both publications. Bligh seemed to have felt little need to revise his first impression of these men. Though there are a few moments in the published accounts in which Bligh retroactively attributes occasional signs of discontent to crew members who later proved mutinous, these changes were of limited significance: unsubtle revisions of keywords, a single retrospective speculation about the cause of a broken cable.[20]

The passages that Bligh worked hardest to revise were those that concerned his own character. The dignified and assured portrait he gave of himself dominates both the *Narrative* and the *Voyage*. But the very detail of this portrait invited contradiction. The supporters of the men who had remained on the *Bounty* did not have to vindicate Christian and his comrades, they only had to prove that the case Bligh had built for his lack of culpability in instigating the mutiny was flawed. In what follows

[19] See e.g. Richard Hough, *Captain Bligh and Mr. Christian: The Men and the Mutiny* (New York, 1973).
[20] For an instance of an unsubtle revision, see the account of the first punishment that Bligh had had to inflict on a crew member: 'I found it necessary to punish Matthew Quintal, one of the seamen, with two dozen lashes, for insolence and mutinous behaviour' (Bligh, *A Voyage to the South Sea*, 26–7)— the original log read that Quintal's fault had been 'Insolence and Contempt' (William Bligh, *The Log of the Bounty* (2 vols.; London, 1937), i. 110). For the example of retrospective speculation, see *A Voyage to the South Sea*, 126.

I will suggest further that Bligh even failed to see his culpability as a serious concern, preoccupations with authorship—and his image as an author—clouding his understanding of the potential significance of the mutiny as an event.

The earliest reports of the *Bounty* mutiny gave Bligh near complete control of how the events were to be presented to the public. When Bligh returned to England on 14 March 1790, he was accompanied by only two of the *Bounty* crew—Bligh's clerk and one of the *Bounty*'s cooks (the remainder of the launch survivors remained in Batavia until their passage to England could be secured on a transport vessel).[21] This was a situation which he was quick to exploit. An early report of the mutiny in the *Gentleman's Magazine* concluded, 'This officer [Bligh] only holds the rank of Lieutenant in our navy . . . the distresses he has undergone entitle him to every reward . . .'[22] Such leaders were followed a few months later by Bligh's publication of *A Narrative of the Mutiny on Board H.M.S. Bounty* (1790), which did much to focus public sympathy for the launch party and for Bligh. In October of the same year Bligh was acquitted by a court martial of the charge of losing the *Bounty* and simultaneously promoted to the rank of post-captain. From this comfortable position Bligh set about rewriting his *Narrative*, originally published as a pamphlet 'for the purpose of communicating early information concerning an event which had attracted the public notice'[23] in a less ephemeral form.

The complete history of the *Bounty* voyage, *A Voyage to the South Sea* (1792), was published in a handsome quarto volume, complete with plates. In the opening chapter of the account Bligh casts the voyage as a culmination of the noble effort of all the former voyages to the Pacific:

The object of all the former voyages to the South Seas, undertaken by the command of his present majesty, has been the advancement of science, and the increase of knowledge. This voyage may be reckoned the first, the intention of which has been to derive benefit from those distant discoveries.[24]

This grand declaration set Bligh's voyage on a par with Cook's—a weighty voyage of discovery. With such prestige would also come the financial reward of writing the official account. Bligh's account, like those of Cook's voyages, soon found itself competing on the book market with two editions of an unauthorized account of the *Bounty*'s

[21] According to Edward Christian, both men were Bligh cronies who would not have taken issue with the inaccuracies of Bligh's account. The second of these men (John Smith, the cook) was in Bligh's service as late as 1794. See Edward Christian, *Short Reply* (London, 1794), 5.

[22] *Gentleman's Magazine*, 60 (May 1790), 464. The accuracy of this report's list of the provisions that the mutineers supplied to the launch suggests access to Bligh's account.

[23] Bligh, *A Voyage to the South Sea*, sig. a1.

[24] Ibid. 5.

voyage, seeming further testimony to the potential for profit in the publication of such voyages of discovery.[25]

Bligh's determination to cast his voyage as an important voyage of discovery raised several problems that the body of the account failed to resolve. He had 'Published by permission'—not, significantly, by order—'of the Lords Commissioners of the Admiralty'. The stake in making the story public was Bligh's, not the Admiralty's. The stature that he claimed to himself for those elements of the voyage that had been successful had not been formally conceded to him by the Admiralty.[26] Further, although the unauthorized accounts against which Bligh was competing may appear to be in the tradition of the accounts that competed with Cook (among others) for the market in discovery voyage books, this appearance is illusory. Rather than offering a second (or third) viewpoint of the voyage, as written from the journal of a secondary officer, these accounts were a bookseller's attempt to cash in on the notorious aspect of Bligh's *Voyage*, as the title itself makes clear: *An Account of the Mutinous Seizure of the Bounty: with the succeeding Hardships of the Crew. To which are added Secret Anecdotes of the Otaheitean Females.* The text of this work printed verbatim Bligh's description of the 'Pirates' issued from Timor.[27] The representations of the mutiny itself were diverting attention from Bligh's vision of the voyage as one of 'uninterrupted prosperity'[28] overturned by a surprising and unexpected moment of violence. Bligh, concentrating on constructing his voyage as a prestigious event, neglected to counter this depiction of the mutineers as important in themselves.

Bligh's construction of a prosperous voyage was of greater importance to his ambitions than sustained depiction of Christian and his men as an alien 'tribe of armed ruffians'[29] who had thrown over links of gratitude and friendship after a sophisticated concealment of their true natures. It

[25] The unauthorized account was *An Account of the Mutinous Seizure of the Bounty: with the succeeding Hardships of the Crew. To which are added Secret Anecdotes of the Otaheitean Females* (London, 1790; 2nd edn. 1792). This *Account* has been reprinted recently, ed. Stephen Walters (Genesis Publications, Surrey, 1987).

[26] If the *Bounty* voyage was not a voyage of discovery, and could not naturally be accorded the prestige and status of such a voyage, neither was it the first voyage to derive benefit from Cook's discoveries. In 1787, the year the *Bounty* set sail, the settlement in New South Wales was already on its way to being established. Portlock, along with other ex-members of Cook's expedition, had already established a profitable fur trade from Nootka Sound (Withey, *Voyages of Discovery*, 415–16).

[27] Other contemporary productions seeking to capitalize on the *Bounty*'s notoriety were a play performed on 5 May 1790 (just six weeks after the Admiralty was informed of Bligh's return) and the somewhat belated *Letters of Fletcher Christian containing a Narrative of the Transaction on board H.M.S. Bounty, Before and After the Mutiny, with his subsequent Voyages and Travels in South America* (London, 1796), a bizarre grafting of a speculative escape by Christian to South America on to what appears to be a genuine account of a tour of the west coast of South America by a displaced Englishman.

[28] Bligh, *A Voyage to the South Sea*, 153.

[29] Bligh, *A Narrative of the Mutiny, on Board His Majesty's ship Bounty* (London, 1790), 5.

has been argued that Bligh made exclusions in the published accounts 'to the advantage of the mutineers and not himself'.[30] His characterization of the mutineers is certainly minimal. Even so significant a figure as Christian is mentioned a spare half dozen times, twice as a parenthetical tag designating 'an officer (Mr. Christian)' whom Bligh has instructed to carry out some small task. But Bligh extended these erasures of identification beyond the mutineers to include members of the 'loyal' crew. Only Nelson, the botanist who shared Joseph Banks's patronage with Bligh, retains anything like a character (Bligh describes some of the work Nelson completed at Tahiti). The pattern of Bligh's marginalia in King's account suggests that such erasures were most probably conducted less with the intention of giving advantage to the mutineers than with the intention of advancing Bligh's credibility as the commander of the voyage, an appropriation for his own purposes of self-serving editorial techniques similar to those that Bligh had condemned in King's writing. 'Cronies' and the central narrator have their exploits elaborated, whether of significance to the voyage or not, while those outside the clique simply make no appearance. The careful revisions Bligh made to mask his strained relations with his officers, including those who remained 'loyal' to him, would become one of the most controversial aspects of Bligh's accounts.

The log Bligh had kept during the launch journey had accused two of the launch crew of mutinous behaviour. Though Bligh retained this accusation in his published accounts, he eliminated direct identifications of the guilty parties, opting instead to emphasize the difficulties he had suffered personally in retaining control over a hard-pressed crew. He first published the passage to read:

On this occasion . . . One person, in particular, went so far as to tell me, with a mutinous look, he was as good a man as myself. It was not possible for me to judge where this might have an end, if not stopped in time; I therefore determined to strike a final blow at it, and either to preserve my command, or die in the attempt: and, seizing a cutlass, I ordered him to take hold of another and defend himself; on which he called out I was going to kill him, and began to make concessions. I did not allow this to interfere further with the harmony of the boat's crew, and every thing soon became quiet.[31]

This is a substantive change from the episode as it was originally recorded in the unpublished log-book. At the time he initially recorded his reaction to the incident, Bligh wrote of himself as isolated, and even alienated, from the remaining 'loyal' members of his crew. In

---

[30] Gavin Kennedy, in his Introduction to George Mackaness (ed.), *The Book of the Bounty* (London, 1981), p. ix.

[31] Bligh, *Narrative*, 55.

the log-book version the carpenter, Purcell, is named as the 'particular' person. His actions are recorded much as in the above passage. The sentence 'I did not allow this to interfere further with the harmony of the boat's crew, and every thing soon became quiet', however, is a substantial revision of Bligh's original log entry, in which:

[the carpenter] called out that I was going to kill him, and began to make concessions. I was only now assisted by Mr. Nelson, and the Master very deliberately called out to the Boatswain to put me under an Arrest, and was stirring up a greater disturbance, when I declared if he interfered when I was in execution of my duty to preserve Order and regularity, and that in consequence any tumult arose, I would certainly put him to death the first person. This had a proper effect on this Man . . .[32]

This is a spare account of a tense moment, but the brief characterization of Fryer, the master, speaking to the Boatswain without heat, 'very deliberately', has a suggestion of considered premeditation in it that Bligh would eliminate from his published *Narrative*. If Bligh believed the master to be at fault, it is curious that he should have suppressed his report of such behaviour. The question of Fryer's right as second in command to put Bligh 'under an Arrest' according to a general agreement among the officers (i.e. support from the Boatswain) seems to have been one that Bligh was unwilling to air, let alone to investigate.

In the first published version of the episode Bligh advanced an explanation for the 'mutinous' behaviour of the carpenter 'On this occasion', hypothesizing that 'fatigue and weakness so far got the better of their sense of duty, that some of them began to mutter who had done most'. This somewhat mitigated the circumstances of the incident, though the impression of a sullen and disaffected crew remained. In the 1792 *Voyage*, Bligh's last published version of the episode, the muttering 'expressed their discontent at having worked harder than their companions'.[33] The original image of a surly antagonized group of sailors was transformed in the final published version into one in which hard-working companions calmly articulate grievances.

The fact that Bligh offered justification for Fryer and Purcell in his revised accounts has been interpreted as an appeasement strategy to buy their silence as to Bligh's own behaviour. In this view Bligh's men would be those who retained a 'sense of duty', and were willing to make sacrifices for a greater goal than the immediate gratification of their own

[32] William Bligh, *Log of the Bounty Launch*, ed. Owen Rutter (London, 1935), 192.
[33] Bligh, *A Voyage to the South Sea*, 209.

senses, in contrast to the loose-charactered mutineers for whom the corrupting prospect of 'a more happy life among the Otaheiteans, than they could possibly have in England; which,' in Bligh's opinion, 'joined to some female connections, have most probably been the principal cause of the whole transaction'.[34] But Bligh's account creates no such juxtaposition of opposing factions within the crew. He devotes a bare seven pages to the events of the mutiny—including everything that he conjectures might have occasioned such a revolt. From the log entry of April 1789 through to the published *Voyage* of 1792 there are few changes or expansions—and none of these significant. If anything there is a reduction of the information.[35] The revisions of the Purcell and Fryer incident similarly reduce the specifics of the circumstances. The effect in both episodes is to subordinate the importance of the actions of individual crew members, de-emphasizing the seriousness of their threat to Bligh's command. This change moves Bligh from a stance isolated from the crew to a position of centralized control. Bligh's final words on the incident describe himself as 'regulating the mode of proceeding'.[36] This is firm unemphatic language that casts the incident as an isolated deviation. This assessment of the role he played towards his crew pertains to his larger purpose in the *Voyage*: to create himself as a respected (if not venerated) figure of authority in the tradition of James Cook.

By playing down how isolated he had become from both his officers and his men in the course of the voyage, by writing out his comprehensive lack of trust and his feelings of insecurity (he wrote of his officers in his log-book 'I have no resource, or do I ever feel myself safe in the few instances I trust them'), the mutiny was convincingly depicted as a shocking and startling event, juxtaposed against the background of a serene and well-regulated voyage. 'The secrecy of this mutiny is beyond all conception. . . . With such close-planned acts of villainy, and my mind free from any suspicion, it is not wonderful that I have been got the better of.'[37] In the version of 1792 the final phrasing of the preceding sentence was amended to 'that I fell a sacrifice'.[38] Bligh was seeking a martyred status equivalent to Cook's with this narrative. He was indeed to achieve a martyred status, but it was not to be along the lines he expected.

[34] Bligh, *Narrative*, 9.
[35] The *Voyage to the South Sea* describes how Bligh's endeavours to call his men to action at the moment of mutiny were answered 'with threats of death' (p. 155). In *The Voyage of the Bounty's launch as related in William Bligh's Despatch to the Admiralty*, Charles Churchill is particularly identified as having threatened him with these words (p. 31).
[36] Bligh, *A Voyage to the South Sea*, 210.
[37] Bligh, *Narrative*, 10.
[38] Bligh, *A Voyage to the South Sea*, 163.

'Where Captain Bligh have wrote single he should have wrote plurel'

Bligh's policy of omitting names from his published narratives was one which did not serve him well, for reasons that he might have been able to predict had he considered the implications of the mutiny for members of the crew other than himself. His personal experience of being the character omitted from a narrative had not put him in a position to feel more than resentment. In his own experience with King's *Voyage to the Pacific Ocean*, Bligh had had no pressing motive to publish his objections. Though his charts had been plagiarized for the published account and he resented King's appropriation of credit for the voyage's success to himself and his cronies, with one-eighth of the account's proceeds in his pocket there was nothing pressing Bligh to make a public protest. The launch-party and the mutineers, however, had material reasons for exposing Bligh's effacement of individual crewmen's actions: his refusal to offer any of the surviving crew public commendations. Every member of the *Bounty* crew faced court martial or criminal trial. Bligh, intent on his own aggrandizement, failed to take into account the implications of the threat that his text posed for the careers of those who had sailed with him in the *Bounty*, mutinous or otherwise.

John Fryer, the *Bounty*'s Master, had initially believed that 'the People in England will hear of our misfortunes and forget them before we get home'. After reading Bligh's *Narrative of the Mutiny*, he began to prepare a counter-narrative.[39] Although his manuscript remained unpublished until the twentieth century, his frequent calls to 'the reader' to witness points as he makes them emphasizes that he was preparing this account for publication, meaning to go on the record with his catalogue of resentments:

I will now refer the reader to Captain Bligh Narrative which is true and just except for some few omittinces, where Captain Bligh have wrote single he should have wrote plurel—Mr Bligh say that there was no one in the boat that know any thing about Timor but himself—Now Mr Peckover the Gunner was the first that mentioned Timor as he had seen the Island when he came through the Straits of New Holland with Captain Cook—and from this circumstance we lookd into Hammilton Moors Book and likewise the Requisite Tables—which were in the boat belonging to Mr Hallet Midshipman . . . —therefore I knew where Timor lay as well as Captain Bligh—but as Captain Bligh has not mentiond any body['s] services but his own I must till my Friends that there was

---

[39] This was Fryer's retrospectively written journal (tentatively dated 1790), first published in *The Voyage of the Bounty's launch as related in William Bligh's Despatch to the Admiralty.*

others in the Boat that would have found their way to Timor as well as Captain Bligh and made every one with them more pleasant.[40]

Bligh had created himself as the one navigator aboard the launch capable of getting the boat to Timor: 'I was solicited by all hands to take them towards home . . . I told them no hopes of relief for us remained . . . till I came to Timor.'[41] Considering what Fryer says about the lieutenant's 'omittinces' on this occasion, this is a peculiarly ironic claim. Years earlier, the one point Bligh considered publicly protesting in King's *Voyage to the Pacific Ocean* was the suppression of his role as navigator.

Bligh's challenge of King's depiction of Cook's death is echoed in the passage in which Fryer defends himself against Bligh's description of the cutlass incident. Bligh's words 'I did not allow this to interfere further with the harmony of the boat's crew, and every thing soon became quiet' are revealed as a compression of far more complicated events than even Bligh's unpublished log acknowledged:

I here tell the reader how that matter Happened and he will be a judge whether this man was mutinous or not— . . . [Bligh called the man] a damn scoundrel &c what have I brought you here when if I had not been with you, you would have all aperished, yes Sir the carpenter said, if it had not been for you we should not have been here—what's that you say Sir—I say Sir if it had not been for you we s[h]ould not have been here—you damn'd scoundrel what do you mean—I am not a scoundrel Sir the carpenter said. I am as good a man as you in that respect—[42]

Fryer depicts his own involvement in the scene as that of a moderator, entering the fray only to come to the Carpenter's protection. Bligh's outrage at the Carpenter's suggestion (which amounts to the accusation that Bligh was responsible for the mutiny that was the ultimate cause behind their being at the island) is presented as impassioned. The Carpenter, by contrast, controls his anger: his words conceal their insult rather than betraying open insubordination. When Bligh seizes a cutlass the Carpenter has the strength of mind not to respond in kind, refusing to take up arms against his superior officer. Fryer's reaction is mixed: amusement fades to a comprehension of how seriously Bligh has lost his temper:

I could not help laughing to see Captain Bligh swagering with cutless over the carpenter's head—when I said no fighting here—I put you both under arrest—Captain Bligh turn his conversation on me. By God Sir if you offerd to

[40] *The Journal of John Fryer*, ed. Rutter, 67–80. The spelling and grammatical oddities are Fryer's.
[41] Bligh, *Narrative*, 22. See also p. 30, Bligh's description of Timor.
[42] *The Journal of John Fryer*, ed. Rutter, 70–1.

tuch me I would cut you down—I said Sir this is a very wrong time to talk of fighting . . .[43]

Fryer's declaration that he threatened to put '*both* under arrest' touches on—and modifies—the point Bligh made in his log but did not carry over to his published accounts. Where Bligh had written single in his log-book: 'the Master very deliberately called out to the Boatswain to put me under an Arrest',[44] Fryer again insists on the plural. His act, he insists, was an attempt to stop *both* the Captain and the Carpenter from continuing to provoke each other. This insistence on describing the men's reactions as a crew, each member of which has a defined responsible position in a complex hierarchy, is directly at odds with Bligh's depiction of himself as the all-responsible commander.

In the discussion which Fryer holds with Bligh following the incident with the Carpenter, Fryer attempts to explain the motivations behind his threat. Fryer stages this discussion as a private conversation between officers, emphasizing his own ability to control his emotions in front of the men—in vivid contrast to Bligh.

[Bligh.] Me wrong sir—
[Fryer.] yes sir you wrong—you put yourself on a footing [with] the carpenter when you toke up a cutless and told him to take another; if he had done so and cut you down it is my opinion that he would have been Justifiable in so doing . . . there [were] other methods in making people do as they were orderd without fighting them . . .[45]

The key moment in this passage is surely the statement in which Fryer accuses Bligh of lowering himself in his combative confrontation with the Carpenter. Whether Fryer's report of the words that passed between the Carpenter and Bligh is exactly accurate or not, whether Fryer offered to arrest both the Captain and the Carpenter or the Captain alone make little odds: Bligh had lost his temper, and with it the poise and detachment suitable to his rank. To have moved from this loss of equilibrium to a construction of himself as a controlled harmonizer cannot be other than a conscious construct. Bligh's is a literary rather than a literal regulation of the 'mode of proceeding'.[46]

Fryer (the Master) and Purcell (the Carpenter) both ranked as officers in the eighteenth-century navy. At the time of the mutiny, Fryer—second in command aboard the ship—was barely on speaking terms with Bligh.[47] By Fryer's own account, when Christian took over the ship, Fryer's first effort to dissuade Christian from his course of action was an

---

[43] Ibid. 71.   [44] Bligh, *Log of the Bounty Launch*, ed. Rutter, 192.
[45] *The Journal of John Fryer*, ed. Rutter, 72.   [46] Bligh, *A Voyage to the South Sea*, 210.
[47] See Owen Rutter, Introduction, in *The Journal of John Fryer*, 19.

offer to confine Bligh to his cabin, if Christian would agree to hand back the ship.[48]

Acts of mutiny were not uncommon in the eighteenth-century navy. 'The ejection of intolerable officers was a proper and traditional object of mutiny.'[49] In the naval mutinies of 1797, ship after ship threw out their officers (Bligh was to suffer his second dispossession[50]) in expression of discontent with poor working conditions exacerbated by the changing technology of ship design. Yet despite the fact that these mutinies went forward at a time of war, reprisals were limited to the most outspoken of the mutineers' leaders.[51] Mutiny could be, as N. A. M. Rodger has observed, 'a means of safeguarding the essential stability of shipboard society, not of destroying it',[52] a prelude to investigation of shipboard affairs by the Admiralty and—perhaps—to ejection of incapable officers. So long as physical violence was avoided, the Admiralty was willing to look with forgiveness on such acts, and punishment for the crime was rarely capital. Such mutinies generally took place while ships were in port or at anchor, with access to central authority for mediation (the 1797 mutinies were concentrated at the Nore, an island barely a mile away from the Admiralty's seat at Greenwich). 'Mutiny' as such was analogous to the eighteenth-century concept of 'Riot'—a quasi-legitimate means by which popular sentiment could be brought to a governing body's notice.

The *Bounty* mutiny, while respecting the code of non-violence, was notable as a rare example of a mutiny that took place far away from the seat of Admiralty power. Fryer's offer to Christian was after all not so startling that he hesitated to repeat it as evidence as a mitigating factor during the trial of the mutineers who were brought to England by the *Pandora* voyage in 1792.[53] Had Christian accepted Fryer's offer, he and the rest of the mutineers would have avoided the concomitant act of piracy that ensured that the punishment for the initial act of mutiny would have been capital.

With this alternative scenario in mind—Bligh, by consent of the whole crew, ignominiously confined below decks for the remainder of the

---

[48] *The Journal of John Fryer*, ed. Rutter, 58.

[49] N. A. M. Rodger, *The Wooden World* (London, 1986), 239. My discussion of eighteenth-century mutiny is indebted to Rodger's research on this topic.

[50] He was deprived of the command of *The Director* during the mutinies at the Nore. See George Mackaness, *The Life of Vice-Admiral William Bligh* (London, 1951), 308–9.

[51] For a contemporary account of these reprisals, see *An Impartial Account of the Life of Richard Parker, who was president of the delegates at the Nore* (London, 1797).

[52] Rodger, *The Wooden World*, 244.

[53] See Stephen Barney, *Minutes of the Proceedings of the Court-martial*, with an Appendix by Edward Christian (London, 1794; facsimile edn., Melbourne, 1952). See particularly Fryer's testimony (ibid. 7), and William Cole's testimony (ibid. 15).

voyage (or until an Admiralty outpost was reached)—it is not surprising that Bligh modulated his tone in so far as general observations about his officers went. For Bligh not to be at fault, he needed to prove that he was the victim of an unpredictable faction of the crew, rather than the fomenter of a general shipboard discontent; that his behaviour during the course of the voyage had been moderate, appropriate to his station, and, indeed, that he had not allowed his temper an unjustifiable free rein, the very quality, according to Fryer's account, that had cost Bligh the respect of his fellow officers. But such aims meshed uneasily with Bligh's broader efforts to establish himself historically as the sole exemplar of control and authority on board. Bligh did not wish to be remembered as a victim, he wished to be remembered as a successful and resourceful captain.

Bligh's description of the mutiny, like that of his dealings with Fryer and the carpenter Purcell, is a literary rendering of his own mode of proceeding that masked not only the strained relations with his officers but what also must have been a changed atmosphere—one of fear and alienation—on board the *Bounty* following the brief stop to reprovision at the island of Annamooka. This is an episode in the *Voyage* that has been little attended to, largely because Bligh himself depicts it as unimportant. He omits it entirely from the 1790 *Narrative of the Mutiny*, the action of which commences on the day following the incident. But it was important enough for Fryer to choose to frame the opening of his account of the mutiny and its fall-out with a description of this incident, and it is clear that the Master viewed it as intimately related to the action that followed it. It contains within it the first bloodshed of the *Voyage*, as well as the first acts of violence charged with lethal potential. The worst of the events at Annamooka occurred a scant day-and-a-half before the mutiny.

Bligh's *Voyage to the South Sea* mentions the loss of an axe, an adze, a spade, and a grapnel to native pilfering in the course of efforts to procure wood and water for the ship. A friendly islander, known to Bligh from his visit to the island in 1777 with Cook, is described as recovering the spade for them; as for the other hardware,

the croud of natives was become so great . . . that it was impossible to do any thing, where there was such a multitude of people, without a chief of sufficient authority to command the whole. I therefore ordered the watering party to go on board, and determined to sail . . .[54]

Bligh accompanied his determination to sail with a decision to detain three Annamookan chiefs, telling them that, unless the grapnel was

[54] Bligh, *A Voyage to the South Sea*, 152.

returned, he would not allow them to leave the ship. Having secured the chiefs and returned safely on board, Bligh casts this as a re-enactment, this time successful, of the failed kidnapping tactic that had got Cook murdered at the Sandwich Islands.

Bligh's version of the events on Annamooka is a detached, ship's-eye view that gives little hint of the difficulties experienced by the wooding and watering parties. Fryer, onshore, moving casks with Matthew Quintal, had a particularly unnerving experience. 'Quintal call'd out Mr. Fryer there['s] a man going to knock you down with his club—I turn myself round rather surprised, when I saw the Man Brandishing his club over my head, but as soon as he found I knew his intentions he set off into the Plantation—I was not arm'd even with a stik—'.[55] That Bligh had little sympathy for or understanding of these difficulties is clear from his reaction, as noted in his log. The watering party, those responsible for the loss of the grapnel, came in for a strongly worded attack:

The men cleared themselves of the Neglect as they could not comply with every part of their duty and keep their Tools in their Hands, and they therefore merit no punishment. As to the Officers, I have no resource, or [sic] do I ever feel myself safe in the few instances I trust them.[56]

Written down two days before the mutiny, that 'ever' is worthy of notice. It bespeaks a lack of trust, of alienation, absent from the *Voyage*, except, perhaps, as a nuance lying behind this retrospective comment: 'Had their mutiny been occasioned by any grievances, either real or imaginary, I must have discovered symptoms of their discontent, which would have put me on my guard'.[57] Reacting to symptoms of discontent by aggressively going on 'guard', rather than making attempts to alleviate the cause behind the symptoms, reveals something of the extent of Bligh's alienation from his crew. This is the same alienation that Bligh suppressed in the public account of his proceedings, the alienation, the jealousy of purpose, that undermined his captaincy.

Neither Bligh's log nor the published *Voyage* convey a sense of what it must have been like for his crew to confront a beach full of islanders whose intentions seemed far from friendly. This tension on the beach was followed by a period of more than six hours (from noon to sunset) during which the chiefs detained on board subjected themselves to horrendous acts of self-mutilation, beating themselves 'about the face and eyes' until even Bligh began to think that 'this distress was more than the grapnel

[55] *The Journal of John Fryer*, ed. Rutter, 54.
[56] Bligh, *The Log of the Bounty*, ii. 116.
[57] Bligh, *Narrative*, 11; *A Voyage to the South Sea*, 163.

was worth',[58] relented, and allowed the chiefs to go off into the canoes that had followed the *Bounty* out to sea.[59]

Bligh writes as if the matter had ended there, but it was otherwise for members of his crew. William Peckover, the gunner (one of the few crew members who had previous experience of the South Seas, a veteran of all three of Cook's voyages),[60] reported at the trial that when he woke up on the morning of the mutiny and was told that the *Bounty* had been taken his first thought was that the ship had been attacked by natives in canoes.[61] An undertone of violence rises to taint events both before the mutiny (the trouble on Annamooka) and after (the cutlass threats). The non-violence of the act of mutiny itself, a strange, quasi-legitimate act, rises to stand in stark contrast to the violent displays of temper that surround it. Bligh acquires a shadow of violence that would later develop into the myth of Bligh as a tyrannous violent man. It is a myth that, for all Bligh's textual manoeuvring and revision, had enough of a basis in fact to sustain itself.

'Circumstances of envy and jealousy': Bligh and Authorial Paranoia

By December 1792 Bligh appeared to be well on his way to total vindication from responsibility for the mutiny. He had seen the publication of his *Narrative* and its favourable reception in London in 1790,[62] had organized the publication of the *Voyage* in the mode of a weighty voyage of discovery, and, now in command of HMS *Providence*, was about to anchor off St Helena on the last leg of a successfully completed second voyage to Otaheite for breadfruit. His stature seemed unassailable. Bligh could not have known that he was about to return to London to embroil himself in a pamphlet war with Edward Christian, Fletcher's brother, that Bligh was going to lose. Although Edward Christian's work has been derided as biased, and 'self-contained',[63] the work of a man

---

[58] Ibid. 152.

[59] Bligh commented on the event, 'I have little doubt but that we parted better friends than if the affair had never happened' (*A Voyage to the South Sea*, 153). Fryer directly contradicts this view: 'Mr Bligh at last made those poor fellows presents and releast them, when those saw it in the canoes that there was some hopes of getting their cheefs back they cut their heads with their paddles, the blow you might hear at a considerable distance, the Blood run down their faces really a melancholy sight to see—lucky for Mr Bligh he did not get to Annamooka in the Boat' (*The Journal of John Fryer*, ed. Rutter, 55).

[60] See Fryer's comments on finding Timor, above at n. 40. Madge Derby, *William Peckover of Wapping: Gunner of the Bounty* (London, 1989), offers a brief biography.

[61] Barney, *Minutes*, 24.

[62] George Mackaness writes that Bligh's *Narrative of the Mutiny* was even an instigating factor in sending out HMS *Pandora* to capture the mutineers (*Life of Bligh*, 190).

[63] Ibid., 107.

ignorant of sea matters and discipline, it nevertheless exposed an aspect of Bligh's performance as a captain that, because it had been hidden, would rise to damage his credibility permanently.[64] This reversal was the beginning of the public attack and counter-attack concerning Bligh's reputation that continues to this day, as Bligh's own assessment of his role as a stable commander continues to be debated.

It was just at this juncture, before Bligh's return to London, that his young master's mate, Francis Bond, wrote a letter to his brother which contained an extraordinary passage on Bligh's attitude towards journal-keeping, a passage which reveals something of the intensity of Bligh's efforts at self-construction, and his blindness to the needs of those around him. Bond, who occupied the same position aboard the *Providence* as Christian had held in the *Bounty*, had a number of grievances against Bligh. The relationship between Bond and Bligh suggests something of what it might have been like to be a young officer reliant upon Bligh for advancement:

Among many circumstances of envy and jealousy, he used to deride my keeping a private journal, and would often ironically say, he supposed I meant to publish. . . . Every officer who has nautical information, a knowledge of natural History, a taste for drawing, or anything to constitute him proper for circumnavigating, becomes odious [to Bligh]; for great as he is in his own good opinion, he must have entertained fears of some of the ships company meant to submit a spurious Narrative to the judgment and perusal of the public . . . Tired heartily with my present situation, and even the subject I am treating of, I will conclude it by inserting the most recent and illegal order. Every officer is expected to deliver in their private logs ere we anchor at St. Helena. As our expedition had not been on discoveries, [I] should suppose this an arbitrary command, altho the words *King's request; Good of the Country; Orders of the Admiralty, &c, &c, &c,* are frequently in his mouth . . .[65]

Bligh was still seeking the stature accorded to Cook's *Voyages of Discovery*. The orders with which the Admiralty dignified a voyage of discovery are the shadow behind what might otherwise seem to be Bligh's arbitrary fixation on control. This letter throws some light on Bligh's insistent creation of himself (post-mutiny) as the one man capable of piloting the launch to safety. Bligh moulds himself as a polymath, possessively creating himself as the man most capable in any realm of endeavour, literary or otherwise. There is a blindness in this self-creation that sets itself on a collision course with any man who has a compelling

---

[64] The pamphlets were the *Minutes of the Proceedings* and Christian, *Short Reply.*
[65] National Maritime Museum Library, Greenwich, MS BND/46. See also George Mackaness, *Some Correspondence of Captain William Bligh RN with John and Francis Godolphin Bond* (Sydney, 1949), 71.

need to question the construction. Bligh cannot see the stake that men who need to combat court charges of negligence and criminality have in attacking such a construct. Yet Bond's suspicion that Bligh 'entertains fears' of becoming the victim of a 'spurious Narrative' suggests that doubt as to the propriety of his actions did indeed remain, however repressed.

The attack that was lying in wait for him on his return to England was an event for which Bligh was ill prepared. Standing off St Helena, Bligh would have had no external reason to suggest to him that his final reflection on the *Bounty* voyage was no longer well in place:

my mind was disposed to reflect on our late sufferings, and on the failure of the expedition; but, above all, on the thanks due to Almighty God, who had given us power to support and bear such heavy calamities, and had enabled me at last, to be the means of saving eighteen lives.[66]

Was Bligh the means of saving eighteen lives or of putting forty-two lives (the entire *Bounty* crew) at risk? The portrait he gave of himself may initially have created the image of a stable man of command, but the means by which he chose to do this left too little credit to the men who had shared his distresses. That Bligh had something of a guilty conscience about this construct is suggested by his behaviour on board the *Providence*, aggressively confiscating journals—not an act easily comprehensible to any sailor who has performed his duty unexceptionally, with neither slurs on his commander nor ambitions to publish. That Bligh had a reason for such a guilty conscience is borne out by his altercation with the Carpenter, already quoted earlier this chapter, the echo of which lies behind all the great *Bounty* debate:

what have I brought you here when if I had not been with you, you would have all aperished, yes Sir the carpenter said, if it had not been for you we should not have been here—[67]

[66] Bligh, *A Voyage to the South Sea*, 236.
[67] *The Journal of John Fryer*, ed. Rutter, 71.

PART THREE

The Eighteenth-Century Canon

13 *Parnell, Pope, and Pastoral*

CHRISTINE GERRARD

Roger Lonsdale's two Oxford anthologies have taught us to expect the unexpected from eighteenth-century poetry. Amid the women poets, farm labourers, Dissenters, and other previously marginalized writers who now jostle for our attention, Thomas Parnell's decorous urbanity seems curiously outmoded. Bar his Irishness (a quality barely evident in his published work), Parnell looks like T. S. Eliot's archetypal eighteenth-century poet: a classically educated country parson prone to the 'spleen', one of the school of Pope, a minor member of the Scriblerus Club. His best known poems—'The Hermit', 'An Elegy to an Old Beauty', 'A Night Piece on Death'—have invited praise for their neo-classical elegance, wit, polish, clarity, or (in the case of the last) their 'restrained' emotionalism. Parnell is 'the epitome of early eighteenth-century polite poetry'.[1] Now that we are beginning to discover what the polite 'Augustan' style excluded from the canons, does Parnell really warrant reappraisal?

Claude Rawson's and F. P. Lock's *The Collected Poems of Thomas Parnell* (1989), a substantial 720 pages long, has given pause for thought.[2] Two artistic virtues previously associated with Parnell were brevity and control, qualities exemplified by the short pieces in the posthumous edition of his verse, the *Poems on Several Occasions* (1722).[3] Parnell, who died suddenly, aged 39, on his way home to Ireland in 1718, had only ever had nine poems published in his lifetime. The *Poems on Several Occasions*, a slim, elegant selection of twenty poems and some prose pieces, chosen and edited by his friend Pope, effectively secured for Parnell the literary reputation he had never enjoyed while alive. Although the Parnell corpus was enlarged from manuscript sources at intervals during the eighteenth century, notably in 1758 when the *Posthumous Works of Dr. Thomas Parnell ... Containing Poems Moral and Divine* appeared, Rawson and Lock have recovered and printed from the papers of the Congleton family (Parnell's brother's descendants) sixty-seven new English Parnell poems and seven fragments

---

[1] T. M. Woodman, 'Parnell, Politeness and "Pre-Romanticism" ', *Essays in Criticism*, 33 (1983), 205–19. See also his *Thomas Parnell* (Boston, 1985), for a fuller assessment of Parnell's place in the 'polite' tradition.

[2] *The Collected Poems of Thomas Parnell*, ed. Claude Rawson and F. P. Lock (Newark, Del., 1989) (hereafter *CP*).

[3] Published Dec. 1721, though with 1722 on title-page.

as well as several Latin poems and some hitherto unseen early versions of poems which later appeared in revised form in the *Poems on Several Occasions*. The editors are modest about their volume's appeal to a readership wider than Scriblerian devotees, but it is hard to ignore an edition which claims such a substantial enlargement of a minor poet's *œuvre*.

Much of the new material reproduced in the *Collected Poems* was written prior to 1711, before Parnell became involved in London literary life. Readers of the 1758 *Posthumous Poems*, where some of Parnell's juvenilia first appeared, were dismayed to encounter not polished, arch couplets, but long, earnest, biblical paraphrases of a decidedly evangelical turn. Could such an 'elegant, pure and spirited a Writer', asked a reviewer for the *Critical Review* in 1758, really have written pieces 'which resemble the wild and nonsensical hymns of a mad Moravian'? No. 'These poems are spurious,' he asserted, since 'Nothing sure can be more unlike Dr. Parnell.'[4] The reviewer's confident assumption that he knew the 'real' Parnell begs the question which Roger Lonsdale's students have learnt to ask of eighteenth-century poetry: how influential is the selection, editing, and packaging of poetry in defining how subsequent generations pigeonhole their poetic predecessors? The *Critical Review*'s 'Dr. Parnell' was the Parnell who Pope bequeathed to the public through the 1722 *Poems on Several Occasions*. Yet a large amount of Parnell's earlier unpublished work, we now discover, was very different and by no means risible. It espoused values, both moral and political, strikingly at variance with the Tory politics, Scriblerian wit, and worldly sophistication suggested by the *Poems on Several Occasions*.

Parnell's family background was Commonwealth and regicide. His parents had moved to Ireland after the Restoration of Charles II. Born in Dublin in the autumn of 1679, he was early destined for a clergyman, and entered Trinity College Dublin at the early age of 13, a low-Anglican, impassioned Anglo-Irish Whig whose admiration for William and Mary went beyond obligatory Protestant piety.[5] His first poem on the death of the 32-year-old Queen Mary, written when he was only 15 (1694), may be rough, but it is plangent—'The Persians us'd at setting of yᵉ sunn | To howl, as if he nere again should runn | They onely acted it but we indeed | Must doot'.[6] The simple refrain 'all that lovely was is fled | all that was great good Just & vertuous Dead' is far more sincere than the baroque artifice of his 1713 Tory poem 'On Queen Anne's Peace'.

---

[4] *Critical Review* (Aug. 1758), 121.
[5] See e.g. 'On The Trust', *CP* 351–2; 'On yᵉ Plott against King William', *CP* 334–5.
[6] *CP* 332.

Many of Parnell's early works, concerned with Irish politics, are unusually hostile to the English parliament. He wrote a vigorous tribute to
Jeremy Collier[7] implicitly comparing his essay on the 'debauchd' Restoration stage with Spenser's Guyon destroying the Bowre of Blisse. Collier's attack 'shew[s] the sodom wch you teach to shun'—and this
included (so it seems) William Congreve's comedies, a blot on his reputation as Queen Mary's elegist. From the so-called 'Satires' notebook,
Rawson's and Lock's most important discovery, emerge Parnell's satires
on secular themes—the nature of virtue, poetry, the law, the court, the
spleen. These were probably written after the biblical paraphrases, between 1702 and 1711.[8] 'The Spleen' is a very engaging Billy-liar fantasy
in which the poet imagines himself as statesman, antiquarian, lover, and
soldier in turn. In Satire 4 the 'Pretty Gentleman' of its title comes to a
sticky end in debtor's prison from too much theatre-going and modelling
himself on Etherege's Dorimant, 'a man of air a beau | Nay poet too'.[9]
This puritanical progress-piece against wit, plays, 'wine & whores &
games' was written around the time that Pope was posturing as a
hard-drinking Restoration rake, 'fairsexing it' round London in the
company of William Wycherley and Henry Cromwell. Given Pope and
the Scriblerians' endless ridicule of the Whig Sir Richard Blackmore's
Arthurian epics on William, it is striking how much the young Parnell
admired them. 'B———r in Epicks may be still inspir'd, | by men of sence
approv'd by all ye rest admir'd.'[10] The heroic William's 'thickned law-
rells' will 'crowne ye poet wch adorns ye King'.[11]

Parnell's friendship with Swift may have dated back to as early as 1704
when both held minor offices at St Patrick's, Dublin. His first excursions
to London probably began as early as 1706, but the visits became regular
after his wife's death in 1711. Through Swift, Parnell became friendly
with the Whig writers Richard Steele and Joseph Addison, who printed
some of his lyrics and essays.[12] In the last years of Anne's reign, as the
political antagonisms between the Whig and Tory parties became more
acute, Parnell, through Swift's influence, was drawn into Tory circles. By

---

[7] Ibid. 341–2.
[8] The 'Satires' notebook (CP 344–408) contains thirty-seven items, of which twenty-eight are new
poems and nine are versions of eight previously published poems. The items can be dated from internal
references as running from *c*.1700 through to *c*.1713–14.
[9] CP 363.
[10] Cf. Pope, *Essay on Criticism* (1711), l. 391, 'For Fools *Admire*, but Men of Sense *Approve*.'
Parnell's line predates Pope's probably by some ten years. Pope's allusions to Blackmore in this poem
are very different from Parnell's.
[11] CP 345.
[12] Parnell contributed two allegorical prose 'visions' to the *Spectator* (nos. 460, 501) and two to the
Guardian (nos. 56, 66). The fifth vision of a library appeared in print for the first time in *Poems on
Several Occasions*. He also contributed four short pieces to Steele's *Poetical Miscellanies*, published at
the end of Dec. 1713.

1713 he was friendly with the Tory ministers Robert Harley and Henry
St John, Viscount Bolingbroke, and was meeting informally with Pope,
Swift, Gay, and Arbuthnot, the nucleus of what was soon to become the
Scriblerus Club. Parnell's poetry inevitably changed, most would claim
for the better. He developed a sense of humour, the piety became less
pronounced, the roughness was smoothed out and replaced by sophistication. Parnell may not have wanted to be remembered for his earlier
verse. Yet one of the problems is that he seems to have been totally
indifferent to *any* kind of literary fame: 'I seek no praise & keep me safe
from shame | Not known to many & unknown to fame.'[13] Apparently
devoid of ambition, he was particularly susceptible to manipulation by
stronger forces, notably Pope. And, although Parnell would probably not
have found a place in eighteenth-century literary history had it not been
for Pope, the *Collected Poems of Thomas Parnell* raises certain important questions about the motives behind Pope's posthumous tribute to his
friend, about the choices and decisions he made for the *Poems on Several
Occasions*. For the first time we can see Parnell spread out in full—not
only the range of Parnell's unpublished work but earlier manuscript
versions of poems such as 'An Allegory on Man' and 'Health: An
Eclogue', to add to the earlier versions of 'Hesiod', 'A Night Piece on
Death', and 'The Hermit' which had previously come to light in the
1755 *Works in Verse and Prose*.

It is impossible to reach any definite conclusions about the extent of
Pope's 'shaping' of Parnell. Parnell evidently trusted Pope's superior
judgement in literary matters. After he returned to Ireland for good in
late 1714, he continued an active correspondence with Pope. In 1716 he
gave Pope some of the poems which later appeared in the 1722 volume,
intending Pope to prepare them for publication on his behalf. They may
have been designed for the 1717 *Miscellany* that Pope was putting
together, or perhaps for a separate Parnell edition. In March or April
1717 Pope wrote to Parnell, 'in the poems you sent I will take the liberty
you allow me . . . Let me know how far my commission is to extend, and
be confident of my punctual performance of whatever you enjoin.'[14]
Parnell's unexpected death the next October probably meant that Pope
never received the guidance he had requested. Pope put Parnell's work on
one side until 1720, when he wrote to Jervas of 'Parnelle . . . to whose
Memory I am erecting the best Monument I can. What he gave me to

[13] 'Satyr 5: Verse', CP 365. This is an interesting and apparently autobiographical piece: perhaps
written before Parnell's association with Pope.
[14] *The Correspondence of Alexander Pope*, ed. George Sherburn (5 vols.; Oxford, 1956), i. 395.
Pope here mentions having read Parnell's 'Pandora' ['Hesiod'] and the 'Eclogue upon Health', neither
of which appeared in *Pope's Own Miscellany* of 1717.

publish was but a small part of what he left behind him, but it was the best, and I will not make it worse by enlarging it.'[15] We can never be sure how far the *Poems on Several Occasions* represented Parnell's own intentions. Pope burnt all his Parnell manuscripts, thereby effacing all evidence of his sources. Rawson and Lock show us that Parnell himself was capable of revising his own poems: Pope may have been working from some now lost manuscripts, brought to their near final state by Parnell himself. Although 'there can be little doubt that Pope made some improvements to the texts of his friend's poems',[16] Rawson and Lock are cautious (over-cautious, perhaps) in pointing the finger anywhere specifically at Pope. In any case, their consistent use of the term 'improvements' rather than 'alterations' accords with their generous estimate of Pope's benign influence on Parnell, both as friend and editor. In producing the *Poems on Several Occasions*, Pope, they claim, selected the best and discarded the rest. Had Parnell lived, he 'would probably have thought himself fortunate in the friendship of a great poet and a tactful editor'.[17] But Donald Davie, in an important review article, raises a more sceptical voice. Given Pope's lifetime habit of pressing into service the writings, even the private confidences, of his friends to bolster his own literary reputation, could it be that the 'Monument' which Pope erected to Parnell was also, in some way, a monument to himself?[18]

Neither Pope nor Swift was devoid of ulterior motives in encouraging Parnell as a poet. Swift recognized Parnell's talent, and prided himself on drawing him to Bolingbroke's and then Harley's attention, on 'making the Ministry desire to be acquainted with Parnell, and not Parnell with the Ministry', partly to foster the Tory administration's reputation for artistic patronage and learning.[19] It was Swift who in 1712 persuaded Parnell to insert some fulsome compliments to Bolingbroke in his *Essay on the Different Styles of Poetry* (not an improvement from an artistic viewpoint), and pushed him to finish the revisions so that he could finally get it published in 1713. With Pope, Parnell enjoyed a particularly affectionate relationship. Yet Pope probably needed Parnell as much, if not more than Parnell needed him. Oliver Goldsmith was probably right in his later observation that 'the commerce between them was carried on to the common interest of both'.[20] By the time the pair met, probably around 1711, Pope, smarting from the savagery of the elderly critic John Dennis's nasty personal attack following his *Essay on Criticism*, was discovering that the life of wit was truly 'a

[15] Pope, *Corr.* ii. 24.
[16] *CP* 24.   [17] Ibid. 23.   [18] *TLS*, 8–14 Dec. 1989.
[19] Swift, *Journal to Stella*, ed. Harold Williams, (Oxford, 1947), 646.
[20] Oliver Goldsmith, *The Life of Parnell* (London, 1770), 34–5.

warfare upon earth'. Pope needed to gather literary allies as rapidly as he made literary enemies, and his friendship with Parnell was played out against the backdrop of increasing animosities between the Whigs and the Tories.

Political and literary affairs during the last years of Anne's reign were closely interconnected, in part because during this period writers could still play an active role in public life. Addison and Prior were both diplomats, and many other writers, including Parnell himself, sought lesser office.[21] Pope, whose Catholicism debarred such ambitions, prided himself on his non-partisanship, at least up to 1713. Despite the closeness of his friendships with eminent Tories such as William Trumbull and Lord Lansdowne, both he and Swift kept on good terms with Steele, Addison, and other lesser Whig wits who frequented Button's Coffee House: men such as Thomas Tickell, Ambrose Philips, and Addison's cousin Eustace Budgell. Yet the increasing tension between the Whig and Tory parties, especially during and after the Tory-negotiated Treaty of Utrecht (1713), placed a strain on literary neutrality. Anne's severe ill health deepened the Whigs' anxieties over the security of the Protestant Hanoverian succession. They accused the Tories of negotiations with the exiled Stuarts, and Pope's own *Windsor-Forest* contained lines that confirmed Whig suspicions that Pope was 'disaffected'. Hostilities first broke out over the rival merits of Pope's and Ambrose Philips's respective *Pastorals* (to be shortly discussed) in spring 1713. By that autumn, Addison had turned against Pope. It was probably at Addison's suggestion that the Oxford Whig Thomas Tickell began work on a translation of Book I of the *Iliad* (with plans for a translation of the entire epic) which was almost certainly an attempt to spoil the success of the subscription edition of the *Iliad* that everyone knew Pope was preparing. Tickell's first book appeared two days after Pope's in June 1715, 'at a time' (as Parnell wrote) 'when it cou'd not but appear as a kind of setting up against you'.[22]

Parnell was a skilled classicist who gave Pope invaluable advice and assistance. He stayed with him at Binfield all through the spring and summer of 1714, preparing Homer. Pope's lack of confidence in his own expertise emerges in his coy letter to Parnell: 'You are a Generous Author, I a Hackney Scribler, You are a Grecian & bred at a University, I a poor Englishman of my own Educating.'[23] As late as July 1717, Pope

---

[21] Apparently Swift tried, but failed, to obtain for Parnell a post with the Commission that was to accept the surrender of Dunkirk. See Woodman, *Thomas Parnell*, 5.

[22] Pope, *Corr.* i. 299. George Sherburn, *The Early Career of Alexander Pope* (Oxford, 1934), contains the fullest account of the political and literary conflicts of this period with their *dramatis personae*.

[23] Pope, *Corr.* i. 225–6.

was still requesting Parnell's help with Homer. If Parnell 'could yet throw some hours away, rather on me than him, in suggesting some remarks upon his 13th, 14th, 15th and 16th books, it would be charitable beyond expression'.[24] One wonders if Pope's promise to edit Parnell's poems was not some kind of friendly quid pro quo for all Parnell's help with Homer. In the same letter Pope tried to excuse his tardiness: 'I only meant to have told you the reason that your poems are not published.' The political conflicts to which he vaguely alludes (the 1717 split in the Whig party) can have had little bearing on Parnell's own verse. Pope was probably too busy at this stage with his own literary affairs. It seems clear that the only Parnell compositions Pope was ever really keen to publish were, in fact, those which advertised his own work and defended his own literary reputation—namely, Parnell's *Essay on the Life, Writings and Genius of Homer* with which Pope prefaced Book I of his *Iliad* (1715), the *Life of Zoilus*, a satirical attack on Homer's pedant critic Zoilus, and Parnell's translation of *Homer's Battle of the Frogs and Mice* (published together, May 1717).[25]

Pope later complained of the stiffness of Parnell's prose—but the *Essay on Homer* was a useful formal vindication of Pope's principles of versification and translation by an 'authority', a classical scholar: and its very dryness contrasted admirably with the 'fire' of Pope's translation. The *Life of Zoilus* not only by implication attacked Dennis and Pope's other detractors, but enhanced Pope's own reputation by drawing attention to him as Homer's heir: Zoilus predicts that there 'shall arise a poet in another nation, able to do Homer justice, and make him known amongst his people to future ages'.[26] Parnell's translation of Homer's miniaturist mock-epic, the *Batrachomuomachia*, done at Pope's suggestion, borrowed elements of Pope's *Rape of the Lock*, as well as advertising Pope's own translation of the *Iliad* by a translation of Homer's caricature of the poem.[27] All of this, as Richard Dircks noted, was designed 'not so much to destroy the critics of Pope as to enhance the reputation of the poet'.[28] Pope spent over two years extracting these works from Parnell. 'Let *Zoilus* hasten to your friend's assistance'; 'the thing I wish above all

---

[24] Ibid. 415–16.

[25] The complex role played by these three interrelated works is charted by Richard Dircks, 'Parnell's "Batrachomuomachia" and the Homer Translation Controversy', *Notes and Queries*, 201 (Aug. 1956), 339–42.

[26] Parnell, 'The Life and Remarks of Zoilus', repr. in *Poetical Works of Thomas Parnell*, ed. Revd J. Mitford (1833), 161.

[27] See Pope–Parnell, 6 July 1717: 'to say that I like it still the better . . . because it was done at my desire is no more than you know already' (Pope, *Corr.* i. 415). Pope probably suggested the *Zoilus* prose too: cf. his caricature of Zoilus in *Essay on Criticism*, ll. 464–5: 'Nay shou'd great *Homer* lift his awful Head | *Zoilus* again would start up from the Dead.'

[28] Dircks, 'Parnell's "Batrachomuomachia" ', 340.

things, it is to see you again; the next is to see here your treatise of Zoilus
with the Batrachomuomachia.'[29]

Did Parnell continue to serve the same function even after his death,
enshrined in the *Poems on Several Occasions* as Pope's friend, supporter,
and admirer, a lesser but complementary literary talent who reflected, by
comparison, Pope's greater glories? In 1717 Pope had erected a handsome monument to his own precocious genius in the *Works of Mr. Pope*.
Parnell's eulogistic poem 'To Mr. Pope' first appeared among the com-
mendatory verses prefixed to the volume. Its moving last lines, dramatiz-
ing Parnell's exile in Ireland 'Far from the joys that with my soul agree, |
From wit, from learning—very far from thee', said as much for Pope's
personal charisma as did its glowing comparisons with the greatest
classical poets Horace, Virgil, and Homer for his literary pre-eminence.
'To praise, and still with just respect to praise | A Bard triumphant in
immortal bays.'

> O might thy Genius in my bosom shine!
> Thou shoud'st not fail of numbers worthy thine;
> The brightest Ancients might at once agree
> To sing within my lays, yet sing of thee.[30]

A generous tribute from an older to a younger man, and 'one of the finest
compliments that ever was paid to any poet'.[31] Pope reprinted 'To Mr.
Pope' in the Parnell 1722 *Poems on Several Occasions*—ostensibly to
commemorate their friendship. Yet there is something undeniably self-
serving about choosing for a modest volume of another man's verse a
poem which celebrates one's own very substantial achievements (the
Pastorals, *Windsor-Forest*, the *Rape of the Lock*, *The Temple of Fame*,
the Homer translations). Parnell presents himself as Pope's acolyte: 'O
might thy Genius in my bosom shine', 'Still, as I read, I feel my bosom
beat, | And rise in raptures by another's heat'. Another piece in the *Poems
on Several Occasions*, 'A Translation of Part of *The Rape of the Lock*',
had also previously appeared in 1717, the only Parnell piece to find its
way into *Pope's Own Miscellany*. According to Scriblerian apocrypha,
Parnell produced this Leonine Latin version of the description of Belinda's *toilette* one night after listening to Pope's recital of the poem he was
composing. He brandished it the next morning as the 'original source'
from which Pope had stolen his lines. A Scriblerian *jeu d'esprit*, affection-
ately reproduced, yet one that neatly served to remind the Parnell reader
of Pope's own poetic powers. Pope had more Parnell material in hand

[29] Pope, *Corr.* i. 285 (18 Mar. 1714/15); 333 (Feb. 1715/16).
[30] *CP* 119–21.
[31] Goldsmith, *Life of Parnell*, 45.

than appeared in the volume. Swift was surprised at the omission of the *Essay on the Different Styles of Poetry*, Parnell's most substantial independent poetic work in print. Pope may have left it out because of its praise of the now exiled Jacobite Bolingbroke. Yet political prudence did not stop him dedicating the entire volume to the now disgraced Robert Harley, and in any case the compliments could have been removed as easily as they had been added. Pope may have felt that Parnell's essay would inevitably suffer unfavourable comparison with his own *Essay on Criticism*, yet it is not impossible that he preferred not to publish another poem on a subject which he had made very much his own. Of the 217 pages of text in the volume, only 165 are taken up with Parnell's own poems: the rest are occupied by Pope's own dedicatory poem, the Latin translation of the *Rape*, the Latin source for the 'Vigil of Venus' and some of Parnell's rather inferior prose contributions to the *Spectator* and *Guardian*. As Rawson and Lock suggest, Pope may have wanted to record both Parnell's and his own associations with these papers.[32]

What were the principles at work behind the *Poems on Several Occasions*? Rawson and Lock deduce that 'the general aim [was one] of classical permanence. This was clearly the effect that Pope (and presumably also Parnell) wanted'.[33] The paring down and polishing of individual poems may be seen from textual changes which occurred between earlier manuscript versions and their final printed form. Manuscript versions exist for nine of the fourteen poems which first appeared in the *Poems on Several Occasions*. In some the changes made are slight, in others they are more substantial. Diction is refined and made more 'Augustan', yet (one feels) not always for the better. Some of Parnell's extended similes are omitted, sometimes to aid clarity, yet at a price. Although the 1722 version of 'An Allegory on Man', Parnell's reworking of an old fable about Care's ownership of mortal man, is undoubtedly more concise, something is lost from the early version: the haunting if imprecise seasonal metaphors for man's brief life, when *'Nature's* harvest fully grown | Bows with the Mellow'd ears of grain, | And longs to Prostrate on ye plain' until cut down by Time's 'long promiscuous blow'. These lines were cut, the last replaced with the makeweight 'Time draws the long destructive blow'.[34] In 'The Hermit', a rather dark theodicy about the ultimate rightness of God's designs, Pope was almost certainly responsible for turning the original Christian 'God' into a deistic or

---

[32] *CP* 19. [33] Ibid. 20.

[34] Ibid. 400; cf. 167. This point is also made by Donald Davie, *TLS*, 8–14 Dec. 1989. For other discussions of Pope's revisions to various Parnell poems, see Woodman, *Thomas Parnell*, 48–50; A. P. Hudson, 'The Hermit and Divine Providence', *Studies in Philology*, 28 (1931), 218–34; A. H. Cruikshank, 'Thomas Parnell, or What was Wrong with the Eighteenth Century?', *Essays and Studies*, 7 (1927), 57–81.

Newtonian 'Maker', a 'Him' to an impersonal 'It'. The devout Parnell would probably not have approved of the replacement of

> Eternal God the world's foundations laid,
> He made what is, and governs what he made

with

> The Maker justly claims that World he made,
> In this the Right of Providence is laid.[35]

A handful of the *Poems on Several Occasions* originally contained many more contemporary references, both literary and political. Cutting them may have won Parnell 'classical permanence', but at the cost of topical vigour. Pope's own poetry, it might be argued, had never suffered from its engagement with the specific, and suspicion invariably hovers over any form of political editing. Pope was unlikely to retain references which suggested that Parnell may have supported views and opinions other than his own, or that Parnell was politically neutral where he was partisan. Parnell may not have been so ready to renege on his Whig sympathies as Pope would have liked after 1714 and the Homer affair. The 1722 *Poems on Several Occasions*, even though it prints two short lyrics which first appeared in Steele's *Miscellanies*, none the less creates an impression of Parnell's unambiguously Tory sympathies: an impression reinforced by the dedicatory poem to Harley. This reminder of the friendship between Parnell, Harley, Swift, and Pope places the volume within the context of the Tory ministry of Anne's last years. Yet Goldsmith in his *Life of Parnell*, describing the period when the 'Whig wits held the Tory wits in great contempt, and these retaliated in their turn', claimed that Parnell 'was a friend to both sides, and with a liberality becoming a scholar, scorned all those trifling distinctions, that are noisy for the time, and ridiculous to posterity'.[36] An early version of 'The Book-Worm',[37] Parnell's mock-heroic pursuit of the monster roaming his library shelves, suggests that Parnell, at least up to 1714, remained politically neutral. It contains topical references one would certainly not expect in this year from a man who was friends with 'men who approved the Treaty of Utrecht and disliked the duke of Marlborough'.[38] One was a six-line Whiggish paean to Marlborough, the 'mightier *Heroe* . . . | Who forct the strength of *Gaul* to bow, | While *Blenheim* hills returnd thy name'. These lines were later removed; so, too, Parnell's lines deliber-

[35] CP 176; cf. 530.
[36] Goldsmith, *Life of Parnell*, 8.
[37] CP 162–4; variants at 518–20.
[38] Goldsmith, *Life of Parnell*, 8.

ately linking Whig and Tory writers, '*Pope* and *Addison*', '*Row Steel Pope Addison* and *Swift*'. Parnell made a plea for harmony: 'Sense may they seek, and less engage | In papers fill'd with Party-Rage.' This line was retained, but not the subsequent illustration mixing Whig and Tory writers indiscriminately together:

> Here's Fame to *Pope*, and Wealth to *Steel*,
> And all to *Addison* he will,
> May *Garth* have Practice, *Congreve* sight:
> May *Row* have many a full third night;
> Be Gentle *Gays & Tickels* lot
> At least as good as Budgel got.

Rawson and Lock argue that in the case of 'The Book-Worm', the revisions almost certainly point to Pope.[39] The 1722 version is not quite devoid of topical reference. Pope retained Parnell's compliments to Gay's 'Blouzelind' from his *Shepherd's Week* and his own 'Belinda', and four lines mocking John Dennis and Ambrose Philips, with his 'rustick strains', both mere 'mortal bards'—thereby giving the poem an anti-Whig bias it did not have in the earlier version.

The reference to Ambrose Philips leads us into a consideration of one area—pastoral—where Parnell's attitudes were certainly more mixed than this reference to Philips implies. Something that looks suspiciously like censorship seems to have taken place on one particular piece in the 1722 edition—'Health, an Eclogue'—which originally showed Parnell at work rethinking pastoral for himself and not necessarily agreeing with Pope. The Whig poet Philips, also secretary of the Hanover Club, wrote six pastorals which appeared alongside Pope's in the sixth part of Tonson's *Miscellanies* (1709). Pope's youthful exercises in classical decorum were highly praised, perhaps overpraised; but Philips, lionized by the Whig wits, began to attract more public critical notice. Five *Guardian* essays of April 1713, probably by Thomas Tickell, puffed Philips's *Pastorals* to the pointed and deliberate exclusion of Pope's, which were nowhere mentioned. The row which brewed up between Pope's Tory friends and Philips's Whig supporters focused on the critical debates over pastoral style and decorum, each side taking opposing views.[40] Philips's

---

[39] See CP 515–16.
[40] Accounts of the row are to be found in Sherburn, *Early Career of Alexander Pope*, 114–123; *Twickenham Edition of the Poems of Alexander Pope*, ed. John Butt *et al*. (11 vols.; London, 1939–69), i. 11–48. Both Pope's and Philips's pastorals were themselves politically encoded with covert references to Anne's illness and the succession crisis. Philips dedicated his to Lionel Sackville, duke of Dorset, Whig envoy to Hanover; Pope's *Pastorals* contained emblems with possible Jacobite allusions and were dedicated to Tories with Jacobite associations. For Philips, see Annabel Paterson, *Pastoral and Ideology: From Virgil to Valery* (Oxford, 1988), 218; for Pope, see John Aden, *Pope's Once and Future Kings* (Knoxville, Tenn., 1978), 62–3. The 'Prologue' to Gay's *Shepherd's Week*,

Pastorals, written in imitation of archaic rustic dialect, and drawing on British folklore and peasant names—Cuddy, Colin, Lobbin—were an attempt to continue the Spenserian tradition of a vernacular 'realistic' pastoral. Pope, conversely, followed what he believed to be classical precedent in stressing the 'Golden Age' pastoral world which required some 'illusion' to render it delightful: easy, simple, refined diction rather than crabbed, quaint dialect; classical shepherds named Strephon, Daphnis, and Alexis, not 'rustic' swains. In the manuscript version of the *Discourse on Pastoral Poetry* (c.1704) in which Pope set out his views, he had originally described his indebtedness to Spenser, but he was forced to expunge this reference in the printed version of 1717 after his clash with Philips.[41] On 27 April 1713 Pope took his revenge on Philips and his Whig supporters in his *Guardian* essay on pastoral, in which an 'anonymous' critic quoted and praised all the silliest-sounding rustic bits in both Philips and Spenser, then damned Mr Pope for deviating into 'downright poetry', claiming for him a classical lineage which included Bion and Virgil. Philips was apparently so incensed that he hung up a rod in Button's coffee-house to beat up Pope. John Gay rallied with his famous *Shepherd's Week*, finally published (after some delay) in April 1714, on the one hand a parody of Philips's rustic manners, on the other an affectionate, acutely observed minor masterpiece of rural realism which (paradoxically) helped prepare the deathblow to the kind of neo-classical Arcadianism epitomized by Pope's *Pastorals*.

Parnell, like the other Scriblerians, entered into the fray. Two of his six Scriblerian epigrams recently discovered by Rawson and Lock centre on the affair.[42] 'After the French Manner' describes Pope's and Gay's conversation accusing Philips of trying to bribe the publisher Tonson to delay the publication of the *Shepherd's Week* with money entrusted to him as secretary of the Hanover Club—money intended by its members for subscriptions to Pope's Homer translation. 'On a Certain Poets Judgement between Mr. Pope and Mr. Phillips done in an Italian Air' dramatizes the row between Pope and Philips through the story in Ovid's *Metamorphoses* 11 of Pan's and Apollo's singing contest. The rustic Pan (appropriately) is Philips, the divine Apollo, Pope. Midas the judge (perhaps Tickell) foolishly adjudicates in Pan's favour. Apollo exacts his revenge (an allusion to Pope's *Guardian* essay) by taking two laurel leaves from his own crown and sticking them on Midas's head, where

with its compliments to Harley, Bolingbroke, and Arbuthnot (ministering to the sick Anne) was an unmistakable declaration of Tory loyalties.
[41] See *Poems of Pope*, i. 13–33.
[42] Repr. in *CP* 417–18, commentary 650–1. Discussed by Rawson and Lock, 'Scriblerian Epigrams by Thomas Parnell', *Review of English Studies*, 33 (1982), 148–57.

they become ass's ears. Yet Pan, the 'Rustick [who] to his Fauns withdrew', is not an entirely absurd figure. His quiet withdrawal contrasts rather favourably with Apollo's spiteful revenge.

In the end, the row between Pope and Philips proved, in creative terms, far more positive than negative. It liberated pastoral from the neo-classical stasis epitomized by Pope's *Pastorals*, unleashing an enormous amount of imaginative generic cross-fertilization. It spawned Swift's plans for the 'porter, foot-man, or chair-man's pastoral' and the oxymoronic 'Newgate pastoral, among the whores and thieves', genesis of Gay's *Beggar's Opera*, as well as Mary Wortley Montagu's *Town Eclogues* (1717).[43] Parnell's own 'The Flies. An Eclogue', one of the *Poems on Several Occasions*[44] owes something to this burlesque application of pastoral style to incongruous subject: two flies perched on a milk-pail near a ditch engage in an amoeban singing match on the rival charms of Favonia and Zephyretta. In July 1714 Pope and Parnell penned a joint invitation to Arbuthnot which showed that they, like Gay, could slip in and out of Philips's rustic garb with ease:

> How foolish Men on Expeditions goe!
> Unweeting Wantons of their wetting Woe!
> For drizling Damps descend adown the Plain
> And seem a thicker Dew, or thinner Rain;
> Yet Dew or Rain may wett us to the shif[t]
> We'll not be slow to visit Dr. Swift.[45]

After 1714—a year marked by the accession of George I and the fall of the Tories—a more sombre note entered. Pope, Swift, Gay, and Parnell were much preoccupied with the theme of exile from Arcadia. Swift and Parnell returned to Ireland, and Pope finally left his family home at Binfield for good in March 1716 in a new political climate more punitive to Catholics. Two verses from Virgil's first eclogue, Meliboeus' lament on being forced to leave his homeland, recur repeatedly in their letters.[46] On 26 March 1716 Gay wrote to Parnell:

---

[43] Swift–Pope, 30 Aug. 1716, Pope, *Corr.* i. 360. For a stimulating discussion of the transmutation of pastoral convention to rural poetry via burlesque in Gay *et al.*, see Margaret Doody, *The Daring Muse: Augustan Poetry Reconsidered* (Cambridge, 1985), 99–109.
[44] *CP* 158–60.
[45] Pope, *Corr.* i. 235.
[46] For the Gay letter to Parnell, 26 [?] Mar. 1716, see Claude Rawson, 'Some Unpublished Letters of Pope and Gay, and some Manuscript Sources of Goldsmith's Life of Parnell', *Review of English Studies*, 10 (1989), 377–87, at 380. Pope quoted the same line from *Eclogue* 1.3 in a letter to Parnell written around the same time referring to the 'Solitary hours of your Eremitical Life, in the mountains'. See Rawson, 'Some Unpublished Letters', 377. Pope quoted it to his Catholic friend Caryll, 20 Mar. 1715/16 (Pope, *Corr.* i. 337). Rawson conjectures that Pope may have been applying it to the possibility that he might have to leave the country if the situation for Catholics grew any worse.

nos Patriae fines & dulcia linquimas arva, I don't love Latin quotations, but you must consider him as a pastor and a w[riter]. Binfield alas is sold. The Trees of Windsor Forest shall now no more listen to ye tunefull reed of the [?Popeian] swain.

Something of the feel of this letter lies behind Parnell's 'To Mr. Pope'.[47] Parnell, who as a classicist must have valued the 'correctness' to which Pope aspired, pays Pope the highest compliment by picturing him in a singing match with Virgil himself (Strephon and Daphnis): 'smile, all ye valleys, in eternal spring, | Be hush'd, ye winds! while *Pope* and *Virgil* sing.' The poet's reverie of the literary Arcadian landscape of rills and flowers merges with his own personal memories of the last summer he spent with Pope at Binfield.

> Thus in the wood, when summer dress'd the days,
> When *Windsor* lent us tuneful hours of ease,
> Our ears the lark, the thrush, the turtle blest,
> And *Philomela* sweetest o'er the rest.
> The shades resound with song—O softly tread,
> While a whole season warbles round my head.

Yet this idyllic *locus amoenas* in Pope's company is juxtaposed with scenes of exile and alienation in a far harsher and very un-Arcadian Irish landscape.

> For fortune plac'd me in unfertile ground.
> Far from the joys that with my soul agree,
> From wit, from learning—very far from thee.
> Here moss-grown trees expand the smallest leaf;
> Here half an Acre's corn is half a sheaf;
> Here hills with naked head the tempest meet,
> Rocks at their side, and torrents at their feet;
> Or lazy lakes, unconscious of a flood,
> Whose dull, brown *Naiads* ever sleep in mud.

The unhappy poet in his landscape anticipates George Crabbe's self-portrait in *The Village*, 'No, cast by Fortune on a frowning coast | Which neither groves nor happy vallies boast'.[48] Both poets contrast the unforgiving terrain of their birthplace—Derry's bogs and hills, Suffolk's thistles and sterile sands—with the smooth fictions of neo-classical pastoral. Parnell may not (as does Crabbe) blame pastoral poetry for deceiving socially complacent readers with false pictures of country bliss. But his

---

[47] CP 119–21.
[48] *The Village*, i. 49–50, in *George Crabbe: Complete Poetical Works*, ed. N. Dalrymple-Champneys and A. Pollard (3 vols.; Oxford, 1988), i. 158.

juxtaposition of the real with the ideal creates certain ironies. The 'pastoral Age of Gold in which the miseries of human life are carefully concealed' may, in the end, have that 'fatal irrelevance to human actuality' posed by the hard facts of a life lived close to the soil.[49]

This was the message first written into Parnell's early draft of 'Health, an Eclogue'.[50] When it appeared in the *Poems on Several Occasions* it was much shorter (78, as opposed to 116 lines) and served as a companion piece to 'The Flies'. The 1722 'Health', which seems to owe as much to the georgic as to the pastoral tradition, describes a youth Damon's retreat to a bower where he sings the praises of health, country life, and rural sports, followed by friendship, books, 'flutes and innocence', Virgil, and Theocritus. The blithe, optimistic ending accords with the light mood of the poem as a whole: 'These soft *Amusements* bring *content* along, | And *Fancy*, void of Sorrow, turns to song.' The earlier version in the 'Satires' notebook, probably written in 1714, was simply called 'An Eclogue' and did indeed explore pastoral issues—with some sophistication. Damon's happy song of the 1722 version was originally framed by lines which questioned the status of his literary fantasies, and the relationship between real and fictional representations of the shepherd's life. It might in its way be described as anti-pastoral. It is hard to know if the changes were all Pope's, but it seems likely.[51] In the early version 'Damon' was originally called 'Harry'—a very unclassical British name. The alterations were verbal as well as substantial. The 'Satires' manuscript begins:

> Now early shepherds ore y[e] meadow pass
> And print long foot-steps in the glittering grass;
> The cows unfeeding near the cottage stand,
> By turns obedient to the Milkers hand,
> Or loytring stretch beneath an Oaken shade,
> Or lett the suckling Calf defraud the maid.[52]

In Pope's version it reads:

[49] *Poems of Pope*, i. 49 (Introduction to *Pastorals*).
[50] *CP* 401–3. The 1722 shorter version is repr. in *CP* 156–8. Rawson and Lock (*CP* 22) rather oddly claim that 'The Book-Worm' was the only poem substantially altered between manuscript and Pope's text (thirty-six lines shorter). 'Health, An Eclogue' loses thirty-eight lines.
[51] Rawson and Lock (*CP* 22) claim that 'they cannot be attributed conclusively either to Pope or Parnell'. Parnell had gone some way towards preparing the longer MS version in the 'Satires' notebook for publication. He had punctuated the text, revised it (i.e. striking out a couplet), and done an accurate line-count. The 'Eclogue upon Health' was one of the poems Pope mentions having read in his letter to Parnell of March 1717, describing it as one of the most 'beautiful things' he had ever read (*Corr*. i. 396). This may indicate that Parnell had already removed some of the complimentary references to Pope's enemies himself, but not necessarily. Pope may not have read the poem closely. Even if Parnell had taken out these lines himself, it would have been in order not to offend Pope.
[52] *CP* 401.

> Now early Shepherds o'er the Meadow pass,
> And print long Foot-steps in the glittering Grass;
> The Cows neglectful of their Pasture stand,
> By turns obsequious to the Milker's Hand.[53]

Pope's version loses Parnell's last couplet of closely observed rural detail, the cows 'loytring' beneath the shade, the calf suckling its mother's milk. The substitution of the ornately anthropomorphic 'Cows neglectful of their Pasture' for the simpler 'cows unfeeding', the loss of the locational 'near the cottage', and the replacement of 'obedient' with 'obsequious' comes closer to the latinate, literary language of Pope's own *Pastorals*. It is a change for the worse. It makes what was originally fresh and immediate seem trite and conventional. So, too, the alterations to Parnell's natural descriptions, from:

> Ore the flat Green refreshing Breezes run
> To make young Dazys blow beneath the sun:
> While limpid waters to the bottom seen
> Lave the soft margin of the lovely Green.[54]

to

> O'er the flat Green refreshing Breezes run,
> The smiling Dazies blow beneath the Sun,
> The Brooks run purling down with silver Waves,
> The planted Lanes rejoice with dancing Leaves.[55]

'Smiling Dazies' instead of 'young Dazys', purling brooks, silver waves (almost clichés from the *Essay on Criticism*).[56] The loss of Parnell's image of slow-moving, transparent water, and of the liquid alliteration 'limpid ... lave ... lovely', is a pity. But it is from line 6 that the first major changes occur. This is the later version:

> When *Damon* softly trod the shaven Lawn,
> *Damon* a Youth from City Cares withdrawn;
> Long was the pleasing Walk he wander'd thro',
> A cover'd Arbour clos'd the distant view;
> There rests the *Youth*, and while the feather'd Throng
> Raise their wild Musick, thus contrives a Song.[57]

The 'Satires' manuscript version runs thus:

[53] Ibid. 156.   [54] Ibid. 402.   [55] Ibid. 156.
[56] See ll. 349–53 on trite pastoral description. See also Pope's own 'Winter', ll. 61–5, for similar epithets.
[57] CP 156.

> When Harry softly trod the shaven lawn,
> Harry a youth from Citty care with drawn,
> Unlike the lowly swains Arcadia bore,
> Their Pipes but sounded in the days of yore:
> Now Gales regardless range the Vaults above,
> And No fond swain believes they sigh for love,
> No more the Waters sympathising weep;
> Our Lads unskilld in musick tend the sheep;
> For Tom and Will our Yellow Ceres waves,
> And Kate instead of Chloris binds ye sheaves.
> Sicilian Muse thy higher strains explore,
> Thy higher strains may suit with nature more.[58]

Parnell debunks the pathetic fallacy central to Pope's famous 'Where-e'er you walk, cool Gales shall fan the Glade' passage in his 'Summer'.[59] Nature does not sympathize with man's emotions, and real rural swains are much more likely to be found gathering in the harvest than composing love-songs. The Arcadian shepherds of classical pastoral have vanished—perhaps they never existed. These lines anticipate something of the anti-pastoralism of Crabbe's *The Village*:

> Fled are those times, when, in harmonious strains,
> The rustic poet prais'd his native plains;
> No shepherds now in smooth alternate verse,
> Their country's beauty or their nymph's rehearse;
> Yet still for these we frame the tender strain,
> Still in our lays fond Corydons complain,
> And shepherds' boys their amorous pains reveal,
> The only pains, alas they never feel.[60]

Yet the more tolerant tone of Parnell's passage seems closer in mood to Stephen Duck's 1735 *The Thresher's Labour*. Tom and Will replace Damon and Strephon, the English Kate replaces the classical Chloris. Parnell's homely descriptions are an attempt to define pastoral in terms of a rustic British landscape—essentially as Spenser, Philips, and Gay had done.

It is thus not surprising to note that, in the earlier version, the four-line passage praising Theocritus and Virgil had originally introduced a longer discussion of more recent British pastoral poets.

---

[58] Ibid. 401.

[59] 'Summer', ll. 73–6. Cf. also Parnell's 'Colin' in the 'Satires' notebook (CP 375–7); 'tis true the rivers did not cease to run I the winds still blew tho still the shepheard sung.'

[60] *The Village*, i. 7–14, in Crabbe, *Complete Poetical Works*, i. 157.

> Great Maro's Muse, that in the finest light
> Paints Country prospects and the charms of sight;
> Strong Spencers Calendar, whose Moons appear
> To trace their Changes in the rural year;
> Sweet Pope whose lays along with Nature run,
> Through all the seasons which divide ye sun;
> The tender Philips lines, who lately tryd
> To plant Arcadia by the Severn side;
> And Gentle Gays that happily explore
> Those British Shepheards Spencer sought before.[61]

Were these lines cut in the interests of 'classical permanance'? Or was it because they showed Parnell adopting views essentially antagonistic towards Pope's own conception of pastoral? Parnell praises Pope—a couplet lost along with the rest in the 1722 version. Pope would not have usually axed compliments to himself. Yet here, unlike in 'To Mr. Pope', which presents Pope and Pope alone as the great modern pastoral poet, Virgil's heir, Pope is only one on Parnell's list of writers who have excelled in the pastoral vein. Pope's own classical 'sweetness' seems marginalized by the 'strong' British rustic tradition of Spenser, Philips, and Gay. Parnell here pays genuine tribute to the 'tender' Philips's efforts to create a vernacular pastoral by trying to 'plant Arcadia by the Severn side'. Parnell praises Gay's recent *Shepherd's Week* not as a witty burlesque but as a happy 'exploration', a development of Philips's aims in the Spenserian vein.

Also lost from the 1722 version was the detailed description of the arbour to which Harry/Damon retreats to sing his song. In the early version it is a screened-off pergola with 'cross-sloping railes' and a 'lattice front' covered in flowering woodbine: an artificial shelter designed to blend with, yet to block out nature. It is the symbolic equivalent of Harry's song, which presents only an idealized version of nature, not nature itself. The artificial and the real come into conflict in the final six-line coda. This was lopped altogether from the 1722 version, which ends with Damon's innocuous song: 'Here Beauteous Health for all the year remain, | When the next comes I'll sing of thee again.' The 'Satires' manuscript version ended thus:

> So sung the Youth. But now ye cool wthdrew;
> The sun had dryd the shaking drops of dew,
> Then ragd with flames insufferably bright,
> & shot the lattice with a checq'ring light;

[61] CP 403.

> The Zephirs fall, tho' not to hear his lay,
> And in his shade the Flyes offensive play.[62]

Not 'inoffensive', as one might expect, but annoyingly 'offensive'. Just as the blazing sun pierces uncomfortably through Harry's latticework shelter, so flies buzzing in the heat intrude on his polished Arcadian song. Parnell struck out his original bathetic last couplet which shows crude nature triumphant: the flies 'sting his face they buzz with humming tone | & break his music while they make their own'.

The early 'An Eclogue' is a far more subtle and ironic poem than 'Health, An Eclogue' as it appeared in the *Poems on Several Occasions*. It is hard not to concur with Donald Davie that 'something in Parnell was mutilated by his association with the Scriblerus Club'.[63] A loose sheet among the Congleton manuscripts, printed for the first time in the *Collected Poems*,[64] contains the following undated, untitled poem:

> Oft have I read that Innocence retreats
> Where cooling streams salute ye summer Seats
> Singing at ease she roves ye field of flowrs
> Or safe with shepheards lys among the bowrs
> But late alas I crossd a country fare
> And found No Strephon nor Dorinda there
> There Hodge & William Joynd to cully ned
> While Ned was drinking Hodge & William dead
> There Cicely Jear'd by day the slips of Nell
> & ere ye night was ended Cicely fell
> Are these the Virtues which adorn the plain
> Ye bards forsake your old Arcadian Vein
> To sheep those tender Innocents resign
> The place where swains & nymphs are said to shine
> Swains twice as Wicked Nymphs but half as sage
> Tis sheep alone retrieve ye golden age.

Here the Strephons and Dorindas of neo-classical pastoral are vacuous fictions compared with the Hodges, Williams, and Neds who form the 'real picture' of the rural poor. Hodge is, of course, the generic name for the English rural labourer: the backbiting 'Cicely and Nell' are the rustic cousins of Parnell's spiteful nymphs Caelia and Sabrina who vie for the favours of Thyrsis in another rather anti-pastoral piece he wrote, 'Thyrsis, a young and amorous swain'.[65] Yet these country 'nymphs' are

[62] Ibid.   [63] Donald Davie, *TLS*, 8–14 Dec. 1989.   [64] *CP* 421–2.
[65] Ibid. 132–3. The ironic deflation of the pastoral lyric (the romantic shepherd Thyrsis's disillusion) is discussed by Woodman (*Thomas Parnell*, 54–5).

well and truly fallen. Nor are their 'slips' portrayed with the generous humour of Gay's portrait of the liberal Susan in the *Shepherd's Week*.[66] The tight-lipped irony is again uncannily like Crabbe's line, 'Nor are the nymphs that breathe the rural air | So fair as Cynthia, nor so chaste as fair'.[67] Crabbe responded to centuries of Arcadian falsifications by describing villagers in their real habitat—drinking, slandering, fornicating, and punching each other up on the village green. His own anti-pastoralism was fuelled by a clergyman's social conscience and by his deep-seated distaste for the isolated rural community into which he was born and from which he escaped as fast as he could. The Parnell who left London in disappointment in 1714 to return home to Ireland 'made out a gloomy kind of satisfaction in giving hideous descriptions of the solitude to which he retired . . . that scarce a bog in his neighbourhood, was left without reproach'.[68] He had almost certainly not absorbed the early advice given him in 1706 by Archbishop King: that the man coming straight from civilized company 'is apt enough to despise the roughness or plainness of his country brethren'.[69] Had Parnell lived beyond the age of 39, he might have found this the irritant which would have transformed him from a 'polite' to a not-so-polite poet. His return to the cheerless 'Derry's oaten soil & frozen air' he had described in an early poem might have inspired verse which sounded less like Pope's, and more like an Irish version of that later 'Pope in worsted stockings', Crabbe.[70]

---

[66] See 'Friday; Or the Dirge'.
[67] *The Village*, ii. 49–50, in *Complete Poetical Works*, i. 169.
[68] Goldsmith, *Life of Parnell*, 21–2.
[69] See George Aitken, *Poetical Works of Thomas Parnell* (London, 1894), p. xi.
[70] The line is from Parnell's poem to a friend, 'To——' (CP 354–5). Parnell did not seem to have been as ready as Swift to write about a specifically *Irish* version of rustic life, e.g. Swift's 'A Pastoral Dialogue' between Dermot and Sheelah in which the 'Nymph and Swain' grub for potatoes among the thistles with wet backsides. But see his 'For Philip Ridgate Esq.' (CP 422) for a reproduction of Irish dialect and description of peasants dancing a 'bory'.

14 Poetry from the Provinces: Amateur Poets in the Gentleman's Magazine in the 1730s and 1740s

ANTHONY D. BARKER

Thomas Carlyle was particularly struck by an episode from Hawkins's *Life of Johnson* (1787), in which Johnson was taken to a Clerkenwell tavern to meet the champion of the *Gentleman's Magazine* poetry contests, Moses Browne.[1] According to Hawkins, Johnson,

being introduced by Cave, dressed in a loose horse man's coat, and such a great bushy uncombed wig as he constantly wore, to the sight of Mr Browne, whom he found sitting at the upper end of a long table, in a cloud of tobacco-smoke, had his curiosity justified.[2]

The curmudgeonly Hawkins's recollection of the scene diminishes everyone—Browne is invisible to posterity in a cloud of his own mediocrity, the magazine proprietor Cave is crassly unaware of his new hireling's superiority, and Johnson is the bumpkin in his coat and wig. Carlyle, reproducing the incident in *Fraser's Magazine* nearly a century after it happened, finds Johnson a giant among pygmies and transfers the wig to Cave's head. Thrice referred to as a 'dull oily Printer', Cave is finally dismissed metonymically as 'the great bushy wig'. The writing of eighteenth-century literary history has consistently worked thus, selecting a few peaks for prominence and levelling out the surrounding terrain. Pope initiated many of the confident assertions and dismissals of the first half of the century, and, even when his verse fell into disfavour in the next century, he was still regarded as a reliable guide to what was redeemable in his own age. T. S. Eliot is echoing Pope's judgements in *An Epistle to Dr Arbuthnot* and elsewhere 200 years later when he described the poetry of the century as essentially that of 'retired country clergymen and schoolmasters'.[3] Also castigated by Pope were maudlin poetesses, and *The Dunciad* of 1743 alludes to magazines as the place where the work of these amateurs began to appear. They are described as 'Miscellanies in

---

[1] *The Works of Thomas Carlyle in Thirty Volumes* (London, 1899), xxviii. 103.
[2] Sir John Hawkins, *The Life of Samuel Johnson* (2nd edn., London, 1787), 49–50.
[3] Introduction to the Haslewood edition of *Johnson's London and the Vanity of Human Wishes* (London, 1930), repr. in *The New Pelican Guide to English Literature*, iv. *From Dryden to Johnson*, ed. Boris Ford (London, 1982), 228–34.

prose and verse, in which at some times—new-born nonsense first is taught to cry; at others, dead-born Dulness appears in a thousand shapes.'[4] 'Verses, Epigrams, Riddles & c.' are listed as being 'equally the disgrace of human Wit, Morality, and Decency'. The *Gentleman's Magazine* was rehabilitated within two generations of its inception (Burke referring to it in the *Annual Register* (1780) as 'one of the most chaste and instructive Miscellanies of the age' and thereby hinting at its future as a staid antiquarian journal). Yet magazine poetry has had to wait until recent years to receive any serious attention.[5] The focus of this chapter is on this 'new-born nonsense' in verse and the extent to which it represents the voices of a misprized (if not actually despised) provincial middle class who had only limited access to the centres of literary influence. The *Gentleman's Magazine*, because it was expressly targeted at the country reader, was the principal conduit for, and preserver of, mid-century diversity in poetry.

Much has been written about the impact of editorial policy on rising sales of the *Gentleman's Magazine* during the 1730s and 1740s, most of it assuming that selection of matter or improved quality of content was a determining factor in establishing its primacy over its rivals. Johnson's parliamentary reporting is often adduced as a key factor. Those closer to events at the time, Cave's trading competitors, ascribed it to another cause. As the printer John Watts put it, 'I have been certainly inform'd his Agents give out that Mr Cave can command the Sale of an Edition of any thing he publishes, be it ever so paltry, by the Privileges he has of dispersing it thro' the Country.'[6] The *London Magazine* and the *Grub-street Journal*, a paper plundered and finally put out of business by the magazines, also refer to these 'Privileges'. Here is the latter's editor, 'Bavius', in the final editions of his paper: Cave, he writes,

might very safely offer to the Public a Pamphlet of three sheets and a half, in a very small character, for six-pence, containing more in quantity, and greater variety, than any Book of the kind and price. In the dispersing of which, he had likewise a very great advantage by his place in the Post-office; which gave him continual opportunities to prevent the progress of other Papers into the coun-trey, and to promote that of his own Pamphlet, without the expense of postage to his customers.[7]

[4] *Dunciad*, bk. 1, l. 42 and n.

[5] Most influential in reappraising eighteenth-century poetry have been Roger Lonsdale's anthologies *The New Oxford Book of Eighteenth-Century Verse* (Oxford, 1984) and *Eighteenth-Century Women Poets: An Oxford Anthology* (Oxford, 1989). For a general discussion of new approaches, see Karina Williamson, 'The Eighteenth Century and the Sister Choir', *Essays in Criticism*, 40 (Oct. 1990), 271–86.

[6] This allegation comes from a bifolium 'Letter to the Publick', dated June 1737, bound in with the Bodleian copy of the *London Magazine* (Hope Adds. 392).

[7] *Grubstreet Journal*, no. 417, 22 Dec. 1737.

Certainly up to January 1738 magazines were being sent into the country from the GPO Inland Office under the frank of the Clerks of the Roads.[8] Cave was a senior official of this Office and the Inspector of Franks. From the squeals of dismay coming from his rivals, it is clear that the *Gentleman's Magazine* alone possessed this advantage. Cave had the right to frank all his own letters, and there is every reason to believe that most if not all communication between the magazine and its country customers passed free of charge. Even after Cave's death, letters to the editor of the magazine were directed through the Clerks of the Road.[9] The Post Office had a crucial but for the most part now unquantifiable influence in establishing the pre-eminence of the *Gentleman's Magazine* over all its competitors, and the desire to exploit this trading advantage gave it a particularly provincial orientation. Apart from his Post Office connections, Cave cultivated excellent relations with the country through provincial newspaper proprietors. A former printer/editor of a Norwich newspaper himself,[10] Cave had operated in the 1720s as a supplier of news, especially parliamentary affairs, to provincial customers via newsletters.[11] He had at various times collaborated with Robert Raikes of the *Gloucester Journal*, William Dicey of the *Northampton Mercury*, James Abree of the *Kentish Post*, Thomas Gent of the *York Mercury*, and William Thompson of the *Stamford Mercury*.[12] There is no doubt that the newsmen who supplied country customers with these papers also delivered the *Gentleman's Magazine* to them. Elizabeth Carter wrote to Cave in June 1739 asking him to include a book for her 'when you send the Magazines to Mr. Abree . . .'[13] A similarly reciprocal relationship existed between Cave and many provincial booksellers—he was in communication with the Dublin bookseller George Faulkner,[14] supplied Thomas Warren of Birmingham with books from London when his credit was no longer

---

[8] GPO Headquarters, St Martin Le Grand, London: *Minute Books 1737–1774*, i. 4–9, details the struggle of the Post Office Governors to understand what forms of private enterprise were going on in the Inland Office and put a check on them.

[9] David Henry received a letter in 1757 from the Revd Samuel Pegge of Chesterfield, directed to Thomas Ravenhill, assistant to a Clerk of the Road (BL Stowe 748, fo. 189).

[10] David Stoker argues convincingly that it was the *Norwich Post* and that Cave was running it around 1712, in his 'Edward Cave and the *Norwich Post*', *University of East Anglia Bulletin*, 7/2 (1975), 1–5.

[11] The details of Cave's arrest and interrogation for breach of parliamentary privilege by distributing newsletters are given in *Journal of the House of Commons (1727–34)* (London, n.d.), xxi. 104, 108, 115, 117, 127.

[12] A reissue of the *Gentleman's Magazine* (hereafter *GM*) for Feb. 1731 mentions the first four provincial newspapermen in its imprint. Thompson was later included with them in the sale of other Cave-owned pamphlets, but his paper was in any event taken over by the Dicey family upon his death in May 1732.

[13] BL Stowe 748, fo. 169.

[14] Ibid., fo. 170.

good there,[15] and in the Quaker bookseller and printer–proprietor of the *Newcastle Journal*, Isaac Thompson, he had an essayist and contributor to the poetry columns of the magazine.[16] Also, Cave's brother-in-law and successor as editor of the *Gentleman's Magazine*, David Henry, was engaged in running the *Reading* and *Winchester Journals* and in a position to distribute the magazine throughout the central southern counties and the Isle of Wight. These trading alliances are the background to the prodigious success of the magazine in its first two decades and have a bearing on the kind of poetry the *Gentleman's Magazine* promoted.

The magazine did not appeal primarily to a metropolitan élite, who could amuse themselves with the whole range of London periodicals and papers at the coffee-houses if they so desired—it was aimed at the news-hungry and culturally isolated provinces and at the urban lower middle classes with little disposable income, for whom the charge against Cave, that he gave 'the Publick too much Paper and Print for their Money',[17] would have been ample endorsement. We can glimpse the former grouping of customers in a letter sent to Cave by Thomas Dodd of Chester, dated October 1735, which accompanied some proposed contributions to the magazine:

If for the encouragement of the Authors inclos'd who are 8 miles off any Bookseller you wou'd favour them with one years Magazines sent hither monthly by the Post you'd probably find a retaliation from some of their performances each alternative month or the favour otherwise acknowledged, since it coming so late from the Bookseller & perusing it one after another the month is at an End before 'tis well read over by them, so that by yr next I shou'd be glad if hopes thereof might be afforded them . . .[18]

The essential point here is that readers and contributors are one and the same people. Scholarly concentration on the magazine as a vehicle for advancing the careers of professional authors in London has obscured the real editorial situation. Johnson, Hawkesworth, and their kind were not typical contributors, but rather contracted specialists. It was by the talented amateur poet, scholar, mathematician, or controversialist that the monthly magazines succeeded or failed. Cultivating these people was the prime editorial task.

[15] The letters of Cave to Thomas Warren, detailing some of their commercial dealings, were printed in the *Birmingham Weekly Post* for 22 and 29 Aug. 1891, shortly before being destroyed in a fire.
[16] Thompson published a volume of his own poetry, *A Collection of Poems Occasionally Writ on Several Subjects* (Newcastle, 1731). Two essays on religious matters by him appeared in *GM* 7 (July 1737), 415–18; 8 (June 1738), 291–2.
[17] Quoted by Cave in his *Northampton Mercury* denunciation (see at n. 12 above).
[18] BL Stowe 748, fo. 143.

In its early years, the *Gentleman's Magazine* appropriated poetry in the same way that it lifted news and political comment from the daily and weekly papers, usually acknowledging the source. Under competition from the *London Magazine*,[19] it became more anxious and evasive about these thefts. It is difficult to determine what proportion of the work extracted appeared with the approval of its authors or copyholders—the excerpts from Pope's *Essay on Man* which were published all through 1734 were probably unlicensed,[20] whereas the piece in 1736 from Thomson's *The Seasons* may well have been sanctioned.[21] In August 1733 Cave reprinted Savage's 'To a Young Lady' from the *Grubstreet Journal* and found himself confronted by an irate author. The matter was resolved amicably shortly afterwards when the poem was reprinted in the magazine in a corrected text,[22] but the incident illustrates the precarious legal and moral position of the early magazines. It was, therefore, imperative that Cave forage for original verse contributions. The idea for poetry competitions, according to Cave, was suggested by a correspondent a year earlier. The immediate stimulus, however, seems to have been a prize essay competition run by the Royal College of Surgery in Paris.[23]

Poetry contests are usually cited as instances of Cave's naïvety. Beginning with Hawkins, commentators have puzzled over a defective judgement which could none the less pioneer a new type of literary organ and earn the respect of contemporaries like Johnson. Most explanations have pointed to the genius of his editorial assistants, when it is in fact the case that the magazine was already an assured success before better-known writers appeared on the scene. Poetry contests were an adroit solution to the problem of how to rise above origins in literary piracy, acquire a reputation for 'encouraging learning', and generate some cheap copy. They were never going to attract 'the first authors of the kingdom'[24] and in the first instance were intended only as a casual amusement. In all, eight competitions were launched between April 1733, when the first

[19] Since the *GM* had stolen some features from, and the market for, the *Monthly Chronicle*, which was partly owned by the *London Magazine* proprietors, it was a moot point who was behaving in the more piratical manner.

[20] *GM* 4 (1734), 43, 97, 157, 212–13, 325, 382, 442, 501, 561, 619, 694, 747; 5 (Jan. 1735), 41. The Feb. 1734 extract is accompanied by the assertion that the poem appearing in the *GM* can only help its sales, strongly suggesting that it was taken without Pope's permission.

[21] By the late 1730s Cave and Thomson were dining companions, probably through both knowing Savage. Clarence Tracy (*The Artificial Bastard* (Toronto, 1953), 124) suggests there were masonic connections. Certainly, Thomson's 'To his Royal Highness the Prince of Wales. An Ode' in *GM* 7 (Sept. 1737), 569, was printed with his approval.

[22] The defective text appeared in *GM* 3 (Aug. 1733), 433–4; the authorized one in *GM* 4 (Mar. 1734), 157.

[23] This is alluded to in the original proposal for a competition (*GM* 3 (Apr. 1733), 208).

[24] Johnson, 'Life of Cave', *GM* 24 (Jan. 1754), 55–8, was reprinted with textual changes by the author in *Biographia Britannica* (2nd edn., London, 1784), iii. 313–15.

was proposed on a theme of the Queen's grotto in Richmond, and April 1739, when the result of the last 'On the Divine Attributes' was announced. The difficulties which Cave encountered were no more than one would expect from the novelty and populism of the idea. Only the third ('On Life, Death, Judgment, Heaven and Hell') and the last had cash prizes, although for the penultimate ('On the Christian Hero'), Cave had a special medal cast as the prize.[25] Johnson's comment that Cave thought 'the influence of fifty pounds extremely great'[26] is a curious one, since it clearly was very influential to someone like himself, who at this time undertook many a dreary task for less reward. Competitions affected would-be professional writers in their *amour propre*—pride fought with penury in the Oxford-rejected scholar Johnson and the self-created nobleman Savage. Denigrated or ignored from this quarter, contests were also reviled in rival publications, where there was some jealousy of the stir they created. But they undoubtedly succeeded with the readership of the *Gentleman's Magazine*, with professional people, students, country clergymen, non-conformists, provincial ladies. Contestants were protected from the taint of exploiting their talents for gain by pseudonyms; indeed identities were so well concealed that it was complicated determining where and to whom to send the prizes.[27] Far from being a fiasco, they filled the poetry columns with much-needed copy, generated useful publicity for the magazine, and attracted entries from Ireland and the Continent (in Latin). The same Johnson who was to jeer at the £50 prize wrote to Cave from the Midlands in November 1734 offering his services to the magazine proprietor and alluding to the prize as evidence of his munificence as a patron of poetry.[28] More pertinently, he also offered him *London* to publish a few years later.[29]

Judging these competitions was no simple matter. Anyone could enter them, but the judges had, plausibly, to be authorities. Yet setting themselves up as arbiters in these matters made gentleman-authors look as though they had pretensions to being 'looked upon under the character of a Critick', as Joseph Spence put it to Cave.[30] Both he and Pope were approached and both politely but firmly declined the office.[31] Isaac

[25] John Gough Nichols (in 'The Autobiography of Sylvanus Urban', *GM* 201 (Aug. 1856), 137) gives an account of the problems Cave had in finding suitable subjects to be honoured on his medal.

[26] 'Life of Cave', *Biographia Britannica*, 315.

[27] Entrant no. VI for the 'Life, Death . . .' contest had given a Dublin address for correspondence, but three months after the results were announced, had not made any effort to identify him or herself and collect the prize (see *GM* 6 (Apr. 1736), 228).

[28] *The Letters of Samuel Johnson*, ed. Bruce Redford (5 vols.; Princeton, NJ, 1992–4), i. 5–6.

[29] For full details, see my 'The Printing and Publishing of Johnson's *Marmor Norfolciense* (1739) and *London* (1738 and 1739)', *Library*, 6th ser., 3/4 (1981), 287–304.

[30] BL Stowe 748, fo. 155.

[31] *The Correspondence of Alexander Pope*, ed. George Sherburn (5 vols.; Oxford, 1956), iii. 499.

Watts, in his capacity as poet and author of a work on astronomy, agreed to adjudicate the prize poems on astronomy. In his written judgement, he offered some objections to scurrilities in the poetry columns. Cave was quick to apologize and to propose that future competitions be on 'Sublime Subjects', as well as soliciting a poem from Watts himself.[32] The *London Magazine* mocked the whole enterprise and printed its own entries for the epigram competition, which were openly abusive of Cave and the *Gentleman's Magazine*.[33] So much was to be expected. Criticism was either partial or disdainful of the practicalities of running a large-circulation contributory literary miscellany. In retrospect, it seems a pity that Cave felt obliged to offer sacred and abstract subjects for his main competitions. It meant that his poets were straining for sublimity when it was neither their strength nor that of the age. Johnson, who disapproved of devotional poetry and had low expectations of occasional verse, was at least consistent in his dislike. An additional problem was that the same poets tended to win each time. These were Moses Browne and John Duick, Dissenting cousins who were Clerkenwell pen-cutters by trade. Browne's success was a source of embarrassment to Cave, laying him open to the charge of favouritism,[34] but, ironically, the uniformity of result probably testifies to his probity. Browne was quite a decent poet in a lighter vein. Although opinion was divided as to the lesser placings, few challenged Browne's poems. Duick, the perpetual runner-up, had no great talent to declare but was a ready versifier of the kind which the magazine needed, for the poetry columns rapidly attracted contributors who addressed poems to one another. Identities were eventually discovered, correspondence was exchanged between people in different parts of the country, friendships developed, and before long *Gentleman's Magazine* poets had formed a clique. The columns served a social function not dissimilar to the letters page of a modern newspaper; grievances were aired, public issues commented upon, compliments paid, occasionally private griefs were shared. A bantering style of light verse predominated, at which Cave himself was an adept. Long sequences of poetic expostulations and retorts, animadversions and defences were printed, under the benign editorial control of 'Sylvanus Urban'. The influence of poetry in the magazine was at its height during the second half of the 1730s, regularly comprising eight double-column pages a month. The more metropolitan *London*

---

[32] The two letters of Cave to Watts and Watts's reply to the first are given in Thomas Milner, *The Life, Times and Correspondence of the Rev. Isaac Watts DD.* (London, 1834), 507–11, 515–16.

[33] *London Magazine*, 3 (Sept. 1734), 487.

[34] In a poem entitled 'Urban and Will his Attorney: A Dialogue', in the *London Magazine*, 6 (Jan. 1737), 48, a very heavy hint is dropped that the £50 prize was a reward for services rendered.

Magazine, with its better book-trade connections, extracted more from newly published verse and did not build up a network of contributors to the same degree.

Many of the competition entries and most of the contributions to the columns came from the provinces. The only semi-reputable status of the contests now makes it difficult to break through the conventions of disguise which the entrants adopted. Some had no truck with pseudonymity, like the Revd John Hulse of Yoxhull, near Lichfield, previously of Hulm's Chapel in Cheshire,[35] although it got him no nearer the astronomy prize with his fellow Dissenter Isaac Watts. Another Midlands entrant B. Drake wrote to Cave to complain that his poem was not printed in the *Gentleman's Magazine Extraordinary* devoted to the 'Life, Death . . .' contest, whereas Latin poems from the Continent, excluded from the competition, were.[36] The first epigram contest was won by 'Vario' of Durham, with a woman, 'Corinna', in second place.[37] A modern jury would probably dissent from this verdict and put 'Corinna' in first place—the poems of 'Vario' are elegant rather than amusing. 'Corinna', however, produces poems which are both well crafted and funny. Her first epigram, 'On a Gentleman whose Thigh was put out of joint, by a Young Lady whom he attempted to kiss, as she was playing on her Spinnet', only just fails to live up to the splendour of its title, perhaps because it takes a rather indulgent line on sexual harrassment. Her third, 'On a Short Clergyman', manages to conjure comedy out of the contemporary fashion for high church-pews and pulpits:

> I went to M–r–d–n one sabbath even
> To hear the priest direct the way to heav'n;
> I heard, but cou'd not see; the stately pew,
> And lofty pulpit, hid him from our view;
> With heav'nly truths he charms our list'ning ears,
> The truths we hear; the preacher ne'er appears;
> Then laugh no more when *Homer's* tripods walk,
> Since now our desks can pray, and pulpits talk.

Browne's epigrams were much admired but Cave must have been relieved to award the spoils to two poets entirely unknown to him. John Nichols, quoting the poem above and identifying the place as Meriden, near

---

[35] Hulse did not enter the £50 prize contest. Instead he provided the prefatory poem, 'On the Dignity of Divine Poetry', addressed to the Revd William Broome (presumably one of the judges) in the *GM Extraordinary* (following July 1735).
[36] BL Stowe 748, fo. 144.
[37] Results announced in *GM* 5 (Sept. 1735), 556.

Coventry, observed that the better epigrams were often reprinted in eighteenth-century collections.[38] The Revd John Bunce of St Stephen's near Canterbury sent a letter acknowledging receipt of third prize in the 'Christian Hero' competition.[39] A letter survives from George Smith of York, in which he offers his own verdict on the 'Life, Death . . .' contest.[40] Clearly an entrant himself but disavowing any interest in the prize money, Smith accepts the superiority of Browne's poem, but disagrees with the choices for second and third places. Smith was a regular contributor to the magazine on subjects like mathematics and astronomy. This was his first and, if he is to be believed, only competition entry. Other letters testify to the interest generated by these events. An essay appeared in the *Barbados Gazette* for 1 October 1735 commending the idea of poetry contests and praising the quality of epigrams received.[41] The essayist made a belated entry of his own with three epigrams signed 'Americanus'. Poems and correspondence about poems swelled the postbags of England during the mid-1730s. Cave's primary objective had been attained. By the end of February 1738 he could assert that every poem in that month's number was an original offering, and that, should a reader see one elsewhere, it was sure to have been pirated from the *Gentleman's Magazine*. The abandonment of contests in 1739 may well have had more to do with the political scene than their supposed failure to catch with the public. In October 1739 war broke out against Spain and from then until the peace of Aix-la-Chappelle in 1748 the magazine strove to keep pace with naval engagements, European campaigns, the protracted attempts to oust Walpole, and the events surrounding the Rebellion of 1745. Parliamentary reporting, political journalism, and hard news displaced poetry as the chief editorial concerns. Poetry averaged only five pages per number throughout the 1740s, and often one of these was given over to a song, complete with sheet music. Moreover, the character of much magazine poetry changed, perhaps sobered by these momentous events. Poets essayed more public themes, and the columns increasingly began to reflect the contents of other parts of the magazine. Cave's passion for promotions turned towards maps, plates, illustrations, and scientific curiosities.[42]

Pat Rogers has argued that mid-century poetry had no centre.[43] The few poets of established reputation wrote from the provincial fastness of

---

[38] John Gough Nichols, 'The Autobiography of Sylvanus Urban', *GM* 201 (Aug. 1856), 135.
[39] BL Stowe 748, fo. 164.
[40] Ibid. fo. 145.
[41] It was extracted in *GM* 6 (Jan. 1736), 52, as was, in the next number in February, a letter from 'G.W.' of 'Bamff', Scotland, commending the epigrams by women (ibid. 107).
[42] These subjects are treated more fully in my 'Edward Cave, Samuel Johnson and the *Gentleman's Magazine* 1731–54' (Oxford D. Phil. thesis, 1981), ch. 6, 'Expansion and Diversification in the 1740s'.
[43] *The Augustan Vision* (London, 1974), 143.

Cambridge, Northampton, Halesowen, Chichester, and so on. This might help to explain the relative sparsity of canonical poetry from between 1740 and 1760. For the Augustans, it would have been sufficient explanation in itself. Johnson's comment on Thomson, that 'He easily discovered that the only stage on which a poet could appear, with any hope of advantage, was London; a place too wide for the operation of petty competition and private malignity where merit might soon become conspicuous', makes the familiar identification of the provinces with constraint and mean-spiritedness.[44] Clearly, he is referring exclusively to would-be professional authors, men such as himself. The remark takes no account of people with another profession to pursue, or no profession at all, or those not yet of an age to take up a career, or those who lacked the courage to take on the capital penniless. These were the groups of people whom the *Gentleman's Magazine* reached and whose contribution to its success has been consistently undervalued, in comparison with the attention given to jobbing hacks and minor scholars.

One of the largest identifiable groups of amateur poets would seem to be the country clergy. Having acquired the standard classical education of their day, young men, usually of middle-class backgrounds, took orders and were dispatched to different parts of the kingdom as curates. If they were lucky or well connected, they might be preferred to livings. Many felt no vocation for the church, but equally placed no faith in the life of writing for the booksellers, which talent and education might suggest as an alternative. Since stipends were usually modest, many, if not most, took private pupils or ran schools. A career in the church, therefore, blends almost indistinguishably with that of teacher. Literary ambitions might then spring out of and complement these professions. Many not prolific or confident enough to produce a volume of poetry contented themselves with sending their occasional poems to the magazines. 'Sylvanus Urban' was a useful man to know, for he accepted, as well as verse, mathematical puzzles, learned disquisitions, scientific theories, translations, even extracts from sermons on topical matters. Take the case of the Revd Robert Luck, Master of Barnstaple School.[45] He had been tending to his Devon parish and school since 1699, and was approaching 60 when the *Gentleman's Magazine* began printing his poems. Cave arranged a printing by subscription of his *A Miscellany of New Poems*, which duly came out in March 1736, followed by a second

[44] 'Life of Thomson', *Johnson's Lives of the Poets*, ed. G. B. Hill (3 vols.; Oxford, 1905), iii. 283.
[45] This school produced several famous men, including John Gay, Aaron Hill, John Jewel, Bishop of Salisbury, and William Fortesque, Walpole's Private Secretary and later Master of the Rolls (for Luck, see Joseph Foster, *Alumni Oxoniensis (1500–1886)* (8 vols.; Oxford, [1891]), iii. 946).

impression in 1737. Two years later Cave published by subscription the *Poems on Various Subjects* of his competition champion Moses Browne, whose career was on an opposite trajectory to that of Luck. Unable to support his large family by poetry and literary odd jobs, Browne renounced his Nonconformity as he approached 50 and took orders in the Church of England.[46] He thereafter lived out the rest of his long life in relative comfort, with few further incursions into poetry. Perhaps the best known of the priest contributors to the poetry columns was Pope's collaborator on the *Odyssey* translation, William Broome, who acted as a judge in more than one of the poetry contests.[47] The magazine had a particularly active group of contributors amongst the clergy of Kent, including Nicholas Carter of Deal, Samuel Pegge of Godmersham, John Bunce of Canterbury, John Clough of Ashford, and John Sackette of Folkestone.

Many who subsequently became priest–pedagogues had their first poems published in the *Gentleman's Magazine*. Minor figures such as William Rider,[48] Stephen Barrett,[49] and William Dodd[50] were either still students or newly graduated when their work started to appear in the columns (as was William Collins). Indeed, nurturing young poets was one of the strengths of the magazine. In April 1737 Cave began to receive poems from a correspondent signing himself 'Marcus'. This was Mark Akenside, then a 16-year-old pupil at a Dissenters' academy in Newcastle. In all, five of his early poems appeared in the magazine and one, 'A British Philippic', signed 'Britannicus', was published in folio simultaneously in August 1738 from St John's Gate.[51] At this stage, the poet was still unknown to Cave, although he had identified himself in a letter before the reissue of the poem as 'The Voice of Liberty'. The reissued poem was still in the original text, as 'corrected' by Moses Browne, despite the fact that Akenside's letter contained his own corrections.[52] When the magazine took an extract of 'The Pleasures of the Imagination'

---

[46] He had seven children when he wrote to Thomas Birch seeking a job at the Royal Society in 1745 (BL Add. MS 4301, fo. 333). The poet Cowper in the 1750s was unsure whether Browne had ten or twelve—the Revd James Hervey maintained it was thirteen children.

[47] Two letters from him to Cave about judging the contests are in BL Stowe 748, fos. 153, 154.

[48] Rider contributed poems under the name 'Philargyrus' between 1741 and 1752. His anonymous pamphlet *An Historical Account of the Lives of the Living Authors of Great Britain* (London, 1762) is chiefly remembered for its flattering piece on himself.

[49] Barrett kept a MS book which is in the Osborn Collection in Yale University Library. It contains an anecdote of how poetry was corrected for the magazine (see James M. Osborn, 'Dr Johnson's "Intimate Friend" ', *TLS*, 9 Oct. 1953, 652).

[50] For the role of the *GM* in launching the literary career of Dodd, see my 'The Early Career of William Dodd', *Transactions of the Cambridge Bibliographical Society*, 8 (1983), 217–35.

[51] The poems, 'The Virtuoso', 'Ambition and Content', 'The Poet: A Rhapsody', 'A British Philippic', and 'Hymn to Science' appeared in magazines for April, May, July, and August 1738, and October 1739.

[52] BL Stowe 748, fos. 163, 168.

in 1744, Cave felt able to refer to its author as an 'old friend'.[53] Akenside may stand for the type of writer that the *Gentleman's Magazine* helped to bring to light. He was young and unknown, a Dissenter who had lived all his early life away from London, and was pursuing a profession outside writing, eventually taking up a career in medicine. From Hawkins, we learn that Cave drew contributions in verse and prose from two academies just outside the city, one in Spitalfields run by Thomas Watkins and another in Moorfields run by John Eames.[54] These, like the Stoke Newington school which both Defoe and Watts attended, had reputations for academic excellence and produced just the kind of middle-class professional man by whom the magazine prospered. Since all poetry was printed under the hostile glare of rival publications looking to expose weaknesses in the magazine, it was usual to include the age of the poet whenever he or she was a child. These poems were routinely corrected by the editors and in most cases this was not objected to. Typical of these would be 'An EPISTLE from H. W. *Aetat.* 12, to her Cousin A. L.' in August 1737.[55] No doubt H. W. got a double dose of benevolence for being female as well.

On the principle that contributors were also customers, the poetry columns were particularly open to women writers. Elizabeth Carter wrote from St John's Gate during one of her stays in London: 'Female Scribbling goes on most successfully. St. John's Gate is hourly attacked by whole vollies of Rhyme from a jingling Club.'[56] Here we find the characteristic jocular tone towards women's poetry which the magazine editors could not help adopting from time to time. The difference was that the *Gentleman's Magazine* mitigated its shows of gallantry with unusual receptivity and even solicitude towards it. Cave may have shared many of the prevailing assumptions about what constituted worthwhile poetry, but his commercial interest lay with a wider public than the one which had established these views two generations earlier. Female poets were still quick to declare the limitations of their sex, education, and experience, yet there was now more of a sense of polite formality about these declarations of unfitness.[57] Equally, the attitude of male writers towards them contained an element of merely token magnanimity. Thomas Dodd, in the same letter quoted above, gives an idea of the

[53] *GM* 14 (Apr. 1744), 219.
[54] *Life of Johnson*, 48. There are entries for Watkins and Eames in the *DNB*.
[55] *GM* 7 (Aug. 1737), 509.
[56] Gwen Hampshire, 'Elizabeth Carter's Unpublished Letters' (Oxford B.Litt. thesis, 1971), 18.
[57] An example might be that of 'Ophelia' of Yorkshire, who sent a poem, 'To Dr Young on his Night Thoughts', requesting the usual 'favourable allowances to my sex and want of learning' (*GM* 21 (Jan. 1751), 36). The editor deflects this with *his* sense of obligation and a request for further poems.

respectful camaraderie of the poetry columns when, in extenuation of some of the grosser epigram contest entries, he writes

As the Mag: seems to be a Ragout with diff.ent ingredients in the saver, so it may possibly hit the tast of several diff.ent persons but to say 'tis calculated for Numbers of a more delicate tast than what is chiefly adapt'd to the Fair is surely no great Compliment to your Fidelia's, Melissa's, Grierson's, Barber's.

Although Cave gave some offence by correcting contributors' poems, as in the case of the Reading Bards affair,[58] which was picked up and exploited by the *London Magazine*, it was generally the case that he printed whatever he could and that he went to some lengths to satisfy his readers' desire to see themselves in print. Take the case of the following note inserted in the September 1737 magazine: 'The Lady of 18, has not put in an advantageous Metre her Poem on Recovery from the Small-Pox: But if she knew whose Opinion this is, she would probably chuse to give it another Measure. We are at Liberty to send her some Intimation on that Head.'[59] By tactfully invoking an unnamed eminent practitioner, the desired revision took place and 'A Solemn Thank-offering to God for Recovering from the Small-Pox' duly appeared in November 1737.[60] Compare this with the preface to the *London Magazine* for 1737 which, as well as claiming to contain only 'full Copies, or proper Extracts, of all remarkable Dissertations, Essays, and Poems publish'd in this great City', asserted that 'we shall take care not to publish any Original, but what we know to be the Production of some Genius of establish'd Character' and that 'we have no occasion to sue for, or to purchase insignificant scraps at a low rate, from obscure Persons, or from Authors of no Name in the Commonwealth of Learning, or from Poets who were never heard of . . .'. This was meant as a guarantee of quality, but it can and perhaps should be interpreted as excluding and silencing many sectors of the population at large. Small wonder, therefore, that the *London Magazine*, despite being more stylishly printed and often one step ahead of its rival in procuring parliamentary and other information, was less successful commercially and is a less important historical repository of its age.

Elizabeth Carter was the first poetess to establish a reputation in the *Gentleman's Magazine*. As a 17-year-old in 1734, when she sent her first poems to the magazine, she was clearly desirous of praise. Cave would have been happy to hail 'Eliza' as a prodigy, but she saw to it that fame

---

[58] Cave gives an account of this literary squabble with contributors from Reading in *GM* 6 (Supplement, 1736), 785–6.
[59] *GM* 7 (Sept. 1737), 568.
[60] *GM* 7 (Nov. 1737), 692–3.

was courted discreetly. After producing a small, privately printed collection of poems and two unsigned book-length translations,[61] she declined to appear in the magazine again until Richardson's unlicenced use of her 'Ode to Wisdom' in *Clarissa* gave Cave a pretext for printing it as well.[62] Although retaining him as a useful contact, the Carters felt uneasy about Cave's commercial instincts and disliked the company Elizabeth's poems were obliged to keep in the magazine.[63] She withdrew from the poetry columns just at the moment when an understandable youthful desire to shine might be interpreted as a woman in her twenties seeking the limelight and thereby forfeiting some respectability. Interestingly, the *Gentleman's Magazine* was the means by which Jane Brereton re-emerged from obscurity in North Wales. She had appeared on the London scene twenty years earlier as half of a literary couple, but, following a painful public separation from her husband, she retired to Denbighshire, the region of her birth, to raise her children. She recovered the respectability which the separation had put in jeopardy, flattered her Welsh connections with poems in the magazine, and re-established a link with literary London through the same agency. Under the pseudonym 'Melissa', she and her vintner-poet neighbour Thomas Beach, using the pseudonym 'Fido', entertained magazine readers in 1735 and 1736 with a long-running verse dispute on the woman's role in courtship.[64] Cave, Browne, and Duick also contributed poems under their pseudonyms. That Jane Brereton belonged to the clique of *Gentleman's Magazine* poets is evident from her 'Verses from a Mother to her Daughter, with Dr CARTER'S SERMONS',[65] which shamelessly puffs a book printed at St John's Gate, and rounds off the praise with the following lie (Jane Brereton and Elizabeth Carter had corresponded since being introduced the previous year):

> This, to the Merit of the Work is due;
> The Preacher quite unknown, to me and you.

After Jane Brereton's death in August 1740, Cave published proposals for her *Poems on Several Occasions*, probably for the benefit of her two

[61] These were *Poems on Particular Occasions* (London, 1738), *An Examination of Mr Pope's Essay on Man from the French of Crousaz* (London, 1738), and *Sir Isaac Newton's Philosophy Explain'd for Ladies* (London, 1739) from Algarotti's Italian, all printed at St John's Gate.

[62] GM 17 (Dec. 1747), 585.

[63] Elizabeth says as much in a letter to Catherine Talbot dated 5 Mar. 1755 (see *The Correspondence of Elizabeth Carter and Catherine Talbot from 1740 to 1770*, ed. Montagu Pennington (4 vols.; London, [1809]), ii. 203).

[64] The mock-debate generated 40 poems for the GM, 11 by Brereton, 10 by Beach, and 7 by 'Fidelia' of Lincoln (who started it off). Changes of pseudonym and various games of duplicity were involved, before the joke went sour with Beach's suicide on 17 May 1737 (reported in *The Old Whig*, 16 June 1737).

[65] GM 9 (Mar. 1739), 155.

daughters. The book came out only in 1744, however, and with just a modest list of subscribers. Charlotte, one of her daughters and an active contributor to the poetry columns under the name of 'Carolina', returned the favour with a poem, 'The Progress of Charity', in aid of the North-ampton County Hospital, a charity of which Cave was one of the principal patrons.[66]

Leaving aside the young and the exceptionally confident, it was gener-ally only under certain conditions that women broke cover and wrote for publication. The traditional obstacles are well known—the opposition of family and friends, self-consciousness about lack of education, and a social and religious training that subordinated all other activities to domestic duties. Even here, magazines eased the path, for the very ephemerality of poetry in them lent an air of casualness to those who wrote it and sent it in. Household chores need not have been neglected and the prevailing conventions of pseudonymity protected authors and families from unwanted attention. The push or patronage of a male figure was almost a prerequisite for overcoming literary reticence. Esther Lewis ('Sylvia') of Holt in Wiltshire was lionized by Dr Samuel Bowden of nearby Frome, who promoted her poems in the *Bath Journal* and then in the *Gentleman's Magazine*.[67] It seems that Sarah Dixon got similar encouragement from the competition poet, John Bunce. Cave himself became the patron of Mary Masters, and must have been instrumental in getting Johnson to correct her work.[68] She eventually became a member of his household, as Anna Williams came to live with Johnson. Indigence played a part in this, and, although difficult for a poetess to admit, it was tacitly understood to be sufficient justification for writing for the press. The magazine proprietors sometimes paid for poetry, but it would not have been assumed that anyone sent a poem for gain. Finally, death put a woman's poetry in the public domain; no self-seeking motive or imputation of frivolous dereliction could be attached to posthumous publication. This is why it was easier to do justice to the achievement of women poets after the mid-century, by which time a number of the people here mentioned had died, suggesting a lineage to which living writers could be added. Within a few short years, George Ballard had published his *Memoirs of Several Ladies of Great Britain who have been Celebrated for their Writing* (1752), Robert Shiells[69] included fifteen

---

[66] GM 13 (July 1743), 377–8, and in a separate folio half-sheet. See D. F. Foxon, *English Verse 1701–1750* (Cambridge, 1975), no. P. 1107.
[67] Bowden's poem, 'To a Young Lady at Holt on her late Ingenious Poems' in GM 19 (Apr. 1749), 179, seems like a ploy to set her before a larger audience.
[68] *Boswell's Life of Johnson*, i. 242.
[69] Johnson's *Dictionary* amanuensis, whose poem *The Power of Beauty* (1750) was printed in quarto at St John's Gate.

women in his *Lives of the Poets* (1753), John Duncombe published *The Feminiad* (1754), and Colman and Thornton's influential anthology *Poems by Eminent Ladies* (1755) appeared in two volumes. These projects were not without some polite condescension, but they played a part, along with Richardson's recent efforts to give prominence to female concerns and sensibility in his fiction, in challenging inhibiting prejudices and preconceptions about women and their writing. These works register an opening-up of opportunities for women to show what they could do, and are in part predicated upon over twenty years of magazine-publishing. As well as being a vehicle carrying some to fame, the *Gentleman's Magazine* is just as important for preserving the work of countless others who may never be identified but who existed and left a small mark of themselves. The claim is not that magazines contain a lot of great poetry, but rather that they contain *different* poetry from what we might expect from our schooling in the hitherto rather static canon of eighteenth-century poetry. What, for example, would prepare us for the playful eroticism of the following anonymous lines, which were, according to the editor, 'Sent home with a young Lady's repeating *Watch*'?

> Go, go, you little tatler, go
>   And dangle by her side
> Thou emblem of a modern beau
>   In all his glittering pride.
>
> When in her bed, you hang in air,
>   And measure out dull time,
> Say—joy and love shou'd be her care
>   Now beauty's in its prime.
>
> When first she wakes at Jenny's knock,
>   (Then thoughts are frank and free)
> Tell her—instead of what's o'clock,
>   'Tis time to think of me.
>
> Tell her—a lover in her arms,
>   His pulse would beat as true,
> His heart would spring with love's alarms,
>   And vibrate quick as you.[70]

A closer inspection of magazine verse, in the light of changing tastes and interests, has begun to reveal and will go on revealing work of more than sociological or historical significance.

[70] *GM* 14 (May 1744), 272.

15 William Collins and the Idea of Liberty

PAUL WILLIAMSON

The essentially Neoplatonic poetics which William Collins pursued in the *Odes on Several Descriptive and Allegoric Subjects* (1746–7) characterized him as a strange figure.[1] His was a 'deviation in quest of mistaken beauties' (Dr Johnson), while his pursuit of 'pure Poetry' rendered him 'remote from common apprehension' (Mrs Barbauld).[2] For modern critics, Collins's singularity has been further emphasized by the tendency to regard the mid-eighteenth century generally as a transitional period: 'At a time when, unsettled by the empirical philosophy, English thought was puzzling over the relations between the external world and sensory data, between sensory data and the mind, what Collins aspired to was something nearly unique.'[3]

Yet that same uniqueness has made Collins almost the epitome of the Age of Sensibility, the exception which, as it were, proves the rule. This is the picture of Collins as a premature romantic: 'Sublime Personification seems to me an uneasy transitional phase . . . Collins is on the verge of strength, yet hesitant to cross over into it . . . to be an Orphic prophet in the mode of Sensibility was plainly not possible.'[4] Similarly 'Collins opens the way to a new, if still uneasy, nature poetry'.[5]

On a formal level, however, Collins's aspirations are relatively orthodox. His odes divide neatly into the two kinds of lyric, sublime and beautiful, Greater and Lesser, distinguished by neo-classical critics,[6] and his repeated use of the progress structure situates his work in 'one of the most popular poetic genres of the seventeenth and eighteenth centuries'.[7]

---

[1] For chronological details, see R. Wendorf and C. Ryskamp (eds.), *The Works of William Collins* (Oxford, 1979), 122 ff. All references to Collins's work will be to this edition.

[2] Samuel Johnson, 'Collins', in *Lives of the English Poets* (2 vols.; London, 1906, repr. 1975), ii. 382; *The Works of Mr. William Collins*, 'with a Prefatory Essay by Mrs. Barbauld' (London, 1797), p. v.

[3] E. R. Wasserman, 'Collins' *Ode on the Poetical Character*', *English Literary History*, 34 (1967), 100.

[4] H. Bloom, 'From Topos to Trope: Collins's *Ode to Fear*', repr. in H. Bloom (ed.), *Poets of Sensibility and the Sublime* (New York, 1986), 170, 177, 180.

[5] G. H. Hartman, *The Fate of Reading* (Chicago, 1975), 139.

[6] See N. Maclean, 'From Action to Image: Theories of the Lyric in the Eighteenth Century', in R. S. Crane (ed.), *Critics and Criticism* (Chicago, 1952; repr. 1968).

[7] *The Poems of Gray, Collins, and Goldsmith*, ed. R. H. Lonsdale (London, 1969), 160. Also J. R. Crider, 'Structure and Effect in Collins's Progress Poems', *Studies in Philology*, 60 (1963).

The plan to publish his *Odes* jointly with Joseph Warton indicates the extent to which his thinking about the general direction of poetry was in harmony with that of at least some of his generation; as A. S. P. Woodhouse remarks, though the plan for joint publication was abandoned, 'it was through no disagreement in principle'.[8] Even Collins's version of Neoplatonism, peremptorily dismissed by Mrs Barbauld,[9] finds a contemporary analogue in the work of a philosopher expressly admired by Collins, James Harris (1709–80), the nephew of Anthony Ashley Cooper, the Third Earl of Shaftesbury. It will be the purpose of the present chapter to show how Collins's verse is built on this mixture of historical elements. The difficulties of his situation emerged from a willingness to confront the set of formal and intellectual presuppositions with which he was engaged and the recognition that these were inherent in the kind of poetry he was trying to write.

Although James Harris's *Hermes* (1751) postdates Collins's *Odes*, Collins versified his regard for this 'Gentlest Patriot' who wrote in 'Plato's polish'd style', desiring 'To fix fair Science in our careless Isle', and one may presume he would be broadly in sympathy with Harris's anti-empirical views.[10] Harris's doctrine may be summarized in the maxim '*Nil est in* SENSU, *quod non prius fuit in* INTELLECTU', a radical inversion of Thomas Hobbes's formulation, 'there is no conception in a mans mind, which hath not at first, totally, or by parts, been begotten upon the organs of Sense'.[11] For Harris, words are not primarily signs of objects in the natural world, but rather '*symbols* of GENERAL IDEAS'.[12] Although the 'Idea'[13] may be translated into many human languages, it remains constant; the same Idea is referred to in any language whatsoever. The Idea is prior to the word: 'NOW it is of these COMPREHENSIVE and PERMANENT IDEAS, THE GENUINE PERCEPTIONS OF PURE MIND, that WORDS of all Languages, however different, are the SYMBOLS'.[14]

The Ideas, those perceptions of 'PURE MIND', are the '*Internal Forms*' of things; to have an Idea of a material object is: '*to have* A FORM INTERNAL *correspondent to* THE EXTERNAL; only with this difference, that the *Internal Form is devoid of the Matter*; *the External is united with it*'.[15] The '*Forms*' are perceived by the imagination: 'IMAGINATION OR

---

[8] A. S. P. Woodhouse, 'The Poetry of Collins Reconsidered', in F. W. Hilles and H. Bloom (eds.), *From Sensibility to Romanticism* (New York, 1965), 100.
[9] *The Works of Mr. William Collins*, p. xxv.
[10] For the verse epistle addressed to Harris, see Collins, *Works*, 68.
[11] Harris: 'There is nothing in the senses that was not first in the intellect' (*Hermes* (London, 1751; 5th edn., 1794), 391). Cf. *Leviathan* (London, 1914; repr. 1965), 3. For an account of Harris's theories, see R. Marsh, *Four Dialectical Theories of Poetry* (Chicago, 1965).
[12] Harris, *Hermes*, 343.
[13] Henceforth initially capitalized to distinguish Harris's 'GENERAL IDEA' from the modern 'idea'.
[14] Harris, *Hermes*, 372.   [15] Ibid. 375.

FANCY, which however as to its *energies* it may be subsequent to Sense, yet is truly prior to it both in *dignity* and *use*. THIS it is which *retains the fleeting Forms of things*, when Things themselves are gone, and *all Sensation* at an end'.[16] Accordingly, in a highly Platonic formulation:

THE WHOLE VISIBLE WORLD exhibits nothing more, than so many *passing* Pictures of these *immutable Archetypes*. Nay thro' these it attains even a Semblance of Immortality, and continues throughout ages to be SPECIFICALLY ONE, amid those infinite particular changes, that befal it at every moment.[17]

The '*Archetypes*' reside in the mind of God, '*where all things lie inveloped in their Principles and Exemplars . . . essential to the fulness of his universal Intellection*'.[18] It is through such '*permanent and comprehensive*' forms that God views '*at once*' '*all possible productions both present, past, and future*'.[19] The '*immutable Archetypes*' are thus logically prior to nature in the same way as God, in the '*fulness of his universal Intellection*', is prior to the natural world. It is this fact which no purely empirical scheme can comprehend:

the *intellectual* Scheme, which never forgets Deity, postpones every thing *corporeal* to the *primary mental Cause*. It is *here* it looks for the origin of *intelligible* Ideas, even of those, which exist in *human* Capacities. For tho' *sensible* Objects may be the destined medium, *to awaken* the dormant Energies of *Man*'s Understanding, yet are those Energies themselves no more contained in the *Sense*, than the Explosion of a Cannon, in the Spark which gave it fire.[20]

The word '*primary*' explicitly confronts John Locke's Primary Qualities, the powers by which a material body produces ideas in the perceiving mind without the prior existence of '*intelligible* Ideas',[21] while the notion of the '*primary mental Cause*' implies a doctrine of the imagination as the means of perceiving archetypal truth. It is by way of 'IMAGINATION or FANCY'[22] that one perceives those Ideal forms, present in the mind of God, which underlie the transient world of nature. The essential rapport between man, nature, and God is thus recognized and sustained: 'IN short ALL MINDS, that are, are SIMILAR and CONGENIAL; and so too are *their Ideas*, or *intelligible Forms*. Were it otherwise, there could be no intercourse between Man and Man, or (what is more important) between Man and God'.[23]

It is a view of Collins's metaphysics as closely comparable with the sort of system described by Harris that underpins Mrs Barbauld's discussion of the *Ode on the Poetical Character*: 'true Poetry being a representation

[16] Ibid. 354.   [17] Ibid. 383–8; cf. Plato's 'moving image of eternity' (*Timaeus*, 37d).
[18] Harris, *Hermes*, 390–1.   [19] Ibid. 390.   [20] Ibid. 393–4.
[21] Cf. *An Essay concerning Human Understanding*, II. viii. 8–9.
[22] Harris, *Hermes*, 354.   [23] Ibid. 395–7.

of Nature, must have its archetype in those ideas of the supreme mind, which originally gave birth to Nature.'[24] As Mrs Barbauld asserts, poetry which takes such Idealist metaphysics as its starting-point is necessarily sublime, 'pure Poetry, or Poetry in the abstract'.[25] Yet it does not imply a romanticism whose interest is in the poet's psychological state. Rather, as Martin Price remarks of Shaftesbury's conception of the sublime, in this case the emotions 'are not blind; they are tied to an act of recognition'. Sublime 'elevation of the spirit' comes about 'through a persevering faith in cosmic order'.[26] In Harris's terms, the 'act of recognition' becomes the perception of the '*Ideas, or intelligible Forms*' on which rests the possibility of 'intercourse . . . between Man and God'.[27]

In the 'Ode to Liberty' Collins is in quest of a vision of Liberty's 'Shrine' (l. 91); this exists only in its Ideal form, the 'beauteous *Model*':

> Yet still, if Truth those Beams infuse,
> Which guide at once, and charm the Muse,
> Beyond yon braided Clouds that lie,
> Paving the light-embroider'd Sky:
> Amidst the bright pavilion'd Plains,
> The beauteous *Model* still remains.

(ll. 101–6)

The '*Model*' is 'Beyond yon braided Clouds' ('yon', yonder, within view) which 'pave' the 'light-embroider'd Sky', 'Amidst' the 'bright' 'Plains'. Accordingly, the 'Beams' which 'guide' and 'charm' the poet's imaginative sight must be infused with 'Truth' if the poet is to 'see' the model, if his vision is to transcend the realms of mere worldly light to view 'the bright pavilion'd Plains'. As A. D. McKillop remarks, this passage represents a 'cosmic progress' which 'extends the scene to an ideal otherworld, in which the shrine of Liberty stands eternally'.[28] Liberty, that is, is Ideal in the sense described by Harris.

McKillop's phrase, 'cosmic progress', alerts one to a further important element in the poet's attempted vision—the concept of progress. The seventeenth- and eighteenth-century development of the progress poem has been seen as the product of a burgeoning historical awareness.[29] Yet progress may be regarded as a combination of two much older

---

[24] *The Works of Mr. William Collins*, p. xxv.   [25] Ibid., p. xxv.
[26] Martin Price, 'The Sublime Poem: Pictures and Powers', in Bloom (ed.), *Poets of Sensibility and the Sublime*, 32.
[27] Harris, *Hermes*, 395–7.
[28] A. D. McKillop, 'Collins's *Ode to Evening*—Background and Structure', *Tennessee Studies in Literature*, 5 (1960), 80.
[29] See e.g. *Poems of Gray, Collins, and Goldsmith*, ed. Lonsdale, 160.

ideas, *translatio imperii*, the transfer of empire or political power, and *translatio studii*, the corresponding movement of the arts.[30] *Translatio imperii* derives from Eccles. 10:8: 'Because of unrighteous dealings, injuries, and riches got by deceit, the kingdom is translated from one people to another.'[31] Horace's *Epistle* 2.1 is the source of *translatio studii*. For Horace the situation is paradoxical because, following the initial transfer of empire, the arts of Greece reconquered the Latin conqueror:

> Graecia capta ferum victorem cepit et artis
> intulit agresti Latio . . .
>
> (ll. 156–7)

> Greece, the captive, made her savage victor captive, and brought the arts into rustic Latium.[32]

In each case the notion of *translatio* can be connected with a failure of morality; the 'transference of dominion . . . is the result of a sinful misuse of that domination'.[33] In eighteenth-century panegyric such sinfulness is reinterpreted as providential.[34] In 'Liberty', for instance, the historical movement from Greece to Italy and finally to Britain is a sign of the western island's special, holy status as Liberty's destined home: 'The Magic works, Thou feel'st the Strains, | One holier Name alone remains' (ll. 60–1).

Britain is regarded as Liberty's 'last Abode' (l. 88), preserver of her ancient 'Shrine' (l. 91), and British Liberty as the most perfect instantiation of the Idea. Such sentiments were not confined to the poets; Lord Bolingbroke wrote in *The Craftsman*:

> our *Constitution* is brought nearer than any *other Constitution* ever was to the most perfect Idea of a *free System of Government*. . . . this *Constitution* is better fitted than any, ancient or modern, ever was, not only to preserve *Liberty*, but to provide for its own Duration, and to become immortal, if any Thing human could be so.[35]

---

[30] Cf. Crider, 'Structure and Effect'.
[31] *The Apocrypha*, authorized version (Oxford, n.d.).
[32] *Satires, Epistles and Ars poetica*, ed. and trans. H. R. Fairclough (rev. edn., Cambridge, Mass., 1929; repr. 1970), 408.
[33] E. R. Curtius, *European Literature and the Latin Middle Ages*, trans. W. R. Trask (London, 1953; repr. 1979), 29. Cf. R. C. Cochrane, 'Bishop Berkeley and the Progress of Arts and Learning: Notes on a Literary Convention', *Huntington Library Quarterly*, 17 (1953–4); A. L. Williams, *Pope's 'Dunciad'* (n.p., 1955; repr. 1968), 43–8.
[34] For the notion of 'progress as redemption', see E. L. Tuveson, *Millenium and Utopia* (New York, 1964; repr. and corr. from 1st edn., 1949), 153 ff. See also C. A. Moore, 'Whig Panegyric Verse, 1700–1760: A Phase of Sentimentalism', *Publications of the Modern Language Association of America*, 41 (1926).
[35] *The Craftsman* no. 436 (9 Nov. 1734). Quoted from the reprint for R. Francklin (vol. 13, London, 1737).

With respect to Liberty, the progress structure regards history as designed to produce the 'present', British state of freedom and the temporal movement is understood as the progressive embodiment of the Idea. This belief affects the shape of Collins's poem. The 'Ode to Liberty' consists of a dual structure divided stanzaically into strophe and epode on the one hand, antistrophe and second epode on the other. The first movement, in the strophe and first epode, depicts the classical aspect of *translatio imperii*: the 'Historic truth' of Liberty's progress from ancient Greece to ancient Rome, renaissance Europe, and finally to Britain.[36] The second movement, in the antistrophe and second epode, develops the theme of 'native' or 'Gothic' Liberty (l. 118); it describes the endemic conditions that make Britain fit to be Liberty's final resting-place.[37] The components of progress contained in this dual structure are formulaic and generic, a 'ready-made interpretation of history'.[38] In addition to such inherited subject-matter, Collins also inherits the ode-form in which this matter is expressed. The Pindaric is not merely the proper form of the sublime or Greater Ode; on account of its seeming irregularity it was associated with a poetic or formal liberty.[39] In Abraham Cowley's words: 'And though the *Liberty* of them may incline a man to believe them easie to be composed, yet the undertaker will find it otherwise.'[40]

As Cowley suggests, Pindaric irregularity is more apparent than real because the stanzaic structure as well as the meaningful function of each stanza is broadly governed. The Pindaric order is strophe, antistrophe, and epode. Ben Jonson translated these terms as 'Turn', 'Counter-Turn', and 'Stand',[41] by which one presumes he was thinking of the manner in which such an ode may have been performed and relating the idea of its performance to the alternation between action and chorus (movement and commentatory stasis) in the Greek drama.[42] 'Epode', however, means 'song on top' or 'singing over' and its function is that of a refrain. As such it may still be regarded as a form of stasis, a thematic standing-still which follows and, as it were, steadies (by unifying or synthesizing) the contrary movements of 'turning' and

---

[36] A. D. McKillop, *The Background of Thomson's 'Liberty'* (Rice Institute Pamphlet, 38; 1951), 5.

[37] On the 'double tradition' of 'classical' and 'native' liberty, see ibid. 74; and S. Kliger, *The Goths in England* (Cambridge, Mass., 1952).

[38] McKillop, *Thomson's 'Liberty'*, 4.

[39] See Maclean, 'From Action to Image'. For a brief history of the form's revival, cf. *Poems of Gray, Collins, and Goldsmith*, ed. Lonsdale, 156–60.

[40] Abraham Cowley, *Poems*, ed. A. R. Waller (Cambridge, 1905), 11.

[41] In his Pindaric ode 'To the Immortal Memory and Friendship of That Noble Pair, Sir Lucius Cary and Sir H. Morison' (1629).

[42] Choral odes in Greek tragedy may also comprise strophe, antistrophe, and epode. Cf. 'Tragedy' in *The Oxford Classical Dictionary* (OCD) (Oxford, 1970).

'counter-turning'.⁴³ Strophe, antistrophe, and epode contain an almost dialectical force: statement, counter-statement, and a concluding refrain which draws together the contrary themes of the previous stanzas.

In 'Liberty', as in the other Pindaric poems in Collins's *Odes*, the normal Pindaric order is significantly altered.⁴⁴ Collins makes strophe and epode work in parallel with antistrophe and second epode. In terms of theme and stanzaic function the first of these movements is comprised of strophic statement: the classical world enjoyed the blessings of Liberty until the sack of Rome by the 'Northern Sons of Spoil' (l. 22); epodic refrain: 'Remnants' of Liberty's 'perfect Form' (ll. 29–31) resisted destruction, inspiring attempts to reinstate it at later moments during Liberty's *translatio*, until the goddess finds her 'holier' (l. 61) resting-place in Britain. Movement becomes stasis, argument becomes paean: 'Hail Nymph, ador'd by *Britain*, Hail!' (l. 63). In the antistrophe and second epode occurs, firstly, a new thematic or strophic statement: the quasi-mythical 'Tradition'⁴⁵ of Britain's geological separation from France, under the auspices of Liberty and 'consenting Heav'n', such that the British Isles are fit to be Liberty's final dwelling place:

> For Thee consenting Heav'n has each bestow'd,
> A fair Attendant on her sov'reign Pride:
> To Thee this blest Divorce she ow'd,
> For thou hast made her Vales thy lov'd, thy last Abode!
>
> (ll. 85–8)

In the second epode this movement is completed in a further refrain and a further paean: the inhabitants of Britain have never lost their indigenous '*Gothic*' (l. 118) Liberty, so the present poet may once again perceive the 'beauteous *Model*' (l. 106) of Liberty's 'Shrine' (l. 91).⁴⁶ Liberty will be worshipped in Britain until the latter, an ambiguous 'Her', is recognized as supreme by the surrounding nations:

> Her let our Sires and Matrons hoar
> Welcome to *Britain*'s ravag'd Shore,
> Our Youths, enamour'd of the Fair,

⁴³ Notions of movement and stasis were not foreign to performances of the odes. Sir John Sandys regards three of Pindar's odes which have no epodes as 'processional poems'. See his *The Odes of Pindar* (2nd edn., Cambridge, Mass., 1919; rev. and repr. 1961), p. xxxiii.

⁴⁴ Other variations are the 'Ode to Fear' and the 'Ode on the Poetical Character' (strophe, epode or 'mesode', antistrophe), both of which end at a moment of tension not resolution—'Fear' with a conditional, the 'Poetical Character' with a declaration of poetic failure and misplaced ambition. The 'Ode to Mercy' (strophe, antistrophe) ends with a statement of future intent rather than present achievement.

⁴⁵ Collins's word from his footnote to this passage.

⁴⁶ Again, it is worth observing that such concepts are also found in the political writers. Bolingbroke: 'in all these Ages *Britain* hath been the *Temple*, as it were, *of Liberty*' (*Craftsman* 436).

> Play with the Tangles of her Hair,
> Till in one loud applauding Sound,
> The Nations shout to Her around,
> O how supremely art thou blest,
> Thou, Lady, Thou shalt rule the West!
>
> (ll. 137–44)

The same parallelism is at work in more detailed ways. In the contrast between statement and counter-statement, strophe and antistrophe, similar poetic materials are used to create two effects. In the description of the fall of Rome the city is like a statue pushed from its pedestal:

> No, *Freedom*, no, I will not tell,
> How *Rome*, before thy weeping Face,
> With heaviest Sound, a Giant-statue, fell,
> Push'd by a wild and artless Race,
> From off its wide ambitious Base,
> When Time his Northern Sons of Spoil awoke,
>   And all the blended Work of Strength and Grace,
>   With many a rude repeated Stroke,
> And many a barb'rous Yell, to thousand Fragments broke.
>
> (ll. 17–25)

While, in the antistrophe:

> Till all the banded West at once 'gan rise,
> A wide wild Storm ev'n Nature's self confounding,
>   With'ring her Giant Sons with strange uncouth Surprise.
>   This pillar'd Earth so firm and wide,
>   By Winds and inward Labors torn,
>   In Thunders dread was push'd aside,
>   And down the should'ring Billows born.
> And see, like Gems, her laughing Train,
> The little Isles on ev'ry side . . .
>
> (ll. 73–81)

One has the 'Giant-statue' (l. 19) and the 'Giant Sons' (l. 75), an epithet which also recalls the 'Northern Sons of Spoil' (l. 22). The earth, 'so firm and wide' (l. 76), may be compared with Rome's 'wide ambitious Base' (l. 21); the 'Giant-statue' is 'push'd' (l. 20), just as the 'pillar'd Earth' is 'push'd aside' (l. 78). In terms of concept and poetic vocabulary, two apparently opposite events are conflated. The purpose behind this poetic technique is the subordination of the poem to the Idea of Liberty. Viewed in isolation, the destruction of Rome was a dreadful historical moment, and yet, seen in the providential context of Liberty's progress to the British Isles, it was a necessary, indeed contributory, stage. This understanding qualifies the contradictory passage in the strophe where the poet relates precisely that which he has just refused to 'tell':

> Let not my Shell's misguided Pow'r,
> E'er draw thy sad, thy mindful Tears.
> No, *Freedom*, no, I will not tell,
> How *Rome*, before thy weeping Face,
> With heaviest Sound, a Giant-statue, fell . . .[47]
>
> (ll. 15–19)

This seeming reluctance can be understood in terms of the priority of the Idea over the poem. The poet's aim is to convey a vision of Liberty, but the Idea of Liberty, the 'beauteous *Model*', is logically prior to all poetic endeavour, as it is to human history in general. Poetry, like history, is no more than a medium of Ideal recognition, the 'Spark', as Harris would say, which gives 'fire' to the imagination.[48] In the strophe and antistrophe, therefore, two descriptions of destruction jointly signify construction; each breaking—of the 'Giant-statue', as of the British Isles from the European continent—is a means to Liberty's later, British instantiation, a stage in Liberty's *translatio*.

The poetic shape which acts as the vehicle for this schematic view of history negates the poem's own linear progression as well as the linear, temporal basis of progress itself. In Harris's terms, the Idea of Liberty is an '*immutable*' archetype which guarantees the essential unity of Liberty's worldly manifestations, renders them 'SPECIFICALLY ONE', as a whole which is prior to its parts.[49] In the same way the '*Model*' is prior to the poem. As a truthful vision, perceived when the poet's imagination is infused with 'Truth' (l. 101), the Idea is prior to the poetic song and should control it. The poet's vision of Liberty thus dictates a spatial, pictorial, even architectural method and the poet's task is to devise a relationship between the whole and its parts such that the parts stand in a structural or qualitatively subordinate relationship to the Ideal whole.[50] The Ideal, 'mix'd Design' of Liberty's shrine, composed of '*Gothic*' and '*Græcian*' (ll. 118–20) aspects of Liberty's progress, is realized in the

---

[47] Collins's note refers the reader to Callimachus' Hymn, *To Demeter* (13 ff.): 'Nay, nay, let us not speak of that which brought the tear to Deo! Better to tell how she gave to cities pleasing ordinances . . .' (*Hymns, Epigrams, Lycophron, Aratus*, trans. A. W. and G. R. Mair (Cambridge, Mass., 1921; rev. 1955)).

[48] Harris, *Hermes*, 394.

[49] Harris, *Hermes*, 383–8. On the Neoplatonic belief in the subordination of the parts to the whole, cf. E. Cassirer, *The Platonic Renaissance in England*, trans. J. P. Pettegrove (New York, 1970), 136.

[50] Cf. Horace's 'ut pictura poesis' (*Ars poetica*, 361). Cf. R. W. Lee, *Ut Pictura Poesis: The Humanistic Theory of Painting* (New York, 1967), and J. H. Hagstrum, *The Sister Arts* (Chicago, 1958), p. xxii.

intentionally static reordering of the Pindaric norm. Compare the prophetic insight into British history towards the end of the poem:

> There on the Walls the *Patriot's* Sight,
> May ever hang with fresh Delight,
> And, grav'd with some Prophetic Rage,
> Read *Albion*'s Fame thro' ev'ry Age.
>
> (ll. 125–8)

The history of '*Albion*'s Fame' has already been adumbrated in the course of the poem—Gothic and Grecian aspects of *translatio* have been expressed in terms of their Ideal subordination. The poem's linear movement, like historical progress generally, is governed by the Idea and so made to work in parallel as an expression of the contributory role which it plays in the realization of that Ideal. The poem's linear motion is made dual and static and those elements of Liberty's progress described in the course of the poem have been incorporated into the Ideal design—'grav'd' (l. 127) almost ecphrastically on to Liberty's shrine.

Nevertheless, the logic of progress as well as the poem's intrinsic linear force are not so easily denied. Collins shows his awareness of the implications of progress in 'An Epistle: Addrest to Sir Thomas Hanmer, On his Edition of Shakespear's Works'.[51] The poem's skeletal structure is the progress of the arts from Greece to Britain. But even as he states the basic principle, Collins makes an exception of poetry, which 'alone' (l. 19) escapes the normative dynamic:

> Each rising Art by just Gradation moves,
> Toil builds on Toil, and Age on Age improves.
> The Muse alone unequal dealt her Rage,
> And grac'd with noblest Pomp her earliest Stage.
>
> (ll. 17–20)

A few lines later, with regard to Shakespeare, it seems that *translatio studii* has been working normally:

> But Heav'n, still various in its Works, decreed
> The perfect Boast of Time should last succeed.
> The beauteous Union must appear at length,
> Of *Tuscan* Fancy, and *Athenian* Strength:
> One greater Muse *Eliza*'s Reign adorn,
> And ev'n a *Shakespear* to her Fame be born!
>
> (ll. 45–50)

---

[51] (1st edn. 1743, rev. 1744). For the chronology of the poem, see Collins, *Works*, 110–13, and *Poems of Gray, Collins, and Goldsmith*, ed. Lonsdale, 386–9.

But in these lines a twofold and apparently self-contradictory norm is confirmed. In an unusual fulfilment of *translatio studii* Shakespeare is hailed as the 'perfect Boast of Time' (l. 46);[52] in a 'beauteous Union' he unites the virtues of '*Tuscan* Fancy' with '*Athenian* Strength' (ll. 47–8) and his genius is presented as the necessary consequence (l. 47) of an ordered temporal progression in which the 'rising Art' of poetry has indeed moved by 'just Gradation' (l. 17). Yet this apparent proof of the general historico-progressive scheme is termed 'various' (l. 45), an exception to the second principle of order. Shakespeare's timely appearance in Britain contradicts the idea that 'The Muse alone unequal dealt her Rage' (l. 19):

> But Heav'n, still various in its Works, decreed
> The perfect Boast of Time should last succeed.
>
> (ll. 45–6).

These lines contain two opposing ideas. The fulfilment of the normative idea of progress—the best comes 'last' (l. 46)—is understood as a heavenly variation (l. 45) which counters the alternative norm stated earlier (ll. 19–20)—the best comes first. The reason for Collins's artful juxtaposition is intimated in the poem's opening lines:

> While born to bring the Muse's happier Days,
> A Patriot's Hand protects a Poet's Lays:
> While nurst by you she sees her Myrtles bloom,
> Green and unwither'd o'er his honour'd Tomb:
> Excuse her Doubts, if yet she fears to tell
> What secret Transports in her Bosom swell:
> With conscious Awe she hears the Critic's Fame,
> And blushing hides her Wreath at *Shakespear*'s Name.
>
> (ll. 1–8)

Translatio studii entails a great burden for the young poet. If historical progress implies a corresponding progress in the arts, then the latest poem—in which the poet, as Collins acknowledges, is 'ev'n now' engaged (l. 111)—should also be the greatest. The logic of *translatio* is that the present work should be the culminating instance in the progress of the art. Naturally, however, the youthful muse is diffident when contemplating the poetic achievements of the Greeks 'And blushing hides her Wreath at *Shakespear*'s Name' (l. 8).[53]

---

[52] Collins's treatment is unusual because 'the climax is reached with Shakespeare and not . . . in the early eighteenth century' (*Poems of Gray, Collins, and Goldsmith*, ed. Lonsdale, 388).

[53] Cf. R. Wendorf, *William Collins and Eighteenth-Century English Poetry* (Minneapolis, 1981), 75, who argues that two muses are referred to in these lines.

The force of the present moment, expressed in the word 'now' and the use of the present tense, can be overwhelming in Collins's verse.[54] This is most clear in the *Poetical Character* where a question in the mesode, 'Where is the Bard, whose Soul can now | Its high presuming Hopes avow?' (ll. 51-2), immediately provokes an attempted vision, 'I view that Oak' (l. 63), and, in the concluding antistrophe, the end of future inspiration, 'And Heav'n, and *Fancy*, kindred Pow'rs, | Have now o'erturn'd th' inspiring Bow'rs' (ll. 74-5). The 'ev'n now' of the 'Epistle to Hanmer' is repeated in the second epode of the 'Ode to Liberty', at the moment when the poet achieves his Ideal vision of Liberty's shrine:

> Ev'n now before his favor'd Eyes,
> In *Gothic* Pride it seems to rise!
> Yet *Græcia*'s graceful Orders join,
> Majestic thro' the mix'd Design . . .
>
> (ll. 117-20)

As in 'Hanmer', the problematic nature of the poet's personal progress to this weighty historical moment forms part of the poem's thematic concerns:

> Who shall awake the *Spartan* Fife,
> And call in solemn Sounds to Life,
> The Youths, whose Locks divinely spreading,
> Like vernal Hyacinths in sullen Hue,
> At once the Breath of Fear and Virtue shedding,
> Applauding *Freedom* lov'd of old to view?
> What New *Alcæus*, Fancy-blest,
> Shall sing the Sword, in Myrtles drest . . .
>
> (ll. 1-8)

The first word of the poem, an interrogative 'Who', is reflexive, immediately connecting the poem which is now beginning with the 'solemn Sounds' of the '*Spartan* Fife'. The later reference to 'my Shell' (l. 15) further acknowledges the poet's desire to become the 'New *Alcæus*':

> O Goddess, in that feeling Hour,
> When most its Sounds would court thy Ears,
> Let not my Shell's misguided Pow'r,
> E'er draw thy sad, thy mindful Tears.
>
> (ll. 13-16)

[54] 'Ev'n now' ('Pity', l. 26); 'I see, I see thee near' ('Fear', l. 6); 'I see recoil his sable Steeds' ('Mercy', l. 20); 'To Thee we build' (ibid., l. 25); 'Now teach me' ('Evening', l. 15).

The word 'misguided', with its hint of possible failure, counters the implied presumption of the opening lines. The reference to the '*Spartan Fife*' (l. 1), which by its 'solemn Sounds' (l. 2) summons those 'Youths' (l. 3) whose hair is like 'Hyacinths' (l. 4), may indicate the nature of the Alcaean song. This recalls the story of Hyacinthus and the Spartan Hyacinthia, recounted by Ovid through the person of Orpheus.[55] Hyacinthus was killed by Apollo's deflected discus but subsequently reborn in the flower that bears his name.[56] His death was commemorated at the Hyacinthia, a Spartan festival celebrated at Amyclae probably in late spring or early summer. The Hyacinthia lasted three days and was progressive or processional in the sense that the 'solemn Sounds' of the opening day—mourning the death of Hyacinthus—gradually gave way to the joyful worship of Apollo.[57] A ritual progression from mourning to joy, beginning with the 'awakening' of the Spartan 'Youths', also figures in the present poem in the movement from the poem's opening 'solemn Sounds', before the demise of Liberty among the ancients, to the joy of Liberty's triumphant rebirth—her establishment in Britain. At the end of the poem the 'Hyacinthan' 'Youths' become British:

> Our Youths, enamour'd of the Fair,
> Play with the Tangles of her Hair . . .
>
> (ll. 139–40)

Such allusive use of myth would relate to Pindar's own practice,[58] and this is not the only way in which Collins's poetic task is reflected in his Pindaric models. Pindar's odes are primarily songs of praise: of the human victor in the games and of the bond between human and divine which such victory illuminates. The ode from which Collins takes the epigraph for his volume:

many men have striven to win their fame by means of merit that cometh from mere training; but anything whatsoever, in which God hath no part, is none the worse for being quelled in silence . . . our hero hath by the blessing of heaven been born with deftness of hand . . .[59]

Collins's task, for which 'mere training' is also insufficient, is the invocation of Liberty, Britain's own 'blessing of heaven'. Just as the 'common' contrast between 'natural genius and imitative

---

[55] *Metamorphoses* 10.

[56] Cf. OCD, 'Hyacinthus'.

[57] For a near-contemporary account, cf. Diderot and D'Alembert, *Encyclopédie*, viii (Neufchastel, 1765).

[58] OCD, 'Pindar'. Wasserman ('Collins' *Ode on the Poetical Character*', 102) remarks on the 'apparent afunctionalism' of Pindar's myths.

[59] Pindar, *Olympian Odes* 9. Quoted from *Odes of Pindar*, ed. Sandys, 105–6.

accomplishment'[60] is drawn in Pindar's poem, so, underlying Collins's poetic aim, is the need for divine aid. Collins's possible identity as the 'New *Alcæus*' depends on two things: the genuine instantiation of the Idea of Liberty in eighteenth-century Britain—the truth of historical progress—and the poet's ability to celebrate and confirm Liberty's presence in song. But a victory achieved by mere skill 'is none the worse for being quelled in silence', and the poet's own success or failure depends on divine aid, on the inspiratory presence of the 'Soul-enforcing Goddess' (l. 92). The interrogatory 'Who' which opened the poem, signalling the start of the poet's personal progress to the accomplishment of his task, thus translates into 'How':

> How may the Poet now unfold,
> What never Tongue or Numbers told?
> How learn delighted, and amaz'd,
> What Hands unknown that Fabric rais'd?
>
> (ll. 113–16)

The end-point of the poem's internal progress, as of Liberty's *translatio*, is indicated by the word 'now' (l. 113) and its forward motion is apparently fulfilled in the ensuing vision of the 'beauteous *Model*'. The poem's linear progress culminates in a reversion to the Idea. 'Ev'n now' the poem becomes the point where history coincides with the principle by which it is informed, where temporal progress intersects with the eternal Idea. British Liberty, that is, should not merely be symbolized by Collins's ode but contained in it.

The reversion to the Idea at this climactic moment conceals an underlying problem. Linear progress, of the poem as of history, culminates in the vision of Liberty, but that Idea is prior to any of its temporal manifestations and dictates the spatial poetic mode already observed. The linear now resolves into the spatial, and the linguistic organization which carried the poem to this point becomes meaningful because of its Ideal subordination. Yet the poet's vision of the '*Model*' is only fully realized in the poem's conclusion. This is a continuation of the basic principle of progress—temporal succession involving gradual improvement. Just as historical progress precedes Liberty's British instantiation, so the poem's internal sequence precedes the realization of Liberty's shrine. In the parallel between the fall of Rome and Britain's 'blest Divorce' (l. 87), for instance, the significant connection between fragments of the 'Giant-statue' and fragments of land is established in the course of the poem's linguistic development. The dual stanzaic structure

---

[60] Ibid., from the commentary to the same ode.

is realized through the poem's necessarily successive exposition of epithets. History may derive its significance from the informing priority of the Idea but the Idea is nevertheless realized in time. Such an understanding might tend to raise the status of poetic form. As is suggested by the notion of a poetic recreation of Liberty's ancient shrine, as well as by the images drawn from the arts which are used to express Liberty's various manifestations, though the work of art cannot exist without Liberty, the presence of Liberty is confirmed in works of art.[61]

The implied precedence of *translatio studii* over *translatio imperii* recalls Horace's paradox of the conqueror reconquered.[62] It argues a mutual dependence of Liberty and the poem that reflects the larger relationship between Liberty and historical progress. History may be informed by Liberty but the Idea gains expression through its temporal instantiations. For the poet, however, this circle of dependence entails a crisis of priority. The eternal Idea makes history significant by shaping it progressively. Similarly, if the poet experiences the sort of 'translation' by which Collins is identified as the 'New *Alcæus*' then his poetic endeavour, of little intrinsic import in this view, gains significance by its Ideal subordination. Poetry, like human history, acquires value on an absolute scale, as a greater or lesser embodiment of the Idea, while the divine origin of the Idea means that the scale of value is ethical as well as cognitive. Compare Harris: 'the Cause of LETTERS, and that of VIRTUE appear to co-incide, it being the business of both *to examine our Ideas, and to amend them by the Standard of Nature and of Truth*'.[63]

The later the poet, moreover, the greater the responsibility. Yet, when the poet attempts to fulfil the demands of this belief, the poetic process by which a sublime vision would be achieved is ultimately undermined. The criterion of poetic success, the '*Standard of Nature and of Truth*', is extrinsic to *poesis*, the act of making, and the poet's personal action is tantamount to an irrelevance. The basis of this problem is the inherent antipathy between a metaphysics of the Ideal and the work of art. As Erwin Panofsky remarks of Plato:

since Plato applied to the products of sculpture and painting the concept— utterly foreign to their nature—of cognitive truth (i.e., correspondence to the

---

[61] Cf. Crider ('Structure and Effect', 70) on the eighteenth-century belief in 'public liberty' as a 'necessary condition for poetic achievement'. 'Liberty' is full of references to artistic forms. In the strophe: '*Spartan* Fife' (l. 1), the 'beautiful Fragment' of Alcaeus (note to l. 7), '*Wisdom's* Shrine' (l. 9), the 'Sounds' of the poet's 'Shell' (ll. 14–15), and the 'Giant-statue' (l. 19).

[62] *Epistle* 2. 1. 156–7, where the Grecian capture of 'her savage victor' becomes another type of imperial conquest.

[63] Harris, *Hermes*, 406–7.

Ideas) as a measure of value, his philosophic system could have no room for an aesthetics of representational art as an intellectual realm *sui generis*.[64]

Collins's response to this problem, worked out in the 'Ode to Liberty', is essentially Plotinus' answer to Plato:

But if anyone despises the arts because they produce their works by imitating nature, we must tell him, first, that natural things are imitations too. Then he must know that the arts do not simply imitate what they see, but they run back up to the forming principles from which nature derives . . .[65]

As Panofsky argues, the goal of art now becomes that of reducing 'the visible world to unalterable, universally and eternally valid forms, thus renouncing that individuality and originality in which we are accustomed to see the principal criterion of artistic accomplishment'.[66] The poet's aim, therefore, remains the abdication of any personal control or authority in favour of the sovereignty of the Idea, a radical denial of his natural status as maker.

Clearly, such abdication is not possible. Just as the forward motion of 'Liberty' will never be fully reducible to spatial stasis, so the existence of the poem requires action on the part of the poet. Failure, however, though perhaps inevitable, is not absolute. In its final lines 'Liberty' modulates from the sublime to the beautiful. The poet's own vision resolves into a cultural imperative and the burden of responsibility is transferred from the poet on to his society: 'Thou, Lady, Thou shalt rule the West!' (l. 144).[67]

The last word of the poem is 'West', a word which signals the continuation of progress.[68] Despite the poet's apparent vision, Liberty's ultimate Western instantiation has not yet occurred; Liberty does not but 'shall' rule the 'West'. The remaining social requirement is 'to gain' '*Concord*':

> Ye Forms Divine, ye Laureate Band,
> That near her inmost Altar stand!
> Now sooth Her, to her blissful Train
> Blithe *Concord*'s social Form to gain:
>
> (ll. 129–32)

[64] E. Panofsky, *Idea*, trans. J. J. S. Peake (New York, 1968), 4.
[65] *Ennead*, 5. 8. 32 ff. Quoted from *Plotinus*, v, trans. A. H. Armstrong (Cambridge, Mass., 1984). Cf. M. H. Abrams, *The Mirror and the Lamp* (New York, 1958; repr. from 1953 edn.), 42.
[66] Panofsky, *Idea*, 4.
[67] Other examples of this modulation occur in the conclusions of 'Pity' and 'Fear'. For the social associations of the beautiful, later summarized in Edmund Burke's *Philosophical Enquiry* (1757), see Maclean, 'From Action to Image', *passim*.
[68] Cf. Cochrane, 'Bishop Berkeley'.

With this modulation into the beautiful the poet's own position takes on Horatian overtones. The conquest of political empire by an empire of the arts becomes an inverted *translatio* whereby *translatio studii*, exemplified in Collins's poem, precedes *translatio imperii*, which will be fulfilled in Liberty's still later instantiation. Finally, therefore, the present poem represents not the achievement of Liberty but a further stage in its invocation.[69]

The difficulties encountered in Collins's verse arise out of the metaphysical beliefs that underlie his poetics, the elements of which are relatively conventional, and each of the poems in his volume of *Odes* can be regarded as a different response to the same problem. As E. R. Wasserman observes, Collins is 'a philosophic realist rather than the usual eighteenth-century nominalist . . . Instead of ascending from images or impressions to universals and abstractions, Collins' true poet would create by realizing and concretizing "the shad'wy Tribes of Mind", the universal categories, or suprasensible Ideas.'[70]

The realist character of Collins's assumptions begs a question. How can one know that the description of Liberty's shrine, for instance, is not a truthful or accurate expression of the Idea? Any presumption of failure requires an Ideal point of comparison. If the poet concedes that his own 'View' is not Ideal, does he not tacitly presume some knowledge of that other 'View' by comparison with which he recognizes his failure? The assertion of a failure of vision, that is, is validated by the presupposition of some further 'View' whose truly Ideal nature provides the poet with the criterion of failure. At some level, the acceptance of failure paradoxically presupposes a sort of success.[71] Further, however, if the Idea of Liberty is always and everywhere the same, then the ubiquity and sameness of the essence which underlies its various manifestations renders it imperceptible. The Idea dissolves in the logic entailed by its ubiquity and there exists neither a negative nor a positive criterion by which one may judge the proximity of a work of art to the Ideal.[72]

If this point is reached, the debilitating force of the Ideas disappears. The poet is no longer required to be a slavish imitator of given forms and

---

[69] Crider ('Structure and Effect', 72) argues that Collins was 'appealing to traditions of British freedom and concord as inspiration for political liberty and harmony in the present. Such a condition would provide the atmosphere necessary for realizing the achievements which seem to be projected at the end of the odes to Pity, Fear, and Simplicity.'

[70] Wasserman, 'Collins' *Ode on the Poetical Character*', 99. One must question the verb 'create'. Any poetics which depends on 'universal categories, or suprasensible Ideas' is fundamentally imitative.

[71] This is basically R. G. Collingwood's argument against the proposition 'knowing makes no difference to what is known'. See his *Autobiography* (Oxford, 1939; repr. 1967), 44.

[72] Cf. E. Auerbach, *Literary Language and its Public in Late Latin Antiquity and in the Middle Ages*, trans. R. Manheim (New York, 1965), 13.

the way is open to a conception of the imagination as creative.[73] The divine Ideas become subjective 'ideas' and any model which acts as the basis of poetic composition may be found in the poet's subjective imagination rather than the world of universals. As M. H. Abrams notes, the criterion of art would then become 'intuitive and introspective', a step on the emerging path to Romanticism.[74] James Harris, for one, would regard this as a kind of madness:

Either all MINDS have their Ideas *derived*; or all have them *original*; or *some have them original, and some derived.* If all Minds have them derived, they must be derived from something, *which is itself not Mind,* and thus we fall insensibly into a kind of Atheism. If all have them original, *then are all Minds divine,* an Hypothesis by far more plausible than the former.[75]

Collins did not take this route. As G. H. Hartman notes, his attempt to renounce metaphysics for Nature, vision for '*Observance*' ('The Manners, l. 20), remains 'uneasy'.[76] Yet the appreciation of Collins's proximity to the possibilities opened up by intuition and introspection, along with the poet's willingness to address the seemingly insurmountable difficulties which lie at the very heart of his endeavour, have given his poetry an enduring energy and vitality and assured his place in the evolving canon of eighteenth-century literature.

[73] Cf. Panofsky, *Idea, passim.*
[74] Abrams, *The Mirror and the Lamp,* 43.
[75] Harris, *Hermes,* 400.
[76] Hartman, *The Fate of Reading,* 139.

16 Celts, Goths, and the Nature of the Literary Source

NICK GROOM

This chapter examines James Macpherson's sensational *Ossian* (1760–5)[1] and its relevance to Percy's *Reliques* (1765), arguing that Thomas Percy's work, which began as a straightforward response to the Scotsman, was actually predicated upon a crisis within the evolving canon of English literature. I will show that accounts of ancient cultures were determined by problems caused by the nature of the literary source, whether oral or literate. The rival claims of Macpherson and Percy on the literary establishment reveal that the presentation of the source was crucial to the reception of eighteenth-century antiquarian literature and its incorporation into the canon of English poetry: each writer employed an exclusive methodology, derived from opposed theories of British history, to validate his respective ancient poetry. The story of how Percy came to compile the *Reliques* is, therefore, full of significance for eighteenth-century poetic history, and the effects of his critical debate with Macpherson are clearly perceptible in how the literary canon henceforth evolved as a hierarchy of physical texts, distinct from the popular oral traditions which the next century codified as 'folklore'.

To redefine the relationship between *Ossian* and the *Reliques* I take an approach which is chronological and what I will term 'micro-bibliographical': explaining in detail how Percy read and used Macpherson, and how the context of the Ossianic controversy affected his own works. Percy emphasized the written, indeed the physical, status of ancient English poetry—embodied by his folio manuscript and later the *Reliques*. He stated his theory most clearly in *Five Pieces of Runic Poetry*, and it is this work, written as an explicit rejoinder to Macpherson's *Fragments*, upon which I will concentrate. The first part of this chapter explains that the antiquarian background of *Ossian* was a series of competing interpretations of prehistoric Britain. I then describe the impact of *Fragments*

Publication of manuscripts is by kind permission of the British Library and the Bodleian Library.
[1] It is conventional to denote James Macpherson's four published Ossianic works (*Fragments of Ancient Poetry, collected in the Highlands of Scotland, and translated from the Galic or Erse Language* (Edinburgh, 1760); *Fingal, An Ancient Epic Poem, in Six Books: together with several other Poems, composed by Ossian the Son of Fingal* (London, 1761); *Temora, An Ancient Poem, in Eight Books: together with several other Poems, composed by Ossian, the Son of Fingal* (London, 1763); *The Works of Ossian, the Son of Fingal* (2 vols.; London, 1765)) by the collective title *Ossian*.

of *Ancient Poetry* and *Fingal* upon Percy in his letters and in *Runic Poetry*. Finally, I will consider the effects of Richard Hurd's *Letters on Chivalry and Romance* (1762), Hugh Blair's *Critical Dissertation* (1763), and John Brown's *Dissertation on . . . Poetry and Music* (1763) on Percy's construction of the figure of the medieval minstrel as it appeared in the *Reliques*. The act of defining the nature of the literary source within the evolving canon was expressed as a series of attempts to assert a single nationalist ideology over the whole of Great Britain, but what this account shows is that the articulation of these ideologies was a haphazard and contradictory process, delegated to a tiny band of literary antiquarians, and critically influenced by their private whims.

The literary–antiquarian debates of the eighteenth century were all, to a degree, concerned with the ethnographical origins of culture and society: the invention of language, letters, and poetry. Among British antiquarians, these issues posed two related questions: who were the original inhabitants of Great Britain, and who were their descendants? Macpherson and Percy—who were working in the immediate wake of the 1759 'Year of Victories', at the height of the British Empire, and grappling with the definitions of national cultural identity that an emergent international power demanded—both tried to establish the pure racial origins of their material, but the ways in which they went about it were radically different. Each argument developed in a way that legitimated one poetic lineage and excluded the other.

The question concentrated on the Goths and the Celts. The word 'Gothic' is a semantic minefield in the eighteenth century.[2] The historical Goths were a particular tribe who crossed the Danube in AD 376 on their way to sack Rome. Following the sixth-century historian Jordanes, however, the term was used to describe the Germanic tribes in general, including the Angles, Saxons, and Jutes, who had landed with Hengist and Horsa in Kent and invaded England in AD 449. The Goths were reinvented and glorified in the sixteenth century as an aboriginal race originating in the *vagina gentium* ('womb of nations'), and therefore displaying in its purest form the instinctive love of liberty that had enabled them to overcome the tyranny of the Roman empire, and later assert the rights of Magna Carta over the Norman yoke. Consequently the word was used extensively by seventeenth-century Parliamentarians against the absolutist aspirations of the monarch, and subsequently by

---

[2] For definitions of the 'Gothic', see Paul Frankl, *The Gothic: Literary Sources and Interpretations through Eight Centuries* (Princeton, NJ, 1960); Samuel Kliger, *The Goths in England: A Study in Seventeenth and Eighteenth Century Thought* (Cambridge, Mass., 1952); Hugh MacDougall, *Racial Myth in English History: Trojans, Teutons, and Anglo-Saxons* (Montreal, 1982); Michael Meehan, *Liberty and Poetics in Eighteenth Century England* (Beckenham, 1986).

eighteenth-century Whigs to defend the peculiar advantages of the English constitution.

But the word also retained a strong pejorative sense which dated from the Renaissance. This usage deplored the fall of Rome to the Goths and the displacement of classical genius by a barbarism that had heralded the onset of the Dark Ages. Hence the Goths became gradually confused with the medieval, a time despised for its 'Gothic' taste. At the same time, the medieval pageantry of romantic Gothic was itself being revived: in architecture by Horace Walpole, who bought Strawberry Hill in 1748, and in literature by Thomas Warton. The latter's *Observations on the Faerie Queene of Spenser* (1754) was written with an antiquarian zeal that disclosed a conviction of the value of ancient native genius.

There did remain, however, a lingering popular distrust of the Gothic and even Thomas Percy retained a pejorative understanding of the term. On viewing the ruins of Melrose Abbey on the Tweed, he drafted a letter to Henry Revely on 9 August 1766 which gave his opinion of Gothic architecture: 'what I have generally ['ever' deleted] observed as faulty in our old Gothic Churches, has been for the most part a heavy clumsiness in the principal parts; and in the more minute, an injudicious load of fantastic and unnatural ['load' deleted] ornaments, crowded too thick together.'[3]

And there is perhaps one further dimension to the perplexed semantics of 'Gothic'. Lawrence Lipking suggests that the Walpole set 'enjoyed the iconoclastic feeling of daring that accompanied their praise of a word so weighted with derogatory connotations'.[4]

The definition of 'Celtic' is complicated in a different way. As Michael Hechter suggests, the Celts (the Irish, Scots, and Welsh) were imagined as a collection of peripheral peoples, excluded from the central core of power and resources by an English policy of internal colonialism. The Celts had resisted the Roman Invasion and enjoyed an indigenous geographic concentration; they had nurtured their own language, culture, and society, and had ambitions of political self-determination. They therefore had a profound sense of identity and locality which denied them the full integration afforded to the Picts, Frisians, Angles, Saxons, Danes, and Normans.[5]

The rhetoric of the Celtic fringe was also obscured by a rift between the Irish and the Scottish, who both claimed to be the original Celts. The Irish pedigree was the more respectable, originating in the fourteenth

---

[3] BL Add. MS 32335, fo. 12ᵛ.

[4] Lawrence Lipking, *The Ordering of the Arts in Eighteenth-Century England* (Princeton, NJ, 1970), 149.

[5] Michael Hechter, *Internal Colonialism: The Celtic Fringe in British National Development, 1536–1966* (London, 1975).

century with John of Fordun, and in the 1760s this argument was making itself felt through the work of the seventeenth-century historians Geoffry Keating and Roderic O'Flaherty. Central to the Irish claim was the evidence—indeed the very existence—of manuscript archives. Fordun's *Scotichronicon*, reprinted in 1759, relied on written records for its account: 'E Codicibus MSS. editum, cum notis et variantibus lectionibus'.[6] O'Flaherty, whose title-page likewise boasted materials 'Ex Pervetustis Monumentis fideliter inter se collatis eruta', argued that Ireland was nothing less than Homer's fabled island Ogygia, and entirely dismissed Scottish history as 'no more than a fabulous modern production, founded on oral tradition, and fiction'.[7]

In response, the Scottish Celtic, devoid of physical records, was remodelled along the primitive lines of archaic Greek: a symbolic classical stand against the new eruption of the Gothic. It derived from the Aberdeen school of primitivism and in particular the Homeric criticism of Thomas Blackwell.[8] Savage societies bred poets: primitive language was constructed by metaphor, and those metaphors derived from natural images. Poets were nomadic prophets: gliding across social strata, reciting verses in company, and falling into frenzied extemporizations under the influence of the muse. Under these conditions, original poetic genius did not need to be confined to the Greek world, and the description provided an important basis for the development of a comparable Gaelic poet. Macpherson was to invoke Blackwell's Homer in a Scottish Celtic context as a way of actually celebrating his use of oral sources. Ironically, Blackwell also provided a useful model for Percy's ancient English minstrel.

These speculations and researches into racial origins were keenly contested. A great deal of national pride rested on their conclusions. And then on 14 June 1760, James Macpherson erupted on to the scene, with his anonymously published *Fragments of Ancient Poetry, collected in the Highlands of Scotland, and translated from the Galic or Erse Language*: a slim pamphlet containing fourteen prose pieces (fifteen in the second edition) which purported to be ancient Celtic translations. The *Fragments* immediately won fanatical popularity.

From 1756 James Macpherson had begun collecting old Gaelic poetry while working as a teacher in his native Ruthven, Speyside, forming a

---

[6] Johannis De Fordun, *Scotichronicon* (Edinburgh, 1759), title-page (edited from manuscripts with notes and variant readings), 43.

[7] Roderico O Flaherty, *Ogygia* (London, 1685), title-page (collected from antiquarian records faithfully compared with one another); Roderic O'Flaherty, *Ogygia, or, A Chronological Account of Irish Events*, trans. James Hely (Dublin, 1793), i. 226.

[8] Thomas Blackwell, *An Enquiry into the Life and Writings of Homer* (London, 1735).

collection that included both transcriptions of local ballad-singers and manuscripts.[9] His poetic and nationalist aspirations were evident in his strongly partisan six-canto poem *The Highlander* (1758) and pieces which he had published in the *Scots Magazine*, before he turned his full attention to translating old Gaelic poetry.

Macpherson was put to the task of translating by John Home, a Scottish playwright whom he had met in Moffat in 1759. Home had a keen interest in Highland culture, but could not speak Gaelic himself, so he persuaded Macpherson to translate some pieces for him. Macpherson reluctantly did so, and Home excitedly carried them to Edinburgh, showing them to the Scottish literati: Alexander Carlyle, Hugh Blair (who was about to be appointed Professor of Rhetoric and Belles Lettres at Edinburgh University), William Robertson, Adam Ferguson, and Lord Elibank. Having spent a decade searching for ancient Highland verse, these Scottish intellectuals had their own cultural agenda, and Macpherson was rather overtaken by events.[10] Blair managed to persuade him to produce a few more translations, sent copies to Gray, Walpole, and Shenstone, and began making preparations for publication.

Macpherson attributed the poems to a Homerically blind third-century bard called Ossian, the son of Fingal, the last of the Celts. The Blackwellian conception of the bard—a prophetic ancient poet—had recently re-emerged in Thomas Gray's poem 'The Bard' in 1757, but bards were also part of Macpherson's Highland background. Fiona Stafford indicates that the bardic tradition had in some places survived the suppression following the Jacobite Rebellion of 1745, and clan chiefs were still sometimes attended by a bard 'who was responsible not only for the composition of poetry, but also for preserving the history of the Clan'.[11] In Ossian, Macpherson drew together the idealized product of antiquarian poetry with the living poets who recited Gaelic verse.

It should be stressed that *Ossian* was presented as an oral phenomenon. Macpherson made a crucial contribution to the antiquarian debates of racial origins and historiography by postulating that Celtic society was entirely illiterate: it was an oral culture. Macpherson's point was that this did not diminish the historical significance of the culture: on the

[9] See Paul J. deGategno, *James Macpherson* (Boston, 1989); Richard B. Sher, *Church and University in the Scottish Enlightenment: The Moderate Literati of Edinburgh* (Edinburgh, 1985); Bailey Saunders, *The Life and Letters of James Macpherson* (London, 1894); Fiona Stafford, *The Sublime Savage: A Study of James Macpherson and the Poems of Ossian* (Edinburgh, 1988).
[10] deGategno, *James Macpherson*, 24–6; Stafford, *The Sublime Savage*, 78–80.
[11] Ibid. 13. René Wellek comments, 'The Tudor antiquarians, in their patriotic fervour for everything "British", had already raised the status of the bard, who slowly assumed heroic proportions long before Gray's poem and Macpherson's sentimentalized version' (*The Rise of English Literary History* (Chapel Hill, NC, 1941), 126).

contrary, it was an absolute proof of its antiquity. There was already a sense of the primal orality of language in mid-eighteenth-century thinkers as diverse as Johnson and Hume.[12] Macpherson capitalized on this feeling to stress the staggering age of his Celtic fragments and scotch the arguments of Irish antiquarians who relied on the documentary evidence of a later age. Furthermore, the Preface of Macpherson's *Fragments*, ghost-written by Hugh Blair, not only invoked the oral tradition of the Highlands; it actually resisted any indigenous literacy supposedly contemporary with the composition of the poems:

In a fragment . . . which the translator has seen, a Culdee or Monk is represented as desirous to take down in writing from the mouth of Oscian, who is the principal personage in several of the following fragments, his warlike atchievements and those of his family. But Oscian treats the monk and his religion with disdain, telling him, that the deeds of such great men were subjects too high to be recorded by him, or by any of his religion.[13]

It was claimed that the poems had survived only through bardic tradition. Gray, witnessing what appeared to be the incarnation of his 'Bard', was '*extasié*' with the *Fragments*' 'infinite beauty', believing Macpherson was 'the very Demon of Poetry, or he has lighted on a treasure hid for ages'.[14]

This bardic oral tradition defined *Ossian* on every level. The poems themselves constantly stressed their oracy. They were full of sound, several were dialogues, and 'voices' served as a metaphor for poetry, memory, the past, and the present. For example, 'Fragment VIII' ended with Ossian's lament: 'SUCH, Fingal! were thy words; but thy words I hear no more. Sightless I sit by thy tomb. I hear the wind in the wood: but no more I hear my friends. The cry of the hunter is over. The voice of war is ceased.'[15]

Stylistically, the poems were constructed out of accumulating resonances and repetitions, such as alliteration, concatenation, parallelism, and accumulation, which appeared to testify that they were primitive, exotic, and oral.[16] A sense of evanescent orality was also present in the structure

---

[12] Samuel Johnson, *A Dictionary of the English Language* (London, 1755), i. A2ʳ; David Hume, *Enquiries concerning Human Understanding and concerning the Principles of Morals*, ed. L. A. Selby-Bigge, rev. P. H. Nidditch (Oxford, 1975), 224, 241.

[13] Macpherson, *Fragments*, pp. iv–v.

[14] *The Correspondence of Thomas Gray*, ed. Paget Toynbee and Leonard Whibley (Oxford, 1935), ii. 680.

[15] Macpherson, *Fragments*, 40.

[16] Walther Drechsler, 'Der Stil des Macphersonschen Ossian', Ph.D. dissertation (Berlin, 1904); John Dwyer, 'The Melancholy Savage: Text and Context in the Poems of Ossian', in Howard Gaskill (ed.), *Ossian Revisited* (Edinburgh, 1991), 164–206; Robert P. Fitzgerald, 'The Style of Ossian', *Studies in Romanticism*, 6 (1966), 23, 29–31; Stafford, *The Sublime Savage*, 103–11; Janet Todd, *Sensibility: An Introduction* (London, 1986), 59–60.

of the *Fragments*: the collection was a shadow of something larger, a fragment of something complete. The whole work was finely structured through subtle allusion and shifting perspective, which gave the sense of another work struggling to find form: of a lost northern oral epic articulated as a printed pamphlet.

Thomas Percy's interest in literary antiquarianism was as deeply rooted, if differently directed, as Macpherson's. Percy was a country parson living at Easton Maudit in Northamptonshire, with a growing interest in old English poetry.[17] In the 1750s he had obtained a piece of Interregnum flotsam: a seventeenth-century handwritten miscellany of antique popular verse. This folio manuscript was to provide the impetus for his anthology *Reliques of Ancient English Poetry*, published in 1765. By 1760 he was actively cultivating contacts across the country and beyond to help him collect antique verse.

For over two years Percy had corresponded with the respected poet William Shenstone, a vogue leader of taste and incumbent of the Leasowes, who shared Percy's passion for antiquarian ballads. They had transcribed and revised a small number of ballad texts from the folio manuscript, intending that they would eventually publish some sort of selection. But in 1760, both were busy with other projects. It was not until the sudden appearance of Macpherson's *Fragments* that they were roused to begin serious work on what was to become the *Reliques*.

The story of how Macpherson provided the stimulus for Percy and Shenstone to begin the *Reliques* in earnest is important for explaining the accidents and local struggles that were to shape English literary history. On 21 June 1760 Shenstone was sent an early copy of the *Fragments* by John Macgowan, who accompanied the book with an evangelizing letter.[18] Shenstone excitedly informed Percy on 11 August: 'you *must instantly* procure the "antient Fragments" of Scotch Poetry' and Percy coincidentally visited Shenstone shortly afterwards and consulted the new work.[19] The unexpected arrival of Macpherson's *Fragments* at the Leasowes inspired and stimulated Percy, who had as yet done virtually nothing with the *Reliques*, to propose that he compile a comparable anthology of ancient English fragments, under the editorial guidance of Shenstone. Shenstone responded with the suggestion that they be included in a four-volume *Reliques*.

---

[17] See Bertram H. Davis, *Thomas Percy* (Boston, 1981), and *Thomas Percy: A Scholar-Cleric in the Age of Johnson* (Philadelphia, 1989).

[18] Margaret M. Smith, 'Prepublication of Literary Texts: The Case of James Macpherson's Ossianic Verses', *Yale University Library Gazette*, 64 (1990), 132–57.

[19] *The Percy Letters*, vii. *The Correspondence of Thomas Percy and William Shenstone*, ed. Cleanth Brooks (New Haven, Conn., 1977), 68.

Percy's sudden and absorbing enthusiasm about the *Fragments*, and his proposal for a rival anthology, were not merely momentary excitements. His long-standing friendship with Edward Lye, for example, had already grounded him in the field of literary antiquarianism. Lye was an Anglo-Saxon scholar and the parson of Yardley Hastings, Bedfordshire, just a mile and a half away from Percy at Easton Maudit. He was a close and obliging neighbour—on 24 April 1759 he gave away Anne Gutteridge, Percy's bride. Bertram Davis notes that Lye 'seems to have taken a fatherly interest' in Percy, and Percy's memoranda books from their first acquaintance in 1756 to Lye's death in 1767 show that the two antiquarian scholars frequently dined together.[20] In 1757 Lye offered help glossing the folio manuscript and in 1759 he taught Percy the Runic alphabet.[21]

This is why when Shenstone told Percy that he must '*instantly* procure' a copy of Macpherson's *Fragments*, Percy was able, after he had pored over the book at the Leasowes, to respond swiftly with fragments of his own: 'Inclosed I send you an ancient Celtic, (or rather Runic) Poem, translated from the Icelandic. I am making up a small Collection of Pieces of this kind for the Press, which will be about the Size of the Erse Fragments.'[22] Although Percy himself was at this early stage confusing the Celts with the Goths, the first Runic fragments he sent Shenstone in September 1760 were introduced with a scholarly note, the fruit of his dinners with Lye:

It will be difficult to meet with many Celtic pieces so well preserved & so intire as, *the Epicedium of Haco*; or *the Incantation of Hervor* [in dryden's Misc.] [*sic*] because they are only to [be] met with inserted as Vouchers to Facts, in some of the Old Gothic Prose Histories. It will be more easy to meet with smaller fragments, which every where abound in those Histories.[23]

Percy transcribed two short fragments for Shenstone: six lines of 'Gandrode' and nine lines of the 'Death of King Guthlange' and wondered whether he should print the originals, 'which after all nobody will understand'.[24]

---

[20] BL Add. MS 32336, fos. 18–76.

[21] The neglected research of Andrew Deacon ('The Use of Norse Mythology and Literature by some 18th and 19th Century Writers, with special reference to the work of Bishop Percy, Thomas Gray, Matthew Arnold and William Morris', B.Litt. thesis (Oxford, 1964)) describes the collaboration between Percy and Lye in the production of *Runic Poetry*. Percy certainly had some ability at Runes, but, like his tutor, was not a serious Runic scholar, and they both relied heavily on seventeenth-century critics. Deacon compares sources and establishes that Percy's texts were largely derived from Latin versions, and that Lye contributed more to the historical framework than the difficulties of translation.

[22] *Percy Letters*, vii. 70.

[23] Margaret M. Smith, 'Thomas Percy, William Shenstone, *Five Pieces of Runic Poetry*, and the *Reliques*', *Bodleian Library Record*, 12 (1988), 473; Bodl. MS Percy, c. 7, fo. 2ʳ.

[24] *Percy Letters*, vii. 71. It is revealing that during this early and tentative work, Percy was inclined to regard poetry as a footnote to the text of history, for it implies that such fragments can be used to

Shenstone thought that there was 'something good' in the 'Celtic [*sic*]' fragments, but advised not to over-annotate the poems, warning 'The absolute *Necessity* of Notes, will be the Rock that you may chance to split upon'. He suggested that Percy use either a preface, glossary, or endnotes, omit the originals and shorter pieces, and adopt 'a kind of *flowing* yet *pompous Prose*' in paragraphs.[25]

James Dodsley signed the contract for 'five pieces of *Runic Poetry translated from the Islandic Language*' (with *The Song of Solomon*) on 21 May 1761, the day before the *Reliques* deal was struck, and the next month 'The Incantation of Hervor' was published in the *Lady's Magazine*.[26] Although *Runic Poetry* was not published until April 1763, Percy never lost sight of his project as a response to Macpherson, because by June 1761, in the immediate wake of the *Fragments*, Percy had already decided on the title and the contents of *Runic Poetry*, and had edited at least one piece. Nevertheless, he spent the rest of the year hard at work on the *Reliques*: visiting Cambridge to transcribe ballads from the Pepysian Library, assembling his 'Alphabet Collection' of white-letter broadsides from Dicey's warehouse, engaging Thomas Astle, Thomas Warton, and Richard Farmer to aid him in his researches, and commencing printing early in 1762—but he confidently expected *Runic Poetry* to be published in the winter of 1761.[27] On 17 September 1761, Shenstone again wrote encouragingly: 'Let the Liberties taken by the Translator of the Erse-Fragments be a Precedent for *You*. Many old Pieces, *without* some alteration, will do nothing; and, *with your* amendments, will be striking.'[28] He was reminding Percy of Edward Young's *Conjectures on Original Composition*, published in 1759, a highly influential little tract. Indeed, Shenstone urged Percy to read Young: 'even tho' it shou'd dissuade you . . . from undertaking any more *translations*. I should not *murmur* at the *effect*; provided it stimulate you to write *Originals*.'[29]

Young roundly condemned imitations because, unlike colonizing originals, they sprang from over-considered words, books, and texts.

attack or defend interpretations of that history. His hints of a creative synthesis of fragments were realized three years later in the *Reliques*, in which his ballad 'The Friar of Orders Gray' was assembled from parts of ballads quoted by Shakespeare and, moreover, derived from Goldsmith's as yet unpublished 'Edwin and Angelina' (Thomas Percy, *Reliques of Ancient English Poetry* (3 vols.; London, 1765), i. 225–30; *The Poems of Gray, Collins, and Goldsmith*, ed. Roger Lonsdale (London, 1969), 596).

[25] *Percy Letters*, vii. 74.
[26] Bodl. MS Eng. lett. d. 59, fo. 8ʳ (this contract is one of the few omissions from *The Correspondence of Robert Dodsley 1733–1764*, ed. James E. Tierney (Cambridge, 1988), 563); *Lady's Magazine*, 2 (1761), 487–9.
[27] *The Percy Letters*, iii. *The Correspondence of Thomas Percy and Thomas Warton*, ed. M. G. Robinson and Leah Dennis (Baton Rouge, La., 1951), 13; *The Percy Letters*, v. *The Correspondence of Thomas Percy and Evan Evans*, ed. Aneirin Lewis (Baton Rouge, La., 1957), 3.
[28] *Percy Letters*, vii. 118.
[29] Ibid. 26.

Young offered the advice: 'Let us build our Compositions with the Spirit, and in the Taste, of the Antients; but not with their Materials'—precisely what Shenstone consistently told Percy to do.[30] This neatly illustrates the tensions of rival attitudes to the nature of the source: Shenstone had far more sympathy with Macpherson's technique of adaptation and remodelling than with Percy's scrupulous adherence to the text, and in the end the *Reliques* became a compromise between the two.

For reasons I have given elsewhere, *Five Pieces of Runic Poetry* was not published until 2 April 1763, but Percy still placed it in the context of Macpherson: 'It would be as vain to deny, as it is perhaps impolitic to mention, that this attempt is owing to the success of the *ERSE* fragments.'[31] Percy presented the work as a direct, if delayed, response to Macpherson. Like the *Fragments* it was a slim octavo containing short pieces of apparently ancient foreign verse translated into distinctive English prose. Percy, however, emphasized his use of documentary sources; in fact, the entire structure of *Runic Poetry* served as an authenticating mechanism. Its title-page was more elaborate than that of the *Fragments*, and displayed an engraving of a number of untranslated Runes, underlining the palpability of Percy's sources. Like the Chinese characters which adorned Percy's *Miscellaneous Pieces* (1762), these offered an opportunity to authenticate the work. The title-page of Macpherson's *Fingal* (1761) significantly portrayed a blind Ossian extemporizing his verses in the Celtic wilderness with no manuscript in sight.

Both the *Fragments* and *Runic Poetry* quoted Lucan as an epigraph, but there the physical similarities ended. *Runic Poetry* was printed on quality paper, was set more accurately, and the text was enlivened with frequent ornaments. It was not designed to be bound sympathetically with the *Fragments*, but to replace it. Percy's poems were not translated in the Ossianic idiom, and were prefaced with notes, clarified with footnotes, and concluded with endnotes. 'The Incantation of Hervor', for example, had a lengthy Preface 'To prevent as much as possible the interruption of notes', but there were still footnotes throughout the entire piece.[32] Macpherson's collection was lean by comparison: it simply had

---

[30] Edward Young, *Conjectures on Original Composition. In a Letter to the Author of Sir Charles Grandison* (London, 1759), 22. For Young, see Patricia Phillips, *The Adventurous Muse: Theories of Originality in English Poetics 1650–1760* (Uppsala, 1984), 95–110. Percy alluded to Young in his Advertisement to 'Fragments of Chinese Poetry' (*Hau Kiou Choaan or The Pleasing History* (4 vols.; London, 1761), iv. 199).

[31] See my forthcoming article, 'Thomas Percy, Edward Lye, William Shenstone, and *Five Pieces of Runic Poetry*'; Thomas Percy, *Five Pieces of Runic Poetry translated from the Islandic Language* (London, 1763), A4ᵛ. Earlier (in 1761) Percy had placed his 'Fragments of Chinese Poetry' (*Hau Kiou Choaan*, iv. 197–254) in the context of Macpherson's *Fragments*, calling them 'striking and poetical' (iv. 200). This whole section of *Hau Kiou Choaan* was modelled on the layout of the Ossianic pamphlet and possibly was intended to be marketed separately.

[32] Percy, *Runic Poetry*, 6.

a brisk Preface contributed by Blair, and occasional, usually brief, explanatory footnotes.

Here Percy and Shenstone differed. Shenstone approved far more of the latter style, because it presented the pieces as poetry, and he disliked the antiquarian lumber which burdened Percy's poems. Percy in fact apologized for this in a letter to Shenstone: 'You will probably be disgusted to see it so incumbered with Notes; Yet some are unavoidable, as the Piece would be unintelligible without them.'[33] But Percy would not relinquish any critical apparatus which verified the physical existence of his Gothic poetry, and did not appreciate that it was the very unintelligibility that so appealed to Shenstone.

In *Runic Poetry* Percy outlined scholarly precedent, pleaded editorial integrity and verifiable sources, and listed appropriate references. In other words, he placed the work in a diagrammatic scholarly context: the literary establishment of books and writing, rather than the oral bardic tradition claimed by Macpherson. This is demonstrated most clearly in the Runic originals that were appended to the translations, of which he wrote: 'The Editor was in some doubt whether he should subjoin or suppress the originals. But as they lie within little compass, and as the books whence they are extracted are very scarce, he was tempted to add them as vouchers for the authenticity of his version.'[34] In fact, these originals were printed in roman, rather than Runic, characters, because they were themselves Swedish and Latin translations. They were included for the sake of form rather than to encourage scholarly precision: part of a grand textual conspiracy. Without authentic originals, Percy had no way of knowing whether his Gothic translations were more or less accurate than Macpherson's Celtic translations. But what is important about Percy's working of his textual machine is that it fixed the idea of extant manuscripts on to his work, a notion which he emphasized in his account of the Goths.

Percy's Goths were the ancient ancestors of the English, and had laid the foundations of national character, culture, and politics: 'It will be thought a paradox, that the same people, whose furious ravages destroyed the last poor remains of expiring genius among the Romans, should cherish it with all possible care among their own countrymen: yet so it was.'[35] They also invented rhyming verse, a claim Percy could 'prove' because they were inveterate scribblers, or rather carvers, of Runes. Just as the verbal clamour of Macpherson's Ossianic fragments stressed the oral culture of the Celts, so the prodigious textuality of *Five Pieces of Runic Poetry* underlined the literacy of the Goths. Percy

---

[33] *Percy Letters*, vii. 70.   [34] Percy, *Runic Poetry*, A7ʳ.   [35] Ibid. A2ᵛ.

demonstrated that his Goths differed from Macpherson's Celts in the crucial area of extant records, records which were keys to unlock 'the treasures of native genius' and settle the literary–antiquarian debates.[36] The confrontational Preface challenged Macpherson to publish his Ossianic originals: 'till the Translator of those poems thinks proper to produce his originals, it is impossible to say whether they do not owe their superiority, if not their whole existence entirely to himself. The Editor of these pieces had no such boundless field for licence.'[37]

While Percy had been trying to finish *Runic Poetry*, Macpherson published his first Ossianic epic, *Fingal, An Ancient Epic Poem, in Six Books*, on 1 December 1761. *Fingal* was introduced with an account of Macpherson's manuscript-collecting expedition in the Highlands, undertaken in 1760 and sponsored by the Scottish literati, but it still renewed the *Fragments*' commitment to orality, and Macpherson's own account of the trip did not mention tangible manuscripts. Instead he claimed that it was 'in order to recover what remained of the works of the old bards'.[38] This was in spite of his haul of 'two Ponies laden with old Manuscripts'.[39] Macpherson persisted in marginalizing manuscripts from Ossian, and he described the Gaelic oral tradition by analogy with Tacitus' references to song in, ironically enough, the compendium of Gothic culture, *Germania*: 'This species of composition was not committed to writing, but delivered by oral tradition . . . This oral chronicle of the Germans was not forgot in the eighth century, and it probably would have remained to this day, had not learning, which thinks every thing, that is not committed to writing, fabulous, been introduced.'[40] Macpherson disputed the emphasis on written records in eighteenth-century accounts of ancient history, which he claimed had misrepresented the Celts. The literacy of classical nations was crucial to their ensuing historical renown: 'They trusted their fame to tradition and the songs of their bards, which, by the vicissitude of human affairs, are long since lost. Their ancient language is the only monument that remains of them.'[41]

The poem 'Fingal' itself was full of episodes from the *Fragments*, though not told with quite the same sound and fury. There was more emphasis on the singing of the bards as a universal metaphor than on the disembodied voices of the *Fragments*.

The orality of *Fingal* was most clearly demonstrated in Macpherson's use of episodes derived from the *Fragments*, episodes that were substan-

[36] Ibid. A8[r].   [37] Ibid. A4[v].   [38] Macpherson, *Fingal*, a1[r].
[39] Robert Lingel, 'The Ossianic Manuscripts: A Note by Gordon Gallie MacDonald', *Bulletin of the New York Public Library*, 34 (1930), 80.
[40] Macpherson, *Fingal*, p. xiii.   [41] Ibid., p. ii.

tially changed. Macpherson indicated this in his voluminous footnotes—virtually every page of *Fingal* was annotated. Derick Thomson explains Macpherson's extreme footnoting as a contextual frame, but his annotation was also ideologically significant.[42] The fluctuation between versions demonstrated the inherent orality of the verses. Footnotes literally underwrote Macpherson's editing methods, not by positioning the text in the canon of antiquarian scholarship as Percy's did, but by exposing the evolution of the text and preventing closure. Macpherson was not simply pursuing the archetypal *Ossian*, but demonstrating by the constant fluctuation of each version the inadequacy of letters to communicate ancient Celtic poetry.

Neither the public, nor even Percy and Shenstone themselves, held simple or uniform views of Macpherson's project. 'What say you to Fingal—?' asked Shenstone, who had subscribed to the Scottish edition, 'What a treasure *these* for a modern Poet, before they were published!'[43] Percy's opinion was divided, noting 'too little simplicity of narration . . . affected and stiff . . . turgid and harsh . . . not what it is made to pass for', yet richly 'sublime and pathetic'.[44] Macpherson's work had a dramatic effect upon the world of letters. A storm of protest greeted *Fingal*. Irish nationalists, Wilkesites, and textual pedants forged an unlikely alliance against the Scottish literati, poets, and antiquarian cranks. There was a sudden demand for literary antiquarianism, and 1762 saw an explosion of books and pamphlets eager to turn a penny on *Ossian*. For Percy, in the middle of the *Reliques*, the most important of these was Richard Hurd's *Letters on Chivalry and Romance* (1762). This publication defined the place of ancient poetry in the popular imagination, marking the 'enchanted ground' on which Percy's Goths would fight Macpherson's Celts, and it consequently requires detailed consideration.[45]

---

[42] Derick S. Thomson, *The Gaelic Sources of Macpherson's 'Ossian'* (Aberdeen, 1952), 59. Macpherson's sources were probably medieval (1200–1600) oral ballads: see Donald E. Meek, 'The Gaelic Ballads of Scotland', in Gaskill (ed.), *Ossian Revisited*, 19–48.

[43] *Percy Letters*, vii. 138, 125. Percy wrote to Evan Evans on 15 Oct. 1761 that 'hardly one reader in ten believes the specimens already produced to be genuine' (*Percy Letters*, v. 19).

[44] *Percy Letters*, vii. 141–2.

[45] Richard Hurd, *Letters on Chivalry and Romance* (London, 1762), 54. The neatest account of Hurd is Hoyt Trowbridge, 'Richard Hurd's *Letters on Chivalry and Romance*', in his *From Dryden to Jane Austen: Essays on English Critics and Writers* (Albuquerque, 1978), 175–184; see also Audley L. Smith, 'Richard Hurd's *Letters on Chivalry and Romance*', *English Literary History*, 6 (1939), 58–81. Percy borrowed a copy of Hurd's *Letters* from Farmer (*The Percy Letters*, ii. *The Correspondence of Thomas Percy and Richard Farmer*, ed. Cleanth Brooks (Baton Rouge, La., 1946), ii. 5). He had read it twice by 5 June 1762 and was encouraged that Hurd placed 'The Old Romances . . . in a very respectable light' (*Percy Letters*, ii. 7). Notwithstanding this, he wrote to Shenstone on the same subject twelve days later: 'Have you seen Hurd's new Letters on Chivalry? he is clever, but he is a Coxcomb' (*Percy Letters*, vii. 157).

Like Thomas Warton, Hurd was interested in the pervasive influence of the apparently low literature of Gothic Romance (which he had not read) on the great English poets, Spenser, Shakespeare, and Milton (whom he had). Hurd redefined the Gothic by paralleling the cultural and artistic fecundity of ancient Greece with medieval Europe, re-evaluating the medieval by redefining the Hellenic. The petty tyrannies, incessant warring, and feudal values of the Middle Ages were not unlike the martial politics of ancient Greece which had created the institutions of chivalry and bardism.

Hurd's strategy, however, was not simply to impose an anachronistic social and linguistic model on the classical canons of literature and taste, and he was not so naïve as to find classical beauties in Gothic art. Instead, he tried to demonstrate that, if the conditions and therefore execution of Gothic and classical art differed, their theories of composition coincided.

When an architect examines a Gothic structure by Grecian rules, he finds nothing but deformity. But the Gothic architecture has it's own rules, by which when it comes to be examined, it is seen to have it's merit, as well as the Grecian. The question is not, which of the two is conducted in the simplest or truest taste: but, whether there be not sense and design in both, when scrutinized by the laws on which each is projected.[46]

Although he did not support Ossianic revivalism ('I would advise no modern poet to revive these faery tales in an epic poem') Hurd did propose an indigenous autonomy for Gothic art, rather than simply condemning it as mongrel degeneration.[47] In this way, Hurd's *Letters* helped to develop an English aesthetic by placing original genius in the Middle Ages and distinguishing it from the Franco-Scottish Celts.[48]

For a literary antiquarian like Percy, the work was a godsend. Hurd was effectively legitimating the medieval ballads Percy was editing from the folio manuscript for the *Reliques* by endowing them with native Gothic genius. *Runic Poetry* and the putative *Reliques* had an identical Gothic pedigree. The Goths were simultaneously being reinvented in two different ways: both as ancients and as medievals.

Yet even as Percy was developing an English answer to *Ossian*, Macpherson's publications found their defenders among the Scottish intelligentsia, for whom they formed the focus of a whole poetic and critical school. In 1763 Hugh Blair responded to Hurd's argument in his *Critical*

---

[46] Hurd, *Letters*, 61.
[47] Ibid. 101.
[48] Gerald Newman, *The Rise of English Nationalism: A Cultural History 1740–1830* (London, 1987), 110, 111; see also 117–18.

Dissertation, which was designed to be bound into *Fingal*.[49] Blair argued that an archetypal genius was common to all nations at primitive stages of development. This original genius was the modernity of sentiment displayed by Ossian. He therefore attacked Percy's Gothic fragments for their barbaric and bloodthirsty images, which revealed them to be effete and worthless trash.

Blair further postulated that in early societies (for example, in Old Testament times) language was purely figurative. From this childlike state, 'Language advances from sterility to copiousness, and at the same time, from fervour and enthusiasm, to correctness and precision. Style becomes more chaste; but less animated.'[50] Society progressed in a similar way: the four stages of hunters, gatherers, farmers, and capitalists. But although *Ossian* was nominally set in the primary moment of this Aristotelian social theory, it displayed all the artistry and enlightenment of later stages. Blair emphasized this social modernity in the language he used to compare Celtic with Gothic verse: 'When we turn from the poetry of Lodbrog to that of Ossian, it is like passing from a savage desert, into a fertile and cultivated country.'[51] The image was used advisedly. By demonstrating the Augustan sophistication of Ossian he could show that the ancient Celtic verse was both authentic and vastly superior to that of the Goths. 'In one remarkable passage, Ossian describes himself as living in a sort of classical age, enlightened by the memorials of former times, conveyed in the songs of bards; and points at a period of darkness and ignorance which lay beyond the reach of tradition.'[52] The pejorative shades of Gothic were reinscribed, once again merging the shadow of barbarism into the dark night of medieval ignorance: *Ossian* trod a fine, Homeric line between primitivism and enlightenment.

More importantly, Blair made a lengthy case against the Gothic fragments, retranslating the ubiquitous Nordic poem 'Regner Lodbrog'. The response of the Celtic *Ossian* supporters to 'Regner Lodbrog' was profoundly different from that of the Gothic revivalists, and clarifies how ancient poetry was being employed in new nationalist discourses.

[49] Hugh Blair, *A Critical Dissertation on the Poems of Ossian, the Son of Fingal* (London, 1763). A letter to Davies of Cadell and Davies (21 May 1782) shows that the *Dissertation* was based on a lecture Blair sold to Becket for 50 gns. (Historical Society of Pennsylvania, Gratz Collection, Case 10, Box 27). For Macpherson's hand in the published *Dissertation*, see R. W. Chapman, 'Blair on Ossian', *Review of English Studies*, 7 (1931), 80–3: Macpherson effectively wrote the final paragraph. David Punter ('Blake: Social Relations of Poetic Form', *Literature and History*, 8 (1982), 182–205) reads the clash between Hurd and Blair as the antiquity of culture meeting its obverse, barbarism (p. 196). Steve Rizza develops this idea by examining Blair's use of the sublime ('A Bulky and Foolish Treatise? Hugh Blair's *Critical Dissertation* Reconsidered', in Gaskill (ed.), *Ossian Revisited*, 141–3).
[50] Blair, *Critical Dissertation*, 3.
[51] Ibid. 11. [52] Ibid. 15.

William Temple had translated this poem from Latin into English in 1690, but it had of course appeared most recently in Percy's versions in the *Lady's Magazine* and *Runic Poetry*.[53] Blair's version in his *Critical Dissertation* was certainly less florid than Percy's, but he emphasized its bloodthirsty images and formlessness. *Ossian* was completely different, combining 'the fire and the enthusiasm of the most early times . . . with an amazing degree of regularity and art'.[54] Blair discounted claims that the Goths invented rhyme, and characterized the style of Ossian as a 'measured prose' which exhibited all the native, ancient, and original genius of the works.[55]

Macpherson's second epic, *Temora, An Ancient Poem, in Eight Books*, which was also published in 1763, attempted to divide and rule the clamour of opposition that had risen against *Ossian*. As he wryly remarked, 'WHILE some doubt the authenticity of the poems of Ossian, others strenuously endeavour to appropriate them to the Irish nation.'[56]

Macpherson introduced *Temora* with an emphatic attack on the Irish claim to be the original Celts and thereby the composers of *Ossian*. He refuted the Irish in two ways: first, he derided their historians, and, secondly, he gave his own reading of the racial migrations of ancient Britain. Macpherson argued that John of Fordun's history was erroneous precisely because of the very paucity of records that were the hallmark of *Ossian*: 'Destitute of annals in Scotland, he had recourse to Ireland, which, according to the vulgar errors of the times, was reckoned the first habitation of the Scots.'[57] Keating and O'Flaherty were dismissed on the authority of Sir James Ware, whose *De Hibernia*, originally published in 1654, had been reprinted in 1739. Ware had argued for a more flexible approach to sources: 'it is Antiquity, and the Unfaithfulness of Oral Tradition that have created these Errors, and left nothing clear for Posterity to depend on'.[58] Macpherson's own attack lacked the tolerance of Ware: 'Credulous and puerile to the last degree, they have disgraced the antiquities they meant to establish.'[59]

Having combated the immediate threat of *Ossian* being hijacked by the Irish, Macpherson then delivered an Ossianic account of the racial composition of ancient Britain. The Romans invaded south Britain and

---

[53] Frank Edgar Farley, *Scandinavian Influences in the English Romantic Movement* (Studies and Notes in Philology and Literature, 9; Cambridge, Mass., 1903), 59–69.

[54] Blair, *Critical Dissertation*, 11.

[55] Ibid. 53, 4 n.–6 n.

[56] Macpherson, *Temora*, p. xx.

[57] Ibid., p. iii.

[58] *The Works of Sir James Ware concerning Ireland Revised and Improved*, rev. Walter Harris (3 vols.; Dublin, 1739), ii. 13.

[59] *Temora*, p. xi.

drove the Caledonians into the north of the country, which remained unconquered. These Caledonians were the Celts or Gauls who had originally possessed Britain.

In distinguishing the Caledonians from the Romans, British, and Lowlanders, Macpherson rejected Ireland as well. The Irish were denied pure Celtic origins. Their country was initially colonized by the 'Firbolg', 'confessedly the Belgæ of Britain', before being invaded by the Caledonians, in support of which Temora was presented as proof.[60] *Ossian* was more than a cultural product: it was a confirmation of national identity.

Temora also placed the bards in a more contemporary light. Macpherson concentrated on their decline in status: they were expelled from clans for 'dull and trivial' compositions, took to 'satire and lampoon', and were accommodated by 'the vulgar'.[61] They began to invent incredible stories, interpolated the remains of *Ossian* with their 'futile performances', and subsequently created the romance.[62] Macpherson extended his Ossianic theory of the origin of poetry in the wake of Hurd's *Letters*: 'I firmly believe, there are more stories of giants, enchanted castles, dwarfs, and palfreys, in the Highlands, than in any country in Europe' in which, of course, 'the very language of the bards is still preserved'.[63] But Macpherson was actually retheorizing his material and belatedly considering *Ossian* manuscripts. The oral tradition was now defined by manuscripts, a new fidelity of the source:

The reader will find some alterations in the style of this book. These are drawn from more correct copies of the original which came to my hands, since the former publication. As the most part of the poem is delivered down by tradition, the style is sometimes various and interpolated. After comparing the different readings, I always made choice of that which agreed best with the spirit of the context.[64]

The context in fact overwhelmed the poetry. *Temora* was more fictional than earlier works, so Macpherson verified it historically. Fragments and poems that would have graced an earlier collection in their own right were literally reduced to footnotes in a larger argument, to prove the Gaelic language was purely and divinely harmonious. The integrity of Gaelic was its oracy. In other words, the language and style of the poem was not merely a source to settle the Celtic ancestry of the Scots over the Irish; it was the very object of their national quest, their true heritage.

---

[60] Ibid., p. viii.   [61] Ibid. 126 n.

[62] Ibid. 184 n.; see also John Macpherson, *Critical Dissertations on the Origin, Antiquities, Language, Government, Manners, and Religion of the Ancient Caledonians, their Posterity the Picts, and the British and Irish Scots* (London, 1768), 204–6, 213–25, in which James had a hand (Stafford, *The Sublime Savage*, 152–3).

[63] *Temora*, 184 n.   [64] Ibid. 4 n.

The original Celtic was imaginatively reconstructed: 'There is not a passage in all Temora, which loses so much in the translation as this. The first part of the speech is rapid and irregular, and is peculiarly calculated to animate the soul to war . . . The first is like torrents rushing over broken rocks; the second like the course of a full-flowing river, calm but majestic.'[65]

Macpherson claimed that the Gaelic language was universal and sentimental like music, rather than pictorial and abstract like hieroglyphs or runes: 'So well adapted are the sounds of the words to the sentiments, that, even without any knowledge of the language, they pierce and dissolve the heart.'[66] By arguing that the language was inherently musical, Macpherson was able to print an original text. Whether it was an original manuscript or dictated by oral tradition was irrelevant: the vocalic harmony of antique sounds was sufficient evidence for its authenticity. The document comprised twenty pages of what purported to be the ancient Gaelic: 'A SPECIMEN OF THE ORIGINAL OF TEMORA BOOK SEVENTH'. Ossian, for three years an oral phenomenon, at last sought the sanction of literacy.

The effect was disastrous. The introduction of manuscripts was not simply incongruous: it was lethal to the culture Macpherson and Blair had laboured to realize—the bardic oral tradition of the primigenial Highland Celts—because it dramatically increased the demand to see manuscript sources. The demand could not be met and, after an extended public controversy, Ossian was dismissed as a forgery.[67]

This belated literation and its attendant ruinous effect on Macpherson confirmed Percy's formulation of Gothic poetics, which he was rewriting for the Reliques. Ossian trespassed upon the written records of literate ancients like Percy's Goths, and paid the price. The source had become the deciding factor in the antiquarian canonization of literature. Percy's counterattack against Macpherson appeared in the Reliques in 1765 as the 'Essay on the Ancient English Minstrels', written during the summer of 1764—one of the last things he wrote before final publication. Percy considered the medium of literate poetry in a new way. His thesis hinged on the representation and reputation of the ancient poets themselves.

---

[65] Ibid. 50 n.   [66] Ibid., p. xvii.

[67] For the knotty problem of Macpherson's manuscripts, see Howard Gaskill, 'What did James Macpherson really Leave on Display at his Publisher's Shop in 1762?', Scottish Gaelic Studies, 16 (1990), 67–89 (summarized in Gaskill (ed.), Ossian Revisited, 6–16). The controversy blew up again in 1781: see Richard B. Sher, 'Percy, Shaw and the Ferguson "Cheat": National Prejudice in the Ossian Wars', in Gaskill (ed.), Ossian Revisited, 207–45; and Thomas M. Curley, 'Johnson's Last Word on Ossian: Ghostwriting for William Shaw', in Jennifer J. Carter and Joan H. Pittock (eds.), Aberdeen and the Enlightenment (Aberdeen, 1987), 375–431.

Percy's immediate source was John 'Estimate' Brown's *Dissertation on the Rise, Union, and Power, the Progressions, Separations, and Corruptions, of Poetry and Music* (1763).[68] Brown asserted that poetry and music were naturally united, but had been gradually separated by civilized refinement. Uncultivated societies, such as the American Iroquois and Hurons, relied on bards for their history and ultimately for their cultural identity: 'The Profession of *Bard* or *Musician* would be held as very honourable, and of high Esteem. For he would be vested with a kind of *public Character*: and if not an original Legislator, yet still he would be regarded as a *subordinate* and *useful Servant* of the *State*.'[69] Emphasis was placed on the civic duties of the bard. At the cusp of literacy bards remodelled their traditional ancient songs as written verse, severed the connection with music, and broke with the past. The new literacy legitimated itself by rewriting history.

Brown agreed that 'the *Scythian* or *Runic* Songs' were the oldest extant literature in the North, and quoted Odin, who boasted that 'his Runic Poems were given him by the Gods'; but at the same time suggested that *Ossian* had been composed 'during the second Period of Music . . . when the Bard's Profession had separated from that of the Legislator, yet still retained its Power and Dignity in full Union'.[70] His conclusion, 'Of the possible Re-union of Poetry and Music', was strangely expectant, and so Percy's minstrel evolved from Brown's anticipation of cultural and national renewal. He devised a state role for the poet, and defined the relationship of the arts to the court by reviving patronage. For his models, Percy returned to *Runic Poetry* and the scalds.

Percy derived most of his information about ancient Scandinavia from Paul-Henri Mallet's *Introduction à l'histoire de Dannemarc* (1755–6). He had read Mallet by 1761 and, with the help of Lye, began translating it on 21 November 1763, devoting a whole week to the business.[71] According to Mallet, scalds were central to Scandinavian society. Their spiritual father was Odin, inventor of poetry and runes, and their runic poetry was both a divine gift and a social asset: 'Those that excelled in it, were distinguished by the first honours of the state: were constant attendants on their kings, and were often employed on the most important commissions.'[72]

[68] 'Estimate' Brown accompanied Thomas Percy and his charge Algernon Percy on their 1765 tour of Scotland (Davis, *Thomas Percy: A Scholar-Cleric*, 144–6).
[69] John Brown, *A Dissertation on the Rise, Union, and Power, the Progressions, Separations, and Corruptions, of Poetry and Music* (London, 1763), 44.
[70] Ibid. 51, 158–9.
[71] *Percy Letters*, v. 16–17; BL Add. MS 32330, fo. 41ᵛ–42ᵛ.
[72] *Runic Poetry*, A3ʳ.

From a draft of his proposal to the booksellers, it is clear that in *Northern Antiquities* Percy was writing a national myth by perfecting the word 'Gothic':

Here he ['the English reader'] will see the seeds of our excellent Gothic constitution . . . many superstitions, opinions and prejudices . . . that the ideas of Chivalry were strongly rivetted in the minds of all the northern nations from the remotest ages . . . and . . . an ancient Islandic Romance that shews the original of that kind of writing which so long captivated all the nations of Europe.[73]

Percy warned the Welsh antiquarian Evan Evans that Mallet's biggest mistake was to compound the Goths with the Celts, 'a mistake which I shall endeavour to rectify in my translation'.[74] Percy worked hard to expunge all references to the Celts from Mallet's book. He produced a list of page references headed 'Notes concerning the Author's Confounding of Celtic & Gothic Antiquities' and methodically changed every Celt into a Goth.[75]

Thus the stage was set, as Percy sat down to begin his essay in August 1764, for a dramatic remodelling of the transmission of national literature. Percy was ready to draw together the threads of many arguments as he sought to reinvent the English poetic tradition, and it cannot be a coincidence that such an ambitious essay was begun under the eye of Johnson, who was staying at Easton Maudit with Percy at the time. Percy combined his sources: the folio manuscript and the Pepys and Dicey ballads, with his antiquarian research: the scalds and bards. The scalds became the Gothic forefathers of the ancient English minstrels and were disingenuously merged with the bards. He united the different senses of Gothic, attributing the invention of writing and poetry to the scalds, who became almost divine; dehistoricizing the bards by applying the term indiscriminately to scalds and minstrels; and making the medieval minstrels the inheritors of the Runic tradition. He invented a contemporary role, both cultural and ideological, for his English minstrels: they were the embodiment of the Gothic aesthetic.

The 'Essay on the Ancient English Minstrels' began by picking up the thread of Brown's argument: 'THE MINSTRELS seem to have been the genuine successors of the ancient Bards, who united the arts of Poetry and Music, and sung verses to the harp, of their own composing. It is well known what respect was shown to their BARDS by the Britons: and no less was paid to the northern SCALDS by most of the nations of the Gothic race.'[76] Percy argued by analogy, claiming, in Hurd's style, that the bloody ferocity of scaldic society would have produced the institutions of

[73] *Percy Letters*, v. 84–5.   [74] Ibid. 88.   [75] Bodl. MS Percy, c. 7, fo. 42ʳ.
[76] Percy, *Reliques*, i, p. xv.

chivalry. In his essay on metrical romances, the last to be finished for the *Reliques* on 1 November 1764, Percy concluded, 'That our old Romances of Chivalry are derived in a lineal descent from the ancient historical songs of the SCALDS, is incontestible, because there are many of them still preserved in the North, which exhibit all the seeds of Chivalry, before it became a solemn institution.'[77]

Like the scald, Percy's minstrel was originally a 'privileged character' among the Anglo-Saxons and Danes: a historian, genealogist, poet, and harpist. Alfred and later Anlaff adopted minstrel disguises and were able to infiltrate their enemy's camps unchallenged.[78] By obscuring the role of the Welsh bards he was able to annex their court status, yet retain the marginal and indigent nature of the minstrels. The minstrels, moreover, were oral poets. Percy therefore argued that the Gothic literacy of the scalds generated an oral tradition, which was in turn absorbed into the ephemeral publishing of popular balladry and chapbook romance, and ultimately the inaccuracies of the folio manuscript. It is no surprise, considering Percy's absolute emphasis on written sources, that he imagined writing somehow came before speech. To distinguish his noble minstrels from the (usually female) hack ballad-singers who regaled passing Londoners with their wares in the 1760s, he adapted Brown and blended the oral ballads of the minstrels with the press-work of the ballad-singers:

so long as the Minstrels subsisted, they seem never to have designed their rhymes for publication, and probably never committed them to writing themselves: what copies are preserved of them were doubtless taken down from their mouths. But as the old Minstrels gradually wore out, a new race of ballad-writers succeeded, an inferior sort of minor poets, who wrote narrative songs merely for the press.[79]

Percy's account of the decline of the minstrels exactly mirrored that of Macpherson's bards. They 'gave more and more into embellishment, and set off their recitals with such marvelous fictions, as were calculated to captivate gross and ignorant minds' and predictably created the romance.[80]

Percy's response to Macpherson's *Ossian* was to invent a Gothic tradition, and in the end he reinvented himself. He performed all the duties of a minstrel for his patrons the Northumberland Percys: acting as chaplain to the family and tutor to Algernon Percy, cataloguing the books at Syon House and writing a visitor's guide to the Alnwick estate, and ultimately composing a lengthy pastiche of a Northumbrian ballad, *The Hermit of Warkworth* (1771). Indeed, it could even be argued that this social

[77] Ibid. iii, p. iii.   [78] Ibid. i, p. xvi.   [79] Ibid. i, p. xxii.   [80] Ibid. iii, p. iii.

toadying lay behind all of Percy's elaborate construction of state-Gothicism. But in doing so he fundamentally shifted the attention of scholars to the medium of literary remains, and all that that entailed: reading the interfaces of oral, manuscript, and print cultures, and the coefficient of transmission, in terms of national myths or the spatialization of culture. The effect of this endeavour was to confirm the limitations of the evolving canon and to confine it to physical rather than evanescent texts. This effect is also seen in other literature of the period, as diverse as *Tristram Shandy*, Boswell's *Life of Johnson*, and the Gothic novel, where the validity of different literary media (speech, manuscripts, and the press) is explored. Percy's *Reliques* stands not only as an example of the literary–antiquarian taste, an early attempt to assemble the nation's literary inheritance, and an influential anthology of popular verse, it is also a response to Macpherson's *Ossian*, a reinvention of the Gothic, and ultimately a manifesto for a new poetics of the source.

17 Trafficking in the Muse: Dodsley's Collection of Poems and the Question of Canon

MICHAEL F. SUAREZ, SJ

I

In his 'Introduction' to *The New Oxford Book of Eighteenth-Century Verse* (1984), Roger Lonsdale presents a conventional map of eighteenth-century poetry as a well-charted and comfortably domesticated landscape, only to suggest that beyond the well-worn track of our customary excursions there lies a vast and unexplored *terra incognita*. 'Since the landscape of eighteenth-century poetry is now apparently so well mapped and likely to afford so few unexpected perspectives . . .', he writes, 'it will seem outrageous to suggest that we still know very little about the subject.' Nevertheless, Lonsdale insists, 'this must literally be the case', because literary historians and anthologists have typically neglected the great majority of eighteenth-century poetic texts, focusing their attention instead upon a relatively small group of familiar works. According to Lonsdale, 'this situation is explicable only if we recognize the hypnotically influential way in which the eighteenth century succeeded in anthologizing itself'. First among the anthologies Lonsdale singles out is Robert Dodsley's *A Collection of Poems by Several Hands* (1748–58), which Lonsdale notes is 'invariably trusted as definitively representative of the mid-century'.[1]

Originally published in 1748, the *Collection* went through twelve editions in thirty-four years, spawned two unauthorized supplements, and was generally regarded as the epitome of polite taste in poetry during the second half of the eighteenth century. In an Age of Miscellanies, Robert Dodsley's *Collection of Poems* was the best seller of the century. In 1755 the *Edinburgh Review* judged the anthology 'much more valuable than any other of the same kind', and asserted that the 'volumes of

I wish to thank the Bibliographical Society of America for generous support of research associated with this essay.
  [1] *The New Oxford Book of Eighteenth-Century Verse*, ed. Roger Lonsdale (Oxford, 1984), pp. xxxv–xxxvi.

miscellany-poems, published by Mr. Dodsley, are already known to all persons of taste'.[2]

Not surprisingly, the *Collection* was widely recommended as an indispensable addition to every gentleman's library. *Directions for a Proper Choice of Authors to Form a Library* (1766), for example, singled out 'Dodsley's Miscellaneous Collection, 6 vols. 12mo. being some of the best productions of the present time' among the thirty-five great works 'of our own poets' that the discerning reader should acquire.[3] In 1769, writing from his home in Corn Street, Bristol, the 16-year-old Thomas Chatterton remarked to a correspondent that Dodsley's 'Collection of modern and antique poems is in every library'.[4] Some three-and-a-half thousand miles away, Thomas Jefferson, compiling a list of 148 titles his brother-in-law must have in his Virginia library, included only Dodsley's anthology and Pearch's supplement to represent miscellanies of contemporary poetry.[5] John Duncombe, writing in the *Gentleman's Magazine* (1780), appears to have reflected general public opinion in calling the *Collection* 'confessedly the best in our language'.[6]

Robert and James Dodsley were the Faber & Faber of mid-eighteenth-century London. They were the most successful publishers of poetry in their day, and the *Collection of Poems*, one of their most dependable and lucrative products for thirty-four years, was an emblem of that success. Despite its many lacunae—including the virtual absence of works by Young, Prior, Gay, Swift, Pope, and Smart—the *Collection* gradually came to be seen by then-contemporary consumers as the miscellany best representing the highest standards of taste in 'modern' poetry.

In our own century, several generations of literary historians have taken Dodsley's *Collection of Poems* to be the most reliable indicator of the state of poetry in the mid-eighteenth century. 'The collection which best represents the poetry of the middle of the eighteenth century is Dodsley's *Collection of Poems*,' observe H. V. D. Dyson and John Butt. Maximillian E. Novak calls the miscellany 'that repository of the best poetry of the period', while George Sherburn asserts, 'the taste of readers of poetry in the mid-century is revealed by Dodsley's *Collection of Poems by Several Hands*. . . . It was in these volumes largely that people of the

[2] *The Edinburgh Review, for the Year 1755* (2nd edn., Edinburgh, 1818), 51. This periodical has no direct relation to the quarterly publication of the same name founded by F. Jeffrey *et al.* and published by A. Constable from 1802 to 1829.

[3] *Directions for a Proper Choice of Authors to Form a Library* (London, 1766), 40–1.

[4] *The Complete Works of Thomas Chatterton*, ed. Donald S. Taylor (2 vols.; Oxford, 1971), i. 339. To Mr Stephens, 20 July 1769.

[5] *A Virginia Gentleman's Library: As proposed by Thomas Jefferson to Robert Skipworth in 1771 and now assembled in the Bush-Everard House, Williamsburg, Virginia*, intro. Arthur Pierce Middleton (Williamsburg, Va., 1952), 11–15.

[6] *Gentleman's Magazine*, 50 (Mar. 1780), 121.

day read their "contemporary" poetry.' In much the same vein, James Sutherland surmises that 'we are safe in taking the reader of this miscellany as the typical poetry-reader of the period'. John Butt may be closest to the truth when he begins his survey of English poetry from 1740 to 1760 with the remark: 'the most convenient way of examining the state of English poetry at the death of Pope is to turn over the pages of Dodsley's *Collection of Poems*.'[7]

Because Dodsley's miscellany has come to occupy so central a place in chronicling the state of eighteenth-century poetry—and has been the subject of studies by such accomplished scholars as Courtney, Chapman, and Eddy—it seems highly incongruous that we still know very little about the editing, marketing, and readership of the *Collection*.[8] The consequence of this unaccountable gap in our knowledge is that we have virtually no understanding of the relationships among the *Collection*'s bibliographical history, its public reception, and the place subsequently assigned to it by literary historians. In the absence of a reasonably thorough bibliographical profile of the miscellany's 'life history', students of eighteenth-century literary culture have been unable to judge in what ways the editorial, marketing, and readership histories of the *Collection* played a part in determining how the miscellany came to represent the state of poetic production and consumption at mid-century in a seemingly definitive and unassailable way.

Taking up Lonsdale's assertion that 'these compilations were calculated to appeal to a respectable readership at a precise historical moment', this chapter shows the extent to which what began as a coterie collection came to be understood as 'definitively representative', and considers what this case tells us about the relationship between the book trade and the process of canonization. In sum, by putting the 'text' of the *Collection* in the 'context' of its editorial, publishing, and marketing history, I hope to demonstrate by particulars the truth of Lonsdale's general pronouncement that 'the success of [polite] taste lay less in

[7] H.V.D. Dyson and John Butt, *Augustans and Romantics* (London, 1950), 165; Maximillian E. Novak, *Eighteenth-Century English Literature* (New York, 1983), 117; George Sherburn, 'The Restoration and Eighteenth Century', in Albert Baugh (ed.), *A Literary History of England* (New York, 1948), 1006–7; James Sutherland, *A Preface to Eighteenth-Century Poetry* (Oxford, 1948), 54; John Butt, *The Oxford History of English Literature*, viii. *The Mid-Eighteenth-Century*, ed. Geoffrey Carnall (Oxford, 1979), 57. See also Raymond Dexter Havens, 'Changing Taste in the Eighteenth Century: A Study of Dryden's and Dodsley's Miscellanies', *Publications of the Modern Language Association of America*, 44 (1929), 501–36; *The Correspondence of Robert Dodsley 1733–1764*, ed. James E. Tierney (Cambridge, 1988), p. xiv; and Richard Wendorf, 'Robert Dodsley as Editor', *Studies in Bibliography*, 31 (1978), 236.
[8] William Prideaux Courtney, *Dodsley's Collection of Poetry: Its Contents and Contributors* (London, 1910); R. W. Chapman, 'Dodsley's Collection of Poems by Several Hands', *Oxford Bibliographical Society Proceedings and Papers*, 3 (1933), 269–316; Donald D. Eddy, 'Dodsley's Collection of Poems by Several Hands (Six Volumes), 1758 Index of Authors', *Papers of the Bibliographical Society of America*, 60 (1966), 9–30.

governing what was written than in influencing what would be allowed to survive'.[9]

II

The classic status that the *Collection* was to achieve could hardly have been predicted from the publication of the first three-volume edition in 1748. In a letter to Horace Walpole, Thomas Gray complained that the edition was produced in 'whited-brown paper, and distorted figures, like an old ballad. I am ashamed to see myself, but the company keeps me in countenance.'[10] 'The company' was decidedly mixed; it included William Collins, Samuel Johnson, and James Thomson alongside such justly forgotten authors as Hervey Aston, Jacob Hilderbrand, and William Melmoth. Reading through the poorly edited, miserably produced, and comically uneven miscellany, one can scarcely help but wonder what moved Dodsley, a well-established publisher of classical and contemporary poetry, to issue such a second-rate publication.

An analysis of the contents of the 1748 *Collection* appears to indicate at least something of the bookseller's motivation. In this first edition, we find more than one hundred poems by authors who had already published works through Dodsley or his close associate Mary Cooper, and some forty-four poems from periodicals and miscellanies that Dodsley and/or Cooper had previously sold. Among these are twenty-seven from *The Museum: or, Literary and Historical Register* (1746–7), six from *Philomel. Being a Collection of English Songs* (1744), and eight from the *Public Register* (1741). In all, then, over 85 per cent of the poems in the first edition of the *Collection* may be said to come from 'in-house' sources. Moreover, as James Tierney has noted, Dodsley began publishing the *Collection* less than four months after he discontinued *The Museum*, a fortnightly journal containing essays, historical and literary memoirs, and poetry. The miscellany thus may have been conceived as a quick way to sell the substantial backlog of poems left over from his aborted periodical.[11]

Dodsley's expenses for the first edition of the *Collection* were apparently quite low; new poems from the distinguished group of literary friends who met at Tully's Head appear to have been 'donated' to the cause, and the bookseller already owned the copyright to virtually all the

---

[9] *New Oxford Book*, ed. Lonsdale, pp. xxxvi–xxxvii.
[10] *Correspondence of Thomas Gray*, ed. Paget Toynbee and Leonard Whibley, corr. H. W. Starr (3 vols.; Oxford, 1971), i. 143–4. In this letter, Gray assumes that Dodsley 'chose to be œconomical', though he does not speculate why this might be so.
[11] James E. Tierney, '*The Museum*, the "Super-Excellent Magazine" ', *Studies in English Literature 1500–1900*, 13 (1973), 503–15; see especially 509–11.

poems he used from his backlist. Except for Dodsley's sending a complimentary copy of the *Collection* to certain individuals, there is no extant record of payment to any author for the appearance of his work in the *Collection of Poems*. The poor production of the first edition probably reflects Dodsley's reluctance to invest a great deal in the project: the quality of both paper and printing in this edition is far below the usual standard for a publication issued from Tully's Head, and the editorial treatment is inferior to what we find in Dodsley's *Select Collection of Old Plays*, a twelve-volume set that appeared between 1745 and 1746.[12] By all appearances, then, it seems that the bookseller initially had modest expectations for the *Collection*—it was a low-risk enterprise that allowed him to achieve several desirable ends with a single publication.

We might also add the speculation that Dodsley, a bookseller known both for his remarkable sensitivity to the London poetry market and for his impeccable sense of timing, was testing the market for a new multi-volume anthology now that the miscellanies associated with Dryden, Fenton, Steele, Pope, Pemberton, and Lintot no longer occupied a significant place in the London book trade. The former best sellers had run their course and were now dated; perhaps Dodsley sensed that he could occupy the niche left empty by their demise. The bookseller had all he needed to float a trial balloon: a large stock of poetry consisting of some pieces that had already won public approbation and other works that had never appeared in print before, a solid reputation as one of London's leading literary establishments, and sufficient capital to support his plan.

Evidence from the bookseller's surviving correspondence supports the notion that Dodsley himself did not see the first edition of the *Collection* as anything more than a low-budget publishing experiment. Writing to William Shenstone just six days after the miscellany went on sale, Dodsley admonishes his friend: 'I am much oblig'd to You for offering me an improv'd Copy of the School Mistress . . . but I could wish you would not spread the Notion of a New Edition, as that might in some measure retard the Progress of This.'[13] The bookseller was receiving copy for the much-revised and carefully corrected second edition before the first edition had been on sale for a single week!

Thomas Edwards, writing to Daniel Wray on 25 July 1748, offers a fascinating perspective on Dodsley's highly unusual practice of editing a second edition of the *Collection* while the first was still being sold. Upon learning from Dodsley that his sonnets were to be included in the

---

[12] The imprint for all twelve volumes lists 1744 as the date of publication.

[13] Dodsley to Shenstone, 24 Mar. 1748, in *Correspondence*, ed. Tierney, 122. Dodsley's fears were evidently well founded: having received intelligence of the forthcoming second edition, Shenstone himself decided not to purchase the first. See Shenstone to Lady Luxborough, 25 Sept. 1748, in *The Letters of William Shenstone*, ed. Marjorie Williams (Oxford, 1939), 172.

radically revised and substantially enlarged second edition, replacing works by William King and Abel Evans, Edwards became worried that he would be compromised by the bookseller's plan:

> you ought not therefore to have turned Dodsley loose upon me here alone, without sending me at the same time directions how to act, for I think this so ticklish a point, that I do not care to act of my own head. In the first place I cannot but think this scheme a kind of *Popish* trick and a hardship upon the purchasers of the first edition, and that if it is so, I ought not to encourage it . . .[14]

Not wishing to offend his valuable customers, Dodsley soon issued a supplemental fourth volume, bearing a 1749 imprint date and now exceedingly rare, to be given to purchasers of the first edition. Presumably this conciliatory gesture allayed Edward's fears; his writings occupy thirteen pages in volume two of the second edition.

The much revised *Collection of Poems*, which appeared some nine months later, was substantially different in both content and appearance. Nearly one hundred texts were omitted, added, or rearranged. Most significant among the additions were more than twenty-five new poems by Lord Chesterfield, Lord Lyttelton, William Collins, and David Garrick. The inclusion of these works solidified the *Collection*'s literary reputation, while the omission of such pedestrian verses as William King's 'The Old Cheese' was equally in keeping with Dodsley's newly modified programme to make the miscellany a repository of polite taste.

Changes in the physical layout of the text similarly reflect the editor's shifting concerns.[15] This miscellany was printed on high-quality paper by John Hughs, who was soon to become Dodsley's favourite printer. The press is generally well corrected. Forty-five pages were added; the design throughout is larger, with considerably more white space. A new engraving adorned the title-page, and, while the first edition had only eleven ornaments (or one every eighty-nine pages) the second edition sported 234 ornaments and fleurons, a remarkable procession of putti, cornucopia, Roman busts, lyres, flowered borders, and other neo-classical trappings. Page for page, Dodsley's second edition is twenty times more ornamented than the first. In fact, the *Collection* is one of the most highly

---

[14] Bodl. MS 1011, fo. 37.
[15] Dodsley may well have learnt about the great importance of layout and attention to accidentals from his patron; see David Foxon, *Pope and the Early Eighteenth-Century Book Trade*, rev. James McLaverty (Oxford, 1991), 153–236. Cf. Nicholas Barker, 'Typography and the Meaning of Words: The Revolution in the Layout of Books in the Eighteenth Century', in G. Barber and B. Fabian (eds.), *Buch und Buchhandel in Europa im achtzehnten Jahrhundert* (Wolfenbütteler Schriften zur Geschichte des Buchwesens, 4; Hamburg, 1981), 126–65.

ornamented mass-market books of the period. Taken together, these changes in the presentation of the text have an unmistakable effect on the reader, suggesting that the poetic performances collected in these volumes are worthy of close attention and careful preservation.[16] Dodsley's *Collection* no longer gave the impression of a hastily conceived and meanly executed gathering of poetical scraps; its title-page engraving of the nine Muses, its profusion of neo-classical ornaments, and its well-executed illustrations all convey a sense of august sensibility and classical authority that serve to elevate the reader's perception of the poetic texts. This time, Thomas Gray did not complain.

When we consider that the purchasing of paper accounted for about a half of the bookseller's cost for producing a volume, it becomes increasingly clear that Dodsley elected to invest a substantially larger sum in his revised miscellany. Adhering to the standard price of nine shillings for the three-volume set while significantly increasing his printing and paper costs, Dodsley reduced his profit margin for each set of the miscellany. At the same time, however, he sought to ensure that his product would have a longer life in the market. The cost of producing the free supplement to the first edition, nearly 180 pages long, necessarily diminished his profits for the second edition still further. The 'new' *Collection of Poems* was an expensive and somewhat risky business for Dodsley, whose thirteen years as a bookseller had taught him that, in a rapidly changing and highly competitive environment, few miscellanies could sustain multiple editions.[17] Dodsley seems to have made a radical break with his original production and marketing plan for the *Collection of Poems*; at some juncture late in the process of bringing the first edition of the *Collection* to market, Dodsley evidently decided to adopt a longer-term strategy.

Dodsley's business acumen in deciding to change editorial, production, and marketing strategies for his fledgling miscellany is borne out not only by the *Collection*'s subsequent success, but also by the fact that the

---

[16] For an elegant defence of the notion that 'forms effect sense', see D. F. McKenzie, *Bibliography and the Sociology of Texts*, The Panizzi Lectures, 1985 (London, 1986), 1–70, esp. 9–21. Cf. Lucia Re, '(De)constructing the Canon: The Agon of the Anthologies on the Scene of Modern Italian Poetry', *Modern Language Review*, 87 (1992), 585–603: 'The illusion that an anthology is simply made up of texts and that texts are always themselves no matter what container contains them is just that: an illusion' (p. 586).

[17] Cf. Arthur Case, *Bibliography of English Poetical Miscellanies, 1521–1750* (Oxford, 1935). Throughout the late 1730s and 1740s, Dodsley and/or Cooper were involved in a significant number of miscellanies: among the works they published or sold were *The Cupid* (London, 1736); *Philomel. Being a Collection of English Songs* (London, 1744); *The Muse in Good Humour* (London, 1745); *Pastorella; or, The Sylvan Muse* (London, 1746); and *The Theatre of Wit* (London, 1747). Shortly before undertaking *A Collection of Poems by Several Hands*, Dodsley was the principal seller for R. Cross's *A Collection of Poems on Several Occasions* (London, 1747), a miscellany of Restoration verse.

first edition did not sell remarkably well. Although there is no extant correspondence to document exact figures, we may surmise from the pattern of advertisements in the London *Daily Advertiser*, Dodsley's media vehicle of choice at the time, that sales of the *Collection* were not as brisk as its subsequent track record would lead us to imagine. At this time in Dodsley's career, his usual pattern for a major publication was four advance announcements in the *Daily Advertiser*, a notice indicating 'this day is published', and four or five subsequent announcements. The 1751 edition was advertised nine times, for example, while the 1755 edition was mentioned ten times in the *Daily Advertiser*. Later, as the *Collection* became more established, the publisher needed to spend less money giving notice to his product: for the 1758 edition, we find only three notices; with the 1763 edition, Dodsley paid for only two.[18] In sharp contrast, we find the first edition advertised twelve times between 14 January and 8 February, and seven more times between 25 February and 25 March. In addition to these nineteen advertisements, Dodsley placed another on 8 April and still another on 27 May 1748. Good business men do not spend money unless they have to—and Dodsley was an excellent business man. Therefore, this most unusual and otherwise excessive advertising pattern suggests that Dodsley had to keep on paying the editors of the *Daily Advertiser* in order to sell his slow-moving merchandise.[19]

If surviving copies are any indication, it seems that Dodsley may have printed fewer copies of the 'new and improved' second edition than of the poorly produced and rather tatty-looking first edition. One problem in making such an assessment, however, is that book-auction catalogues rarely distinguish between the two 1748 editions. Given that many potential buyers of the second edition would have already purchased the first, and that sales of the first edition were not terribly brisk, the bookseller may have elected to print only 250 copies of the revised miscellany. Yet, if the second edition was not widely disseminated, it was, nevertheless, the model for all subsequent editions of these three volumes.

---

[18] Throughout most of his career, Dodsley advertised in five newspapers: the *Daily Advertiser, General Advertiser, London Chronicle* (which he undertook with Wm. Strahan), *London Evening Post* (in which he owned a 1/15th share), and the *Public Advertiser*. The data from the *Daily Advertiser* should therefore be taken as indicative, rather than exhaustive. On the value of newspaper advertisements as bibliographical evidence, see William B. Todd, 'On the Use of Advertisements in Bibliographical Studies', *Library*, 5th ser., 8 (1953), 174–87.

[19] Ralph Straus, *Robert Dodsley: Poet, Publisher, and Playwright* (London, 1910), 105, asserts that the first edition sold well, but he neither offers any substantiating evidence nor attempts to account for the fact that the second edition was not offered for sale until almost seven months after it went to press. The length of this delay may be explained by Dodsley's unwillingness to offer the second edition before the first had sold out.

III

We can identify seven reasons, all of which can be traced back to this early stage in the *Collection*'s history, for the miscellany's subsequent commercial success. First, there is the niche theory mentioned above. The market seemed ripe for a multi-volume anthology to represent, and indeed to construct, contemporary taste. Dodsley's *Collection* effectively replaced earlier miscellanies and held a prominence in the market that may have discouraged subsequent competition. The time was right and the three-volume miscellany was a bold stroke. Secondly, there is the *Collection*'s close association with Pope. Indeed, as I have argued at length elsewhere, the second edition may fruitfully be read as a memorial to Pope, who had been Dodsley's patron.[20] Let it here suffice to say that virtually all of Dodsley's editors and a striking number of contributors were closely associated with Pope's circle; that the first three volumes of the second edition include over a dozen poems which repeatedly place Pope at the centre of English letters; and, most importantly, that the very nature of the literary project that Dodsley was effecting in the *Collection* had strong ties indeed to Pope's own beliefs about the need to preserve poetry in its proper sphere and to protect it from defilement by 'Smithfield Muses', 'Grub Street', sycophantic laureates, and other compromising, pretentious, or low-born influences.

Closely allied to the *Collection*'s strong ties to Pope and his circle is the third reason for the ascendancy of Dodsley's miscellany: the reputation of the bookseller. The appearance of 'at Tully's Head' on a title-page was an aesthetic imprimatur, for Dodsley had already published Pope, Drayton, Glover, Milton, Dalton, Johnson, Whitehead, Nugent, Duck, Shenstone, West, Young, Akenside, Collins, Swift, Walpole, Chapman, Warton, Mason, and Gray. Although there certainly were other highly reputable publishers of contemporary poetry—Bathurst, Hitch, Millar, the Knaptons, the Rivingtons, and the Tonsons—none could claim a roster of poets as distinguished as Dodsley's.

A fourth reason for the *Collection*'s success is the remarkable group of 'gentlemen' editors, many of whom came to know the bookseller through Pope, who lent their assistance to the project. George Lyttelton, Joseph Spence, Mark Akenside, Richard Owen Cambridge, Gilbert West, Horace Walpole, and quite possibly Joseph and Thomas Warton and Lord Chesterfield, provided Dodsley with an important network for gathering and evaluating poems, and were instrumental in giving the

---

[20] 'Dodsley's *Collection of Poems* and the Ghost of Pope: The Politics of Literary Reputation', *Papers of the Bibliographical Society of America*, forthcoming.

Collection a sufficiently patrician cast.[21] The 'Advertisement' to the miscellany emphasizes this point, suggesting that behind the footman-turned-bookseller stands an oligarchy well qualified to be the arbiter of polite taste: 'This design was first suggested to the Editor, as it was afterwards conducted, by the opinions of some Gentlemen, whose names it would do him the highest honour to mention. . . . nothing is set before [the reader], but what has been approved by those of the most acknow-ledged taste.'[22] Although Dodsley's business acumen and knowledge of the bookselling market were by all accounts outstanding, his 'gentlemen' editors gave the former servant-in-livery the one thing all his industry could not supply: a highly cultivated sensibility attentive to the principles of decorum, refinement, and polite taste. From what fragmentary evidence we have, it is clear that Dodsley relied most especially upon the decisions of Lord Lyttelton in selecting and editing works for the *Collection*.[23]

In much the same vein, a fifth factor contributing to the miscellany's almost unprecedented popularity is its strongly aristocratic associations. That Dodsley's *Collection of Poems* has a distinctively patrician pedigree may be seen both in its gentlemen editors mentioned above, and in the fact that some ninety-five of the 226 poems in these volumes, no less than 47 per cent, are either written by peers or are dedicated or addressed to peers.[24] The deliberately highbrow tenor of the *Collection* is altogether in keeping with the general conduct of Dodsley's business. Tully's Head on Pall Mall traded in the stuff of Augustan sensibilities. The most frequently issued type of publication from Dodsley's firm, for example, was classical poetry, either in the original Greek and Latin, or in translation or imitation in English. If Tully's Head issued a number of works on marriage and domestic affairs, it also published four times as many works on monarchy and nobility.[25] An essential part of Dodsley's success is the appeal of his publications to that privileged sector of the market with incomes sufficiently large to purchase multi-volume sets such as the twelve-volume *Select Collection of Old Plays* and the *Collection of Poems* that was soon to grow to six volumes. The unmistakably aristocratic colouring of Dodsley's miscellany undoubtedly advanced its social

---

[21] Significantly, the only women poets Dodsley and his 'gentlemen' editors judged worthy of inclusion in the first three volumes of the *Collection* (both 1748 editions) were Elizabeth Carter, already a well-established author widely renowned for her intellectual accomplishments, and Lady Mary Wortley Montague, a woman of rank and obvious literary celebrity.

[22] Robert Dodsley (ed.), *A Collection of Poems by Several Hands*, (London, 1748), 1.

[23] See e.g. Dodsley to Shenstone, 10 Nov. 1753: 'I will shew them [Shenstone's poems for volume four] either to Sir George, or Mr. Wm. Lyttelton. Most of those [poems] which compose the first three Volumes, were shewn to Sir George [Lyttelton]' (*Correspondence*, ed. Tierney, 162).

[24] This calculation includes authors who were not peers in 1748, but were subsequently elevated to the peerage.

[25] *Correspondence*, ed. Tierney, 29.

cachet and its attraction for many educated and wealthy readers. The fact
that nearly 50 per cent of the poems in Dodsley's *Collection* are so closely
associated with the aristocracy almost inescapably leads one to recall that
the term *classicus* originally denoted the wealthiest of the five Roman
propertied classes before Aulus Gellius first used the word to signify 'a
first-class and taxpaying author, not a proletarian'.[26]

We have already noted that the new layout of the *Collection*, with its
many ornaments and classically allusive engravings, contributed in no
small way to the overall impression that the miscellany was a distinguished repository of learning and polite taste. The seventh reason for the
Collection's success, though of a rather different nature, may have been
no less carefully planned. In the years while the *Collection* was building
its reputation, a number of its most popular poems were available to the
public only in the miscellany itself. For example, from the time the
Collection was first published, Dodsley never reprinted Johnson's 'London'; anyone who wanted to purchase the poem had to purchase the
entire miscellany.[27]

IV

The acquisition and editing of poems for the *Collection*'s volume four,
which appeared in 1755, and for volumes five and six, published in 1758,
proceeded in much the same way as the earlier volumes.[28] Dodsley
continued to draw extensively from his backlist and to appropriate
poems from periodicals, including his highly successful weekly journal
The World (1753–6). Remarkably, Dodsley's search for fit material to
fill out these volumes even led him to return to his earliest sources for the
Collection, gleaning still more poems from the already once-harvested
contents of *The Museum, Philomel*, and the *Public Register*. Shortly after
the fourth volume went on sale, Dodsley's long-time friend Horace
Walpole wrote to Richard Bentley pronouncing the work 'the worst
tome of the four', despite the fact that it featured Gray's 'Elegy'.[29] The
last two volumes were equally uneven; Dodsley's continued prominence

[26] Ernst Robert Curtius, *European Literature and the Latin Middle Ages*, trans. W. R. Trask (New York, 1953), 250.
[27] As owner of the copyright, Dodsley authorized the 1750 fifth edition of 'London', published by Cave and sold by Dodsley. Until it was reprinted in Oxford in 1759 under the title *Two Satires*, 'London' was available for purchase only in the 1751, 1755, and 1758 editions of the *Collection*.
[28] After the publication of the first two editions of vols. i–iii in 1748, Dodsley produced a third edition in 1751; the fourth edition of the three volumes appeared in 1755 to coincide with the introduction of vol. iv. The full six-volume set went on sale in March 1758 and comprised the fifth edition of vols. i–iii, the second edition of vol. iv, and the first edition of vols. v and vi. Thereafter, all six volumes were issued together in 1763, 1765, 1766, 1770, 1775, and 1782.
[29] *Horace Walpole's Correspondence*, ed. W. S. Lewis *et al.* (48 vols.; New Haven, Conn., 1937–83), xxxv. 241.

as a poetry publisher notwithstanding, the literary standard of volumes four through six is generally inferior to what we find in the second and subsequent editions of the first three volumes. Nevertheless, literary historians may find consolation in the fact that much of the correspondence between Dodsley and William Shenstone survives to document a substantial proportion of the editorial history of these last three volumes.[30] The influence of Dodsley's favourite correspondent, particularly on the 1758 texts, is easily demonstrated by the fact that almost one-fifth of the authors represented in volumes five and six were Shenstone's friends and neighbours.

Although we have a relatively well-developed understanding of who contributed to the *Collection* and how their work came to be included, we know very little about who actually purchased and, presumably, read this best-selling miscellany.[31] In order to trace the provenance of Dodsley's anthology, I have examined more than 200 sets of the *Collection* and have searched through 425 book-auction catalogues covering the years 1750–95. Provenance studies can be fraught with methodological problems, not the least of which is that the average person's books are never sold at auction, nor find their way into Oxbridge college libraries. Moreover, in those rare instances where his books do survive and are signed, it is often impossible to tell where he lived or what he did for a living. What the book-auction and fixed-price sale catalogues can tell us, however, is the extraordinary degree to which the *Collection* did indeed populate the market. For example, in the twenty-six years from the death of Robert Dodsley in 1764 to the French Revolution, 51 per cent of the catalogues listed a copy of Dodsley's *Collection of Poems by Several Hands*. This does not mean that 51 per cent of readers owned this text, however. Many of the catalogues combined the libraries of several gentlemen, and some of the catalogues are huge 'General Sale' affairs from firms like White's and Robson's. Nevertheless, this statistic does indicate that, among the gentry and professional classes, the miscellany was one of the most popular works of its day.

An analysis of the catalogues also tells us that the *Collection* was a great favourite among clergymen—50 per cent of the copies traceable to particular owners belonged to members of the clergy. That clergymen should constitute such a large sector of the anthology's market is altogether congruent with the fact that Classics and imitations, followed

---

[30] Tierney (*Correspondence*, 53) notes that '28 per cent of the entire collection [of Dodsley's extant correspondence] arises out of the nineteen months immediately preceding the last two volumes' of the *Collection of Poems*.

[31] Courtney, *Dodsley's Collection of Poetry* remains the best study of the *Collection*'s lesser-known authors.

by titles in religion, scripture, and clerical affairs, are the two largest categories of Dodsley's publishing and sales activity.[32] Similar logic may help to explain the dearth of lawyers represented, about 5 per cent, since Dodsley published no books on the law. The significant presence of Fellows of the Royal Society, comprising more than 20 per cent of the identifiable purchasers of the *Collection*, may appear to be unusual, but is really quite understandable given both the social status of that group and the fact that Dodsley's fifth largest publishing category is science and medicine.[33] An analysis of the holdings of Oxbridge college libraries and of contemporary instructors' private collections indicates that the miscellany was moderately popular at the Universities, and appears to have become more so as the century progressed.

What the book-sale catalogues also tell us is that many owners had their copies of the *Collection* gilt or specially bound—yet another indication of their sizeable disposable incomes. This is particularly true of the 1765 large-paper edition which frequently appears in bindings by Baumgarten, Robiquet, Payne, and Johnson, selling for two guineas or more.[34] This edition, which James Dodsley issued between the 1763 and 1766 octavo printings, was clearly meant to solidify the miscellany's 'classic' status.[35] In much the same vein, the 1782 edition, like the 1780 reissue of *A Select Collection of Old Plays*, is heavily annotated with learned commentary. These extensive notes by Isaac Reed expanded the market for the miscellany, not only by introducing new matter concerning historical background and the authorship of poems with previously 'concealed names', but also by making the *Collection* compatible with John Nichols's four-volume release of 1780, *A Select Collection of Poems, with Notes Biographical and Historical*.[36] Moreover, if the 1765 edition forwarded an image of the *Collection* as a classic to be acquired, decorated, and displayed by the wealthy, then the 1782 edition no less suggests that, being the worthy object of scholarship and close annotation, the *Collection* has evinced its classic status on another front as well. The book trade has long understood that production and public reception are inextricably linked. It is hardly a coincidence that many copies of the annotated edition also appear in special bindings. Both the

---

[32] *Correspondence*, ed. Tierney, 29.

[33] Ibid.

[34] On the prominence of these London bookbinders, see Ellic Howe, *A List of London Bookbinders, 1648–1815* (London, 1950), p. xxvi.

[35] James Dodsley (1724–97), who was twenty-one years younger than his eldest brother Robert, assumed control of the business at Tully's Head upon Robert's retirement in 1759; his name first appears on the Dodsley imprint in 1753, though there is evidence to suggest that he began learning the trade from his brother in the early 1740s.

[36] On Reed's editing of the 1782 *Collection*, see Arthur Sherbo, *Isaac Reed, Editorial Factotum* (English Literary Studies monograph no. 45; Victoria, BC, 1989), 35–41.

310 *Michael F. Suarez, SJ*

large-paper and annotated editions may be seen as clever attempts to invigorate a market approaching saturation. By modifying the miscellany, James Dodsley created new sales possibilities and helped to extend the life of his product.

We know that the *Collection* went through twelve London editions in thirty-four years, but we have little idea as to the size of the press runs. The only firm data we have is that the 1755 fourth volume, according to the Bowyer ledgers, ran to 1,500 copies.[37] Such a moderately large press run is understandable given that the market for this volume included all the purchasers of the first three editions, as well as those now buying the new four-volume set. Yet, evidence from press figures, and from publication and printing dates, makes it clear that this Bowyer run of 1,500 was in fact a *second* impression. In other words, the *Collection* was selling better at this point than has previously been imagined. It seems most probable that John Hughs's initial printing of volume four ran to at least 1,000 copies and may well have been 1,500. Although the occasional appearance of a 1755 volume four with a new title-page in the 1758 sets indicates that the second press run did not sell out, despite Dodsley's assurance to Shenstone that 'the four first Volumes are now quite out of print, not a book to be had', Dodsley's printing of 2,500 or 3,000 copies indicates that the miscellany was enjoying notable success.[38] Altered press figures and changes in paper stock also indicate two impressions for the 1758 and 1775 editions. Did Dodsley hedge his bets on the large investment required to produce a six-volume set by printing a conservative number of texts and then commissioning a second impression after he had seen how the product was performing? The bibliographical evidence certainly suggests that some kind of market response strategy was here at work.[39]

The extraordinary popularity of the *Collection of Poems* may in no small measure be attributed to the way in which the Dodsleys exercised striking imagination and expertise at every phase of the miscellany's history—editing, production, marketing, and distribution. When we consider that more than 80 per cent of the poems in the second and subsequent editions of volumes one to three of the *Collection* come either from Dodsley and Cooper authors, or from miscellanies or periodicals Dodsley and/or Cooper had previously published, it is remarkable indeed

[37] *The Bowyer Ledgers: the printing accounts of William Bowyer, father and son with a checklist of Bowyer printing*, ed. Keith Maslen and John Lancaster (London, 1991), item 3943, Ledger B362, 457, P1109: 'Dodsley, 10 shts, 1500 crown, dd 25 Mar 55 to Hughs.'
[38] *Correspondence*, ed. Tierney, 332.
[39] William B. Todd ('Concurrent Printing: An Analysis of Dodsley's *Collection of Poems by Several Hands*', *Papers of the Bibliographical Society of America*, 46 (1952), 45–57) was the first scholar to discover two impressions for the 1758 edition.

that this miscellany could be understood for so long to be the mirror of poetic practice in the mid-eighteenth century. When we consider the extent to which Dodsley continued to appropriate works from his previous publications and the manner in which whole sections of the later volumes consist of poems scavenged by Dodsley's gentlemen editors—the strong presence of Shenstone's friends and neighbours is the most notable example—it is highly surprising that this miscellany is routinely adduced as the repository of the best poetry of the period.

One reason for this somewhat distorted view of the *Collection* is that students of eighteenth-century literary history have naïvely accepted then-contemporary pronouncements about the miscellany without considering their sources. For example, *Directions for a Proper Choice of Authors to Form a Library* (1766), which so enthusiastically recommends the *Collection* to prospective book-buyers, was sold by James Dodsley in the same year that he produced an edition of the miscellany. John Duncombe, who in the *Gentleman's Magazine* called Dodsley's miscellany 'confessedly the best in our language', may have been somewhat biased in his critical judgement by the appearance of his own poems in volumes four and six of the *Collection*. Similarly, the encomiastic verses of Richard Graves celebrating his friend Dodsley's great stature in the literary world must be read in light of the appearance of four poems by the then-unknown author in the *Collection*'s fourth volume:

> Where Tully's Bust, the Honour'd Name
>   Points out the Venal Page
> There Dodsley consecrates to Fame
>   The Classics of his Age.
>
> In vain the poets, from their mine
>   Extract the shining Glass;
> Till Dodsley's Mint has stamped the Coin
>   And bade the sterling pass.[40]

Significantly, Graves's poem was edited and submitted for publication in *Aris's Birmingham Gazette* by his neighbour William Shenstone.

V

The editorial, printing, marketing, and readership history of Dodsley's miscellany is not merely bibliographical arcana. The commercial success of the *Collection of Poems* is inextricably linked to its influence upon

---

[40] *Aris's Birmingham Gazette*, 20 Dec. 1756, quoted in *Correspondence*, ed. Tierney, 50; see also Clarence Tracy, *A Portrait of Richard Graves* (Toronto, 1987), 116–18 and n. 54.

312 *Michael F. Suarez, SJ*

literary history. Had it not so thoroughly dominated the market for thirty years and thus effectively determined what was 'allowed to survive', Dodsley's miscellany would not occupy so central a place in the history of eighteenth-century poetry from the death of Pope to the efflorescence of Blake. Until recently, 'publish or perish' was a central axiom of literary historiography even more than it was a shibboleth of academic life. Implicitly and perhaps unwittingly adhering to a creed of bibliographical Darwinism, literary historians and teachers of English letters have routinely assumed that what was often reproduced—and so transmitted to subsequent generations—must have been what was most worthy of survival.

Conflating what Alastair Fowler has called the 'accessible canon' with the 'selective canon', students of the eighteenth century have almost universally subscribed to the belief that Dodsley's *Collection* must be representative of the age, must be most fit for our historical study, because this group of poems more than any other in the century was a conspicuous publishing success.[41] Although the perdurance of a work is often a legitimate index of its merit, the pervasive and powerful forces of bibliography, economy, and ideology must be duly recognized and taken into account when attempting to understand the cultural life of any text. This is especially true in the case of collections comprising works by multiple authors. Modern literary history is most often tied to commercial success, which, in turn, is inseparable from bibliographical and market forces. The canonical status of a text or group of texts is not exclusively a property of the work itself; the question of canonicity is inseparable from the question of transmission.

Of course, Dodsley himself was not in the business of being representative; Dodsley was in the business of selling books. Given the nature of the trade in poetic wares at Tully's Head, it certainly appears that the last thing Dodsley wanted his *Collection* to be was representative. By all appearances, the bookseller wanted his miscellany to be distinctive, even exclusive. Unlike Bell, Cook, Anderson, and Chalmers, Dodsley was not attempting to 'put before the public a cultural heritage apparently vital to be known'.[42] He was marketing poems by his coterie of authors and by the friends of his close associates for a particular readership.

The labours of David Foxon, Roger Lonsdale, and the developers of the *Eighteenth-Century Short Title Catalogue* have challenged many of

[41] Alastair Fowler, 'Genre and the Literary Canon', *New Literary History*, 11 (1979), 97–119.
[42] Thomas F. Bonnell, 'Bookselling and Canon-Making: The Trade Rivalry over the English poets, 1776–1783', in *Studies in Eighteenth-Century Culture* (East Lansing, Mich., 1989), 53–68. See also Douglas Lane Patey, 'The Eighteenth Century Invents the Canon', *Modern Language Studies*, 18 (1988), 23–5.

our old certainties about the landscape of eighteenth-century poetry and the ease with which we tour the well-cultivated estates of the canonical while blissfully ignoring the undomesticated wilds lying outside its familiar borders.[43] To this student of the eighteenth century, the poetic productions of such extra-canonical authors as Alexander Pennecuik, Hetty Wright, and E. Dower are more engaging and, I believe, genuinely more indicative of contemporary compositional practices than are many of the verses found in the pages of Dodsley's 'definitively representative' miscellany.[44] Future scholarship will surely enlighten us further regarding the contributions of these and other relatively unknown poets, even as it alerts us to new perspectives on already established authors and texts. As the revision and re-evaluation of the eighteenth-century poetic canon proceeds, however, we must continue to insist that such critical discussions are appropriately grounded in rigorous bibliographical scholarship.

The case of Dodsley's *Collection of Poems* appears to substantiate the truth of Professor Lonsdale's proposition that 'we still know very little about the subject' of eighteenth-century poetry. New efforts to chart the unexplored regions of the literary landscape will undoubtedly be somewhat disorienting, as old truths are challenged and familiar landmarks recede on the horizon. Students of the period may be consoled, however, by recognizing that it is far better to be asking some of the questions than to be certain that we know all of the answers.

[43] David F. Foxon, *English Verse: 1701–1750: A Catalogue of Separately Printed Poems with Notes on Contemporary Collected Editions* (London, 1975); Roger Lonsdale (ed.), *New Oxford Book*, and *Eighteenth-Century Women Poets: An Oxford Anthology* (Oxford, 1989).
[44] For works by these extra-canonical poets, see *New Oxford Book*, ed. Lonsdale, 148–50, 165–6, and 312.

18 'Sweet native stream!': Wordsworth and the School of Warton

David Fairer

One of the problems raised by the concept of a literary 'canon' is its tendency to encourage static and compartmentalized thinking, either by invoking a 'classic' timelessness (the great work freed from temporal contingencies so as to find a universal meaning) or by the mapping-out of artistic hierarchies and orders. In this scheme 'minor' texts play the subordinate role of providing analogue material that is then left behind by the 'major' text, within which all the interesting critical activity is located. But a poem can be great not by transcendence over other minor or subordinate poems, but by recognizably speaking their language and conducting a dialogue with them. In a satiric context this becomes a state-of-the-culture device, evident in the generic miscegenation between the many analogues of *The Dunciad*, or more elegiacally in *The Waste Land*'s fragmentation of vulgar and sophisticated voices (Pope's anarchy of the pantomime and Eliot's of the radio dial). But the power of a non-satirical poem (Gray's 'Elegy' or Milton's 'Lycidas') can depend on how it makes its sources articulate by absorbing and developing a tradition. Here the relationship with the sources is in a more positive way an organic one: questions of subordination or transcendence are replaced by heredity and kinship—strength is drawn from connection and inherited powers. A 'canon' in these terms becomes a familial relationship between texts, and issues of 'major' or 'minor' have less significance. The 'text' itself may even overrun individual authors, so that the critical emphasis shifts from addressing discrete poems to exploring a poetic continuum. A scenario in which works assert their independence as they write off their debts and make their 'great' statements can be replaced by one in which poems proclaim their intertextual nature and accept responsibility for a shared and developing language.

The later eighteenth century was a period when such issues came to the fore with the growing interest in the writing of literary history. A static and taxonomic model was being replaced by an organic and developmental one in what recent theorists have represented as a 'romantic discourse'. One of the defining characteristics of such a discourse is,

Clifford Siskin and others have argued, a conviction that literary history is best understood in terms of growth and development. A narrative history, one that traces continuities rather than disjunctions, is for David Perkins (following Siskin) a 'romantic project'.[1] 'Romantic', I would want to add, in a Wordsworthian rather than a Blakean sense. To the extent that it draws on a motif of an organic continuum, such a history sits uneasily alongside a revolutionary, rather than an evolutionary, reading of the Romantic impulse. The voice, after all, is that of Burke's *Reflections* rather than Paine's *Rights of Man*; but Burke's image of the nation as an imaginatively living organism, rooted in inherited commitments, values, and affections, has closer affinities to the Wordsworth of *The Prelude* and 'Tintern Abbey', than does Paine's desire to break that thread of inherited connectedness and 'begin the world over again' on virtuous principles.[2]

The aim of this chapter is to attempt a narrative history in these terms of a poem that provides an interesting case-study of textual interplay, Wordsworth's 'Lines written a few miles above Tintern Abbey, on revisiting the banks of the Wye during a tour, July 13, 1798'. Traditionally proclaimed a 'great' work in the old canonical sense, the poem has seemed to encourage, particularly in its sublime passages, notions of transcendence. But something has been lost of the way its power as a poem lies not in how it works at a different level from other texts, but in how it is rooted in them and grows from them. Keats's 'egotistical sublime' is such a wonderful idea that the phrase has been allowed to define the poem unhelpfully. In some ways it is a profoundly unegotistical document. The 'I' of the poem is a voice that throughout, as we shall see, echoes and mirrors others, and the self that it seeks is valued for the relation it bears to earlier selves, not for its un-dependence. Its moments of sublimation discover what is 'interfused' at a deep level. Alongside the individual recollected history (so easily mistaken for egotism) there is what might be termed a bio-history in its literary relations, and this is what specifically concerns me in this chapter.

The full title of Wordsworth's 'Lines' is important: it declares itself to be a poem of the margins, of the 'marge' or river bank, a riparian revisiting that locates itself upstream from the abbey, at the same time

[1] Clifford Siskin, *The Historicity of Romantic Discourse* (New York, 1988); David Perkins, *Is Literary History Possible?* (Baltimore, 1992), 86–7.
[2] John Whale remarks that, 'in *Rights of Man*, Tom Paine goes straight for Burke's philosophical affiliations and turns the argument into one of origins instead. In doing so he immediately short-circuits the whole of history which now stands forlorn, as a rather inadequate product of human invention' ('The Limits of Paine's Revolutionary Literalism', in Kelvin Everest (ed.), *Revolution in Writing: British Literary Responses to the French Revolution* (Milton Keynes, 1991), 121–37, at p. 123).

beyond the tidal inflow and nearer to the source. As Wordsworth's own note to line 4 makes explicit, 'the river is not affected by the tides a few miles above Tintern'. My discussion will attempt to recover the 'inland murmur' of the poem, so to speak. I want to suggest something of its literary topography, working between the ruined abbey and the source or vital spring, following the stream and its margin to the sacred place, and recovering the echoes that sound in muted tones there. Wordsworth's 'Lines' (such must be the appropriate short title) enact a recovery of a sense of connectedness, of belonging to a stream that is in part an interiorized maternal presence, a life-giving transfusion 'felt in the blood, and felt along the heart', but also a wider relationship to a source that has given him a language and made him articulate as a poet. In the poem itself these rhizomic lines of connection are gathered up into the figure of the sister/friend, the climactic sublimation of 'something far more deeply interfused', whose presence throughout is not acknowledged until line 115. In a similar way Wordsworth's poem, though intimated throughout this chapter, will be addressed overtly only at the end. The 'Lines' written along the river bank between the abbey and the springs provide the model for this exercise in organic literary history.

I want, therefore, to attempt a totally different approach from that of Marjorie Levinson, who has written the most influential study of the poem in recent years.[3] In some ways mine is a supplement to hers by being an inversion (not a denial) of her method and conclusions. Where she offers an account of the poem itself by focusing on what it leaves out, mine aims, equally paradoxically, to delineate what is present in the poem by an account that leaves the poem itself out. It is literally an *approach to* Wordsworth's 'Lines', and one that, unlike her 'enabling alienated purchase' on the poem, consciously works along its grain, using its motifs and metaphors in order to trace certain lines of inheritance that issue in the poem and give it life.

In doing so, this chapter resists the kind of universalized history assumed in some recent 'new-historicist' writing, whereby structures are established within which attitudes become generalized, prescribed, or even predetermined. The materials of such history tend, however detailed, to be static ones—they harden into a 'view of' or 'attitude

[3] Marjorie Levinson, *Wordsworth's Great Period Poems: Four Essays* (Cambridge, 1986), 14–57. For Levinson, what is excluded from the poem is the social reality of the abbey site, a haunt of beggars bounded by a polluted tidal river busy with traffic. Her argument that 'Tintern Abbey' enacts a flight from, or displacement of, the political has recently been challenged by Nicholas Roe, who offers a political reading of the poem's picturesque elements in terms of a fallen nature (see *The Politics of Nature* (Basingstoke, 1992), 117–36). Roe (p. 137) would link the 'childish' poems of *Lyrical Ballads* and the *Two-Part Prelude* with Paine's revolutionary 'Adam of a new World' in *Rights of Man*.

towards' a situation or event[4]—and the details themselves become paradigmatic. According to this method, any 'individual' view will predictably be a divergent one that suppresses or denies history-as-reality, and it will therefore be characterized in terms of silences and omissions which it is the critic's task to detect by means of superimposing the chosen paradigm (a mechanism that is the historian's equivalent of the Hinman collator). In face of this inflexible and judgemental technique, where each writer is implicated in a presumed 'social reality', I want to employ a history that is narrative rather than descriptive, personal rather than universal, organic rather than taxonomic, and one that never rigidifies into a paradigm. I therefore prefer the term 'motif', whose musical associations will allow for continual change and development, individually nuanced and given a particular accent or charge.

In the specific case of Wordsworth's 'Lines', for example, to say that the poet does not describe the abbey is not to say, as Levinson does, that it is suppressed or denied,[5] but that, like other subliminal 'presences' in the poem, it makes itself felt without being inscribed through description or direct allusion. In this way I want to raise problems about the issue of 'presence' in poetry and theory, and to suggest some ways in which a poem 'lives along the line' of its own narrative history. Therefore, in refusing to impose a grid of determinate history on the text, the chapter is closer to Siskin's notion of a 'romantic discourse'. History, rather than being viewed deconstructively as an 'event of disruption', becomes a narrative continuity. Nor is the course I wish to follow a teleological one that charts a rising curve of poetic achievement—there are no definite beginnings or ends: the chapter concludes before a discussion of Wordsworth's poem, and it starts with a figure who did not inaugurate but was a vital mediator.

Thomas Warton (1728–90) was the first narrator of English literary history. In place of the earlier encyclopaedic and taxonomic approaches

---

[4] See especially Alan Liu, *Wordsworth: The Sense of History* (Stanford, Calif., 1989). Liu, for example, contrasts the 'French view' of Federation Day (14 July) 1790 with Wordsworth's aestheticized view of it in *The Prelude*. David Perkins challenges the basis of Liu's contextual procedure in *Is Literary History Possible?*, 144–8.

[5] Professor Levinson (*Wordsworth's Great Period Poems*) refers to the 'logical contradiction between title ["Tintern Abbey"] and text' (Introduction, p. 2), and asks: 'Why would a writer call attention to a famous ruin and then studiously ignore it, as it were repudiating its material and historical facticity? . . . its absence from "Tintern Abbey" looks uncomfortably like a suppression' (p. 15). In her reading the poem's 'primary poetic action is the suppression of the social. "Tintern Abbey" achieves its fiercely private vision by directing a continuous energy toward the nonrepresentation of objects and points of view expressive of a public—we would say, ideological—dimension' (pp. 37–8). My view is that the traditional title is misleading, and that the full title locates the poem carefully in relation to the abbey, the river, and its banks, stressing a more dynamic sense of location ('revisiting', 'tour').

that took the form of dictionaries, bibliographies, anthologies, or sketchy outlines of literary 'schools', Warton's three-volume *History of English Poetry* (1774–81) attempted an unfolding narrative from the Norman Conquest to the early seventeenth century.[6] Through his recovery of poetic texts and his tracing of lines of influence and interconnection between them, Warton, more than any other person, gave the British reading public of the 1780s and 1790s a sense of the capacious richness of the literary past, and a model for its infusion into the poetry of the present. It is no surprise that to young poets coming to maturity in the decade following publication of his *Poems* (1777) and the third volume of his *History* (1781) he offered something that was paradoxically old and fresh, a channel of communication with older English poetry that seemed to open up new possibilities. As a teacher with a wide circle of poetical young friends, he was well placed to be a literary mentor to some of them.

In a *Quarterly Review* article of 1824, Robert Southey singled out Warton as a decisive influence on the poetry of the present generation ('if any man may be called the father of the present race, it is Thomas Warton'), and he spoke of Warton's 'school' of poets as 'the true English school'.[7] In the review and elsewhere he mentions four poets as members of this 'school': William Lisle Bowles,[8] Henry Headley,[9] Thomas Rus-

---

[6] Thomas Warton (1728–90), Poet Laureate 1785–90; Professor of Poetry at Oxford 1756–66; Camden Professor of History 1785–90; and fellow of Trinity College 1752–90. On the innovative nature of Warton's *History*, see René Wellek, *The Rise of English Literary History* (Chapel Hill, NC, 1941), 166–201; Lawrence Lipking, *The Ordering of the Arts in Eighteenth-Century England* (Princeton, NJ, 1970), 352–404; and David Fairer, 'The Origins of Warton's *History of English Poetry*', *Review of English Studies*, 32 (1981), 37–63.

[7] Robert Southey, review of William Hayley's *Memoirs*, ed. John Johnson, in *Quarterly Review*, 31 (1824–5), 289.

[8] William Lisle Bowles (1762–1850) came up to Trinity College, Oxford, from Winchester in 1781, and remained there until 1787. His *Fourteen Sonnets* (Bath, 1789) was an immediate success, and its enthusiastic reception by Coleridge and Wordsworth has been frequently noted. Coleridge described Bowles as 'a poet by whose works, year after year, I was so enthusiastically delighted and inspired . . . I made, within less than a year and a half, more than forty transcriptions' (*Biographia Literaria*, ch. 1). An enlarged edition followed in the same year; the sonnets were reprinted in *Sonnets, with Other Poems* (Bath, 1794). See J. B. Bamborough, 'William Lisle Bowles and the Riparian Muse', in W. W. Robson (ed.), *Essays and Poems Presented to Lord David Cecil* (London, 1970), 93–108. My chapter is indebted to his ground-breaking work.

[9] Henry Headley (1765–88), a close friend of Bowles, entered Trinity College, Oxford, from Norwich Grammar School in 1782. Warton helped Headley to have a poem published in the *Gentleman's Magazine* (1785) (see John Nichols, *Literary Anecdotes of the Eighteenth Century* (London, 1812–15), vi. 641). His verse publications were *An Invocation to Melancholy. A Fragment* (Oxford, 1785), and a volume of *Poems and Other Pieces* (London, 1786). In 1787 he published *Select Beauties of Ancient English Poetry*. William Beloe recalled that 'the bias which he took towards ancient English poetry, and the perseverance and zeal with which he pursued and cultivated a knowledge of the earliest English poets, probably arose from his introduction to Thomas Warton, whose History of English Poetry, and other productions in illustration of our ancient bards, were his great and constant favourites' (*The Sexagenarian: or, the Recollections of a Literary Life* (2 vols.; London, 1817), i. 174). He was described by Henry Kett as being devoted to Warton, whom he 'beheld with admiration, and followed with enthusiasm' (Kett's memoir of Headley prefixed to 1810 edn. of *Select Beauties*, p. iv).

sell,[10] and John Bampfylde;[11] and to these I would add a further three, Henry Kett,[12] George Richards,[13] and Thomas Park.[14] Beyond this immediate group, Edward Gardner (whose *Miscellanies* was published at Bristol in 1798) has a noticeable Wartonian accent,[15] as does the

Looking back in 1829, Wordsworth recalled Headley as 'a most extraordinary young man—more remarkable for precocity of judgement than any one I ever read or heard of: in his Poems also are beautiful passages, especially in the "Invocation to Melancholy", that I think is the title, but I have not seen the Poems for thirty years' (Wordsworth to E. H. Barker, 24 July 1824, *The Letters of William and Dorothy Wordsworth*, ed. Alan G. Hill (2nd edn., Oxford, 1979), v. 95). Headley was mourned by Bowles in 'On the Death of Henry Headley', and by Kett in 'Verses on the Death of Mr. Headley'. Kett included both poems in his 1810 edn. of *Select Beauties*, pp. xix–xxii.

[10] Thomas Russell (1762–88) moved from Winchester to its sister Wykehamist foundation of New College, Oxford, in 1780, and he continued to be an admirer of the two Warton brothers. In 1782–3 he defended Warton's *History* in the *Gentleman's Magazine* (52 (1782), 574; 53 (1783), 124). Russell's *Sonnets and Miscellaneous Poems* (Oxford, 1789) were posthumously published by a fellow Wykehamist and dedicated to Joseph Warton. Wordsworth, an admirer of Russell's sonnets, transferred the final quatrain of one of them to his own sonnet 'Iona (upon landing)' as expressing the feeling better than he himself could. See also Wordsworth to Dyce, [c.22 Apr. 1833] (*Letters*, ed. Hill, v. 604). Russell died at Bristol Hotwells in 1788, the same year as Headley. He is featured in Bowles's 'Elegy Written at the Hot-Wells, Bristol', included in the volume, *Monody, Written at Matlock, October 1791* (Salisbury, 1791).

[11] John Bampfylde (1754–97) was, as Roger Lonsdale has shown, also a Wykehamist. Although he studied at Cambridge, he had friends in Oxford, particularly George Huddesford of Trinity, and his sonnet 'On having dined at Trinity College Oxford' was included in his *Sixteen Sonnets* (London, 1778), along with 'To Mr. Warton, on reading his History of English Poetry'. In later life he was confined in a madhouse. Coleridge and Southey were stirred by his poetry and life story, and Southey in particular was instrumental in rescuing a significant amount of both. See *The Poems of John Bampfylde*, ed. Roger Lonsdale (Oxford, 1988).

[12] Henry Kett (1761–1825), like Headley from Norwich Grammar School, entered Trinity College in 1777 and became a fellow 1784. He lived to disown his youthful verse which he collected as *Juvenile Poems* (Oxford, 1793), in a failed bid to become Oxford's poetry professor. He wrote 'A Tour to the Lakes of Cumberland and Westmoreland in August 1798', and interested himself in the reform of the University's syllabus. In 1810 he published a two-volume revised edition of Headley's *Select Beauties* with a sympathetic memoir of his friend and an appendix of Headley's collected poems. He drowned himself in 1825. The three 'Headley' poems included by Southey in his *Specimens of the Later English Poets* (3 vols.; London, 1807) are in fact by Kett. See n. 44.

[13] George Richards (1767–1837) entered Trinity College, Oxford, from Christ's Hospital in 1785, took his BA in 1788, and became a fellow of Oriel College 1790–6. Thomas Warton was assessor when Richards won the Chancellor's Prize in 1789 for an essay on 'The Characteristic Differences between Ancient and Modern Poetry, and the several Causes from which they result'. He published *The Aboriginal Britons, A Poem* (Oxford, 1791) and *Songs of the Aboriginal Bards of Britain* (Oxford, 1792). His two-volume *Poems* (Oxford, 1804) gathered his earlier verse together, much dating from the 1790s. Eventually Richards became Vicar of St Martin's-in-the-Fields, London, 1824–37.

[14] Thomas Park (1759–1834) published his massive *Works of the British Poets* (London, 1805–8), in which Bampfylde and other Wartonians are well represented. Although he attended neither Winchester nor either university, he can claim to be part of any 'School of Warton'. His modestly titled *Sonnets and Other Small Poems* (London, 1797) contains unmistakable Wartonian motifs. Park studied antiquities and was deeply read in older English poetry. His projected completion of Warton's *History of English Poetry* did not materialize, but his notes found their way into nineteenth-century editions of Warton's work.

[15] Little is known of Edward Gardner (?1752–1823), a school friend of Chatterton, later a wine merchant at Frampton-on-Severn, Gloucestershire. His *Miscellanies, in Prose and Verse* (2 vols.; Bristol, 1798) were published by Biggs and Cottle in the same year as *Lyrical Ballads*. The volumes also contained original poems of Chatterton, and vol. i was dedicated to another friend, Edward Jenner, the discoverer of vaccination, about whom Gardner contributed material to John Baron's *Life of Jenner* (London, 1827). Gardner was probably also the author of *Liberty: A Poem* (Bristol, 1776), of which only one copy, at Harvard, has been traced. The library of the Wellcome Institute for the

meditative poetry of Charlotte Smith.[16] The 1795 volume of *Poems* by
Bion and Moschus (Southey and his friend Robert Lovell)[17] contains
material rooted in the Warton school, and during the 1790s the work of
Coleridge and especially Wordsworth is supplied by influences from the
same 'native stream'.

The first seven names in the above list form a group of younger writers
whose work in various ways stood in immediate relationship to Warton's
own; most were bound together by friendship and literary intimacies,
and in different ways all can be said to have regarded Warton as a
father-figure. Four of them (Bowles, Headley, Kett, and Richards) were
at Trinity College, Oxford, where Warton was Senior Fellow, and Bowles, along with Russell and Bampfylde, could boast a twin parentage in
being educated at Winchester School, where Thomas's brother, Joseph
Warton, presided as Headmaster. This was Thomas's second home
during the Oxford vacations, and here the 'Adelphi of poetry' together
nurtured the boys' literary talents.[18] At Oxford the Poet Laureate drew
around him a noticeable group of poetical young men, as Sir Herbert
Croft remarked in 1786: 'the magnetism of Tom Warton draws many a
youth into rhymes and loose stockings, who had better be thinking of
prose and propriety.'[19] Headley, for example, 'poetical from top to toe'

History of Medicine, London, has Gardner's own transcript (MS 2471), dated 1818, of eighteen
unpublished sonnets; they include twelve blank verse sonnets chiefly on religious subjects (three dated
1809–12). His death is recorded in the *Gentleman's Magazine*, 93 (1823), 93.

[16] Charlotte Smith (1749–1806) contributed sonnets to the *European Magazine* (1782), and published *Elegiac Sonnets, and Other Essays* (London, 1784). Joseph and Thomas Warton both subscribed to *Elegiac Sonnets, by Charlotte Smith. The Fifth Edition, with Additional Sonnets and Other
Poems* (London, 1789). *Beachy Head: with Other Poems* was published the year after her death.

[17] Robert Lovell and Robert Southey, *Poems: Containing the Retrospect, Odes, Elegies, Sonnets, &c*
(Bath, 1795). Late in life W. L. Bowles recollected: 'Mr. Cruttwell, the printer, wrote a letter saying
that two young gentlemen, strangers, one a particularly handsome and pleasing youth, lately from
Westminster School, and both literary and intelligent, spoke in high commendation of my volume, and
if I recollect right, expressed a desire to have some poems printed in the same type and form' (*Scenes
and Shadows of Days Departed* (London, 1837), p. xlv).

[18] 'At school I remember we thought we must necessarily be fine fellows if we were but as absent
and as dirty as the Adelphi of poetry' (Sir Herbert Croft to John Nichols, 15 May 1786, in Nichols,
Literary Anecdotes, v. 210). Southey remarked in 1814: 'The Wartons were far from writing purely;
but no men contributed so much to the reformation of English poetry. They brought us back to the
study of the Elizabethan writers; and under the elder brother, Winchester may almost be said to have
become a school of poets'; the review continued with a discussion of Headley, Russell, Bowles, and
Bampfylde as working under the Wartons' influence (*Quarterly Review*, 11 (1814), 89).

[19] Croft to Nichols (see previous note). Thomas Warton's paternal encouragement of the Winchester
schoolboys is recorded in a poem on his death:

> No more, observant of each budding shoot
> Of youthful fancy, shall his count'nance cheer
> Its blushing progress. To each nurtur'd root
> Of genius, that benign regard how dear!
>
> So meek, it bent indulgent ev'n to me;
> All Wykeham's sons confess'd its genial force.
> O Warton! if in heart I bear not thee,
> Its pulse, its feeling's lost, and vital course.

and devoted to Warton, was at the age of 22 clearly following in his master's footsteps, already author of a published volume of poems and of *Select Beauties of Ancient English Poetry*, an anthology of sixteenth- and early seventeenth-century poetry with scholarly notes and biographies.

Besides making a young poet feel in touch with the mainstream of contemporary poetry, Warton showed how that current flowed from long hidden sources. His characteristic impulsion to recover and reanimate the past in a way that traced connecting threads with the present (in sharp contrast to Gray's tragic disjunctions)[20] exemplified how that past could be rediscovered as (personal) history. Along these threads, in a series of 'holy' landscapes, the poet might meditate on relationships, maturity, growth, and change. For this Warton offered a fluid emotional syntax to articulate the characteristic dilemma of continuity facing any organic consciousness. The historian lived within the poet in a symbiotic way.

This interrelationship forms the basis for Southey's characterization of Warton's poems in his *Quarterly Review* article:

they are . . . strongly tinctured by his romantic and chivalrous reading, and by the spirit of our elder poets.

> Nor rough nor barren are the winding ways
> Of hoar antiquity, but strewn with flowers.

Thus he expressed himself, and the truth of this was exemplified in all his writings. No man could at that time have written such poems, unless his studies had qualified him to become the historian of English poetry; nor could any one have composed that history who had not been born a poet.

Southey is quoting the final couplet of Warton's sonnet, 'Written in a blank leaf of Dugdale's Monasticon', a typically Wartonian meditation on the location and recovery of texts:

> While cloyster'd Piety displays
> Her mouldering roll, the piercing eye explores

> How brisk it bounded, when he, smiling, laid
> Light on my auburn curls his plausive hand!
> 'There is some spirit in these lines', he said,
> 'That's not ill turn'd, this not inaptly scann'd' . . .

('Elegy on a Much Respected and Beloved Friend', by 'Philisides', *Gentleman's Magazine*, 61 (Feb. 1791), 165. The author was a 'Mr. Duncan'—either John Shute Duncan (1768–1844) or his brother Philip Bury Duncan (1772–1863), both Wykehamists and fellows of New College, Oxford.)
[20] See David Fairer, 'Thomas Warton, Thomas Gray, and the Recovery of the Past', in W. B. Hutchings and William Ruddick (eds.), *Thomas Gray: Contemporary Essays* (Liverpool, 1993), 146–70.

> New manners, and the pomp of elder days,
> Whence culls the pensive bard his pictur'd stores.[21]
>
> (ll. 9–12)

'New manners' suddenly retrieves something from the 'mouldering roll'. Where we might expect the word 'old', Warton's 'new' inverts the antiquarian impulse and draws a precariously decaying text into the present, turning what is enclosed and static ('cloyster'd Piety displays') into what is penetrative and dynamic ('piercing eye explores'). In a gesture of connectedness Warton sets the retrospective alongside an awareness of future imaginative possibilities. This is how history works for Warton, as a mediation between a living consciousness and its inherited knowledge.

Again and again in Warton's poetry we encounter a lost text—worn away by time, covered in mould, dimly discernible, and usually housed in a remote, concealed place. In the 'Ode Written at Vale-Royal Abbey' he goes

> within the deep fane's inmost cell,
> To pluck the grey moss from the mantled stone,
> Some holy founder's mouldering name to spell[22]
>
> (ll. 74–6)

and in 'Ode on the Approach of Summer' he enters a more mystical space with similar intent:

> As thro' the caverns dim I wind,
> Might I that holy legend find,
> By fairies spelt in mystic rhymes
> To teach enquiring later times . . .[23]
>
> (ll. 249–52)

These texts are 'holy' because they are original and revelatory, drawn from innermost places where legend and history meet. The difficulty of access to their language is somehow a guarantee of the value of discarded truth, of a founding or primal tradition awaiting discovery.

The fact that this is a native tradition is emphasized by his sonnet 'On King Arthur's Round-table at Winchester', where again a text is waiting to be recovered:

> on the capacious round
> Some British pen has sketch'd the names renown'd,

---

[21] Thomas Warton, *Poems: A New Edition, with Additions* (1777; 3rd edn., 1779), 77.
[22] Ibid. 34.
[23] First published in *The Union* (1753). Text from *The Poetical Works of the Late Thomas Warton, B.D.*, ed. Richard Mant (2 vols.; Oxford, 1802), ii. 27.

In marks obscure, of his immortal peers.
Though join'd by magic skill, with many a rime,
The Druid-frame, unhonour'd, falls a prey
To the slow vengeance of the wisard Time,
And fade the British characters away . . .[24]

(ll. 6–12)

The table carries a text that is slipping from view: it is literally a poetic language that is fading and taking with it the 'British characters'—both the words themselves and the people who had once sat around the table. But, Warton ends by saying, the knights live on, 'unconscious of decay', in the pages of Spenser's *Faerie Queene*. That final remark from the literary historian gains resonance from the fact that it was Warton's *Observations on the Faerie Queene* (1754) that had first shown the presence of Malory and Arthurian 'history' in Spenser's poem. Warton's innovative literary source-study (a breakthrough in historical criticism that was praised by Johnson[25] and others) functions silently as his own contribution to the recovery of a narrative history.

In tracing links with the past (and *trace*, as verb or noun, is a crucial word in his poetry, with its suggestion of following the tracks of meaning) Warton becomes an investigator of spaces. His search for hidden writing is associated with a quest for concealed places where such texts might be preserved. This is the subject of a humorous poem by Joseph Warton that issues a fearful curse on his brother and pictures a nightmare in which all Thomas's texts fade and elude him:

But now may curses every search attend
That seems inviting! may'st thou pore in vain
For dubious door-ways! may revengeful moths
Thy ledgers eat! may chronologic spouts
Retain no cypher legible! may crypts
Lurk undiscern'd![26]

(ll. 18–23)

---

[24] Warton, *Poems* (1777), 82.

[25] 'You have shown to all who shall hereafter attempt the study of our ancient authours the way to success, by directing them to the perusal of the books which those authours had read. Of this method Hughes and Men much greater than Hughes seem never to have thought' (Johnson to Warton, 16 July 1754, *The Letters of Samuel Johnson*, ed. Bruce Redford (5 vols.; Princeton, NJ, 1992–4), i. 81). David Nichol Smith remarked that 'it is in Warton's *Observations* . . . that Malory makes his entrance into literary criticism' ('Warton's *History of English Poetry*', *Proceedings of the British Academy*, 15 (1929), 73–99, at p. 76). See also Arthur Johnston, *Enchanted Ground: The Study of Medieval Romance in the Eighteenth Century* (London, 1964), 103–4, 115–16.

[26] 'Epistle from Thomas Hearne, Antiquary, to the Author of the Companion to the Oxford Guide', printed in *The Oxford Sausage* (1764). Text from *Biographical Memoirs of the Late Revd. Joseph Warton, D.D.*, ed. John Wooll (London, 1806), 160.

But in Warton's poems the dubious doorways and hidden entries into the past regularly open, as ruined and empty places are peopled and filled with light and music. In his poem 'The Grave of King Arthur', for example, the ruins of Cilgarran Castle in Wales come to life. The vaulted roof is lit by a thousand torches, the tapestries speak, and the minstrels sing. Inside, Henry II listens to the story of the death of Arthur sung by the bard, who reveals that the King still lies buried in an unmarked grave before the high altar at Glastonbury: 'Away the ruthless Dane has torn | Each trace that Time's slow touch had worn; | And long, o'er the neglected stone, | Oblivion's veil its shade has thrown' (ll. 127–30). On hearing this, Henry vows to recover the body from its obscure resting-place:

> Ev'n now he seems, with eager pace,
> The consecrated floor to trace;
> And ope, from its tremendous gloom
> The treasures of the wonderous tomb . . .[27]
>
> (ll. 165–8)

Warton's own acts of recovery find a suitable image in this kind of imaginative archaeology.

The archetype for so many Wartonian encounters with ruined or neglected places is his 'Ode Written at Vale-Royal Abbey', which moves between the present and the past until, almost surreptitiously, a technique of ironic disconnection becomes one of superimposition, and the scene begins to live as it once did:

> The golden fans, that o'er the turrets strown,
> Quick-glancing to the sun, quaint music made,
> Are reft, and every battlement o'ergrown
> With knotted thorns, and the tall sapling's shade.
>
> The prickly thistle sheds its plumy crest,
> And matted nettles shade the crumbling mass,
> Where shone the pavement's surface smooth, imprest
> With rich reflection of the storied glass.
>
> Here hardy chieftains slept in proud repose,
> Sublimely shrin'd in gorgeous imagery;
> And through the lessening iles, in radiant rows,
> Their consecrated banners hung on high.[28]
>
> (ll. 9–20)

Imaginatively, the thistles hint at knightly plumage, and the tall saplings recall the lofty banners. There is still rich reflection here: even the ivy

---

[27] Warton, *Poems* (1777), 68–71.   [28] Ibid. 30–1.

seems to enhance the tracery of the windows ('where the tall shaft and fretted nook between | Thick ivy twines'). This is not emptiness or dilapidation, but reanimation. Warton's ruins are spaces waiting to be brought back to life by imagination.[29] They contain ancient native writing faded by time, and records of legends and histories. The texts are veiled, worn, or buried, but they speak on behalf of a tradition which has been lost and may be revived.

Linked to these ruins are the many Wartonian secret places, some containing magic springs, which become literally sources from which the poet can draw. In his early 'Invocation to a Water-Nymph',[30] written before he was 20, the poet summons the nymph 'in secret Solitude' where she presides over a magic spring. In seeking permission to drink from the 'silver Lake', the poet invokes not only Milton's Sabrina, but the young Milton himself. (On Warton's part this was to be a lifelong commitment ended only by his edition of Milton's shorter poems which was at press when he died.) Significantly, his final poem, the 'Birthday Ode for 1790',[31] also concerns itself with springs, celebrating a series of health-giving waters: the 'mystic spring' of Bath, the 'dim retreat' in the cliffs at Matlock, the cavernous rocks at Hotwells, Clifton, and the 'rich veins' within the mountains at Malvern. Wartonian ancient spaces are filled with music, echoes, dim or reflected lights, the sounds of springs, whispers, murmurs, or chanting choirs.[32]

If it is not the poet himself who inhabits these special removed places, then it is the child—and specifically the foster-child. In a motif of significance for the concept of the 'School of Warton', and for our meandering approach to a Wordsworthian special place, these children have various benign foster-parents who carry the babe off and nurture it in a secret dwelling. It can be the infant Poetry, nurtured by King Alfred in his Saxon cell, or Edward the Black Prince, the 'royal nursling', reared

---

[29] In his excellent article, 'Wordsworth and the Sonnet: Building, Dwelling, Thinking' (*Essays in Criticism*, 35 (1985), 45–75), John Kerrigan discusses 'Wordsworth's desire for, and fear of not finding, a place for the mind to dwell' (p. 47), and he links dwelling ('the most pressing concern of his imaginative life') with 'that rooting in the settlement of the "repose", the "blended holiness of earth and sky" already felt a few miles above Tintern Abbey' (pp. 51, 53). For Wordsworth 'the fourteen-line structure [was] a uniquely comforting abode in which to dwell' (p. 57). But Kerrigan wishes to dissociate this from 'the Wartons' and Bowles's delight in dilapidation', in that 'few things disturbed the poet of the great decade more than the destruction of a dwelling' (pp. 49–50). The point at which I would depart from Kerrigan's view is his equating Wartonian ruins with mere destruction: I argue that Warton's need to reanimate and repossess scenes of dilapidation, and dwell in them imaginatively, links him very closely to the Wordsworth of Kerrigan's analysis.

[30] Included anonymously in the posthumous volume of his father's poems edited by Joseph Warton, *Poems on Several Occasions. By the Reverend Mr. Thomas Warton* (London, 1748), 21–2.

[31] Warton, *Poetical Works*, ed. Mant, ii. 135–42.

[32] See e.g. 'The Triumph of Isis', ll. 153–6; 'The Pleasures of Melancholy', ll. 201–10; 'Inscription in a Hermitage', ll. 25–30; 'Ode Written at Vale-Royal Abbey', ll. 33–6; and 'Solitude, at an Inn' (Warton, *Poetical Works*, ed. Mant, i. 15; i. 86–7; i. 101; i. 134; i. 140–1).

by his foster-mother, the University of Oxford.[33] The model, from
Warton's 'Pleasures of Melancholy', is the infant Contemplation,

> whom, as tradition tells,
> Once in his evening walk a Druid found,
> Far in a hollow glade of Mona's woods;
> And piteous bore with hospitable hand
> To the close shelter of his oaken bow'r.
> There soon the sage admiring mark'd the dawn
> Of solemn musing in your pensive thought;
> For when a smiling babe, you lov'd to lie
> Oft deeply list'ning to the rapid roar
> Of wood-hung Meinai, stream of Druids old.[34]
>
> (ll. 306–15)

The baby listens to the voice of nature in the sound of an ancient stream,
and the sacred presence fosters the first stirrings of consciousness and the
'musing' imagination.

For his young admirers of the 1770s and 1780s Warton himself
functioned as a kind of foster-parent (in some cases almost literally so)
and nurturer of literary talent. In Warton's company a young poet could
feel he was revisiting the ancient sites, hearing previously lost voices,
brushing the moss from the carved stone, reanimating scenes of ruin and
desolation, and locating waters that were flowing from a pure spring.
These Wartonian motifs offered an emotional landscape that encouraged
gestures of reassessment or rededication. As a father-figure, he was not a
repressively looming authority but a nurturing parent encouraging ar-
ticulateness. Warton, the historian of poetry and the poet of history,
became a channel of communication between young poets and their
literary past.

---

[33] See 'The Triumph of Isis', ll. 216–22 (*Poetical Works*, ed. Mant, i. 21–2), and 'On the Birth of the
Prince of Wales', ll. 45–8 (*Poems* (1777), 21).

[34] Warton, *Poetical Works*, ed. Mant, i. 95. William Lisle Bowles's tribute to his former headmaster
is specific about the Wartonian fostering he had received ('The first inciting sounds of human praise, |
A parent's love excepted, came from THEE'), and he sees Joseph Warton as having guided him into a
romantic valley full of the sound of water and poetry:

> by thee my steps were led
> To that romantic valley, high o'erhung
> With sable woods, where many a minstrel rung
> His bold harp to the sweeping waterfall,
> Whilst Fancy lov'd around each form to call
> That fill the poet's dream: to this retreat
> Of Fancy . . .
> Thou first did guide my not unwilling feet
>
> ('Monody on the Death of Dr. Warton' (1800),
> in *Poems, by the Reverend Wm. Lisle Bowles*,
> ii. (London, 1801), 137–8).

Henry Headley and Thomas Russell were the two protégés most involved in the study of literary history. Russell wrote two scholarly papers for the *Gentleman's Magazine* (1782–3) defending Warton's *History* against Ritson's attack,[35] and Headley's *Select Beauties* (1787) was a work of scholarship prompted by the material in Warton's third volume. Thomas Park was especially deeply read in older English poetry, and he felt closely enough attuned to Warton's work to project his own completion of the *History* (his notes were eventually incorporated into nineteenth-century editions of the work). It is no surprise to find, therefore, that in their poetry these three exploited in a distinctly Wartonian manner the reawakening of Gothic buildings to the songs of old. Headley, in his 'Invocation to Melancholy' (a poem greatly admired by Wordsworth), comes upon a moated hall in a 'lonely dell' obscured by trees, and proceeds to animate it with the sound of the old bards singing their tales of chivalry; lively harping fills the place, and the 'rafter'd roofs' ring to 'the tunes of Chevy Chace and Hardiknute'.[36] Russell's 'Sonnet 1' ('In days of old . . .') does something very similar with the 'proud castle', mixing the minstrel's music with the sound of clashing armour;[37] and Thomas Park, in his sonnet 'Written at Windsor-Castle', even goes so far as to end the poem with a quotation from Warton's 'Birthday Ode for 1787', celebrating those poets

> That round these banner'd walls, and crested bowers,
> Have harp'd the 'noblest Bards of Britain's quire!'[38]
>
> (ll. 13–14)

Southey's early sonnet 'Dunnington-Castle' is shaped out of this Wartonian material. Here the fate of the 'ruin'd relique' is linked to that of its occupant, Chaucer ('envious age', which has eaten away the building, has also 'sapp'd the fabric of his lofty rhyme'), and imagination's reanimation of the building finds a parallel in the activity of the reader or literary historian, who

> still shall ponder o'er the page,
> And piercing through the shadowy mist of time,
> The festive Bard of EDWARD's court recall,
> As fancy paints the pomp that once adorn'd thy wall.[39]
>
> (ll. 11–14)

---

[35] *Observations on the Three First Volumes of the History of English Poetry* (London, 1782) by Joseph Ritson (1752–1803). See n. 10 above.

[36] Headley, *Poems and Other Pieces*, 12–13.

[37] Russell, *Sonnets and Miscellaneous Poems*, 1.

[38] Park, *Sonnets and Other Small Poems*, 8.

[39] Robert Southey and Robert Lovell, *Poems: Containing the Retrospect, Odes, Elegies, Sonnets, &c* (Bath, 1795), 61.

The clearest example of a Wartonian 'ruin' poem, and one directly indebted to the much-imitated Vale-Royal ode, is Headley's 'Written amidst the ruins of Broomholm Priory, in Norfolk', in which the poet contemplates a scene that is rapidly losing its language:

> in vain with curious eye we trace
> The tarnish'd semblance of the sacred place,
> With eye profane its fading tints explore
> That mark the features of the days of yore,
> And fain would eager snatch from ruffian Time
> The moss-grown fragment of a monkish rhyme.[40]
>
> (ll. 13–18).

As in other Wartonian poems of this type, the scene soon comes to life, as his imagination brings the coloured glass back to the windows and rebuilds the tombs.

Henry Kett's sonnet 'To Time' gives an individual twist to these tracings from the past. Here there is an effective contrast between the confident youthful sapling (echoes of the Vale-Royal ode are again clear) and the deep wrinkles scarring the walls of the tower, which become the ancient disintegrating face of Time himself:

> yon moss-mantled tower,
> Whose head sublime derided once thy power,
> Now silent crumbling sinks beneath thy sway.
> The sapling, thy tall streamer, waves on high,
> Whilst thy deep wounds each mazy fissure shows,
> Like wrinkles, furrowing deep thy own grey brows.[41]
>
> (ll. 6–11)

The tracings of Time can, in these Wartonian contexts, link the idea of a personal memory with the quest for a self that has been lost: the text can be a subjective one, like that found by Southey in his 1792 verses 'To Contemplation' ('The ruin'd Abbey's hallowed rounds I trace, | And listen to the echoings of my feet. | Or on some half-demolish'd tomb, | Whose warning texts anticipate my doom, | Mark the clear orb of night ...').[42] In several poems in their jointly published volume of 1795, Southey and his friend Robert Lovell pursue the Wartonian tracings into the area of personal integrity. In 'The Miser's Mansion' Southey begins by pondering on its 'time-trac'd walls', in a poem which moves Warton's Vale-Royal ode firmly towards the moral issues of wealth and selfish-

---

[40] Headley, *Poems and Other Pieces*, 37. In his 'Verses on the Death of Mr. Headley', Kett revisits Broomholm's 'holy walls' and recalls an earlier visit there with his friend (*Juvenile Poems*, 12–15).

[41] Kett, *Juvenile Poems*, 18.

[42] Printed in Robert Southey, *Poems* (Bristol and London, 1797).

ness, as the soul-less building takes on the lineaments of the miser who inhabited it. In a similar way, Lovell's elegy 'The Decayed Monastery' echoes the phrases of Warton's ode and mimics its structure, but ends by investigating the personal human imperatives that lead an individual towards social action. The ruin's 'time-defac'd . . . inscription' is set aside for a more instructive and pressing exhortation.[43]

Underlying these various Wartonian motifs is a sense of the connecting stream of human experience. The images of fostering, of recovering distant voices and lost texts, locating springs and 'holy' places, reaching into the past for meanings to illuminate the present, all these are bound up with a concept of an organic history. Such a history seems in interpretive terms to bind together Wartonian texts themselves, and nowhere is this more evident than in relation to Warton's most personal poem about retrieving a connection with the past. His sonnet 'To the River Lodon' is his most influential poem in the literal sense that its mood, phrases, even syntax, flowed into the work of many 1790s poets. It has reverberations throughout the Warton school and beyond, acting itself almost as an original authentic text, a native stream from which succeeding poets could, directly or indirectly, draw:

> Ah! what a weary race my feet have run,
>> Since first I trod thy banks with alders crown'd,
>> And thought my way was all through fairy ground,
>> Beneath thy azure sky, and golden sun:
> Where first my muse to lisp her notes begun!
>> While pensive memory traces back the round,
>> Which fills the varied interval between;
>> Much pleasure, more of sorrow, marks the scene.
> Sweet native stream! those skies and suns so pure
>> No more return, to chear my evening road!
>> Yet still one joy remains, that not obscure,
> Nor useless, all my vacant days have flow'd,
>> From youth's gay dawn to manhood's prime mature;
>> Nor with the Muse's laurel unbestow'd.[44]

In this meditation on loss, continuity, and gain, the crucial concept is the return to the source, the re-establishing of contact with the 'native stream'. The gap between past and present selves does not close, but each

---

[43] Southey and Lovell, *Poems* (1795), 31–4, 41–5. In the same volume (pp. 51–4) Southey's poem 'Hospitality', ll. 15–46, strongly recalls Warton's Vale-Royal ode.

[44] Warton, *Poems* (1777), 83. In Southey's *Specimens of the Later English Poets* the Loddon sonnet appears twice—once under Thomas Warton, and later also under Joseph Warton (see n. 12 above). Mary Jacobus has examined the development of eighteenth-century landscape poetry in 'Tintern Abbey', including the 'revisit' poem of Warton and Bowles which was useful in 'providing Wordsworth with a means of asserting continuity as well as change' (*Tradition and Experiment in Wordsworth's Lyrical Ballads* (Oxford, 1976), 104–30).

is thrown into relief by the experience. The 'sweet native stream' here is not a Painite originating moment when his identity was inaugurated, but a Burkean continuum of history. 'Tracing back' the interval between, Warton sees 'marks' both of pleasure and of sorrow, but thanks to the river he remains in touch with a sense of his developing life and what it owes to the past.

In some ways this sonnet can be seen as Warton's reclaiming of his childhood river from Pope,[45] that figure who represented for the Warton brothers the interruption of the native poetic tradition of Chaucer–Spenser–Milton, which they had helped restore. Significantly, in Pope's *Windsor Forest* (ll. 171–218) the River Loddon, mythologized as the nymph Lodona, rushes into the mighty Thames, whose 'offspring' she is (an odd reversal of their true relationship). Pope and Warton may have shared the same native river, but Pope's eyes were turned downstream, away from the source towards the current flowing confidently out to the tidal ocean beyond.

For the Wartonians Pope was a commanding figure who, although he had changed the poetic landscape, was inadequate as a creative source for other writers. Rather he was someone against whom they needed to define their own literary principles—they wished to reach back beyond him to neglected places that were still there but ignored.[46] To one Wartonian, for example, the translator of Homer represented a mighty flood that should not be mistaken for a true spring:

[Pope's] translation of Homer, timed as it was, operated like an inundation in the English Republic of letters, and has left to this day indelible marks on more than the surface of our poetry. Co-operating with the popular stream of his other works, it has formed a sort of modern Helicon, on whose banks infant poets are allowed to wander and to dream; from whose streams they are content to drink inspiration, without searching for remoter sources. Whether its waters are equally pure, salutary, and deep, with the more ancient wells of English undefiled, admits of a doubt.

The voice is that of Headley in 1787, measuring his own allegiance to his mentor Warton against the text which in the Johnsonian pantheon had marked the pinnacle of poetic achievement. This topographical passage

---

[45] Warton was born at Basingstoke, then a small market town, standing on the River Loddon, which flows into the Thames near Pope's childhood home at Binfield.

[46] Joseph Warton, *Essay on the Writings and Genius of Pope* (London, 1756; 2nd vol. 1782) controversially demoted Pope to the second rank of poets. Joseph's pupil, William Lisle Bowles, inherited the mantle of his teacher and denigrated Pope in his 1806 edition, becoming entangled in the well-known controversy with Byron. In his article, 'The Eighteenth-Century Construction of Romanticism: Thomas Warton and *The Pleasures of Melancholy*', *English Literary History*, 59 (1992), 799–815, Robert Griffin explores the dynamics of Romanticism in terms of the displacing of Pope, analysing Warton's poem 'for the insights it gives into the genesis of a romantic construction of literary history' (p. 802).

from the preface to his *Select Beauties of Ancient English Poetry* links the putatively personal Loddon sonnet to the broader Wartonian project in literary history—the fostering of a sense of continuity with the 'remoter sources'. In contrast to the Wartonian stream, the banks of Pope's river were impure and overcrowded.

Warton's sonnet had many imitators, and during the two decades after its publication in 1777 it established the revisiting of a river bank as the locus for a meditative self-assessment in terms of past and present. The return to the special place allowed the past to be recovered and a continuum established; underneath the sheddings and accretions, the tragedy of loss weighed against the solace of gain, there could be asserted a sense of the self as a developing organism. Revisiting a river bank, albeit in only fourteen lines, implied a personal history in these terms. Bowles's twin sonnets to the rivers Cherwell and Itchin,[47] for example, revisit the banks, respectively, of his days at Oxford and at Winchester. In the former he begins by juxtaposing the optimistic past ('Cherwell, how pleas'd along thy willow'd edge | Erewhile I stray'd') with the rueful present ('And now reposing on thy banks once more'), and, after reference to his 'melancholy way' through life, he ends by taking stock of the gains to be set against what he has lost ('yet something have I won | Of solace'). The Itchin sonnet plays out a similar temporal arrangement:

> Itchin, when I behold thy banks again,
>> Thy crumbling margin, and thy silver breast,
>> On which the self-same tints still seem to rest,
> Why feels my heart the shiv'ring sense of pain?
>> Is it—that many a summer's day has past
> Since, in life's morn, I carol'd on thy side?
> Is it—that oft, since then, my heart has sigh'd,
>> As Youth, and Hope's delusive gleams, flew fast?
> Is it—that those, who circled on thy shore,
> Companions of my youth, now meet no more?
>> Whate'er the cause, upon thy banks I bend
> Sorrowing, yet feel such solace at my heart,
>> As at the meeting of some long-lost friend,
>> From whom, in happier hours, we wept to part.

Warton's strategic 'Since' and 'Yet' had marked syntactically the structure of his poem; they reappear similarly here as the pivotal moments temporally between the visiting and revisiting, and evaluatively between the loss and gain. A 'since' and 'yet' structure is evident in several

---

[47] The Itchin sonnet was included in Bowles, *Fourteen Sonnets*, the Cherwell sonnet first appeared in the second edition. The texts given here are from the third edition, *Sonnets, with Other Poems* (Bath, 1794), 20, 10.

Wartonian river-bank sonnets: Coleridge's 'To the River Otter', his tribute to his own native stream, sets the 'Visions of Childhood' alongside 'lone Manhood's cares', and opens with the characteristic exclamation:

> Dear native Brook! wild Streamlet of the West!
> How many various-fated Years have past,
> What blissful and what anguish'd hours, since last . . .[48]

(ll. 1–3)

An interesting variation is played by Thomas Park's sonnet 'To the River Witham', which actually uses Warton and his Loddon sonnet as a connective figure. It proceeds with the recollection motif:

> How oft, erewhile, in childhood's happy hour,
> Have I the angler's patient labour plied
> Along thy banks . . .

(ll. 5–7)

The 'yet' section introduces 'memory' to release the temporal interplay, but where we would expect a weighing of loss and gain, the gain is never registered; instead, Warton himself enters the poem:

> Yet memory now,
> E'en o'er these scenes of former joys can pine,
> Care with his rugged furrows marks my brow,
> And past delights, like spectres, grimly shine:
> So did they erst round pensive Warton gleam,
> Warton, the laureate boast of Britain's Academe![49]

(ll. 9–14)

A footnote here recalls the reader's attention to the Loddon sonnet. In a significant gesture Warton himself is introduced to the remembered scene, suggesting that the gain for Park is having his mentor as a companion-figure for the revisiting of his own native stream.

In Edward Gardner's sonnet 'On Revisiting the Banks of the Avon near Bristol Hotwells' the banks reconnect the poet to his childhood innocence:

> Ah me! how oft with slow and ling'ring feet,
> Avon I've trod thy grass-grown sedgy side,
> And here once more thy verdant shore I greet . . .
> Here innocent I pass'd the listless day . . .
> O now again I hear thy murmurs slow,
> I see the alders o'er the low waves bend,

[48] Text from *Poems, by S. T. Coleridge, Second Edition* (Bristol, 1797), 78.
[49] Park, *Sonnets and Other Small Poems*, 25.

And sure these scenes must sweetest peace bestow,
They seem the soothings of a much lov'd friend.

(ll. 1–12)

In this context any loss is not in a present set against the past, but is
evoked as a future possibility ('Farewell dear stream, ah far from thee I
go, I Perhaps from paths of peace to those of tearful woe' (ll. 13–14)).[50]
The temporal permutations of the Wartonian river-bank sonnet can,
therefore, vary, and indeed such variations are a feature of this minor
genre. In Southey's sonnet 'To a Brook near the Village of Corston', as
in Gardner's poem, past and present are not juxtaposed and weighed
against each other. Here instead the current of memory revives the past
as a pale but beautiful picture:

As thus I bend me o'er thy babbling stream
And watch thy current, Memory's hand pourtrays
The faint form'd scenes of the departed days,
Like the far forest by the moon's pale beam
Dimly descried yet lovely. I have worn
Upon thy banks the live-long hour away . . .

(ll. 1–6)

with the result that when the 'yet' finally arrives it does so to reaffirm
continuity; however 'faint' or 'dim', the scene is visually and emotionally
present:

Dim are the long past days, yet still they please
As thy soft sounds half heard, borne on the inconstant breeze.[51]

(ll. 13–14)

These 'recognitions dim and faint' with which 'the picture of the mind
revives again' move us a little closer to the Wye.

It is perhaps no surprise that the line of Warton's sonnet which
encapsulates the organic connectedness of life ('From youth's gay dawn
to manhood's prime mature') is repeatedly reworked in later sonnets and
elegies. Charlotte Smith's sonnet 'To Mrs. G.' looks back to 'when life's
gay dawn was opening to my view',[52] and Edward Gardner's sonnet
'Written under a Lofty Cliff on the Banks of the Severn on a Summer's
Evening' ends with the less than resolute remark, 'On this shore . . . I . . .
O let me waste what yet remains of manhood's prime.'[53] Bowles's poem
on the death of Thomas Russell, 'Elegy Written at the Hot-Wells, Bristol', suitably collapses Warton's line, mourning his Wykehamist friend as

[50] Gardner, *Miscellanies*, ii. 127–8. [51] Southey, *Poems* (1797), 112.
[52] Smith, *Elegiac Sonnets* (1789), 10. [53] Gardner, *Miscellanies*, ii. 133–4.

'the lost companion of my youth's gay prime',[54] and when Coleridge penned his sonnet 'To the Rev. W. L. Bowles' in 1794 he tapped into the addressee's own elegiac language: 'Thro Youth's gay prime and thornless paths I went.'[55]

In a similar way, the exclamation 'Sweet native stream!' that ushers in the sestet of Warton's Loddon sonnet provides riparian poets with a refrain. Charlotte Smith's sonnet 'To Melancholy. Written on the Banks of the Arun, October, 1785' records the sounds along Otway's 'native stream'.[56] The invocation 'Dear native Brook!' that opens Coleridge's Otter sonnet echoes throughout his 'Effusion on an Autumnal Evening. Written in Early Youth':

> So tost by storms along Life's wild'ring way
> Mine eye reverted views that cloudless day,
> When by my native brook I wont to rove
> While Hope with kisses nurs'd the Infant Love.
>
> Dear native brook! like PEACE, so placidly
> Smoothing thro' fertile fields thy current meek!
> Dear native brook! . . .[57]

>   (ll. 79–85)

Coleridge's projected long poem, *The Brook*, was to have been a study in connectedness ('I sought for a subject, that should . . . supply in itself a natural connection to the parts, and unity to the whole. Such a subject I conceived myself to have found in a stream, traced from its source in the hills');[58] and Wordsworth's *The River Duddon, A Series of Sonnets* (1820), written over many years, was eventually to trace a river from spring to estuary. Perhaps in acknowledgement of the Loddon sonnet, what became the first poem of Wordsworth's sequence had for the opening line of its sestet, 'I seek the birth-place of a native Stream.'[59]

When Wordsworth composed his 'Lines written a few miles above Tintern Abbey, on revisiting the banks of the Wye during a tour, July 13, 1798', he was choosing a location for his thoughts which invited a

---

[54] Printed in *Monody, Written at Matlock, October 1791* (Salisbury, 1791), 7–9. Bowles's 'Elegy' consciously echoes Thomas Warton, recollecting the times when he and Russell 'heard the merry bells by *Isis*' stream, I And thought our way was strew'd with fairy flow'rs' (combining the last line of the Dugdale's Monasticon sonnet with l. 3 of the Loddon sonnet), and describing the intervening years: 'Thinking how days and hours have pass'd along, I Mark'd by much pleasure some, and some by tears!' (reworking the Loddon sonnet, l. 8).
[55] *Morning Chronicle*, 26 Dec. 1794. The poem was printed in Coleridge's 1796 *Poems* as 'Effusion 1'.
[56] Smith, *Elegiac Sonnets* (1789), 32.
[57] Coleridge, *Poems* (1796), 106–7.
[58] Chapter 10 of *Biographia Literaria*, ed. James Engell and W. Jackson Bate (Princeton, NJ, 1983), i. 195–6. Jonathan Wordsworth links Coleridge's scheme for *The Brook* with 'Tintern Abbey' and earlier 'nostalgic revisited rivers'. See *William Wordsworth: The Borders of Vision* (Oxford, 1982), 333–4.
[59] *The River Duddon, A Series of Sonnets* (London, 1820), 3.

reading in terms of the riverbank-revisited poem popularized by Warton and his school. But he was also drawing upon a wider Wartonian inheritance that was available to him through its motifs, locations, and temporal manœuvres. Underlying Wordsworth's personalized history of revisiting and recovery there is the concept of an organic narrative history such as Warton and his followers had articulated. It is as though the minor genre itself invited contributors to participate in some more communal revisiting that struck the note, even in the supposedly most private moments, of a shared experience. But the configurations are not that simple. In the *poetic* act the self is temporalized as the individual history, with its unique memories and particular determinations, encounters a more precarious and multiple set of potentialities; rather than settling into a single universal pattern, the history becomes, through syntactical variation, a series of possible narratives. In this way the organicism is more complex and contingent than that *bête noir* of some present-day critical theory.

It is appropriate, therefore, to continue this narrative by entering the Wye Valley itself in the company, not of Wordsworth, but of three Wartonians who offer distinct though related voices beside which Wordsworth's may be heard more clearly.

The first text, Edward Gardner's 'Sonnet Written in Tintern Abbey' (1798), locates the speaking voice within the ruined abbey itself. In this poem, typical of Gardner's simple moralized landscapes, the ruin is the temple of man's body victimized by time; but it still contains religious feelings that can be reawakened through contemplation:

> Admiring stranger, that with ling'ring feet,
>   Enchain'd by wonder, pauses on this green;
> Where thy enraptur'd sight the dark woods meet,
>   Ah! rest awhile, and contemplate the scene.
>
> These hoary pillars clasp'd by ivy round,
>   This hallow'd floor by holy footsteps trod,
> The mould'ring choir by spreading moss embrown'd,
>   Where fasting saints devoutly hymn'd their God.
> Unpitying Time, with slow but certain sweep,
>   Has laid, alas! their ancient splendor low:
> Yet here let Pilgrims, while they muse and weep,
>   Think on the lesson that from hence may flow.
> Like their's, how soon may be the tott'ring state
> Of man,—the temple of a shorter date.[60]

[60] The sonnet first appeared in *European Magazine*, 30 (Aug. 1796), and this text is printed by Roger Lonsdale in *The New Oxford Book of Eighteenth-Century Verse* (Oxford, 1984), 819. I give the text as revised for Gardner's *Miscellanies*, ii. 97–8.

Gardner sustains continuity within the ruinous state: the hymn has merely been succeeded by the lesson, and this remains a place in which the tourist is transposed into the pilgrim. The flow of the river has been replaced by the sententious 'flow' of the *memento mori* moral from the abbey, a sentimental equivalent of its ancient dole of charity and hospitality to the poor traveller.

Henry Kett's sonnet 'To the River Wye' (published 1793) omits the abbey, but creates imaginatively out of the natural scene a comparable retreat from the violent world beyond:

> O Wye, romantic stream! thy winding way
>   Invites my lonely steps, what time the night
>   Smiles with the radiance of the moon's pale light,
>   That loves upon the quivering flood to play.
> O'er thy steep banks the rocks fantastic tower,
>   And fling their deepening shadow cross the stream,
>   To fancy's eye worn battlements they seem,
>   Which on some beetling cliff tremendous lower.
> Hark! Echo speaks, and from her mazy cave
>   Sportive returns the sailor's frequent cry,
>   Ah! how unlike thy old bards minstrelsey
> Warbled in wild notes to the haunted wave!
>   Unlike as seems the hurricane's rude sweep,
>   To the light breeze that lulls thy placid deep.[61]

In this poem of visual and verbal playfulness (the tone, in more ways than one, is set by the moonlight), Wordsworth's 'steep and lofty cliffs' take on the lineaments of an ancient building as the metaphorical verb 'tower' is literalized in the battlements. At one level of reading the valley is a calm retreat from the storms blowing across the sea, and the exclusions are explicit ones in this poem of supposed absences: the building is absent, the bards are absent, the hurricane is absent. And yet each registers its presence with a fluidity that has an almost uncanny effect: what is supposedly present is the sailor's cry, but this is less substantial than echo's mimicry of it, and it is overtaken by the wild notes of the absent bards, which are evoked in terms of the sublime power of the hurricane (another absentee). The final lulling of the present breeze cannot pacify a poem in which it is the absence that disturbs.

Finally, George Richards's ode 'Tintern Abbey; or, the Wandering Minstrel' brings the ruins to life by filling them with light and sound in a very Wartonian manner:

---

[61] Kett, *Juvenile Poems*, 16.

Still is the air, and hush'd the wood;
In soothing silence creeps the flood:
And evening calms with golden gleam
The hoary rocks and glittering stream.
Dark shadowy elms beneath embower
The cloisters and high-fretted tower
Of lonely Tintern: tapers bright
Through lofty windows pour their light;
And, rais'd by chaunting quires, a sound
Celestial spreads a charm around.

(ll. 5–14)

The place is animated further when a minstrel begins to sing, celebrating the holy building as a place of loving nurture, of grace and healing, of the 'wild' being calmed to stillness:

Religion, shrin'd in holy walls,
And watching every bead that falls,
Shall wean the beating heart from pain,
Shall still the wild tumultuous vein,
Shall spread around the faded face
Her holy calm, her solemn grace.

(ll. 75–80)

The holiness in Richards's poem is a function of the exclusion and calmness, yet what is excluded registers itself in softened tones, like the echoes and breezes in Kett's Wye Valley. For Richards the abbey is a sanctuary that will remain accessible long after he has left:

Adieu, ye holy men:—I go
To guilty crowds, and scenes of woe.
Yet oft, to silent virtue true,
These warbling strings shall sound of you.[62]

(ll. 111–14)

Extending the canon of English literature involves the retrieval of lost or seldom heard voices. Sometimes the discoveries can make fresh and powerful individual statements, but in other cases the neglected voices are more modest and become articulate only when they are heard as part of a conversation between texts. The work of Thomas Warton and his 'school' needs to be more widely known, partly in order to challenge the over-categorization of literary history evident in a phrase like 'the first-generation romantics'; but also because an awareness of Wartonian poetry can allow a well-known text such as Wordsworth's Wye Valley

---

[62] Richards, *Poems*, ii. 16–23.

'Lines' to be more effectually heard. What seems a sublime egotistical voice is in fact more socially nuanced, and the poem can be understood as recovering not just a private history, but also a literary history for itself in which its language acknowledges the revisitings and recoveries of other poets.

Wordsworth's poem written along the banks of the Wye locates a lost voice among the echoes of the past. As in Warton's Loddon sonnet, a poet revisits an important source and is conscious of what he owes and what he has left behind. The sounds to which Wordsworth is attuned (and we as readers only barely overhear) are elusive ones, but I hope this chapter has captured something of them. In his poem there is no bard, no minstrel song to echo through the valley; there is no abbey, no holy ground being trodden by spirits from the past, no physical text to be recovered; and yet each of these Wartonian motifs exerts a subtle influence in the poem.

Near the beginning of his final paragraph Wordsworth turns to acknowledge for the first time his sister Dorothy's presence in the poem, and he does so with the phrase 'for thou art with me'. In those words we hear an echo of that other valley of the Twenty-Third Psalm, the 'valley of the shadow of death', which for Wordsworth can be faced thanks to the reassurance of a sacred presence, a 'holier love'. In the company of his 'dear, dear Friend' he has no need of the abbey to focus his contemplation; it is her mind that

> Shall be a mansion for all lovely forms,
> Thy memory be as a dwelling-place
> For all sweet sounds and harmonies.
>
> (ll. 141–3)

The Psalm ends with the prayer: 'Surely goodness and mercy shall follow me all the days of my life: and I will dwell in the house of the LORD for ever.' Far from being excluded from Wordsworth's 'Lines', the Lord's house is present throughout in the contemplative procedure of the poem, and in the way in which a human focus is found for the Wartonian special place. As Wordsworth recovers the holy text from his meditation, he reanimates the indwelling spirit as a companion, as a pledge for the future won from his recovery of his own narrative history.

Index